Accounting for Business

Third edition

Peter Atrill,
David Harvey
and
Edward McLaney

OXFORD AUCKLAND BOSTON JOHANNESBURG MELBOURNE NEW DELHI

Butterworth-Heinemann
Linacre House, Jordan Hill, Oxford OX2 8DP
225 Wildwood Avenue, Woburn, MA 01801-2041
A division of Reed Educational and Professional Publishing Ltd

A member of the Reed Elsevier plc group

First published 1991
Reprinted 1992, 1993, 1994
Second edition 1994
Reprinted 1995, 1996, 1999
Third edition 2001
Reprinted 2001

British Library Cataloguing in Publication Data
Atrill, Peter
    Accounting for business. - 3rd ed.
    1. Accounting
    I. Title II. Harvey, David III. McLaney, E. J. (Edward J)
    657

ISBN 0 7506 4256 4

For information on all Butterworth-Heinemann
publications visit our website at www.bh.com

Typeset by Laser Words, Madras, India
Printed and bound in Great Britain

FOR EVERY TITLE THAT WE PUBLISH, BUTTERWORTH-HEINEMANN
WILL PAY FOR BTCV TO PLANT AND CARE FOR A TREE.

Contents

Part One
Introduction to Accounting

This part, which consists of two chapters, aims to provide you with an introduction to the role of accounting and to the type of accounting information typically provided for a variety of users. It gives you a broad framework within which your subsequent studies can be set.

Chapter 1

The role of accounting in business decision making

1.1 Introduction	This chapter is concerned with introducing the role and nature of accounting, the users of accounting information and their information needs.

On completion of this chapter you should be able to:

1.2 Objectives

- discuss the nature and purpose of accounting;
- identify the main users of accounting information and their needs

1.3 Activities and self-assessment questions

There are activities interspersed throughout this and succeeding chapters. The aim of these activities is to help you find out if you have grasped the points which have been raised and to get you to think about issues which relate to the subjects being discussed. Suggested answers to these questions are provided immediately below each activity. You will also find one or more self-assessment questions within each chapter. These questions are usually more demanding than the activities. They may cover a number of the topics or may try to extend your understanding of particular areas. Answers to the self-assessment questions are given at the end of the book. You should make a serious attempt at each activity and self-assessment question before referring to the answers provided.

1.4 The nature of business and business decisions

Most commercial activity occurs because business people (entrepreneurs) see an opportunity to make a profit, to increase their wealth. Given the nature of the free-market economy, with generally free entry and exit into markets, those ventures which yield high returns (profits) are likely to attract new entrants into the industry, thus pushing profits back down to lower levels. Entrepreneurs who find themselves in ventures which are giving low returns will tend to get out of the industry, leaving the more efficient to remain. Given the ever-changing state of the world economy, changes in technology, and a host of other factors, it is fairly apparent that business is in an ever-changing state of flux. In making decisions entrepreneurs need to be as fully aware as possible of the underlying economic situation, both in terms of general economic conditions, and in terms of the specifics of the particular venture. In order to remain profitable, businesses must be aware of the conditions in the particular market(s) in which they trade. They should be fully aware of the costs they are currently incurring, as well as the current and future prices they expect to be able to charge. Much of this information should be available if records (known as accounts) are kept of the historical transactions in which the business engages. Indeed it is difficult to see how decisions can be made effectively unless records of this sort are kept.

Business decision making usually involves choices between alternative courses of action. These alternative courses of action are often subject to constraints of various types. Alternatives are then evaluated, and the decision made. It is usual to then monitor or check the actual decision to see whether in fact the results were in line with what was expected. If not, questions need to be asked. Monitoring can provide useful insights into what went wrong and how to rectify it.

Business decisions can cover a multitude of different things. Possible decisions might include:

- how much of a product to sell
- how much to charge for a product
- whether to take over another business
- whether to close down a business
- whether to invest in a particular piece of equipment
- choosing between alternative ways of producing something
- how much to spend on research and development

plus a host of alternatives.

In passing it is worth pointing out that, in general, it may be expected that ventures which carry higher degrees of risk will (on average) achieve higher rates of return.

| 1.5 **The role of accounting** |

Accounting is concerned with the provision of economic information which will be useful to those directly (and to some extent indirectly) connected with an organization. The information provided should be useful in assessing both the performance of those who manage the organization and the performance and position of the organization itself. Once these assessments have been made by the interested parties, they will be in a position to make more informed economic decisions concerning the organization.

This view of accounting as an aid to economic decision making has achieved increasing acceptance in recent years. The American Accounting Association adopted this perspective when it defined accounting as 'the process of identifying, measuring and communicating economic information to permit informed judgements and decisions by the users of the information'. Though this is only one of very many published definitions of accounting, it is widely quoted in accounting texts because it emphasizes the primary purpose of accounting as providing information which will help users make decisions.

This decision-making emphasis is one which you should constantly bear in mind. There seems to be a feeling held by many people, including many who work in accounting, that accounting is concerned with getting accounting statements prepared each month or each year as if that were an end in itself. While this may describe what some accountants *do*, it does not describe the *purpose* of accounting. Unfortunately, some textbooks on accounting do not really emphasize that accounting is not, or should not be, carried on for its own sake. You should never lose sight of the decision-making objective of accounting information.

Having established that accounting exists in order to provide information for interested parties to make decisions, it is logical to ask: 'Who are these interested parties?' and 'For what kind of decisions is accounting information required?' Figure 1.1 shows the major groups of people who have an interest in an organization. The figure, as constructed, relates to a private sector business but minor alterations in the titles of the participants would make it equally relevant to any organization – for example, a government, a local government unit, a charity, a nationalized industry, a school or college.

Staying with the example of a private enterprise business, it is possible to identify the types of decision that each of the participants might need to make with respect to the organization and the information required. These are as follows.

Owners

Owners are concerned with making two types of decisions. These are:

- investment decisions; and
- stewardship decisions.

Investment decisions are primarily concerned with increasing the wealth of the owners. Those who own businesses normally do so with the intention of increasing their wealth. Owners will, therefore, wish to assess the extent to which the business has generated financial benefits (profits etc.) and the

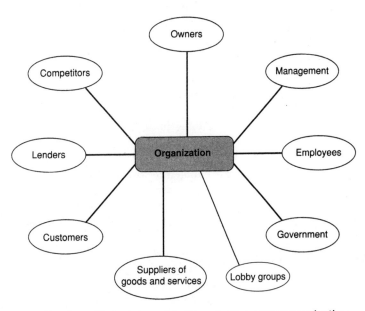

Figure 1.1. *Parties with an interest in the private-sector organization*

likely future prospects of the business. They will also wish to assess the degree of risk associated with their investment in the business. Information relating to associated risks and returns will be useful when deciding whether to hold or sell their ownership interest in the business.

In larger businesses, the owners tend not to exercise day-to-day control over the activities of the business. Instead, managers will often run the business on behalf of the owners. Although managers are expected to operate the business in the interests of the owners, they do have discretion over the way in which the resources of the business are used and there is, therefore, the potential for conflict between managers and owners. This potential conflict creates a need among owners to receive accounting information from the managers which reveals how the resources of the business have been used. The provision of information by managers to owners for this purpose is referred to as *stewardship accounting*. This information may be used by owners, among other things, as a basis for rewarding or dismissing managers.

Government

A government may require information from a business for a variety of reasons. These include:

- *Taxation*
  Businesses are taxed on the basis of their accounting profits (subject to certain adjustments); government (in the form of the Inland Revenue) needs information on each business in order to decide how much tax to charge.
- *Regulation*
  A government may also need information relating to a business for regulatory purposes. For example, information relating to costs and profits may be required in order to decide whether policies promoting greater competition are being adhered to or are necessary.
- *Economic management*
  Governments may also use accounting information relating to businesses to help in the general management of the economy. For example, accounting information may be useful in deciding whether to give support to businesses in a particular industry.
- *Government contracts*
  The government may award contracts on a 'cost plus' basis (i.e. the cost of supplying the goods or service plus an additional profit element) and therefore will be interested in the costs of goods or services supplied by the contractor. This approach is often used when awarding defence contracts. The government will also be interested to see if businesses are making excessive profits as a result of their dealings with the government.

Management

The management of the business is the user group who need most accounting information. Managers are charged with *planning* the activities of the business. They, therefore, require forecast information in order to assess the likely outcome of implementing particular policies in order to decide whether such policies are feasible. Forecast information is also useful in identifying future problems and opportunities for the business, i.e. they may try to ensure that the actual results of the business coincide with the earlier planned results. They therefore require information concerning actual performance and the extent of any deviation from earlier planned performance.

Because managers must plan and control every aspect of the business, detailed information on a wide range of matters is required by them.

Activity 1
Can you think of four types of decisions that a manager of a business might make and which would require accounting information?

Types of management decisions requiring accounting information include:

- *the pricing of goods and services*
- *the quantity of goods to produce*
- *the most appropriate mix of goods to produce*
- *the investment in new equipment, etc.*
- *the raising of finance to maintain or expand the business*
- *the level of payments to make to the owners*
- *the purchase of stock*

This is not an exhaustive list. You may have thought of others.

Of course, managers will also be interested in accounting information which measures financial performance of a business as it may be of direct interest to their future prosperity. For example, good performance may result in a bonus being payable whereas poor performance may result in dismissal.

Customers

These users need information to enable them to answer questions such as 'Will the supplying business be able to remain in business and thus give continuity of supply?' This point may not be important to the domestic consumer buying a tin of peas, but it may well be very important to the supermarket buying the peas from the canner. This is because the supermarket will typically invest quite a lot of time and effort in negotiating a detailed contract with the canner, including visits to the cannery to assess the quality control, etc. If the canner's business fails, this would mean that a different canner would need to be identified and assessed – perhaps a costly business for the supermarket. Accounting information can be useful in trying to assess the ability of a business to survive and to continue to supply its products.

Suppliers of goods and services

As with customers, suppliers will need to satisfy themselves that their customer businesses will be able to honour contracts, etc. Another reason arises from the fact that most commercial sales are made on credit (the goods are delivered or the service is rendered some weeks before cash is paid), so suppliers will be keen to assess the likely ability of customer businesses to meet their obligations.

Lenders

Typically, businesses obtain part of the finance needed to set up and run the business by borrowing from banks, etc. (The other part is supplied by the owners.) Lenders to the business will seek to assess the likely ability of the borrowing business to be able to repay the principal borrowed at the end of the period of the loan (perhaps many years into the future), as well as its ability to pay the interest when it falls due. Lenders may also need to assess the value of any security offered in respect of the loan.

Employees

These are suppliers of a service to the business and their position is much the same as suppliers of goods and other services mentioned above. Employees are typically in a much more profound and long-standing relationship with their employer business than are other suppliers, if only because the employer business may represent the individual employee's only 'customer' at the time and even the only feasible one in the locality. Employees (or their representatives) will therefore have a very direct interest in the ability of the business to survive and to provide employment. They will also be interested in assessing financial performance and position in order to help bargain for improvements in wages and conditions of employment. In some cases, payments to employees may be directly related to the financial performance of the business, e.g. profit-sharing schemes.

Competitors

Competitors have an interest in the accounting information of a business for two reasons:

- They may wish to use the information as a benchmark for measuring their own performance and efficiency. For example, they may wish to see if they are more or less profitable than the business.
- They may wish to assess the financial strength of the business, as a basis for making decisions concerning future policies. For example, competitors may wish to know if the business could withstand a takeover bid or engage in a price-cutting campaign.

Lobby groups

Increasingly activities of private-sector organizations are coming under the scrutiny of lobby groups with an interest in the impact of the organization on social and environmental issues. For example, consider the consequences for a small community which is reliant on one major employer when that employer closes down its local factory. The social costs may be enormous. Whether or not this is or should be the concern of the private-sector business is, of course, debatable, but there is no doubt that accounting information is used in these situations.

The environmental lobby is concerned, among other things, with scrutinizing the impact on the environment, of actions of individual businesses, collectively and separately. There is little doubt that in the past individual businesses have ignored the environmental impact of their actions and effectively passed on the costs to the public. This is now generally seen as unacceptable, but to different degrees. Some business activities still border on environmental vandalism.

Given the growth in interest in social and environmental issues there is now no doubt that even the most single-minded business person needs to be aware of these issues, as they may now directly impact on sales and profits. For example, the sales of recycled products is generally strong. The need for many foodstuffs to be branded as being organic, low-fat, or green in some way all tend to reinforce the increased awareness of social and environmental issues and their importance for the individual business.

These are just a few examples of the types of decision which the different users need to make; in reality, there may be many more.

It is important to recognize that the users identified above represent the major users of accounting information rather than an exhaustive list. There may be others who use the accounting information produced by businesses for particular purposes. For example, community representatives may require information to see whether or not the business is a 'good citizen' and is investing in the community in which it is based. Environmental protection bodies may require information to see whether the business has the resources to make compensation payments for environmental damage it has inflicted. Academic researchers may require information about various aspects of the business to develop or test particular theories, etc.

Activity 2

Are all the users of equal importance when it comes to the provision of financial information? Do you think that a particular user group should be regarded as more important than the others?

There is no single correct answer to this activity. Some may argue that, in a capitalist system, businesses are created by the owners and operate primarily for their benefit. The owners bear the major risks associated with the business, they also incur the costs of producing the financial information. As a result, the owners' information needs (and those of their appointed agents, the managers) should be considered of primary importance. However, others may argue that many of the users identified have a stake in the business. They contribute towards the success of the business and bear risks by being associated with the business. Thus, it would not be appropriate to single out the owners (or any other group) as the most important group.

1.7 Conflict between user groups

It is possible for there to be a conflict of interest between the different user groups. Potential conflict is likely to concern the way in which the wealth of the business is either generated or distributed. For this reason, users may require accounting information to monitor the way in which other users have benefited from the business.

Activity 3

Can you think of an example where accounting information would be useful in dealing with areas of potential conflict between:

- owners and managers
- lenders and owners
- government and owners?

(We have already identified some examples in our earlier discussions.)

We can think of the following examples:

- ***Owners and managers***
  Where managers' pay is linked to performance, the owners may wish to check that the basis for making payments to managers has been properly adhered to and that managers have not been overpaid. This is part of the stewardship role of accounting referred to earlier.
- ***Lenders and owners***
  Lenders may wish to check that the amounts borrowed by the business have been used for their intended purpose and have not been used to make distributions to owners.
- ***Government and owners***
  The government may wish to check to see whether government contractors are not making excessive profits from contracts awarded or that price increases charged to customers by a utility company, such as a gas, electricity or water company, do not exceed the amount stipulated by the government, thereby increasing the owners' wealth.

  You may have thought of other valid examples.

| **1.8**
The usefulness
of accounting
information | You should be clear that accounting information does not provide answers to all the information needs of users; in fact it probably does not provide perfect answers to any of them. However, you should also be clear that accounting as it is practised has grown to its present state because accounting information is perceived as being useful. This is for two reasons: |

- It helps to reduce any uncertainty in users' minds concerning the financial health of the business. Accounting information can give answers to questions such as 'Does the business have the money to repay the loan outstanding?' 'Has the business made enough profit to pay the owners a return on their investment?'
- Other sources of information available may not be as directly relevant, or as reliable, as that produced by the accounting system.

Activity 4
Accounting information does not represent the only source of financial information concerning a business. Can you think of other sources which may be of value when assessing the financial health of a business?

In answering this activity you may have thought of the following:

- *announcement by the business concerning new funds being raised, new contracts won, new products being launched, etc.*
- *newspaper and journal articles reporting on aspects of the business, such as the degree of competition being faced, any reorganization occurring, internal conflict between senior managers, etc.*
- *industry-wide reports on matters such as consumer demand for the products, new government legislation relating to the industry, the impact of new technology, etc.*
- *economy-wide reports on matters such as movements in inflation, levels of consumer confidence, likely changes in taxation or economic policies, etc.*

It should be emphasized that a thorough examination of the financial health of a business should use all the sources of information available and should not rely on a single source. Even though other sources may be less useful than the accounting information produced, each source may help contribute towards the development of a complete picture.

**1.9
Accounting and human behaviour**

The usefulness of accounting reports can be viewed from the perspective of its effect on behaviour. We have seen that accounting exists to provide users with information. The generally accepted definition of information is that it is something which leads to changes in expectations about the outcome of future events, sufficiently large to affect behaviour. Thus accounting reports and statements which do not, and perhaps cannot, affect behaviour are not information, have no practical benefit and are a waste of money.

It is often difficult to judge the usefulness of the accounting information produced by a business. However, there is one area where some assessment can be made of the ability of accounting information to affect behaviour, because the effects can be observed and measured. This is the reaction of investors to the annual accounting profits announced by companies whose shares (portions of the ownership) are traded on the Stock Exchange. There is strong research evidence to suggest that the prices at which the shares are traded change and that the amount of shares that are bought and sold increases when new accounting information is released by companies. This suggests both that investors alter their expectations as to the value of the company (hence changes in share price) and that they take action to buy and sell shares (hence increases in trading volume) as a result of an item of accounting information. What, of course, we do not know is whether the cost of producing the annual accounting report is justified by the benefits it bestows on shareholders, in terms of their ability to put a fairer value on their shares.

| **1.10**
The costs of accounting information | Accounting information can be an expensive commodity. In a business of any size, a large amount of scarce resources can be utilized in paying wages of accounting staff, purchasing computers for the preparation of accounting reports, etc. However, the costs of providing accounting information go beyond the out-of-pocket expenditure incurred. For example, there is also the time spent by managers in evaluating the accounting information received. In addition, the information produced may be employed by users to the disadvantage (cost) of the business and its owners. |

Activity 5

How might accounting information produced by the business be employed by certain user groups to its disadvantage?

Some examples are as follows:

- **Competitors** *may use the information in a way which reduces the competitiveness of a business. For example, a competitor may engage in a price-cutting war in order to improve market share because it knows, from the accounting reports available, that the business is in a weak position to respond to such action.*
- **Employees** *may respond to high reported profits by insisting on high wage increases, thereby reducing the future competitiveness and profits of the business.*
- **Government** *may respond to high reported profits by restricting future price increases to customers of the business (where it has the power to do so) or may levy an excess profits tax.*
- **Suppliers and lenders** *may respond to the reporting of a weak financial position by refusing or withdrawing credit or loan capital.*
- **Customers** *may respond to a weak financial position by going elsewhere for their goods and services to ensure continuity of supplies.*

We have seen earlier that the benefits of producing accounting information are difficult to judge. However, many of the costs of providing accounting information identified above will also be difficult to judge. Nevertheless, when making decisions about the amount and type of accounting information to provide to users, some weighing of costs and benefits should take place.

| **1.11**
Access to accounting information | Without making any judgements about the relative importance of the typical users and their information needs identified in section 1.6 above, it is by the nature of things that managers will have access to as much information as exists or can be compiled within the organization, whereas the other interested groups may be more reliant on what managers are prepared to provide. However, what the 'outsiders' are provided with is not entirely |

determined by managers, since many organizations, public and private, must, as a result of regulations emanating from government, the accountancy profession, or the Stock Exchange, provide prescribed minimum amounts of information. This does not necessarily mean, however, that managers will restrict the amount of information to outsiders to the minimum requirements prescribed by accounting regulations. In some cases managers may be prepared to go beyond these minimum requirements. A business with 'good news' to announce or simply 'nothing to hide' may feel that it is in its best interests to provide additional accounting information to outside users which reveals this. The benefits to the business may take the form of being able to raise future funds more easily and/or at lower cost than might otherwise be the case.

In addition, certain interested groups such as government and lenders (in particular circumstances, such as loan negotiations) may be in a position to demand the information they require. Nevertheless, the outsiders, which include the shareholders in private sector companies, will not normally have free access to the accounting records of the business or be in a position to *demand* information beyond what the various accounting regulations require.

| **1.12 Financial and management accounting** | It was seen above that managers of a business will normally have a need for more comprehensive and detailed accounting information than the other users identified. As a result accounting has developed in two major directions – management and financial accounting. |

| **Management accounting** | Management accounting is concerned with the provision of information to the managers of the business. The major features of this form of accounting are: |

- *Detailed information.* The information provided, as stated earlier, is often very detailed in nature, e.g. information concerning the costs relating to a particular product, the profit made by a particular division of the business, the feasibility of acquiring a particular machine, etc. However, managers will also require accounting reports which provide a general overview at regular intervals to help them retain a proper perspective on the business.
- *Forward looking.* The accounting information provided may incorporate plans as well as information based on actual costs, profits, etc.
- *Frequent reporting intervals.* Feedback of information to managers is provided on a frequent and regularly recurring basis in order to help managers monitor the performance of the business closely. Thus, in a business of any size, some accounting reports are likely to be provided to managers on a monthly basis.
- *Flexibility.* The accounting reports provided to managers can be produced in a form which best suits their needs. There are no regulations governing what accounting information should be produced or in what form it should be provided.

<table>
<tr><td>

Financial accounting

</td><td>

Financial accounting is concerned with the provision of information to the other interested groups identified above. The major features of this form of accounting are:

</td></tr>
</table>

- *Summarized form.* The information is usually in the form of a summary of the performance of the business for the preceding period and a statement of the financial position at the end of the period. Data is often aggregated and so detail may be missing. The information provided is intended to give an overview of the financial health of the business.
- *Backward-looking.* The information is based on actual results and it would be unusual for a business to disclose planned results to outsiders.
- *Infrequent reporting.* Financial accounting reports are usually produced on a regular basis, but not so frequently as is the case with management accounting reports. The majority of businesses produce financial accounting reports on an annual basis, with a few large businesses producing accounting reports more frequently (usually half-yearly but occasionally quarterly).
- *Standardized format.* The financial reports produced by many businesses are subject to accounting regulations from the sources identified earlier. This means that the financial statements are produced in a particular format, will disclose certain minimum information and will adopt certain accounting policies. This requirement for uniformity in financial reporting enables meaningful comparisons to be made between different businesses.

Activity 6
It has been stated earlier that accounting is concerned with decision making and it can be argued that decision making is concerned with the future rather than the past. As a result, would it not be a good idea to provide outsiders with information on planned performance? Why do you think that managers are often reluctant to provide information on planned performance to outsiders?

Some believe that, as the move towards meeting the needs of users gathers momentum, there will be eventual acceptance of the need to produce information on planned performance for outsiders. As managers find this kind of information useful, it is difficult to argue that other users will not. In certain exceptional situations, such as when a company is seeking to raise new capital or is fighting off a hostile takeover, information on planned performance may already be provided to outsiders. However, this is not the norm. Managers are usually reluctant to provide such information to outsiders even though they produce it for their own purposes. There are two important reasons for this:

- *Managers are often concerned that disclosure of plans will damage the competitive position of the business. It may provide competitors with a forewarning of future strategies and policies.*
- *Managers are concerned that the information concerning planned performance will be misinterpreted by some users who may not fully appreciate the risk of error in producing such information.*

It should be mentioned that, for large companies listed on the Stock Exchange, forecasts of future profits are produced by outside investment analysts and made available to investors. Although the evidence is mixed, some studies have shown that profit forecasts produced by investment analysts are as close to the actual profit achieved as the profit plans produced by managers of the relevant companies. If this is the case, it can be argued that there is no need for these companies to produce information on profit plans as profit forecasts provided by other sources are equally useful to investors.

In this book, our primary concern is with financial accounting. We shall examine the major financial statements prepared for outsiders and show how they can be analysed and interpreted. However, it must be emphasized that the division between management accounting and financial accounting is not clear-cut. The financial statements and the techniques of financial analysis which will be discussed are also used by managers to help assess the position and performance of the business.

1.13 Accounting in the private sector – profitability and viability

It was seen above that the different users of accounting information each have different needs. However, when assessing the performance of a business there are two aspects which are likely to be of concern to each group identified. The first aspect is *profitability*. A private-sector business must generate wealth (profits) in order to satisfy the needs of the owners and to ensure that there are sufficient funds to maintain or expand operations. This does not mean, however, that a business must be profitable in every period. It is possible for a business to incur losses, from time to time, provided it is profitable in the long term. The second aspect is *viability*. Profitability and viability are interrelated concepts. In order to survive it is necessary, but not sufficient, for a business to be profitable. A business must also possess a constant capacity to meet its maturing obligations when they fall due. This means that the business must retain sufficient cash (liquidity) in the business. Cash has been described as the life blood of a business. Unless there is sufficient cash available to pay suppliers and lenders when required, the business can be forced to cease trading even though it may be profitable. Viability may also depend on other characteristics such as the way in which the business conducts its operations within the community in which it is based, the degree of risk associated with its operations, etc.

Users of financial reports are likely to share a common interest in these aspects of business performance; however, it is likely that the emphasis placed on each aspect will vary between the different user groups.

Activity 7
Which would each of the following groups be primarily interested in – profitability or viability?

- owners
- lenders

- suppliers
- employees

We think the primary concern of each group is likely to be:

- *Owners – profitability*
- *Lenders – viability*
- *Suppliers – viability*
- *Employees – viability*

**1.14
General-
purpose or
specific-purpose
reports?**

As each user group has different objectives it is possible to argue that each group should receive financial reports which are specifically designed to meet these needs. However, this approach is likely to be extremely costly to a business in relation to the expected benefits. It has been suggested above that, despite the differing objectives of users, it is possible to identify certain aspects of financial performance in which all users are likely to have an interest. Hence, it can be argued that businesses could satisfy the major needs of all users by producing financial reports which deal with the profitability and viability of the enterprise. In practice, businesses produce what are described as *general-purpose reports*, which reveal this information. This approach appears to be broadly acceptable to users.

Although general-purpose reports are capable of covering areas of interest for different user groups it is, nevertheless, a fact that some users of financial information have a more sophisticated understanding of financial matters than others. There may still be a need therefore to provide different types of reports which are aimed at different levels of understanding. In recent years, there has been a growing recognition of this issue by preparers of financial reports. Many large businesses now produce financial reports for employees which are usually a simplified version of the general-purpose financial reports available to outsiders (including employees). In addition, it is now possible for private individuals who own shares (portions of ownership) in a company, but do not have a good understanding of accounting, to receive simplified reports based on the general-purpose reports which are currently being produced.

Activity 8
Do you think it is a good thing to produce simplified reports to help less sophisticated users? What is the argument against producing such reports?

The idea of preparing simplified financial reports for those with a limited under-standing of financial reports has intuitive appeal, particularly as the extent of accounting regulation has increased considerably in recent years, and this has made accounting reports much more complex documents. However, there are potential dangers in providing simplified reports. Businesses can be extremely complex economic organizations and to try to reduce the level of financial complexity of such organizations in order for less sophisticated users to understand may not be possible without seriously distorting the picture which is finally produced. Some argue that it is not the accountant's role to provide potentially misleading information. They believe that if a user cannot understand the financial reports, he or she should seek financial advice from an expert (or study accounting!).

**1.15
Types of
business
enterprise**

A business enterprise will usually take one of three forms. A *sole proprietorship* (or sole trader) is a type of business in which there is a single owner. This type of business tends to be fairly small in size and many small shops, hotels, service contractors (e.g. plumbers, TV repairs, etc.) and farms are of this type. In order to start up and then carry on such a business there are no specific legal requirements to comply with, thus providing the business keeps within the general law of the land, the owner has considerable flexibility in the way in which the business is carried out. In law the business is not regarded as a separate legal entity and, therefore, the business will cease on the retirement or death of the owner. However, for accounting purposes the business is regarded as being separate from the owner. This is an important point, as will be shown later. A sole proprietorship does not even have to keep financial records or prepare accounts except in so far as they are required for taxation purposes. Although there are no formal legal requirements to keep accounts it would, however, be extremely unwise for a sole proprietor not to keep some form of accounts. It is difficult to see how the owner would be able to make sensible economic decisions in the absence of appropriate information.

A *partnership* exists where two or more persons carry on a business with a view to making profits. The maximum number of owners is normally twenty. Once again, partnership businesses tend to be fairly small in size; the amount the partners can afford to invest (known as capital) is usually an important limiting factor to growth. There are no special legal formalities to comply with in order to start up a partnership. The formation of the partnership can take place simply through a verbal agreement or through the actions of the owners. However, it would be unwise not to have some clear written agreement between the parties on how the business should be conducted, the division of profits, the contribution of capital, etc. A partnership does not have to keep financial records or prepare accounts except in so far as they are required for taxation purposes. However, as there is more than one owner, it is probably even more important for a partnership to keep proper accounts than for a sole proprietor. The partnership can carry out its business in any way it sees fit provided the business complies with general legal requirements. Although there is a Partnership Act, this is only designed to cover disputes which arise between partners where they have failed to come to a clear agreement on a particular matter. The law does not recognize a partnership as a separate legal entity and, therefore, a partnership cannot enter into contracts in its own name but must do so through the individuals who make up the partnership. However, for accounting purposes the partnership is treated as a separate entity.

A *limited company* is regarded as a separate legal entity, which means that it can enter into contracts in its own name and is given a perpetual existence which is unaffected by changes in the membership of the company. Limited companies can be very large indeed as there can be no upper limit to the number of people permitted to subscribe capital to the business. This type of business enterprise has limited liability which means that the members of the company are only liable for the debts of the company up to the amount which they have agreed to contribute. This is in contrast to the position of sole proprietors or partners where they will be liable for the debts of the business up to and including the extent of their own personal wealth. In order to start a limited company, documents of incorporation must be prepared which set out the name of the company, the objectives of the business and the way in which its affairs will be conducted. The company will be subject to the accounting regulations set out in the Companies Acts, the accounting standards developed by the accountancy profession and, if it is listed on the Stock Exchange, the requirements of the Stock Exchange. A limited company must keep proper financial records and prepare accounts on an annual basis. Moreover, the accounts prepared must be subject to an independent audit. This means that an independent firm of accountants must examine the accounts and the underlying records and form an opinion as to whether the accounts give a true and fair view of the company's financial performance and position and comply with the Companies Acts' requirements and relevant accounting rules.

Activity 9

When setting up a new business, what factors might you consider in deciding upon the particular form of business enterprise to adopt?

We can think of the following factors:

- **Finance**. *A business may require a large amount of funding from the owners, which is beyond the capacity of a single individual. In this situation, a partnership or a limited company may be appropriate.*
- **Degree of risk**. *The more risky the venture, the more attractive limited liability status may appear to the owners.*
- **Administration costs**. *We have seen that a limited liability company must conform to various legal requirements. This can be both time-consuming and costly and may not appear to the owners to be worth the benefits which flow.*
- **Sharing the burden**. *The responsibilities of ownership may be lightened where there is more than one owner. However, this must be weighed against any loss of control over decision-making which will arise from having multiple ownership.*

- **Flexibility**. *Sole traders and partnerships can be formed, dissolved and restructured in line with the owners' wishes and without having to consider any legal regulations. This is not the case for limited companies.*

In this book the main focus will be on accounting for limited liability companies as this form of business enterprise is, in economic terms, the most significant. Limited companies dominate the economies of most Western industrialized nations. However, it is probably not a good idea to introduce the accounts of limited liability companies at this early stage. Instead, we shall begin by looking at the accounts of a sole-proprietorship-type of business as this is the simplest form of business organization and provides a useful means of introducing the basic principles of accounting. Having examined these principles, which are identical for all three forms of business enterprise, we will then move on to examine the accounts of limited companies.

1.16 Summary

In this chapter we have seen that the purpose of accounting is to help interested parties make economic decisions about an organization. Economic decisions require economic information and it is the role of accounting to provide the economic information required. The use of accounting information should help ensure that users employ the limited resources available to them in the most efficient and profitable manner. A number of groups of users of accounting information can be identified and each group has different objectives to pursue. However, it is possible to argue that each group will have a concern for the profitability and viability of the business enterprise. For those users who have limited access to financial information concerning a business, general-purpose financial reports may be prepared which help reveal the profitability and viability of the business.

Exercises

1 You are the owner of Hope Springs and you have been approached by the management of Goodtime Clocks with a view to your firm supplying clock springs on credit. What information about Goodtime Clocks would be useful to you in assessing the contract?
2 What formal evidence is there that accounting information actually can affect the behaviour of some individuals?
3 Do you agree that lobby groups have legitimate entitlements to accounting information?
4 Does the provision of general-purpose financial reports imply that no one user group can be completely satisfied?
5 What do you think are the main reasons why companies are subject to more detailed accounting requirements than sole trading or partnership businesses?

Chapter 2

The main accounting reports

This chapter provides you with an introduction to the main accounting reports. It also provides a set of desirable qualities (also known as desirable characteristics) which should influence the way in which accounting information is drawn up.

On completion of this chapter you should be able to:

- outline the nature and purpose of each of the major financial statements;
- identify and discuss the desirable qualities of accounting information.

Having discussed the nature and purpose of accounting, we can now introduce the main financial reports which are usually prepared. These reports are designed to give users an insight into the financial position and performance of the business. We will start by considering the problem of simply measuring changes in the cash position of the business as a means of providing users with a picture of the financial health of a business.

**What is wrong
with reporting
cash movements
alone?**

At first sight, since wealth generation is important to users of accounting and wealth is usually measured in monetary terms, it might be thought that a statement of the amount of cash generated, perhaps augmented by some information on how it was generated, would be sufficient for users. However, this would not be the case. To begin with, the amount of cash generated may not be the same as the amount of wealth generated during a period. In order to see why this is, it may be useful to consider a simple example.

Example

Jim, who has been unemployed, decided to start a business selling boxes of matches on a street corner. On Monday he went to the local cash and carry wholesaler and used £20 he had saved to buy £20 worth of boxes of matches. These he sold quite easily during the day for £40. How much wealth (profit) did he generate?

The answer is simply the difference between the amount that he paid for the stock (£20), and what he sold it for (£40), i.e. £20. This is, of course, the difference between the cash he started the day with and that with which he finished the day. So, in this case, the amount of cash generated is the same as the wealth generated. However, let us continue with our example.

On Tuesday Jim decided that since the trip to the cash and carry was time-consuming, it would be useful to buy two days' supply. With this in mind, he bought £40 worth of matches. During Tuesday Jim sold exactly half of the matches for £40. When he came to assess how well the day had gone Jim (a simple soul) was alarmed to realize that he had no more cash at the end of the day than he had at the start. He deduced from this that he had generated no wealth (profit) and that he had therefore wasted his time. Was he correct?

Clearly, he was incorrect since he had actually increased his wealth from the £40 in cash with which he started the day, to £40 in cash plus £20 worth of matches by the end of the day, i.e. a £20 increase in wealth.

This example shows that cash increases and decreases are inadequate as a measure of wealth generation (profit) since wealth can be, and usually to a great extent is, held in other things of value instead of cash. Thus, in order to assess wealth generation, we need to look more widely than just at cash.

The circumstances arising on Tuesday are much more like the typical business where much of any wealth generated will find its way into such things as stock-in-trade, new buildings, new machinery, etc. This should not lead us to the conclusion that where cash comes from, where it goes to and how much is left is not important to businesses. Cash is the life blood of the business and managers need to monitor it, but as a measure of success and achievement, cash is inadequate.

In much of the public sector, where economic wealth generation is not necessarily the objective, the emphasis is often rather less on this and more on other factors. However, even here considerable interest is found in increasing the wealth of society in general, and the measurement of surpluses and assessment of efficiency remain important factors.

The need for more than one financial statement

If Jim, the matchseller in the above example, were to be asked what he needed to know about his business at the end of each day (or perhaps less frequently) his answer would probably be along the following lines:

(a) A statement of how well he had done as far as trading was concerned, i.e. how much wealth he had generated during the day in question. This statement is referred to as the *profit and loss account* or *income statement*. It will take his sales figure and deduct from it the costs incurred relative to those sales. The resulting figure would not necessarily be his net increase in cash, as we have seen, because payment for the stock does not necessarily occur on the day on which it is sold.

For Tuesday (from the above example) such a statement would be something like the following:

Profit and loss account (income statement) for Tuesday

	£	£
Sales of matches		40
Purchases of matches	40	
Less: closing stock of matches	20	
Cost of matches sold		20
Net profit (increase in wealth)		20

(b) A statement of where cash had come from and gone to during the day. This is known as a *cash flow statement*. As we have seen, though cash is not the only form that wealth can take, it is very important, if only because generally it is the only form of wealth which can readily be converted into other forms (i.e. spent).

For Tuesday, such a statement would show the cash received from sales and the cash paid out in buying stocks. The difference between these can then be added to (or subtracted from) the opening cash balance in order to establish the closing cash balance.

Cash flow statement for Tuesday

	£	£
Receipts from sales		40
Less: payment for stock		40
Net increase in cash		Zero
Opening balance		40
Closing balance		40

From this Jim can see why, though he made a profit, he is not better off in cash terms.

(c) A statement of where his business wealth lay at the end of the day. This statement is referred to as the *balance sheet* or *financial position statement*. For Tuesday such a statement would be as follows:

Balance sheet (position statement) as at end of Tuesday

	£
Stock of unsold matches	20
Cash (closing balance on Tuesday)	40
	60
Therefore:	
Jim's business wealth is	60

Obviously, in the very simple circumstances of Jim's business activities on Tuesday, the information contained in the statements could be deduced without any formal written statements. However, it does not take much imagination to see that, if we were dealing with a business any larger than that of Jim, or even Jim's business over a longer period than a day or two, this would not be possible.

These three statements are what is produced periodically by most private-sector, and by many public-sector, organizations. Between them they can give interested parties valuable insights concerning what has taken place within the organization. When used as the framework for projections, they can also give very valuable information on the probable future direction of the business, in financial terms.

The early part of this book is concerned with the preparation of these statements, particularly Chapters 3, 4 and 5. However, as the book progresses, much more emphasis will be placed on the use of these statements, and their analysis and interpretation.

Activity 1

On Wednesday Jim started the day with £20 worth of matches. For some reason trade was bad on that day and Jim had great difficulty in selling the matches. In fact he had to resort to selling them at less than his usual price to sell them at all. Even then he was left with matches which had cost him £5. His takings for the day totalled £25.

Show the three standard accounting statements for Jim's business for Wednesday.

Jim – Profit and loss account for Wednesday

	£	£
Sales of matches		25
Opening stock of matches	20	
Less: closing stock of matches	5	
Cost of sales		15
Net profit for the day		10

Jim – Cash flow statement for Wednesday

	£
Receipts from sales	25
Less: payment for stock	Zero
Net increase in cash	25
Opening balance (Tuesday's closing balance)	40
Closing balance	65

Jim – Balance sheet as at end of Wednesday

	£
Stock of matches	5
Cash (closing balance on Wednesday)	65
	70
Jim's business wealth	70

(Note that Jim's business wealth has increased from £60 on Tuesday to £70 on Wednesday, the amount of Wednesday's profit.)

This answer assumes that Jim, for the time being, regards the cash generated by the business as part of his business wealth. In practice, of course, he may well withdraw cash to live on.

Self-assessment question 2.1

Russell was following a business studies course at his local university. As the summer was approaching, he decided to try to earn some extra money to help finance a holiday in France. As he lived in a seaside town, he decided to try to sell ice cream on the beach. He had £100 to invest and was able to buy 10 boxes of ice cream from a local manufacturer at a cost of £10 per box. He expected to sell the ice creams in each box for a total of £15. On the first day, he sold 8 boxes and stored the unsold boxes in his parent's freezer overnight. The next day he bought a further 10 boxes and managed to sell 11 boxes at £15 per box. On the third day he bought another 10 boxes, but only managed to sell 4 boxes as the weather had turned cold. As the long-term forecast was not good, Russell decided to abandon this venture and sold the remaining boxes at £8 per box.

Required:
(a) Prepare a profit and loss account and cash flow statement for each of the four days of trading.
(b) Prepare a balance sheet at the end of each day's trading.
(c) What do you deduce from an examination of the statements you have prepared?
(The answer to this question is given at the end of the book.)

2.4 Desirable qualities of accounting information

It was mentioned above that accounting information should be useful as a basis for decision making. In order to determine what sort of accounting information will be useful for this purpose, it is possible to identify certain desirable attributes or qualities which accounting information should possess. It can be argued that *relevance* and *reliability* are the two primary attributes which financial information must have in order to be useful.

Relevance means that the information produced should be capable of influencing the decision to be made. In order to be relevant to decision makers, accounting information should have:

- predictive value and/or
- confirmatory (feedback) value

Predictive value means that the information should be capable of helping the decision maker to predict likely future outcomes. This does not necessarily imply that the information should take the form of a prediction. It can mean that the information would be useful in helping to form a prediction. For example, an oil company may announce that its oilfields in a foreign country have been expropriated by the foreign government without compensation. Such information is not a prediction but rather a statement of what has already happened. It may, nevertheless, be extremely useful in helping to predict future profits of the oil company.

Confirmatory value means that the information should help in confirming or correcting expectations about past events. This is extremely important for decision makers. Information relating to past performance or events can be used to compare actual performance with earlier planned performance which can be used to identify past problems or difficulties. It can also help in confirming or revising predictions about the future.

Activity 2
Can you think of an example where a particular piece of accounting information can help in both predicting the future and confirming the past?

Information concerning the amount of sales made during a period may be of value in forming a prediction about likely sales in the following period. It can also confirm earlier predictions concerning the likely sales for the period.

You may have thought of another example where a piece of financial information could serve this dual purpose.

Reliability is concerned with portraying what is supposed to be portrayed. In order to be reliable, the accounting information provided must possess a number of characteristics. These are shown in Figure 2.1.

To be reliable, accounting information must also be *neutral*. This means that the methods of measurement used and those who measure should be free from any bias. Neutrality is important in giving accounting reports credibility in the eyes of users. If users suspect that the information they receive is biased, it will undermine the perceived value of the reports. Accounting information should also possess *representational faithfulness* in order to be reliable. This means that the information provided should be a valid description of what it purports to represent and should be free from error. Users must be satisfied that the accounting numbers and any descriptions used faithfully reflect the underlying economic conditions which they are attempting to represent.

Accounting information should also be *complete* in order to be reliable. A significant omission from the information may create a false impression and may mislead users. This, of course, would render the information unreliable. Many believe that accounting information should also be *prudent* and any estimates or judgements made should be done with a degree of caution. It would certainly be misleading to paint a rosier picture of the position and performance of the business than is actually the case. However, in exercising

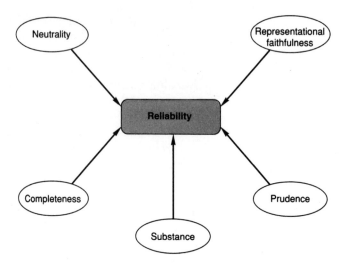

Figure 2.1. *The main characteristics of reliability*

prudence we must be careful not to paint a gloomier picture than is warranted by the facts.

Accounting information should also portray the *substance of the transaction rather than its legal form*. If, for example, a business does not own a particular resource but nevertheless has control over it, then for all intents and purposes, it belongs to the business and this fact should be portrayed in the financial statements. Suppose a business decides to lease a machine for the whole of the machine's working life. This transaction will give the business effective control over the machine and it will become a resource of the business. The fact that the legal ownership still rests elsewhere should not prevent us from recognizing that the machine is part of the economic resource base of the business and so should be included as such in the financial statements. This portrayal of underlying economic reality is more important than excluding the machine from the total resources shown simply because the legal title is not held by the business.

Although, in an ideal world, accounting information should be both relevant and reliable, we must recognize that, at times, a conflict may occur between the two.

Activity 3

A business owns a piece of land which was purchased earlier in the year. When the land was purchased it cost £100,000 but the owners believe it has a current market value of £120,000. How can these two different values create a conflict between relevance and reliability, when producing accounting information?

It may be argued that the current value of the land is likely to be more relevant than the original cost for many types of decisions, e.g. when considering an offer to sell the land. However, the current market value may be difficult to establish with a high degree of reliability. The more unique the item being valued, the more subjective any valuation is likely to be and the greater the likelihood of error. The original cost, on the other hand, can usually be verified and this figure will normally have a high degree of reliability. However, this information may be of limited value for decision-making purposes.

In practice, it may be necessary to trade off one quality against another. Which quality is to be traded off is often a matter of judgement; however, the overriding aim should always be to meet the decision-making needs of users.

Timeliness is closely related to the qualities of relevance and reliability discussed above. This refers to the time lag in reporting accounting information and it can influence both the relevance and reliability of accounting information.

Activity 4

Timely reporting is considered to be essential in providing relevant information. Why is this, do you think? Can the timely reporting of accounting information undermine the quality of reliability?

Although the production of timely reports does not, of itself, ensure relevance, the absence of timeliness can destroy the potential relevance of accounting information. If the time lag in reporting is too long, then the usefulness of the information can diminish or perhaps disappear. For example, if a manager wished to make a decision in November on the results of the business in October, eventual production of the financial reports in December would mean that the information could not be used. However, timely reporting may impair the reliability of the reports. Timely reporting can increase the risk that errors will be made and may increase the need for estimates to be made as all information concerning a particular item may not be known at the time of reporting.

In addition to the primary characteristics of relevance and reliability, accounting information should also possess two secondary characteristics to be useful. These are *understandability* and *comparability*. Understandability means that accounting information should be presented in a form which is readily understandable. However, this raises the question, understandable by whom? We saw earlier that there are compelling reasons for not attempting to simplify complex economic reality in order to satisfy the needs of unsophisticated users as there is a real danger that the message will be distorted. This has led some to argue that we should only seek to address the needs of sophisticated users (e.g. bankers, accountants, investment analysts, etc.). However, many prefer to take a less extreme position than this and believe we should meet the needs of users who have a *reasonable knowledge of accounting* and are prepared to study the financial information with *reasonable diligence*. What is meant by the term reasonable in this context, however, is open to debate.

Comparability has two dimensions. The first concerns the adoption of accounting policies and procedures by a business in a consistent manner between periods. This characteristic is important as users must be able to make comparisons from one period to another in order to assess changes in performance and position. Unless the business adopts the same methods of accounting over time, any such comparisons would be hindered. The second dimension concerns the consistency of accounting policies in relation to other businesses. This can be important when making comparisons between businesses.

In order for users to assess the degree of comparability which exists, it is important for a business to reveal its accounting policies and to indicate when any changes have been made.

2.5 Summary

In this chapter we have seen the limitations of relying on reports which are solely based on cash. We worked through a simple business situation and produced three financial statements which provided different insights. These statements were the profit and loss account – which is a statement which shows how, and by how much, wealth was generated in a period, the cash flow statement, which shows cash movements over the period, and the balance sheet, which provides a statement of financial position at a particular time, usually at the end of the period for which the other two statements are drawn up.

We also saw that accounting information produced for users must have certain qualities if it is to be useful for decision-making purposes. These are relevance, reliability, understandability and comparability. In practice, it is not always possible to provide information which supplies all of these qualities to a high degree and it may be necessary on occasions to trade off one quality against another.

Exercises

1 Helen, a student, has decided to try to earn some extra income in order to purchase a new motor-car. She has been appointed an agent for her region for a business which manufactures a new type of squash racquet. She has agreed to buy from the manufacturer at £24 per racquet and intends to sell at £36 per racquet. In the first month of trading Helen purchased 30 racquets and managed to sell 25 of these. In the second month she purchased 40 racquets and sold 22. In the third month Helen decided that the new venture was taking up too much of her time and therefore decided to cease trading. She purchased no further racquets during the month and sold off her remaining stock at £20 per racquet.

   Required:
   (a) Prepare a profit and loss account and cash flow statement for each month of trading.
   (b) Prepare a balance sheet at the end of each month.
2 Identify and explain the constituent parts of relevance and reliability in the context of the provision of accounting information.

Part Two
Accounting Statements: Nature and Preparation

This part consists of six chapters. It aims to provide you with an introduction to the nature and purpose of the balance sheet and the profit and loss account. The underlying rules, known as conventions, relating to the preparation of financial statements, are identified and their limitations discussed. Some of the important problems associated with measuring profit are also dealt with.

Chapters 3–8 aim to provide you with a framework which can be used to prepare financial statements from a limited number of transactions. Given the aim of this text, this framework should be sufficient to enable you to understand the basic principles of the accounting process, which can then be applied to more complex issues.

Chapter 3

The balance sheet

3.1 Introduction

This chapter aims to set out the nature, form and content of the balance sheet. This is the first of the major financial statements to be studied in detail.

3.2 Objectives

On completion of this chapter you should be able to:

- explain the nature and purpose of a balance sheet;
- define the terms asset, liability and capital;
- identify the typical form and content of a balance sheet;
- explain the major conventions which underpin the balance sheet;
- explain why a balance sheet on its own does not provide an adequate record of events.

3.3 The nature and purpose of a balance sheet

A balance sheet is a *statement of the assets of, and claims against, a business at a particular point in time.* It may therefore be viewed as a statement of financial position. An asset is, in simple terms, something which provides a benefit to the business, while a claim is a financial obligation of the business to a person, group of people, or an organization. However, in practice, rather more precise criteria exist with regard to the inclusion of an item in a balance sheet as either an asset or a claim.

An *asset* may be more formally defined for accounting purposes as a right or other access to probable future economic benefits obtained and controlled by a particular business. This benefit is typically the result of some current or past transaction or event affecting that business. In order to be recorded in a business balance sheet, an asset should normally have the following characteristics:

- The benefits to be obtained must relate to the future. So, if no future benefits remained from an asset at the date of a balance sheet, it would stop being included in the balance sheet.
- Access to the benefits is controllable by the business. A car hired by a business for a week would not be included as an asset of that business, since access is controlled by the hire company.
- The benefits must have been acquired as the result of a past transaction or event. Typically, this will have involved the business in some kind of money sacrifice, or led to it incurring some future liability. This provides the basis for quantifying or measuring the asset.

Activity 1
Which of the following would be defined as an asset for accounting purposes?

- A chief executive who has succeeded in increasing profits by £1m per annum since her appointment.
- Goodwill from customers which has been built up by the business over the years as a result of the quality of its products.
- The M4 motorway which is used daily by a parcel delivery business in order to deliver on time.
- A piece of equipment owned by the company which is obsolete and has no scrap value.
- A new machine purchased by a business for £2,000 and which should lead to cost savings but has not yet been paid for.

Your answer to this activity should be along the following lines:

- *The chief executive would not be regarded as an accounting asset as the business does not control access to its employees.*
- *The goodwill would not be an asset as it did not arise as a result of a past transaction.*
- *The M4 motorway would not be an asset of the business because it cannot control the access of others to the motorway.*
- *An obsolete piece of equipment would not be an asset as it can provide no future benefits.*
- *The new equipment would meet the criteria for an asset. The fact that payment for the asset has not yet been made does not affect the situation.*

This activity illustrates that not all resources which are of value to the business may be defined as an asset for accounting purposes.

As with the definition of an asset, so the definition of a claim as an obligation of the business requires further clarification. A more formal definition is that a *claim* is an existing obligation to provide goods (including money) or services (i.e. to transfer economic benefits) to an individual or organization outside of the business, at some time in the future. To be recorded in a business balance sheet, a claim should normally exhibit the following characteristics:

- The claim exists at the time of the balance sheet. In other words, the transaction or event causing the obligation must already have occurred.
- There is a reasonable expectation that the claim will have to be met.

It is important to note that *potential* future claims, frequently associated with such things as legal cases and the possibility of some future award for damages, are not recorded in a balance sheet. Such claims are known as *contingent liabilities*. While not recorded in the balance sheet, knowledge of such claims is clearly important, since they represent potential problem areas. Contingent liabilities tend to be shown as a separate note to the financial statements.

Claims fall into two distinct types, with further subdivision into categories being found within these two broad types.

- External claims, i.e. liabilities to parties outside of the business.
- Claims by the owners or investors in a business, also known as *capital* or *equity*.

In order to explain the idea of capital or equity it is necessary to introduce the convention of the *business entity*. In essence, the business entity convention says that, for accounting purposes, a distinction needs to be drawn between the owners of a business and the business itself. The financial statements, which include the balance sheet, are prepared *for the business*, and the owners' entitlement is shown as a claim on the business. The business entity convention may be viewed as being technically necessary, since without it, the balance sheet would not balance. It is important to recognize, however, the different nature of the owners' claim, as compared with other external claims.

Once the business entity convention has been introduced, it is possible to summarize the balance sheet as a statement in which:

Assets = claims (capital + external liabilities)

This sets out on one side of the equation the resources of the business which provide future benefits, and on the other side of the equation the claims on those resources.

The above equation is referred to as the *balance sheet equation* and it will always hold. If, for example, an owner introduced £5,000 cash into a new business, the effect would be to increase the assets (cash) of the business, and to increase the owner's claim (capital) of the business. The resulting balance sheet after this transaction would be:

Assets		*Claims*	
	£		£
Cash	+5,000	Capital	+5,000

This shows the assets equal to the claims. (In this case, the only claim is from the owner.)

If a friend of the owner loaned the business £2,000 cash, the effect would be to increase the assets (cash) and to increase the external liabilities (loans) of the business. The balance sheet after this transaction would be:

Assets		*Claims*	
	£		£
Cash	+5,000	Capital	+5,000
	+2,000	Loan	+2,000

We can see that, after these transactions, the balance sheet equation still holds (assets = claims).

We are now ready to look at a more detailed example concerning the balance sheet equation.

| **Example** | This example shows how a balance sheet may be built up from a series of business transactions. You are given the following transactions and asked to prepare a balance sheet showing the resulting financial position. |

(a) Jean Jones invests cash of £10,000 in a new business.
(b) The business buys goods which it plans to resell (known as stock or inventory) for £5,000 cash.
(c) It buys a further £1,000 worth of stock on credit (i.e. it undertakes to pay for them at a later date).
(d) It sells stock which had cost £1,000 for £1,500 cash.
(e) It acquires a new machine for £4,000 cash.

At this stage let us prepare a simple list of assets and claims and record the impact of each transaction on our list. The final position will be as set out below:

Workings

Assets	+	−	Net	Claims	+	−	Net
Cash				Capital			
(a)	+10,000			(a)	+10,000		
(b)		−5,000		(d)	+ 500		
(d)	+1,500						
(e)		−4,000					
Stock							
(b)	+5,000			Creditors			
(c)	+1,000			(c)	+1,000		
(d)		−1,000					
Machinery							
(e)	+4,000						

The effects of the above transactions are shown below.

(a) Assets increase by £10,000 (cash)
    Claims increase by £10,000 (capital, due to the business entity convention)
(b) Assets do not change in total but cash goes down by £5,000 while stock goes up by £5,000. No change in claims
(c) Assets go up by £1,000 (stock)
    Claims go up by £1,000 (creditors, i.e. people to whom the business owes money)
(d) This transaction is a little more difficult than the earlier transactions. The effect on the assets side of the balance sheet will be as follows:

Assets go up by a net amount of £500 with stock going down by £1,000 and cash going up by £1,500

If assets go up by a net amount of £500 (i.e £1,500 − £1,000), then claims must also go up by £500, for the balance sheet to remain in balance. We therefore need to ask if there is any obvious claim which can be increased. The answer is provided by the business entity convention. The transaction in (d) has led to an increase in assets as a result of trading, namely a profit. The essence of most commercial enterprises is the search for profits, with a consequent risk of losses. If a profit or a loss results we need to ask who is the beneficiary (or loser)? The answer must be the owner. Hence, profitable transactions increase the owner's claim, while loss-making transactions reduce the owner's claim. In transaction (d) the remaining entry is therefore:

Claims go up by £500, namely capital.

(e) Assets do not change in total but cash goes down by £4,000 while machinery goes up by £4,000. No change in liabilities

On completion of these five transactions the business balance sheet would therefore be:

Balance sheet as at (say) 31 December 2000

	Assets £		Claims £
Cash	2,500	Capital	10,500
Stock	5,000	Creditors	1,000
Machinery	4,000		
	11,500		11,500

It should be noted that a balance sheet prepared for a business at a particular date (and hence headed Balance Sheet as at (say 31 December 2000) would normally only include the final figure for each type of asset or claim, and not the cumulative workings shown earlier. The workings shown above represent the effect of a series of transactions on the balance sheet and may therefore be seen as a series of balance sheets relating to the financial position after each transaction. For the purposes of this chapter, this method of working enables us to appreciate the impact of various transactions on the balance sheet. Indeed, for many small exercises (and some examination questions), such an approach is both quick and effective.

Clearly when a business becomes fairly large and complex this approach is not feasible and other ways must be introduced to deal with this added complexity. More practical methods will be dealt with in later chapters.

Activity 2
Using the layout given below, prepare a balance sheet to reflect the effect of the following transactions on the business.

(a) Helen Watkins invested £20,000 cash in a business.
(b) The business buys stock for £5,000 cash.
(c) The business buys stock for £1,000 on credit.
(d) Stock which cost £1,000 is sold for £1,500 on credit.
(e) New machinery costing £4,000 is purchased on credit.
(f) £500 is paid to creditors.
(g) £10,000 is borrowed from A. Wood.

Balance sheet

Assets	+	–	Net	Claims	+	–	Net
Cash				Capital			
Stock				Creditors			
Debtors				Loan			
Machinery							

The effect on the balance sheet of the above transaction is as follows:

(a) Helen Watkins brings in cash to the business (an increase in cash) which increases her claim on the business (an increase in capital).
(b) The purchase of stock is reflected in the balance sheet as an increase in stock. The fact that it is paid for in cash is reflected in a reduction in cash.
(c) The purchase of stock on credit is reflected in an increase in stock and an increase in the amount owed, namely creditors.
(d) The sale of stock results in a reduction in the stock figure amounting to £100. It also results in an increase in the amount owed to the business (debtors) of £150. The resulting profit is reflected in an increase in capital.
(e) The purchase of machinery results in an increase in an asset (machinery). As this was not paid for, but purchased on credit, there will be a corresponding increase in a liability (creditors).
(f) Payment of an amount due to creditors will reduce both cash and creditors.
(g) Borrowing from A. Wood will result in an increase in cash and a corresponding increase in a liability.

The effect of these transactions can be seen below:

Assets	+	−	Net	liabilities	+	−	Net
	£	£	£		£	£	£
Cash	2,000a	−500b	2,450	Capital	2,000a		2,050
	1,000g	− 50f			50d		
Stock	500b	−100d	500	Creditors	100c	−50f	450
	100c				400e		
Debtors	150d		150	Loan	1,000g		1,000
Machinery	400e		400				
			3,500				3,500

Note: The letters shown above relate to the transaction.

Activity 3

(a) Briefly outline the main purpose of a balance sheet. Can you suggest an alternative name?
(b) Why is it always necessary to include a date in the title of a balance sheet?

The main purpose of a balance sheet is to set out the assets and claims of a business at a particular point in time. As it aims to show the financial position of a business, the **financial position statement** *is a possible alternative name.*

The balance sheet is a statement of financial position at a particular point of time. The date at which the balance sheet is drawn up is therefore important.

Self-assessment question 3.1

Show the effect that each of the following transactions has on the balance sheet. The first answer has been entered as an example.

	Assets	Liabilities
(a) Purchased a vehicle for cash	+ vehicle	
	− cash	

(b) Paid an amount owing to a supplier
(c) Purchased a piece of equipment on credit
(d) Received money owed by a customer
(e) Borrowed money from E. Mac
(f) Purchased stock for cash
(g) Purchased stock on credit
(h) The owner withdrew cash from the business

3.4 Other important conventions

The business entity convention is just one of a number of rules, or conventions, which we apply in preparing the financial statements of a business. The earlier example and activity should help reinforce in your mind this particular convention. It is important to recognize its implications in terms of entries under capital or equity.

- Capital will be increased as a result of initial injections of cash or other assets, further injections by the owners, and profits.
- Capital will be reduced as a result of trading losses, and withdrawals of cash or other assets by the owners.

However, the earlier example and activity also illustrate other conventions. One important convention is that of *duality*. When working through the example and activity you may have noted that every transaction has two aspects. For example, an injection of cash by the owner will increase cash and will also increase the owner's capital; a purchase of a car by cash will decrease cash and will also increase the car asset, etc. By reflecting both aspects of each transaction in the balance sheet we ensure that the balance sheet will balance.

Another convention is that of *money measurement*, which holds that financial statements are concerned only with those items which can be measured in money terms. There are a great many factors which may be important to the well-being of a business which, nonetheless, cannot be objectively measured in money terms. These include such things as a good reputation, good staff morale, a skilled labour force, etc. Factors such as these, while undoubtedly important in any assessment of past success or future prospects, will not usually be found in a balance sheet. It can be argued that, for some businesses, the most valuable resources may be excluded from the balance sheet because of this convention. As a result the value of the balance sheet as a financial model of the business is undermined.

A further convention deserving attention is the historic cost convention. In essence, this convention states that assets should normally be shown at their historic cost, i.e. *the amount at which they were acquired*. Such an approach is based largely on arguments about objectivity, since the use of historic cost can be seen to be most in line with traditional ideas on objectivity. Alternative valuations for assets are typically seen as involving rather too much subjectivity (i.e personal opinion), and many argue that, wherever possible, financial statements should be based upon facts rather than opinions. In fact, changing price levels may well make financial statements, based upon the historic cost convention, less useful than those based upon alternative asset values. In recent years current value has been accepted as a valid alternative measurement base. This leads to a mixed measurement system (also known as the modified historical cost basis). The measurement basis used will be determined by reference to other factors such as the nature of the assets or liabilities and the particular circumstances. Problems arise with mixed measurement as we might appear to be adding apples and oranges. As against this, it can be argued that adding together figures expressed at historic cost is doing exactly that when assets were purchased at different times. For example, if one building was bought ten years ago for £50,000 and a similar second building was bought a year ago for £100,000, what does the resulting figure of £150,000 mean? Expressing both assets at current value (say £110,000 each) would appear to be more meaningful. This problem will be discussed in more detail in later chapters. At this stage, it is sufficient to note that historic cost is the normal valuation base.

Activity 4

(a) Which of the following could be found in a balance sheet? Give reasons for your answers.

- That the business has good staff morale
- That the business owes £10,000 to a creditor
- That the owner is very good at getting the best from the employees
- That the assets of the business could be used for a variety of other purposes
- That the business owns vehicles
- That increases in VAT are likely to result in lower sales volume in the future

(b) What is the common denominator of things appearing in the balance sheet?

The answers are:

(a) Good staff morale, while extremely important, will not be found in a balance sheet. It is difficult to measure its value in monetary terms, particularly with any degree of objectivity. It is unlikely that the benefits obtained from good staff morale can be attributed to any particular past transaction or event.

Amounts owed to creditors will be included in a balance sheet. However, it will usually not show amounts owed to individual creditors. Only the total amount owed to creditors is usually shown.

The fact that the owner is very good at getting the best from the employees will not appear in a balance sheet, for similar reasons given above relating to good staff morale.

> *The fact that assets can be used for a variety of purposes cannot normally be gleaned from a balance sheet.*
>
> *If a business owns vehicles they will appear in the balance sheet, providing they can produce future benefits.*
>
> *Likely increases in VAT will not appear in the balance sheet. Such increases do not fit with the characteristics of assets or claims. They cannot be measured in monetary terms, nor are they the result of a past transaction or event relating to the business.*
>
> (b) *The common denominator is the fact that the things included are capable of being measured in money terms (convention of money measurement).*

In addition to the above conventions, two further conventions are implicit in preparing the balance sheet. The first of these is the assumption of *continuity*, frequently referred to as the *going concern* convention. Unless there is good evidence to the contrary, the balance sheet is prepared on the assumption that the business will continue to exist in future accounting periods. This assumption has the effect of weakening the objections to historic cost being the main basis of asset values in the accounts, and provides a justification for depreciation, which is the spreading of the cost of assets with long lives over the period of those lives. (This will be dealt with in more detail later.) Without the assumption of continuity, liquidation (sales) values of assets would be a more sensible basis of asset valuation.

The second assumption is that traditional accounting statements are prepared on the basis of a *stable monetary unit*. In other words, no adjustments are made for inflation. In recent years, such an assumption has been somewhat unrealistic, and various proposals have been made to adjust financial statements for inflation. These proposals are dealt with in later chapters. At this stage, it is important to bear in mind this assumption, and its limitations, when analysing and interpreting financial statements which have not been adjusted for inflation.

Self-assessment question 3.3

(a) Why should a balance sheet always balance?
(b) Enter the missing amounts in each of the following:

Assets	£15,000	Liabilities	£5,000	Capital	£	
Assets	£30,000	Liabilities	£12,000	Capital	£	
Assets	£30,000	Capital	£15,000	Liabilities	£	
Assets	£20,000	Capital	£12,000	Liabilities	£	
Liabilities	£5,000	Capital	£15,000	Assets	£	
Capital	£25,000	Liabilities	£10,000	Assets	£	

(c) Jones has just bought a new car for £5,000. Indicate whether you would expect this to appear in the business balance sheet, giving reasons for your decision.

(d) You are asked by a business person to explain why capital in the business is shown as a claim.

**3.5
A detailed
example**

This section illustrates how a balance sheet reflects the effect of the following transactions.

(a) C. Mille invests cash of £15,000 in a business known as Polyprint & Co.
(b) The business borrows £3,000 from the bank.
(c) It purchases plant for £10,000 cash, and a van for £3,000 cash.
(d) It purchases £7,500 of stock on credit.
(e) It purchases £2,000 of stock for cash.
(f) It sells stock which had cost £6,500 for £11,000 on credit.
(g) It receives £8,000 cash from debtors.
(h) It pays £5,000 cash to creditors.
(i) It pays £500 in wages.
(j) It pays £250 rent.
(k) C. Mille withdraws £500 for personal use.

The logic for recording each of these transactions is given below, and their cumulative effect is shown in the balance sheet list following.

		Assets	*£*	*Claims*	*£*
(a)	Cash increases by £15,000	Cash	+15,000		
	Capital increases by £15,000			Capital	+15,000
(b)	Cash increases by £3,000	Cash	+3,000		
	Liabilities (a loan) increase by £3,000			Loan	+3,000
(c)	Plant increases by £10,000	Plant	+10,000		
	Vehicles increase by £3,000	Vehicles	3,000		
	Cash decreases by £13,000	Cash	−13,000		
(d)	Stock increases by £7,500	Stock	+7,500		
	Creditors increase by £7,500			Creditors	+7,500
(e)	Stock increases by £2,000	Stock	+2,000		
	Cash decreases by £2,000	Cash	−2,000		
(f)	Stock decreases by £6,500	Stock	−6,500		
	Debtors increase by £11,000	Debtors	+11,000		
	Capital increases by £4,500 (the profit)			Capital	4,500
(g)	Cash increases by £8,000	Cash	+8,000		
	Debtors reduce by £8,000	Debtors	−8,000		

		Assets	£	Claims	£
(h)	Cash reduces by £5,000	Cash	−5,000		
	Creditors reduce by £5,000			Creditors	−5,000
(i)	Cash reduces by £500	Cash	−500		
	Capital reduces by £500			Capital	−500
(j)	Cash reduces by £250	Cash	−250		
	Capital reduces by £250			Capital	−250
(k)	Cash reduces by £500	Cash	−500		
	Capital reduces by £500			Capital	−500

Balance sheet as at——

Assets	+	−	Net	Claims	+	−	Net
	£	£	£		£	£	£

Cash	15,000a 13,000c
	3,000b 2,000e
	8,000g 5,000h
	     500i
	     250j
	     500k
			4,750	Capital	15,000a
					4,500f
						500i
						250j
						500k
							18,250

Plant and equipment	10,000c		10,000	Loan	3,000b		3,000
Vehicles	3,000c		3,000	Creditors	7,500d	5,000h	2,500
Stock	7,500d 2,000e	6,500f	3,000				
Debtors	11,000f	8,000g	3,000 23,750				23,750

The figures shown in the net columns reflect the balance sheet after the completion of all the transactions.

**3.6
Capital, revenue
and expenses**

At this stage, it is useful to consider in more detail the transactions which relate to capital, since these sometimes cause a certain amount of confusion; also to provide a more detailed introduction to the profit and loss account, and its relationship to the balance sheet.

In general terms, it may be said that most people invest in a business in the expectation of making a profit, but with the risk of loss. Such people may increase the amount of their capital by injecting further sums into the business. Similarly, they may reduce their claim by withdrawals of capital (drawings). Profits are added to the capital of the owner (his/her claim on the business), while losses are subtracted from it. The effect of transactions on the capital account may thus be summarized as follows:

Opening capital	x
+ Injections	x
+ Profits/ − Losses	$\underline{x}$
	x
− Drawings	$\underline{x}$
= Closing capital	$\underline{\underline{x}}$

The transactions included in the last example can now be reconsidered in the light of this summary. Transactions affecting capital are (a), (f), (i), (j) and (k).

- Transaction (a) reflects an initial injection of capital.
- Transaction (k) reflects a withdrawal of capital (drawings).
- Transactions (f), (i) and (j) together reflect the impact on capital of trading transactions, and will give the overall profit or loss resulting from trading, namely £3,750.

It is useful to keep these three types of transaction separate in practice, since their separation will lead to more useful information.

It is clear from earlier chapters that a profit and loss account (also known as an income statement) is generally seen as one of the most important financial statements. It is important to note at this stage that *the profit and loss account is nothing more than a summary of the effect of trading transactions on capital*. As such, it should be seen as being inextricably linked to the balance sheet. In fact, as will be shown in Chapter 4, it is effectively an appendix to the balance sheet.

Before considering this in more detail, two further terms need to be introduced, namely *revenues* and *expenses*. In broad terms (and subject to subsequent qualification and clarification in later chapters), a revenue is an increase in capital (the owner's claim) which results from trading, while an expense is a decrease in capital which results from trading. *Revenues less expenses equals the profit or loss*.

It should be pointed out that expenses cover more than just the cost of any goods which are sold (the cost of sales). Transactions involving such things as rent, rates, heating and lighting, insurance, wages, etc. all reduce the owner's claim and should be seen as expenses.

When considering transactions relating to the sale of goods, the introduction of the idea of revenues and expenses enables such transactions to be broken down into two constituent parts. Consider (by way of example) transaction (f) above, the sale of stock which had cost £6,500, for £11,000 on credit. This transaction may be viewed as having two constituent parts:

- the sale, which brings in an asset (debtors) amounting to £11,000;
- the handing over of goods to the customer which had cost £6,500.

These two separate parts can be dealt with differently from the way set out earlier, in a way which more obviously reflects duality. The two parts are:

- The sale on credit may be seen as increasing debtors by £11,000 and increasing capital by £11,000, this latter increase being a revenue (sales), an increase in capital as a result of trading.
- The handing over of goods may be seen as reducing stock by £6,500 and reducing capital by £6,500, this latter decrease being an expense (cost of sales), a decrease in capital as a result of trading.

The capital will at this stage be showing a revenue (+£11,000) and an expense (−£6,500), which together give the correct profit figure of £4,500 on the transaction. Transactions (i) and (j) reflect the incurring of other expenses, with a consequent reduction in capital.

    Although the final result is the same, this approach enables all aspects of trading profits or losses to be separately identified. This is important, since most users of accounts will want to know not only *how much* profit has been made, but also *how* it has been made. A profit of £1,000 may be achieved by selling goods which had cost £3,000 for £4,000; by selling goods which had cost £100,000 for £101,000; or a variety of other combinations of revenues and expenses. Knowledge of the actual revenues and expenses will provide useful insights into past performance, and help in making decisions for the future. In the example shown above, revenues (sales) amount to £11,000, with expenses being (cost of sales) £6,500, (wages) £500, and (rent) £250, giving an overall profit of £3,750.

    At this stage, all revenues are entered as additions to capital on the balance sheet, while expenses are entered as deductions from capital. In practice, revenues and expenses are collected separately in a profit and loss account (income statement), with only the net profit or loss being transferred to the capital section of the balance sheet. This will be dealt with in more detail in Chapter 4. It is worth restating at this point that:

- revenues are increases in capital as a result of trading
- expenses are decreases in capital as a result of trading

with recordings being made to reflect this.

Activity 5

Show the effect of the following transactions on the balance sheet. Where transactions relate to capital indicate whether the entry is an injection, a drawing, a revenue or an expense.

(a) Stock is purchased on credit for £500
(b) The owner withdraws £250
(c) The owner brings his own car into the business, for use solely by the business. The car is currently valued at £3,000
(d) Goods which cost £500 are sold for £600 cash
(e) Rent of £200 is paid
(f) Goods which cost £1,000 are sold for £1,250 on credit

(g) Bank interest of £50 is paid
(h) Receive £1,000 from debtors
 (i) Purchase equipment for £4,000 with a loan from the bank for the full amount.

The effect of the above transactions on the business balance sheet are shown below:

Assets	Claims
(a) Stock + £500	Creditors + £500
(b) Cash − £250	Capital − £250 (drawings)
(c) Vehicles + £3,000	Capital + £3,000

(d) Earlier in the chapter you would probably have shown the effect of this transaction as:

Stock − £500	Capital − £100 (the profit)
Cash + £600	

In order to provide more detailed information about profit you should split this transaction into the following:

Stock − £500	Capital − £500 (an expense)
Cash + £600	Capital + £600 (a revenue)
(e) Cash − £200	Capital − £200 (an expense)

(f) As with *(d)* this transaction should be shown as:

Stock − £1,000	Capital − £1,000 (an expense)
Debtors + £1,250	Capital + £1,250 (a revenue)
(g) Cash − £50	Capital − £50 (an expense)
(h) Cash + £1,000	
Debtors − £1,000	
(i) Equipment + £4,000	Loan + £4,000

3.7
Types and classification of assets and liabilities

In order for users to analyse and interpret the balance sheet more easily, it is useful to classify assets and liabilities in a generally recognized manner. Standard classifications mean that less explanation is required from users concerning the nature of assets and liabilities shown in the balance sheet. Assets are normally classified under two main headings for balance sheet purposes:

- Fixed assets
- Current assets

Fixed assets are those assets which are held by the business to earn profit. They are not held primarily to resell, but are used to make the business more efficient in carrying out trading operations. Therefore, in a manufacturing business, plant and machinery will be a fixed asset while the goods manufactured by them are not.

Physical (or tangible) assets such as land, buildings, equipment, etc. are the more obvious fixed assets held by businesses. It should be remembered that only assets which cost the business something and which can be measured in money terms appear in the balance sheet. For example, the reputation that a business starting from scratch has built up over the years will not be shown in the balance sheet, even though it may be of considerable importance in assessing both past performance and future potential. However, if a good reputation is purchased, say in the form of a business name, rather than built up, it will be included in the balance sheet, provided that some benefits remain. Such purchased goodwill is an example of an *intangible asset* (one which cannot be physically touched). Other intangible assets which might appear on a balance sheet include such things as the acquisition of patents, copyrights, licences, etc. which involve the business in a cost and provide benefits in the future.

Current assets are those assets which form the basis of business trading, in that they circulate and change in the short term. They include stock, short-term debtors and cash.

It should be borne in mind that an item could be classified as a fixed asset in one type of business, whereas in another business, exactly the same item could be classified as a current asset. The crucial factor determining the heading under which an asset will be shown is the intention with regard to the use to which the asset will be put. For instance, a motor van in a motor dealer's business would normally be a current asset, while in a grocery business it would be a fixed asset. The tendency is for fixed assets to remain in a business for some years, whereas the typical current asset has a much shorter life in the business. It is important to appreciate, however, that the length of life of the asset in the business is not a consideration when classifying assets as either fixed or current.

Claims are classified under three main headings for balance sheet purposes:

- Capital (or owner's equity)
- Long-term liabilities
- Current liabilities

Capital represents the owner's claim on the business and has already been dealt with in some detail. *Long-term liabilities* are those which have to be cleared at a future date more than twelve months from the balance sheet date. *Current liabilities* are those in respect of which settlement could be demanded by the claimant within the next twelve months.

Activity 6

Which of the following are fixed assets in a manufacturing business?

	Yes	No
(a) land and buildings		
(b) raw materials stocks		
(c) stocks of finished goods		
(d) debtors		
(e) plant and equipment		

(a) and (e) are fixed assets. The remainder are current assets.

Self-assessment question 3.4

Which of the following are current assets in a retailing business?

	Yes	No

(a) stocks of goods for resale
(b) sales counters
(c) shop premises
(d) outstanding accounts due to the
      business–debtors
(e) goodwill
(f) cash
(g) tills
(h) rent paid in advance

**3.8
Balance sheet
formats**

In order to help users find their way around the balance sheet, it is also useful to have the capital and the various classes of assets and liabilities arranged in some kind of logical order. An example of one format for a balance sheet is given below.

Balance sheet as at——

	£	£		£
Fixed assets			*Capital*	x
Premises		x		
Fixtures and fittings		x		
Plant and equipment		x		
Vehicles		x̲		
		x		
			Long-term liabilities	
			Loans	x
Current assets				
Stock	x		*Current liabilities*	
Debtors	x		Creditors	x
Cash	x̲			
		x̲		—
		x̲̲		x̲

This form of presentation shows the assets on the left-hand side and reveals a progression from the most fixed to the most liquid, while on the claims side the progression is from long-term to short-term. This format is a particularly useful one to use initially, since it clearly reflects the balance sheet equation:

$$\text{Assets} = \text{claims}$$

Claims consist of capital and external liabilities, therefore we can extend the equation so that:

$$\text{Assets} = \text{capital} + \text{liabilities}$$

This format, however, is rarely used nowadays. In practice, the balance sheet is typically presented in a *narrative* or *vertical* format, rather than in the two-sided way shown above. An example of such a presentation is given below.

Balance sheet as at———

Fixed assets		
Premises		x
Fixtures and fittings		x
Plant and equipment		x
Vehicles		<u>x</u>
		x
Current assets		
Stock	x	
Debtors	x	
Cash	<u>x</u>	
	x	
Less *Current liabilities*	<u>x</u>	
Working capital		<u>x</u>
		x
Less *Long-term liabilities*		<u>x</u>
Net assets		<u><u>x</u></u>
Financed by:		
Capital		<u><u>x</u></u>

It should be stressed that this format represents nothing more than a rearrangement of items in a two-sided balance sheet. Effectively it is saying:

$$\text{Assets} = \text{capital} + \text{liabilities}$$

Therefore:

$$\text{Assets} - \text{liabilities} = \text{capital}$$

Capital has been defined as the claim of the owner on a business. It should be clear that at any time this claim must be reflected by the sum of the assets less external liabilities.

In the narrative format, current assets minus current liabilities gives a figure known as *working capital* or *net current assets*. In practice, a business is likely to need to tie up funds in a variety of short-term, circulating assets, such as stock, debtors and cash, which are just as essential to the effective running of the business as fixed assets. Some of these can be funded by short-term liabilities, particularly creditors. The above layout makes clear the amount of working capital tied up in the business.

A two-sided format for the balance sheet will be used for the remainder of this chapter and the next, unless you are told anything to the contrary, since this will reinforce the underlying convention of duality. Thereafter, increased emphasis will be placed on presentational issues and so the narrative format will be used. However, even at this stage, the classification of assets and liabilities discussed earlier should be used.

**3.9
Miscellaneous
points on the
balance sheet**

It is often the case that, when a new business is created, a number of different assets and liabilities may be brought into the business.

For example, suppose that Ashok starts a business into which he brings equipment of his own, valued at £5,000, his own vehicle (for sole use by the business) valued at £3,000, and £2,000 cash. The opening balance sheet would thus be as follows:

Balance sheet as at——

	£		£
Fixed assets		*Capital*	£10,000
Equipment	5,000		
Vehicle	3, 000		
	8,000		
Current assets			
Cash	2, 000		
	£10,000		£10,000

The capital is calculated by adding together the assets brought in, and subtracting from this total the sum of any liabilities brought in (i.e. $C = A - L$). The capital at any stage of a business may be calculated along similar lines.

In practice, most fixed assets will be used up over time. A piece of equipment which costs £5,000, and is expected to last for five years, may legitimately be recorded at cost when it is purchased, but after five years its future benefit is likely to be low and may even be zero. In reality, therefore, the cost of the asset, less any residual value expected, must be written off (i.e. treated as an expense) over the expected life of the asset. In other words, part of the asset's cost must become an expense – known as depreciation – as the asset is used up. This will result in a reduction in the figure shown under assets in the balance sheet, and a reduction in capital – an expense.

Self-assessment question 3.5

D. Wood owns and manages an agricultural engineering business, which he started three years ago. In discussions with him you ascertain the following facts as at 31 December 1999.

(a) When he started the business premises were bought for £20,000.
(b) Equipment is owned which cost him £8,000.

(c) Stock of raw materials, work in progress, and finished goods are valued at £10,000.
(d) A letter from the building society confirms that £12,000 is still owing on the mortgage taken out to buy the premises.
(e) A schedule of amounts owing for credit sales totals £15,000.
(f) Unpaid invoices for stock and expenses total £10,000.
(g) The bank statement shows that £3,000 remains in the current account. £250 is held in cash on the premises.
(h) D. Wood tells you that he originally put in £25,000 into the business,

Prepare a balance sheet for the business at 31 December 1999.

Depreciation will be dealt with in more detail later in the book. It is mentioned at this stage to alert you to its existence. For many businesses depreciation is an important expense.

3.10 Summary

This chapter has provided an introduction to the nature and purpose of a balance sheet. It has also provided an introduction to the conventions underlying this basic financial statement. The rationale for these conventions, and their importance and limitations, should be carefully noted, since they are important when analysing and interpreting financial statements. The balance sheet contains much information which is useful, but its limitations need to be fully recognized by users of accounting information. This chapter has examined the effect of a variety of transactions on the balance sheet, and you should be familiar with these. In particular, it has considered the effect of transactions on the claim of the owner on the business, and it has distinguished between injections, drawings, revenues and expenses. A thorough understanding of these terms is necessary before moving on to the next chapter. At this stage you should be clear that revenues less expenses equals profit. The next chapter will provide an introduction to the profit and loss account, the second major financial statement, and will build on the ideas introduced in this chapter relating to revenues and expenses.

Exercises

1. Show the effect of each of the following transactions on the assets and liabilities (including capital) of a balance sheet.

   (a) Purchased on credit, goods for resale amounting to £2,000.
   (b) Paid creditors accounts amounting to £200, by a cheque for £190, the remainder being allowed as discount.
   (c) Received an invoice for repairs to buildings amounting to £250.
   (d) Paid annual interest of £150, relating to a long term loan.
   (e) Purchased new machinery on credit for £1,500.
   (f) Fire insurance of £100 is paid which relates to the buildings.

    (g) Fuel for machinery is purchased for £500.
    (h) Trade debts of £25 were written off (i.e. treated as an expense) as bad (i.e. unlikely to be paid)
    (i) Machinery was depreciated by £500.
    (j) The owner withdrew £150 for his own use.
    (k) Stock which had cost £250 was sold for £350 cash
    (l) Leasehold property (on a ten year lease) is purchased for £10,000.
    (m) The owner used stock to the value of £75 in his own home.
    (n) During the year the owner won £5,000 on a bet on a horse race, which he paid intact into the business bank account.
    (o) Wages of £100 were paid in cash.

2. Write brief notes on the conventions and assumptions introduced in this chapter.
3. Record the following transactions on a list of assets and claims, showing each particular type separately. Show the balance sheet on completion of all the transactions.

    (a) G. Mawgan started a business with £20,000 cash.
    (b) The business borrowed £5,000 from the bank.
    (c) Fixtures and fittings were purchased on credit for £1,500.
    (d) Stock was purchased for £500 cash.
    (e) Further stock was purchased for £3,500 on credit.
    (f) A vehicle was purchased for £3,500, with a deposit of £1,000 being paid by cash.
    (g) Faulty stock was returned to suppliers. The invoice value of this stock was £250.
    (h) A small workshop unit was purchased for £15,000 cash.
    (i) Mawgan won £1,500 on the football pools, and put this money immediately into the business.
    (j) A creditor was paid £1,200.
    (k) Stock which had cost £500 was sold for £700 on credit.
    (l) £300 was received from debtors.
    (m) Creditors were paid £2,000.

4. Record the following on a balance sheet list, and show the balance sheet as it appears on 31 January.

    (a) 1 January   D. Harvey puts in £10,000 to start a new business of his own, calling it Wight Enterprises.
    (b) 1 January   Borrows £5,000 from P. Perks.
    (c) 1 January   Buys equipment for £3,000 cash.
    (d) 2 January   Buys stock for resale for £800 cash.
    (e) 3 January   Buys further stock of £2,200 on credit.
    (f) 4 January   Stock which cost £600 is sold for £600 cash.
    (g) 5 January   Stock which cost £200 is sold for £200 on credit

(h)	7 January	Cash of £800 is paid to creditor.
(i)	8 January	Cash of £200 is received from debtor.
(j)	11 January	Harvey withdraws £500 cash from the business for his private use.
(k)	11 January	Harvey pays the creditor £400 from his personal funds
(l)	12 January	Goods which cost £600 are sold for £800 cash.
(m)	13 January	Goods which cost £100 are sold on credit for £90.
(n)	15 January	Stock to the value of £2,000 is bought on credit.
(o)	15 January	Rent of £30 is paid.
(p)	18 January	Stationery is bought for £100 cash.
(q)	20 January	Miscellaneous expenses of £50 are paid in cash.
(r)	28 January	Goods which cost £500 are sold for £750, £250 cash being received and £500 due at the end of February.

On 31 January it was discovered that only £80 of stationery was still in hand.

Chapter 4

The profit and loss account – nature and purpose

4.1 Introduction

The need for, and importance of, the profit and loss account have already been discussed in Chapters 1 and 2. This chapter aims to provide an understanding of the nature, form and content of the profit and loss account (also known as the income statement); the way in which profit is measured; and the way in which basic profit and loss accounts and balance sheets are prepared from a series of business transactions.

4.2 Objectives

On completion of this chapter you should be able to:

- explain the nature and purpose of the profit and loss account;
- set out the basic form of the profit and loss account and explain its relationship with the balance sheet;
- explain the major conventions underpinning the profit and loss account;
- explain the major principles involved in measurement of profit.

4.3 The nature and purpose of the profit and loss account

Chapter 3 made it clear that changes in capital (owner's claim), over time, may be attributable to:

- further injections of capital by the owners
- profits or losses from trading operations
- drawings by the owner.

Injections of capital are likely to occur relatively infrequently. Drawings by owners, on the other hand, are likely to occur rather more frequently, often at regular intervals. Both may be of considerable importance to a business. However, the essence of most commercial businesses is the search for profits, and the number of transactions arising from this search may be enormous. In practice, profits provide a very substantial part of the inflow of new finance to the business sector of the economy. The recording and measurement of profits or losses are, therefore, important parts of the accounting process.

We have already seen that profits or losses from trading operations are arrived at by deducting expenses from revenues. A revenue represents an *increase* in capital as a result of trading operations, while an expense is a *decrease* in capital as a result of trading operations. It should be clear from Chapter 3 that a balance sheet drawn up at a particular time will reflect any profits or losses made to date. However, consideration of the examples and activities of Chapter 3 should also make it clear that the balance sheet alone will not show how profit has been made, or what has happened in terms of transactions carried out.

The balance sheet only shows the *end result* of the transactions. While such a statement is undeniably useful, it is not enough. Information about *how* a profit or loss has been made is also necessary, if a useful picture is to be built up. A separate statement covering this, the profit and loss account or income statement, is therefore usually prepared. Such a statement is necessary if users of accounts are to understand fully the impact of trading operations on the financial position of the business. It is also likely to provide a means of assessing the efficiency of past performance, and to provide indicators which may be useful in improving performance in the future.

The overall purpose of this profit and loss account or income statement is to set out the financial results of trading operations for a particular period.

At this stage it is worth emphasizing that a profit and loss account relates to a period, whereas a balance sheet relates to a particular point in time. This can be illustrated as follows:

At the end of a financial period, users will usually be presented with both statements in order to help them assess financial performance and position. They will receive a profit and loss account for the period and a balance sheet as at the end of that period. The profit and loss account and balance sheet are together often referred to as the *final accounts*.

Activity 1

What piece of information do you think should be included in the title at the top of a particular profit and loss account?

The time period covered by the statement should be included. It would not be appropriate to head it as at a particular date, since it relates to a period. Hence, it should be headed **Profit and loss account for the year (or month etc.) ended 31 December** (*or whatever date the period ended*).

It is common to find profit and loss accounts prepared to cover periods such as one month, six months and a year, together with a balance sheet as at the end of the period covered. For example, financial statements for tax purposes are typically needed every year. Limited companies are required to prepare accounts annually. Companies listed on the Stock Exchange are required to prepare accounts on a half-yearly and an annual basis. More frequent accounts (e.g. monthly) are prepared by most larger businesses, for purposes of internal decision making and control. In the final analysis, virtually every business has to produce financial statements on an annual basis at least, if only for tax purposes. Profit and loss accounts covering shorter periods are prepared as necessary, with usefulness and cost being important considerations.

The profit and loss account, being a statement of the increases and decreases in capital which result from trading, is in essence nothing more than a summary, in convenient form, of entries in the capital area of the balance sheet which relates to trading operations. These have already been outlined as:

- Revenues, i.e. increases in capital attributable to trading operations, and
- Expenses, i.e. decreases in capital attributable to trading operations.

Hence : Profit = revenue less expenses

To help analyse performance, it is useful if revenues and expenses can be identified in some detail. Thus, in the profit and loss account, we show each source of revenue generated and each type of expense incurred, providing that the amounts are significant.

Activity 2

Revenues generated by a business can come from various sources. Can you think of *four* different sources of revenue?

In answering this activity you may have thought of the following:

- *Sales revenue from goods or services*
- *Rent receivable*
- *Commission receivable*
- *Fees receivable*
- *Interest receivable*

This is not an exhaustive list. You may have thought of others.

Activity 3

Expenses incurred by a business in carrying out trading operations can take various forms. Can you think of *six* different forms of expense?

You may have thought of some of the following expenses:

- *Rent payable*
- *Rates payable*
- *Salaries and wages*
- *Interest payable*

- *Postage and telephone expenses*
- *Heat and light*
- *Printing and stationery*
- *Accountancy fees*

There are many others which you may have identified.

**4.4
Introduction to form and content of the profit and loss account**

We have seen that, at any particular point in time:

$$\text{Assets} = \text{capital} + \text{liabilities}$$

We have further seen that after a period of trading:

The *Assets* held at the end of a period	=	The *Capital* at the beginning of the period + *Injections* of new capital + *Net profit/ − net loss* (i.e. revenues − expenses) − *Drawings* + *Liabilities*	The net figure resulting from this represents the capital figure at the end of the period

---

Activity 4
Is it necessary to know all the detailed revenues and expenses in order to complete the balance sheet?

---

*Knowledge of all the individual revenues and expenses is not necessary for completion of the balance sheet. Insertion of the **overall** figure of net profit or net loss into the balance sheet will be sufficient.*

However, it is useful if a separate summary of revenues and expenses can be made elsewhere (i.e. in the profit and loss account), from which the net profit or loss can be calculated. An outline framework for such an approach is shown below:

Balance sheet as at ——

	£	£		£
Fixed assets			*Capital*	
Premises		x	Opening capital	x
Fixtures and fittings		x	+New injections	x
Plant and equipment		x	+Net profit/ − net loss	$\underline{x^*}$
Vehicles		x		x
			−Drawings	$\underline{x}$
			= Closing capital	x
Current assets				
Stock		x	*Long-term liabilities*	x

Debtors	x		
Cash	x	*Current liabilities*	x
	x		–
	x		x

Profit and loss account for the . . . . (period) ended on . . . .

	£		£
Expenses	x	*Revenues*	x
listed and totalled		listed and totalled	
Net profit*	x	(or net loss*)	x
	x		x

*The resulting net profit or loss is transferred to the balance sheet, thereby preserving its balance. You should remember that the profit and loss account is a supplement or appendix to the capital section of the balance sheet.

The following example should help reinforce some of the points made.

Example

Let us reconsider the detailed example shown in section 5 of Chapter 3, in which you were required to prepare a balance sheet resulting from the following transactions.

(a) C. Mille invests cash of £15,000 in a business known as Polyprint & Co.
(b) The business borrows £3,000 from the bank.
(c) It purchases plant and equipment for £10,000 cash and a van for £3,000 cash.
(d) It purchases £7,500 worth of stock on credit.
(e) It purchases £2,000 worth of stock for cash.
(f) It sells stock which had cost £6,500 for £11,000, on credit.
(g) It receives £8,000 cash from debtors.
(h) It pays £5,000 cash to creditors.
(i) It pays £500 in wages.
(j) It pays £250 rent.
(k) C. Mille withdraws £500 for his own use.

Suppose now that you are asked to prepare final accounts for the business, i.e. both a profit and loss account covering the period in question, and a balance sheet as at the end of the period. In fact, the only changes needed to the treatment in Chapter 3 relate to revenues and expenses (i.e. transactions (f), (i), and (j)). All other transactions are treated exactly as before.

Transaction (f) will result in:

- a reduction in stock of £6,500, matched by a reduction in capital, an expense of £6,500;
- an increase in debtors of £11,000, matched by an increase in capital, a revenue of £11,000.

The revenue and expense will now be recorded initially in the profit and loss account, rather than in the capital account. The two sides of the balance sheet will still agree, provided that the profit and loss account figures are included.

Transactions (i) and (j), the incurring of expenses, will both result in decreases in cash and decreases in capital (expenses). These expenses will now also be recorded initially in the profit and loss account, rather than capital, but again with the understanding that they will be included in the calculation of the net profit figure.

The solution to this example should now look like that shown below:

Polyprint and Co
Balance sheet as at———

	£ +	£ −	£ Net		£ +	£ −	£ Net
Fixed assets				*Capital*			
Plant and equipment	10,000c		10,000	Opening capital +net profit	15,000a		15,000 3,750*
Vehicles	3,000c		3,000				18,750
				−Drawings		500k	500
Current assets				= Closing capital			18,250
Stock	7,500d 2,000e	6,500f	3,000				
Debtors	11,000f	8,000g	3,000	*Loan*	3,000b		3,000
Cash	15,000a 3,000b 8,000g	13,000c 2,000e 5,000h 500i 250j 500k	4,750	*Current liabilities* Creditors	7,500d	5,000h	2,500
			23,750				23,750

*Inserted from the profit and loss account

Profit and loss account for the period ended———

	£ +	£ −	£ Net		£ +	£ −	£ Net
Expenses				*Revenues*			
Cost of sales	6,500f		6,500	Sales	11,000f		11,000
Wages	500i		500				
Rent	250j		250				
			7,250				
Therefore net profit (i.e. revenues less expenses)			3,750				
			11,000				11,000

You are advised to check through this answer carefully to ensure that you fully understand it, then attempt Self-assessment question 4.1.

Activity 5

Prepare a profit and loss account for January and a balance sheet as at 31 January from the following transactions.

(a)	1 January	D. Harvey puts in £10,000 to start a new business of his own, calling it Wight Enterprises.
(b)	1 January	Borrows £5,000 from P. Perks.
(c)	1 January	Buys equipment for £3,000 cash.
(d)	2 January	Buys stock for resale for £800 cash.
(e)	3 January	Buys further stock of £2,200 on credit.
(f)	4 January	Stock which cost £600 is sold for £600 cash.
(g)	5 January	Stock which cost £200 is sold for £200 on credit.
(h)	7 January	Cash of £800 is paid to creditor.
(i)	8 January	Cash of £200 is received from debtor.
(j)	10 January	Harvey withdrew £500 cash from the business for his private use.
(k)	11 January	Harvey pays the creditor £400 from his personal funds.
(l)	12 January	Goods which cost £600 are sold for £800 cash.
(m)	13 January	Goods which cost £100 are sold on credit for £90.
(n)	15 January	Stock to the value of £2,000 is bought on credit.
(o)	15 January	Rent of £30 is paid.
(p)	18 January	Stationery is bought for £100 cash.
(q)	20 January	Miscellaneous expenses of £50 are paid in cash.
(r)	28 January	Goods which cost £500 are sold for £750, £250 cash being received and £500 due at the end of February.

On 31 January it was discovered that only £80 of stationery was still in hand.

These transactions formed the basis of Exercise 4 in Chapter 3, so their treatment should not pose particular problems. The emphasis of this question is on the preparation of a separate profit and loss account.

Wight Enterprises
Balance sheet as at 31 January

	+ £	− £	Net £		+ £	− £	Net £
Fixed assets				**Capital**			
Equipment	3,000c		3,000	Opening balance	10,000a		10,000
				Injection	400k		400
				Net profit	340		340
							10,740
				less drawings		500j	500
							10,240
Current assets							
Stock	800d	600f	3,000				
	2,200e	200g					

				Loans	5,000b		5,000
	2,000n	600l					
		100m					
		500r					
Stationery	100p	20 adj	80				
Debtors	200g	200i	590				
	90m			Current liabilities			
	500r			Creditors	2,200e	800h	3,000
Cash	10,000a	3,000c	11,570		2,000n	400k	
	5,000b	800d					
	600f	800h					
	200i	500j					
	800l	30o					
	250r	100p					
		50q					
			18,240				18,240

Profit and loss account for January

	+ £	− £	Net £		+ £	− £	Net £
Expenses				**Revenues**			
Cost of sales	600f		2,000	Sales	600f		2,440
	200g				200g		
	600l				800l		
	100m				90m		
	500r				750r		
Rent	30o		30				
Misc. expenses	50q		50				
Stationery	20adj		20				
			2,100				
Net profit			340				
			2,440				2,440

Self-assessment question 4.1

The balance sheet of James and Co., a small retailing business, showed the following position at 31 October 1999.

Balance sheet as at 31 October 1999

	£	£		£
Fixed assets			Capital	35,000
Premises	35,000			
Fixtures and Fittings	5,000		Long-term loans	15,000
Vehicles	3,600			

		43,600	*Current liabilities*	
Current assets			Creditors	10,600
Stock	7,000			
Debtors	5,000			
Cash	5,000			
		17,000		
		60,600		60,600

The following transactions were recorded during the month of November:

(a) Cash received from debtors £3,000
(b) £2,000 was paid back on the loan
(c) Cash sales amounted to £7,000
(d) Credit sales amounted to £4,000
(e) Stock was purchased on credit, amounting to £3,200
(f) Cash was paid to creditors, amounting to £5,600
(g) The cost price of goods sold was £6,500
(h) Wages were paid for the month totalling £1,200
(i) Other expenses paid for the month totalled £1,800
(j) The vehicle shown in the balance sheet (book value £3,600) was sold for £3,000
(k) A new vehicle was purchased for £5,000. £2,500 was paid immediately, and a loan was taken out for the remainder
(l) Interest on the long-term loan for the month was paid; amounting to £250
(m) The owner withdrew £500 from the bank and £100 worth of stock for his own use
(n) In addition to the sales listed above, damaged stock costing £150 was sold for £100 cash.

Prepare a profit and loss account for November, and a balance sheet as at 30 November.

4.5 **The** **measurement of** **profit**

Measurement of **revenues**

Revenues were defined earlier as an increase in capital resulting from trading activities. This seems straightforward enough at first sight, but closer investigation shows that there is still doubt about exactly *when* revenue is recognized. If a business sells goods it could logically recognize revenue at one of several points of time, e.g.

• when the goods in which it deals are purchased
• when an order is received from a customer
• when goods are delivered to the customer
• when payment is received from the customer

Obviously, it would be useful if there was general agreement on when revenue should be recognized. The *realization convention* provides a basis for the recognition of revenue. This convention states that revenue should be recognized when:

- it is capable of objective measurement (i.e. the selling price is established), and
- the asset value receivable from the customer is reasonably certain.

A variation to this states that revenue should be recognized when the legal title to the goods passes to the customer.

For most practical purposes, this means that when goods or services are sold, the revenue is normally recognized when they are delivered to, and accepted by, the customer. At these stages, the revenue (the price charged) will normally have been agreed, and, assuming that the customer is creditworthy, the asset value receivable (the amount included in debtors) can also be looked upon as reasonably certain. In most cases, legal title will pass with delivery.

For *example*, suppose that a business received an order for goods in December. Suppose further that the goods in question were handed over in January, and paid for by the customer in February. If monthly profit and loss accounts were prepared it would be necessary to decide whether the revenue would be recognized in December, January or February. Using the criteria outlined above, the revenue would be recognized in January.

Clearly some records relating to the order should be maintained by the business, but it is generally considered inappropriate to record the sale until the goods or service pass to the customer. Thus nothing will be included in the accounts which anticipates any revenue or profit.

The transactions will be first recorded in the accounts in January, on delivery of the goods to the customer as follows:

- reduce stock by the cost of the good sold
- increase cost of sales by the cost of the good sold
- increase debtors by the sale proceeds
- increase sales by the sale proceeds.

On receipt of the cash from the customer in February, the following recordings will be made:

- decrease debtors
- increase cash.

Activity 6
When would revenue have been recognized if the goods had been handed over in December? How would the transactions be reflected in the accounts?

If, in the above example, goods had been handed over in December, revenue would have been recognized in December. Whenever the goods are handed over the transaction would then be recorded as follows:

- *increase debtors by the amount of the sale*
- *increase revenues (sales) by the amount of the sale (effectively an increase in capital)*
- *reduce stock by the cost of sales*
- *increase expenses (cost of sales) by the cost of sales (effectively a reduction in capital).*

That is the same transaction as had the sale been recognized in January, but a month earlier.

In fact, the possible options for revenue recognition can become quite complex. For *example*, suppose that an order is received in December, along with the necessary cash from the customer to pay for the goods ordered. Assume that sufficient goods are not on hand, and have to be ordered. The order for these goods is made in January. They are received, and then delivered to the customer, in February. Payment for them is made to the creditor in March. If profit and loss accounts were prepared monthly, the question must be asked as to the appropriate month in which to recognize revenues? Following the rules of the realization convention, revenue would normally be recognized in February, on delivery of the goods to the customer. It might be argued that the two criteria – objective measurement and reasonably certain asset value – would be satisfied in December, when the order was received with cash. However, at this stage, the obligation of the business to the customer has not been satisfied, and, in practice, the second criterion is not deemed to have been met until the obligation has been satisfied.

From the above it can be seen that the recognition of revenue is not necessarily linked with the receipt of cash. In practice, revenue can be recognized:

- before the receipt of cash
- at the same time as cash is received
- after the receipt of cash.

This area of accounting is one of the more difficult, mainly because of the problem of deciding what constitutes *objective measurement*, and what *reasonably certain* means. In certain types of business, the adoption of the realization convention can be a problem.

Activity 7

What problems might be found in applying the realization convention to the following:

(a) a business selling goods on hire purchase?
(b) a civil engineering business involved in a large number of long-term contracts?

(a) *In businesses which sell goods on hire purchase, which typically is associated with a high proportion of bad debts, application of that part of the realization concept relating to relative certainty of receipt frequently results in revenue being recognized piecemeal, as the cash is received, rather than at the time of delivery.*

(b) *A civil engineering business would have problems with obtaining an objective measure of revenues for partially completed contracts, as well as some degree of uncertainty regarding payment. However, it would be hard for a business if it could only recognize revenues on completion if most contracts ran for several years. Typically, revenue is recognized on the basis of a proportion of certified work completed.*

Self-assessment question 4.2

(a) A business sells goods on credit to a customer in December 1999, amounting to £1,500. Cash is received in January 2000. How much would be shown as a revenue under the heading 'sales' in a profit and loss statement prepared for the year ending 31 December 1999? What figure, if any, relating to this transaction, would be shown in the balance sheet as at 31 December 1999? What heading would it be shown under?

(b) A business rents out part of its property at an annual rental of £6,000 per annum, commencing 1 January 1999. During the year to 31 December 1999 cash received amounts to £5,000. How much would be shown as a revenue under the heading 'rent receivable' in a profit and loss statement prepared for the year ending 31 December 1999? What figure, if any, relating to this transaction, would be shown in the balance sheet as at 31 December 1999? What heading would it be shown under?

(c) Assume the same information as in (b) except that during the year to 31 December 1999 cash received amounted to £7,500.

The matching convention

The identification of revenues for a particular period is an important stage in the process of measuring profit for that period. However, it still remains necessary to identify the expenses for the period. In order to do this, we apply the matching convention. This convention states that *all the expenses connected with a particular revenue are to be recognized in the same period as that revenue*. This convention enables the calculation of a logical profit figure in respect of the revenues generated. Application of the matching convention means that if, for example, stock was purchased for £100 cash in December, and sold for £150 cash in January, the revenue of £150 would be recognized in January, and the expense of £100 would be matched with it in January. Thus both the £150 sale and the £100 expense would appear in January's profit and loss account.

With some types of expense, for example cost of sales (i.e. the cost of the goods which are the subject of the sale), it is fairly straightforward to match expenses to revenues in a direct way. This is because it is possible to match the *particular* expense to the *particular* revenue. Thus, it is quite straightforward, to establish the cost of a particular item of stock which has been sold. However, not all types of expense can be dealt with quite as precisely as the cost of sales expense. There are many other types of expense which either cannot be matched with a particular revenue, or where no effort is made to do so because of the cost of doing so outweighs any benefits derived. Under these circumstances, it is usual to *match on a time basis*, so that the revenues recognized in a particular period are matched with the expense incurred (but not necessarily paid for, in that period). If, for *example*, a business pays rent of £1,000 per month, which is impossible to trace to specific sales, it will normally be treated as an expense of the period to which it relates. Thus, if accounts were prepared on a monthly basis, the £1,000 rent due in (say) December would be charged as an expense against revenues earned in December, etc. Note it is the rent *incurred* rather than the actual rent paid which is the relevant expense item.

The accruals convention

Following the realization convention, revenues are normally recognized when the goods pass to, and are accepted by, the customer. It has also been shown, following the matching convention, that expenses should be matched with those revenues. The accruals convention complements these two by asserting that profit (or loss) for a period is the difference between the revenues recognized in that period and the expenses matched with those revenues. Profit (or loss) is *not* the difference between cash payments and cash receipts. As has already been shown, revenues can be recognized before any associated cash receipt, at the same time as any associated cash receipt, or after any associated cash receipt. The same possible relationships exist between expenses and any associated cash payment. In many cases, cash receipts *are* the same as revenues for a period, and cash payments the same as expenses. However, there are also many instances where this is not true, and the relationship between profit and cash changes is tenuous.

The measurement of expenses

It is important to remember that all transactions affect the balance sheet, whereas only certain transactions affect capital. For example, the purchase of an asset will affect the balance sheet, but will not necessarily affect capital. Such a purchase does not give rise to an expense immediately. In accounting, the name given to such an acquisition is an *expenditure* or a *cost*.

Assets are normally bought to generate wealth for a business over a period of time. Given a long enough period of time, most assets will be used up in the normal course of operations. When an asset has some part of its benefit to the business used up, that part becomes an expense. So the acquisition of an asset gives rise to an immediate cost but this will not immediately affect capital. However, as the benefit is used up, so capital will be reduced. Thus, an *expense* may be defined as an *expired cost*. An asset is an *unexpired cost*.

For *example*, suppose a business spent £2,000 on stationery in 1999, and used a quarter of it in 1999 and three-quarters in 2000, there will be an expenditure of £2,000 in 1999 and expenses of £500 and £1,500 in 1999 and 2000 respectively. If balance sheets were drawn up at 31 December 1999 and 31 December 2000 they would show £1,500 (£2,000 − £500) and nil respectively for the current asset of stationery.

Obviously small amounts of stationery are used up each day, so theoretically a small reduction should be made in the asset each day, giving rise to an equivalent reduction in capital. This would necessitate the preparation of a new balance sheet every day, since a balance sheet is at a single moment in time. This, even if possible, would prove to be extremely expensive, and in practice is not normal. As we have seen, most businesses are content to know the effect on capital over a period of, say, a month or a year, with balance sheets being drawn up at the beginning and end of these periods. This means that the amount of benefit used up only needs to be calculated once for each period in which a calculation of the effect on capital is required. In the example used above if such a calculation were only required annually then the calculation of the benefit used up which was given above (£500 in 1999 and £1,500 in 2000), would be sufficient. Further breakdown of these expenses would only be required if profit and loss accounts were required at shorter intervals.

The next important thing to be remembered is that, in calculating the effect on capital, it is not necessarily true that expenditure and expenses, or cash receipts and revenues, will have kept in step with each other. In other words, it is not necessarily true that the benefit of an asset will be used up in the same period as it is paid for.

For *example*, consider goods (stocks) which are acquired for the purpose of resale. When they are purchased they are an asset to the business. When they are sold they cease to be an asset and become an expense. It does not matter when they are paid for, they will cease to be an asset when they are handed over to the buyer. Stock for resale which has not been sold would be shown in the balance sheet as a current asset. The timing difference between cost (expenditure) and expenses can be more clearly seen when considering fixed assets, which usually have a life of several years. An expenditure will typically occur when the asset is first purchased. As its useful life shortens, the part of an asset which is deemed to have been consumed will be treated as an expense known as *depreciation*. The expenses associated with the earlier expenditure will thus be spread over a number of years, to match the expenses with the revenues generated.

There is often a tendency to think only of tangible items as being assets. However, services which are due to the business (i.e. which have been paid for) are also treated as assets until they are rendered. These are included in the balance sheet as *prepaid expenses*, or prepayments, as one of the items under current assets. Examples of prepaid expenses include rates paid in advance and insurance paid in advance. Once the service has been rendered, it will become an expense for the period and will cease to be shown as an asset because no further benefit can be obtained from them.

For *example*, consider a telephone rental of £75 paid quarterly in advance on 1 January. At the date this is paid there is three months' benefit remaining. At this stage, the rent paid is thus strictly an asset. However, if a balance sheet were to be drawn up at the end of January only £50 of the amount paid could reasonably be included as an asset, with the other £25 benefit having been used up in January, and hence having become an expense of January.

The above discussion relates to prepaid expenses, but in certain cases benefit can also be obtained from something before it has been paid for, as is illustrated by the following activity.

Activity 8

Suppose that on 1 December goods were purchased on credit for £1,000 and paid for on 1 January. These were subsequently sold for £1,500 cash on 15 December. If monthly profit and loss accounts were prepared would the £1,000 be treated as an expense in the December or the January profit and loss account?

The answer is December, since the stock was used up in December, and could not be shown as an asset at the end of December. A moment's reflection should also make it clear that the sale of goods for £1,500 on credit would result in an increase in debtors of £1,500, and an increase in revenues (sales) of £1,500. The revenues relate to December and will be included in the December profit and loss account. To calculate the profit, the corresponding expense should be matched with the revenue, in effect to make a net profit of £500 on the transaction. Inclusion of the expense in the January profit and loss account would lead to an understatement of expenses of £1,000 being shown in December and an overstatement of expenses of £1,000 in January. The result of this is that this particular transaction would appear to be causing profit to increase by £1,500 in December, and to decrease by £1,000 in January. Such a treatment is misleading, since the two aspects of the transaction are interrelated, and the profit and loss account should reflect this.

It can be seen from the above activity that the obligation to pay for something which has already been treated as an expense (benefit having already been used up) will be shown as a liability until payment is made. Such amounts are usually known as *accruals* or *accrued expenses*.

In summing up this section on expenses, it may be said that:

- a payment which relates to the period in which it is due will be treated as an expense, with a corresponding reduction in cash
- a payment which is made in advance will be treated as a current asset, labelled prepayments, with a corresponding reduction in cash
- an amount which is due but unpaid will be treated as an expense and as a current liability.

A more detailed example

A business is started on 1 January 1999, and a profit and loss account is to be prepared to cover the period 1 January to 31 December. Included in the transactions during the year are the following;

(a) Cash sales of £100,000
(b) Rent of £5,000 paid to cover the year to 31 December
(c) Loan interest of £2,500 paid to cover the year to 31 December
(d) Credit sales of £250,000 of which £200,000 is received in cash by 31 December
(e) Rates of £1,250 paid to cover the period 1 January 1999 to 31 March 2000
(f) Invoices for electricity paid up to 30 September, amounting to £3,000
(g) Equipment purchased for £10,000 on 1 January 1999, which is expected to last for five years.

Each of these transactions will affect the profit figure in some way or another, as follows:

(a) Cash sales of £100,000 will result in:
  • an increase of £100,000 in cash and
  • a revenue (sales)of £100,000.
  In this case the amount of revenue is the same as the amount of cash received.
(b) Rent of £5,000 paid. Since this all relates to the year to which the profit and loss account is being prepared, it will all be treated as an expense. Hence the double entry will be:
  • reduce cash
  • increase an expense (effectively a reduction in capital).
  In this case the amount of the expense is the same as the amount of cash paid out.
(c) Loan interest of £2,500 paid. Essentially the same as (b), so the double entry will be:
  • reduce cash
  • increase an expense (loan interest).

In practice in a great many transactions cash receipts and payments relate entirely to the relevant period, so cash flows and the associated revenue or expense are identical, as in the three cases shown above. In other transactions this is not the case, as can be seen below.

(d) Credit sales of £250,000 will result in:
  • a revenue of £250,000 matched by
  • an increase in debtors of £250,000.
  As these debtors pay:
  • the amount shown under debtors will decrease and
  • cash will increase (in this case by £200,000).
  In effect the revenue will result in an increase in assets of cash (£200,000) and debtors (£50,000).

(e) Rates of £1,250 were paid. Since this covers a period which is not the same as the period for which profit is being calculated it is necessary to split it into its component parts, so as to identify that part which is to be treated as an expense of the year to 31 December 1999. In practice detailed information is usually available to enable such a figure to be calculated fairly precisely. In the absence of such information an estimate needs to be made. In this example the period covered by the £1,250 is fifteen months. In the absence of any information to the contrary it is probably reasonable to assume that the rates were spread evenly over time. On this basis the expense for the year ending 1999 would be £1,000, and this figure should be included in the profit and loss account. However, this still leaves £250 which has been paid, but which relates to the following period. This will be shown as an asset on the balance sheet as at 31 December 1999, since some future benefit remains from the payment made, which will be included as 'prepayments', under current assets. By the end of 2000 this remaining amount will have ceased to be an asset, since the benefit will have been used up, and will be added to the expense for the year ending 31 December 2000.

(f) Invoices for electricity paid up to 30 September, amounting to £3,000. The double entry for this transaction will be:
- increase an expense (heat and light) and
- decrease cash.

However, at the end of the year, 31 December 1999, the accruals convention requires that the expenses identified should include all those which are due for the year, and not simply those which have been paid for. In fact the £3,000 paid only covers the first nine months of the year ending on 31 December 1999. A further three months' bills need to be included if the correct expense is to appear in the profit and loss account. It may be that an invoice has been received to cover this period, but has not yet been paid. In such a case the amount of the adjustment to be made is clear. If no invoice has yet been received an estimate will need to be made, based on the best information available. In either case the adjustment will require:
- an increase in the expense in the profit and loss account and
- an equivalent increase in a current liability – an amount due – in the balance sheet.

Such amounts due are known as 'accrued expenses' or 'accruals'.

(g) Equipment purchased for £10,000 which is expected to last for five years. The acquisition of this will result in:
- an increase in a fixed asset – equipment – and
- the reduction of cash (or the incurring of a liability).

As the equipment is used up, so the remaining expected future benefit will reduce, until by the end of the five years of its life its value will be much lower, being related to some kind of disposal or salvage value. The value may even be nil. It is necessary to reduce the balance sheet value of the asset in line with the reduction in expected future benefits. In other words, part of the asset will become an expense (known as depreciation) as the benefit is used up. In the above example, if we presume that the benefits are used up evenly over the five years, and that disposal value is expected to be zero, it will be necessary to:

• reduce the asset by £2,000, to £8,000 and
• to increase the expense (depreciation) in the profit and loss account for the year ending 31 December 1999 by £2,000.

Assets which are used up in this way effectively become expenses over time.

These last few examples provide an indication of the kind of circumstances which can arise which cause cash flows and accounting flows (i.e. revenues and expenses) to differ.

Activity 9

Complete the following table to show the relationship between expenditure, expenses, assets and liabilities.

	Balance sheet as at the beginning of the year		Expenditure during year	Expense for year	Balance sheet as at the end of the year	
	Assets	Liabilities			Assets	Liabilities
	£	£	£	£	£	£
Stationery	25		125	x	20	
Fuel	50		220	200	x	
Equipment	1000		1000	x	x	
(depreciate @ 20% of balance at year end)						
Wages		10	900	x		20
Heating		30	300	x	30	
Rent	50		x	250		50
Rates	75		300	x	85	
Stock	1250		x	7750	1000	
Lighting		15	x	65		25
Property	5000		5000		x	
(no depreciation)						

Solution:

	Balance sheet as at 1 January		Expenditure during year	Expense for year	Balance Sheet as at 31 December	
	Assets	Liabilities			Assets	Liabilities
	£	£	£	£	£	£
Stationery	25		125	130	20	
Fuel	50		220	200	70	

Equipment	1000			1000	400	1600	
(depreciate @ 20% of balance at year end)							
Wages			10	900	910		20
Heating			30	300	240	30	
Rent	50			150	250		50
Rates	75			300	290	85	
Stock	1250			7500	7750	1000	
Lighting		15		55	65		25
Property	5000			5000		10,000	
(no depreciation)							

Self-assessment question 4.3

(a) Stationery costing £500 was purchased on 1 January 1999. At 31 December 1999 £150 worth was left. How much would be shown as an expense under the heading 'stationery' in a profit and loss account prepared for the year ending 31 December 1999? What figure would appear in a balance sheet prepared as at 31 December 1999 relating to stationery? What heading would it be shown under?

(b) Electricity bills were paid during the year ending 31 December 1999 amounting to £450. All of these bills relate to the year ending 31 December 1999. One bill remains unpaid, covering the period 1 November 1999 to 31 January 2000, amounting to £150. How much would appear as an expense under the heading 'heating and lighting' in a profit and loss account prepared for the year ending 31 December 1999. What figure would appear in a balance sheet prepared as at 31 December 1999 relating to electricity? What heading would it be shown under?

(c) Rates of £200 were paid on January 1 2000. They relate to the period 1 October 1999 to 31 March 2000. How much would be included as an expense under the heading 'rates' in a profit and loss account prepared for the year ending 31 December 1999? What figure would appear in a balance sheet prepared as at 31 December 1999 relating to rates? What heading would it be shown under? Assume that the level of rates is constant over the years concerned.

Self-assessment question 4.4

The following items appear in the balance sheet of a business at 31 December 1998.

Under Current assets		Under Current liabilities	
Debtors and prepayments		Creditors and accruals	
Rates	200	Rent	500
		Electricity	100
		Deferred revenue	
		Interest receivable	200

During the year to 31 December 1999 the following cash receipts and payments were recorded:

Receipts

Interest – covering the six months from 1 April to 30 September		£400

Payments

Rent – covering the quarter ending	31 December 1998	£500
	31 March 1999	£500
	30 June 1999	£500
	30 September 1999	£500
	31 December 1999	£500
	31 March 2000	£500
Electricity – covering the quarter ending	31 January 1999	£150
	30 April 1999	£120
	31 July 1999	£70
	31 October 1999	£120
Rates – covering the six months ending	30 September 1999	£450
	31 March 2000	£450

Show the revenues and expenses which would appear in the profit and loss account prepared for the year ending 31 December 1999, and the extracts from the balance sheet as at 31 December 1999 which relate to the above transactions.

4.6 Summary

This chapter has provided you with an appreciation of the nature and purpose of a profit and loss account, and its likely format. In particular, it has emphasized that the profit and loss account is effectively an appendix to the capital section of the balance sheet, presented in a form which is rather more useful to users of accounting information. The profit (or loss) for a period is calculated by deducting expenses from revenues. The realization convention was explained, and applied to the definition of revenues. Expenses were then matched against appropriate revenues to calculate profit. Particular attention was paid to this aspect of profit measurement, and to the explanation of the accruals convention. Profit is the difference between revenues and expenses, not the difference between cash receipts and cash payments. Differences between cash payments and expenses will be reflected in prepayments or accruals in the balance sheet, while differences between cash receipts and revenues will be reflected in the balance sheet as debtors or deferred revenues.

Exercises

1 The following balance sheets relate to Pat Trill & Co.

Balance sheet as at 31 December 1999

	£		£
Fixed assets		*Capital*	50,000
Buildings	50,000		
Plant and Equipment	20,000	*Long-term loans*	30,000
Vehicles	10,000		
Current assets		*Current liabilities*	
Stock	5,000	Creditors	25,000
Debtors	10,000		
Cash	10,000		
	105,000		105,000

Balance sheet as at 31 December 2000

	£		£
Fixed Assets		*Capital*	55,000
Buildings	50,000		
Plant and Equipment	25,000	*Long-term loans*	30,000
Vehicles	12,000		
Current Assets		*Current liabilities*	
Stock	6,000	Creditors	27,000
Debtors	11,000		
Cash	8,000		
	112,000		112,000

In order to illustrate that the balance sheets alone do not show what has happened in the course of a period, but only the *effect* of what has happened, you are required to suggest:

(a) a set of transactions which could have caused the above changes, resulting in a profit for the year
(b) a set of transactions which could have caused the above changes, resulting in a loss for the year.

2 The following cash payments are made relating to electricity for a business:

Payment date	Period covered	Amount
15 April 1999	1 January to 28 February 1999	£200
1 July 1999	1 March to 31 May 1999	£350
30 September 1999	1 June to 31 August 1999	£200
20 December 1999	1 September to 30 November 1999	£350

10 April 2000	1 December 1999 to 28 February 2000	£300
5 July 2000	1 March to 31 May 2000	£300
1 October 2000	1 June to 31 August 2000	£200
1 January 2001	1 September to 30 November 2000	£350
1 April 2001	1 December 2000 to 28 February 2001	£450

Assuming that the business has a financial year from 1 January to 31 December, show:

(a) the expense for electricity which will be included in the profit and loss accounts for the years ending 31 December 1999 and 2000.

(b) any amounts relating to electricity which will be included in the balance sheets as at 31 December 1999 and 2000.

3 (a) One business lends £10,000 to another business on 1 January 1999, at an annual rate of interest of 15%. Its financial year is from 1 October to 30 September. Cash received relating to interest on the loan is as follows:

30 June 1999	£750
1 January 2000	£750
30 June 2000	£750
31 December 2000	£750

Show how the revenue (rent receivable) would appear in the profit and loss account for the years ending 30 September 1999 and 2000, and any related entries in the balance sheets as at 30 September 1999 and 2000.

(b) A business rents a property to a tenant from 1 January 1998 at an agreed rental of £10,000 per annum. Its financial year runs from 1 January to 31 December.
Cash relating to the rental is received as follows:

1 January 1998	£5,000
30 June 1998	£5,000
31 December 1998	£5,000
1 July 1999	£5,000
1 January 2000	£5,000

The tenant was in financial difficulties from mid 2000, and it is agreed that any arrears of rent will be paid in 2001.
Show how the revenue (rent receivable) would appear in the profit and loss accounts for 1998, 1999 and 2000, and any related entries in the balance sheets at the end of these years.

4 Complete the following table:

| | Balance sheet as at the beginning of the year | | | | Balance sheet as at the end of the year | |
	Assets	Liabilities	Receipts/ Payments during year	Revenues/ Expenses for year	Assets	Liabilities
	£	£	£	£	£	£
Rates	300		1,000	1,200	x	
Rent payable		250	2,000	x	500	

	Assets	Liabilities	Receipts	Revenues	Assets	Liabilities
Wages		300	x	10,000		500
Heat and light		x	3,000	2,000	500	
Sales/debtors	10,000		48,000	50,000	x	
Sales/debtors	5,000		x	30,000	6,000	
Interest receivable	250		1,250	x	500	
Rent receivable		300	1,500	x	300	

5 Complete the following to show the relationship between revenue, receipts, assets and liabilities:

	Balance sheet as at the beginning of the year				Balance sheet as at the end of the year	
	Assets	*Liabilities*	*Receipts during year*	*Revenues for year*	*Assets*	*Liabilities*
	£	£	£	£	£	£
Rent receivable	100		900	x	200	
"	100		900	x		200
"		100	x	800	100	
"		100	x	500		200
Sales/debtors	2000		x	10000	2500	
"	2000		10000	x	3000	
"	1000		8000	9000	x	
"	x		9000	8000	3000	

What is the name given to a liability in the balance sheet which relates to a revenue?

6 Complete the following table:

	Balance sheet as at the beginning of the year				Balance sheet as at the end of the year	
	Assets	*Liabilities*	*Receipts/ Payments during year*	*Revenues/ Expenses for year*	*Assets*	*Liabilities*
	£	£	£	£	£	£
Rent payable		150	270	x		180
Rent receivable		300	540	x		360
Sales/debtors	3,000		12,000	x	3,500	
Cost of sales	1,500		11,000	x	3,250	
Wages	80		x	5,500	230	
Rates	200		500	1,000		x
Interest receivable		75	x	225		45
Heating	x		100	120	30	
Lighting		20	90	70		
Plant	3,000	1,500		x	x	
(depreciate at 15% on cost)						

7 Pat Trill rents a property from which he runs a retailing business. The annual rental payable is £4,000. The property has three floors, and Pat decides to sub-let one floor to a firm of solicitors who wish to open a small branch office in the town. The annual rent receivable is £1,500.

Pat's accounts are made up for the financial year ending 30 June.

The balance sheet prepared for Pat's business on 30 June 1997 showed, among other things, the following:

Debtors and Prepayments
Rent receivable   £375
Prepaid rent   £1,000.

During the following years the following cash transactions are made relating to rent payable and rent receivable

	Rent paid	Rent received
	£	£
Year to 30 June 1998	4,000	1,875
Year to 30 June 1999	3,000	1,125
Year to 30 June 2000	3,000	2,250.

Show:

(a) the amounts which will be included for the revenue 'rent receivable' and the expense 'rent payable', for each of the three financial years ending 30 June 1998, 1999 and 2000;
(b) the relevant figures in the balance sheets prepared at the end of these three financial years.

Chapter 5

The profit and loss account – form and content

5.1 Introduction

This chapter deals with some of the practical implications of preparing final accounts. The system of pluses and minuses introduced in Chapter 4 is developed further to enable the balance sheet and profit and loss account to be built up from a series of more complicated transactions. The chapter concludes with more detailed consideration of formats, reflecting a variety of types of businesses.

5.2 Objectives

On completion of this chapter you should be able to:

- prepare a profit and loss account and a balance sheet from basic transactions;
- set out profit and loss statements in an appropriate form.

5.3 Practical implications of accruals accounting for the preparation of final accounts

Section 4.4 sets out the basic form of final accounts, together with associated examples. The accruals convention and its associated measurement implications complicate the preparation of accounts somewhat. For example, the payment of cash for, say, rates may result in both an expense and a prepayment. Stationery purchased may be used, in which case its cost becomes an expense, or remain on hand, in which case it is an asset. Expenses may not all be paid for when due, with the result that accruals may need to be introduced into the balance sheet. Such complications make it rather less obvious, when cash flows in and out of a business, whether these flows relate to revenues, expenses, assets or liabilities. In practice, it is usual to record transactions under an appropriate heading, and then, *at the end of the period* for which accounts are being drawn up, to allocate the total amount between assets, liabilities, revenues and expenses.

Example

The following is the balance sheet of Shah & Co. as at 31 December 1998:

Balance sheet as at 31 December 1998

	£	£		£
Fixed assets			Capital	20,000
Buildings		8,000		
Equipment		5,000		
Vehicles		3,000	Loan	5,000
		16,000		
Current assets			Current liabilities	
Stock	5,000		Creditors	3,500
Debtors	3,000			
Cash	4,500			
		12,500		
		28,500		28,500

Given below is a summary of the transactions which took place during the year to 31 December 1999. (*Note*: This list does not reflect the order in which transactions took place.)

(a) Stock purchased on credit £42,000.
(b) Sales for cash £10,000 (original cost of goods £6,000).
(c) Sales on credit £40,000 (original cost of goods £24,000).
(d) Cash received from debtors £36,000.
(e) Cash paid to creditors £35,000.
(f) Cash paid for wages (all relating to the year) £5,000.
(g) Cash paid for other expenses £3,000.
(h) Rent paid amounts to £1,500, covering the period 1 January 1999 to 31 March 2000.
(i) Rates paid amount to £750, covering the period 1 January 1999 to 30 September 1999.
(j) The owner withdrew £2,500 in cash.

At the end of the year you note the following:

(a) A rates demand has been received, relating to the period 1 October 1999 to 31 March 2000, amounting to £500;
(b) Depreciation of equipment is to be taken, amounting to £1,000, together with depreciation of vehicles, amounting to £600.

The first stage is to record all the transactions in the way described earlier, other than the two adjustments set out above. The result, before totalling, should appear as follows:

Balance sheet as at 31 December 1999

	+ £	− £	Net £		+ £	− £	Net £
Fixed assets				Capital			
Buildings	8,000			Opening balance	20,000		
Equipment	5,000			+ Net profit			
Vehicles	3,000			− Drawings		2,500	
Current assets							
Stock	5,000	6,000b		Loan	5,000		
	42,000a	24,000b					
Debtors	3,000	36,000d		*Current liabilities*			
	40,000c			Creditors	3,500	35,000e	
					42,000a		
Cash	4,500	35,000e					
	10,000b	5,000f					
	36,000d	3,000g					
		1,500h					
		750i					
		2,500j					

Profit and loss account for the year ended 31 December 1999

Expenses	+ £	− £	Net £	*Revenues*	+ £	− £	Net £
Cost of sales	6,000b			Sales − cash	10,000b		
	24,000c			− credit	40,000c		
Wages	5,000f						
Other expenses	3,000g						
Rent	1,500h						
Rates	750i						
Net profit							

At this stage note needs to be taken of any adjustments needed. As well as the two identified above, it is important to note that the amount paid for rent was recorded initially as an expense, even though part of this amount relates to the following year. A further adjustment is thus needed for this, giving three adjustments to be made overall:

(a) *Rent.* Of the £1,500 paid it may reasonably be inferred that £300 relates to the period 1 January to 31 March 2000. The adjustment needed is thus:
  • reduce the expense rent by £300
  • increase an asset (prepayments) by £300.
(b) *Rates.* Since the period of profit calculation is 1 January to 31 December 1999, the rates due for this period should be included as an expense. Only nine months have so far been included, so an additional

£250 should be added to the expense (relating to the period 1 October to 31 December), with the appropriate amount outstanding being shown as an accrual. The adjustment needed is thus:

- increase the expense rates by £250
- increase a liability (accruals) by £250.

(c) *Depreciation*. Since the asset is being used up and becoming an expense the adjustments needed are:
Equipment:

- increase an expense (depreciation of equipment) by £1,000
- reduce the asset equipment by £1,000.

Vehicles:

- increase an expense (depreciation of vehicles) by £600
- reduce the asset vehicles by £600.

These adjustments, and the resulting final accounts, are shown below.

Balance sheet as at 31 December 1999

	+ £	− £	Net £		+ £	− £	Net £
Fixed assets				*Capital*			
Buildings	8,000		8,000	Opening balance	20,000		20,000
Equipment	5,000	1,000adj	4,000	+ Net profit	8,200		8,200
Vehicles	3,000	600adj	2,400				28,200
			14,400	− Drawings		2,500	−2,500
							25,700
Current assets							
Stock	5,000	6,000b	17,000	Loan	5,000		5,000
	42,000a	24,000b					
Prepayments	300adj		300				
Debtors	3,000	36,000d	7,000	*Current liabilities*			
	40,000c			Creditors	3,500	35,000e	10,500
					42,000a		
Cash	4,500	35,000e	2,750				
	10,000b	5,000f		Accruals		250adj	250
	36,000d	3,000g					
		1,500h					
		750i					
		2,500j					
			41,450				41,450

Profit and loss account for the year ended 31 December 1999

Expenses	+ £	− £	Net £	*Revenues*	+ £	− £	Net £
Cost of sales	6,000b		30,000	Sales − cash	10,000b		10,000
	24,000c			− credit	40,000c		40,000
Wages	5,000f		5,000				

Other expenses	3,000g		3,000	
Rent	1,500h	300adj	1,200	
Rates	750i		1,000	
	250adj			
Depreciation				
equipment	1,000adj		1,000	
vehicles	600adj		600	
			41,800	
Net profit			8,200	
			50,000	50,000

Period-end adjustments of this nature are commonly found to be needed for the following:

(a) prepayments and accruals
(b) prepayments to a business and deferred revenues
(c) depreciation
(d) debtors (to cover any bad debts)
(e) stock (depending upon the approach used, see below).

The adjustments for prepayments and accruals have been seen above. A similar process is needed for adjustments related to prepayments to a business and deferred revenues, albeit on opposite sides. The adjustments needed for depreciation have also been seen above, although a more informative treatment will be discussed in Chapter 6. The adjustment for debtors relates to bad debts and effectively results in part of the asset debtors becoming an expense.

Activity 1

Milly commenced business as a florist on 1 January 1999. The following information has been collected concerning the business transactions over the first two months of trading.

January 1   Paid £60,000 cash into the business
              Borrowed £20,000 from her parents (interest free)
      2   Purchased a property for £55,000 cash
      3   Purchased a delivery van for £3,000 cash
           Paid road tax and insurance for the van for one year – ending 31 December 1999. Total amount £360
      4   Purchased new till £500
      5   Paid £2,000 cash for shop fittings
           Arranged with bank that overdraft facilities up to £5,000 would be available as required
      6   Acquired stock costing £2,000 on credit.

On 7 January the shop was opened for business and the following is a summary of the transactions up to the end of February:

(a) Further stock purchased on credit £4,200
(b) Cash sales £5,000 (cost of sales £2,900)
(c) Credit sales £2,000 (cost of sales £1,250)
(d) Shop assistant's wages £500
(e) Vehicle expenses £150
(f) Goods returned to suppliers at cost £150
(g) Paid to suppliers for goods supplied £3,500, in satisfaction of debts of £3,600, the difference being discount
(h) Received from debtors £1,800
(i) Paid rates on the shop for the period 2 January to 31 March, amounting to £300
(j) Paid an electricity bill for January, amounting to £75
(k) Milly withdrew £1,000 to cover her salary for the period.

You have been asked to prepare a profit and loss account for the period 1 January to 28 February and a balance sheet as at 28 February. By the time you do this a telephone bill covering the ten weeks to mid-March has been received, amounting to £60. Depreciation of vehicles is to be calculated at the equivalent of 20% per annum on cost.

Solution – Milly

Balance sheet as at 28 February 1999

	+ £	– £	Net £		+ £	– £	Net £
Fixed assets				*Capital*			
Premises	55,000		55,000	Opening balance	60,000		60,000
Fittings	2,000		2,000	Net profit	1,742		1,742
							61,742
Vehicles	3,000	100	2,900	less drawings		1,000	−1,000
Till	500		500				
			60,400				60,742
Current assets							
Stock	2,000	2,900	1,900				
	4,200	1,250					
		150		Loans	20,000		20,000
Debtors	2,000	1,800	200				
				Current liabilities			
Prepayments	300adj1		400				
	100adj2			Creditors	2,000	150	2,450
					4,200	3,600	
Cash	60,000	55,000	20,415				
	20,000	3,000		Accruals		75adj3	123
	5,000	360				48adj4	

1,800	500		
	2,000		
	500		
	150		
	3,500		
	300		
	75		
	1000		
	83,315		**83,315**

Profit and loss account for the two months ending 28 February 1999

	+ £	– £	Net £		+ £	– £	Net £
Expenses				Revenues			
Cost of sales	2,900		4,150	Sales	5,000		7,000
	1,250				2,000		
Wages	500		500	Discount recd	100		100
Vehicle expenses	360	300adj	210				
	150						
Rates	300	100adj2	200				
Electricity	75		150				
	75adj3						
Telephone	48adj4		48				
Depreciation							
– vehicles	100adj5		100				
			5,358				
Net profit			1,742				
			7,100				7,100

Notes:

Adjustment 1 relates to the fact that the road tax and insurance relate to a full year, whereas the period of account is only two months.

Adjustment 2 relates to the fact that rates paid cover three months, with a resulting prepayment for one month.

Adjustment 3 relates to the fact that no electricity bill has been included for February. An estimate thus needs to be made, with a resulting accrual in the balance sheet.

Adjustment 4 relates to the need to incorporate an appropriate amount to cover telephone expenses to the end of February (estimate 8 of the 10 weeks for which a bill has been received – namely £48), and its related accrual.

Adjustment 5 relates to depreciation of vehicles – 20% on cost of £3,000 – for 2 months – £3,000 × 20/100 × 2/12 = £100.

Note that withdrawals by the owner are shown as drawings, whatever they are called (e.g. salary).

5.4
Form and content of profit and loss accounts

The guidance given so far on the form of the profit and loss account has been somewhat limited, effectively saying that it consisted of revenues on the one hand, and expenses on the other. In practice, rather more thought is given to grouping revenues and expenses under appropriate headings, and the profit and loss account is typically split into various sections, according to the type of activity in which the business is engaged.

Trading businesses

This section is particularly concerned with trading businesses, essentially those being engaged in buying and selling goods.

For trading businesses, it is common to split the profit and loss account into two sections:

- one which matches cost of sales with sales, to show a figure known as *gross profit*;
- a second one which deducts any remaining expenses from the gross profit.

The first section is referred to as the *trading account*. The second section is typically referred to as the *profit and loss account*. The trading account is in fact nothing more than a subdivision of the profit and loss account or income statement. An overall heading of '*Trading and profit and loss account for the year ended* ···' is frequently used. Many users of accounts feel that highlighting the gross profit figure is useful, hence the existence of the trading account.

If a two-sided format is used, following on from the approach used to date, the layout is broadly as shown below:

Trading and profit and loss account for the year ending———

	£	£		£	£
Opening stock		x	Sales		x
Purchases	x		Less returns		x̲
Plus carriage in*	x̲				x
	x				
Less returns	x̲				
		x̲			
		x			
Less closing stock		x̲			
Therefore cost of sales***		x			
Gross profit		x̲			
		x̲			x̲
*Administration expenses***			*Gross profit*		x
Rent/rates/insurance/heat and light/telephone/stationery	x				
			Other revenues		
			Discount received	x	
*Finance expenses***			Rent	x̲	
Interest	x		Interest	x̲	
Bad debts					x

Selling and distribution expenses**

Salesmen's salaries/ commission/transport/ advertising/carriage out*	$\underline{x}$	
	x	
Net profit	$\underline{x}$	–
	$\underline{\underline{x}}$	$\underline{\underline{x}}$

*Note that carriage in (carriage on purchases) is treated as an addition to purchases in the trading account, while carriage out (carriage on sales) is treated as an expense relating to selling and distribution. This is because the cost of stock in trade should include any costs incurred in getting it to its current location.

**These headings are suggestions only. Each business should choose headings which are appropriate to its line of business. Further sub-divisions into individual expense headings are also dependent upon the needs of the business. Indeed, the idea of having expenses grouped in some way is only a suggestion, and they are certainly not necessary to most examination questions.

***In some businesses the owner will use stock for his own purposes. This is effectively a drawing. The entries for this would be to reduce the cost of sales by the amount of stock withdrawn, and increase drawings (i.e. reduce capital).

In practice it is more common to present profit and loss accounts in a narrative or vertical form. The two-sided format shown above is modified into a vertical format below.

Trading and profit and loss account for the year ended——

	£	£
Sales		x
Less cost of sales		$\underline{x}$
Gross profit		x
Add Other revenues		
Rent	x	
Interest	$\underline{x}$	
		$\underline{x}$
		x
Less Other expenses		
Administration*	x	
Finance*	x	
Selling and distribution*	$\underline{x}$	
		$\underline{x}$
Net profit		$\underline{\underline{x}}$

*These headings are suggestions only. Each business should choose headings which are appropriate to the information needs of its accounts' users. Further subdivisions into individual expense headings are also dependent upon the needs of the business.

This format will be used in subsequent chapters and so it is important to be familiar with it.

Self-assessment question 5.1

On 1 January Janet has the following balances in her accounts:

Premises	£25,000	Equipment	£6,000	Loan (interest at 10%)	£10,000
Vehicles	£3,500	Stock	£3,000	Debtors	£4,500
Cash	£2,000	Accrued wages	£300	Accrued rates	£500
Prepaid rent	£200	Creditors	£2,000	Capital	£31,400

During the year the following transactions took place:

(a) Purchased stock for £30,000 on credit
(b) Returned purchases amounting to £500
(c) Cash sales amounted to £20,000
(d) Credit sales amounted to £40,000
(e) Returns of credit sales £300
(f) Carriage paid on purchases £500
(g) Carriage paid on sales £300
(h) Rent paid £3,000
(i) Wages paid amounting to £8,000
(j) Janet withdraws £5,000 cash and £1,500 of stock for her own use
(k) Rates of £2,000 are paid
(l) Stationery amounting to £250 is purchased
(m) General expenses amounting to £2,500 are paid
(n) Cash of £38,000 is received from debtors, in satisfaction of debts of £39,000
(o) Cash paid to creditors £27,000 in satisfaction of debts of £28,000
(p) Fuel and electricity bills are paid amounting to £1,000
(q) Motor expenses of £1,250 are paid
(r) During the year some equipment with a book value of £300 was sold for £200

At the year end the following information is available:

(i) Closing stock is valued at £4,000
(ii) Stationery on hand is valued at £150
(iii) An unpaid electricity bill amounting to £150 exists, covering the last quarter
(iv) £100 of the motor expenses relates to tax for the following year
(v) General expenses of £250 are outstanding

> (vi) Depreciation on equipment of £800, and on vehicles of £1000 is to be provided for.
>
> Prepare a trading and profit and loss account for the year and a balance sheet as at the year end.
> *Hint*: In order to calculate the cost of sales you will need to use figures for opening stock, purchases (and returns) and closing stock.

Service businesses

Where a business provides a service, rather than goods, the profit and loss account will simply deduct expenses from revenues, without the use of a trading account.

Manufacturing businesses

It should be clear that in manufacturing businesses goods will typically be produced, rather than bought in. Manufacturing brings with it its own associated costs, and these are generally shown in a manufacturing account. Cost of manufacture may then be substituted for purchases in the trading account. An illustrative manufacturing, trading and profit and loss account is shown below. A two-sided format is given but modification to a vertical format follows the same principles as discussed under trading businesses.

Manufacturing, trading and profit and loss account for the year ending———

	£	£		£
Direct materials				
Opening stock	x		Cost of manufacture to trading	x
Purchases	x		account	
	x			
Less closing stock	x			
Cost of materials used		x		
Direct wages				
Factory wages		x		
Manufacturing overheads				
Factory power	x			
Rent rates insurance*	x			
Factory expenses*	x			
Depreciation of factory equipment*	x			
		x		
Cost of production		x		x
Opening stock – finished goods		x	Sales	x
Cost of manufacture		x		
		x		
Less closing stock		x		
Cost of sales		x		

Gross profit		*x*			
		x			*x*
Administration			*Gross profit*		*x*
Wages/salaries*	*x*				
Stationery	*x*		*Other revenues*		
Heat and light*	*x*		Discount received	*x*	
Rent rates etc.*	*x*		Rent	*x*	
Depreciation of fixtures*	*x*		Interest	*x*	
		x			*x*
Finance					
Interest	*x*				
Bad debts	*x*				
		x			
Selling/distribution					
Salesmen's salaries	*x*				
Packaging/distribution	*x*				
Advertising	*x*				
		x			
		x			
Net profit		*x*			
		x			*x*

*Note that these items will need to be allocated to the appropriate section. Expenses relating to production should appear in the manufacturing section. Expenses relating to administration should appear in the profit and loss section.

The section down to cost of production is the manufacturing account. From that point down to the gross profit is the trading account. The last section down to the net profit is the profit and loss account. The manufacturing account shows the cost of the finished manufactured goods which were made available for sale during the period. The trading account deduces the cost of sales and compares it with the sales revenue to calculate the gross profit for the period. The profit and loss account compares the expenses for administration, finance and selling and distribution with the gross profit, to calculate the net profit.

Activity 2

The following information was extracted from the books and other records of A. Messer, a manufacturer, on 31 December

Raw materials purchased	120,000
Factory expenses	300,000
Selling expenses	80,000
Stocks 1 January	
Finished goods	80,000
Raw materials	20,000

Stocks 31 December

Finished goods	70,000
Raw materials	10,000
Sales	750,000
Debtors	60,000
Creditors	20,000
Plant and Machinery	200,000
Furniture and Fittings	20,000
Capital – 1 January	400,000
General and administration expenses	50,000
Factory wages	150,000
Cash	70,000
Drawings	20,000

The following adjustments are to be brought into account

(a) Amounts outstanding at 31 December
    Factory wages   £2,000
    Advertising   £1,000
(b) Amounts prepaid at 31 December
    General expenses £10,000
(c) Of the debtors £1,000 was deemed to be irrecoverable
(d) Depreciation is to be written off the balance of Plant and Machinery and Furniture and Fittings at 10% per annum.

Prepare manufacturing, trading and profit and loss accounts for the year ending 31 December and a Balance Sheet as at that date. Use the vertical form of presentation.

Manufacturing, trading and profit and loss statement for the year ending 31 December

			Workings
Sales		750,000	
Opening stock of finished goods		80,000	
Direct materials			
Opening stock of materials	20,000		
Purchases	120,000		
	140,000		
Less closing stock	10,000		
Cost of materials used	130,000		
Direct wages	152,000		150,000 + 2,000
Overheads			
Factory expenses	300,000		
Depreciation of plant	20,000		
Cost of manufacture		602,000	
		682,000	

Less closing stock of finished goods	70,000	
Cost of sales		612,000
Gross profit		138,000
Less **Other expenses**		
General and administration costs	40,000	50,000 − 10,000
Depreciation − furniture and fittings	2,000	
Bad debts	1,000	
Selling expenses	81,000	80,000 + 1,000
		124,000
Net profit		14,000

Balance sheet as at 31 December

Fixed assets			
Plant and Machinery		180,000	200,000 − 20,000
Furniture and fittings		18,000	20,000 − 2,000
		198,000	
Current assets			
Stock–materials		10,000	
Stock–finished goods		70,000	
Debtors		59,000	60,000 − 1,000
Prepayments		10,000	
Cash		70,000	
		219,000	
Less **Liabilities due within the next year**			
Creditors	20,000		
Accruals	3,000		2,000 + 1,000
	23,000		
Net current assets		196,000	
Net assets		394,000	
Financed by:			
Capital			
Opening balance		400,000	
Net profit		14,000	
		414,000	
Less drawings		20,000	
		394,000	

5.5 Summary

Further illustrations were given relating to practical aspects of the preparation of final accounts. The kind of formats commonly found were identified and applied to trading, service and manufacturing businesses. You should now be able to prepare a profit and loss account and balance sheet, in good style, from a set of basic transactions.

Exercises

1 The following is the balance sheet of a business at the beginning of a year – 1 January 2000.

	£		£
Fixed assets		Capital	80,000
Buildings	50,000		
Equipment	20,000		
	70,000		
Current assets		*Current liabilities*	
Stock	10,000	Creditors	20,000
Debtors	10,000		
Cash	10,000		
	100,000		100,000

The following is a summary of the transactions which took place during the next year:

1 Stock was purchased for £50,000 cash
2 Stock was purchased for £80,000 on credit
3 Cash sales were £200,000 (original cost £100,000)
4 Credit sales were £50,000 (original cost £25,000)
5 Wages paid were £20,000
6 Rent of £5,000 was paid covering the 15 months to 31 March 2001
7 General expenses of £5,000 were paid
8 Debtors paid cash amounting to £40,000
9 Creditors were paid £70,000
10 Further equipment was purchased for £20,000, financed by a loan (interest free)
11 The owner withdrew £10,000 in cash

At the year end general expenses of £5,000 were owing.
Prepare a profit and loss account for 2000 and a balance sheet at 31 December 2000.

2 A part-time business has the following assets and liabilities at 31 December 2000:

	£		£		£
Buildings	11,000	Motor Vehicles	3,000	Prepaid rent	80
Plant	2,200	Stock	5,300	Debtors	3,700
Cash	2,200	Loan (12%)	3,000	Creditors	2,600
Accrued Heat and light	90				

During 2001 the following transactions took place:

(a) Purchased stock
  • on credit for £27,000
  • for cash for £5,600
(b) Paid creditors £23,000
(c) Made sales
  • cash £23,000
  • credit £27,000
(d) Received cash from debtors amounting to £28,500
(e) Carriage on purchases of stock was paid amounting to £400.
     Carriage on sales – expenses of packing/dispatch, etc. were paid
     amounting to £750
(f) Wages amounting to £9,800 were paid, £300 of which related to
     2002. This included £3,000 for the proprietor
(g) Rent of £800 was paid, covering a period of 10 months
(h) Heating and lighting of £780 was paid
(i) Administration expenses of £2,100 were paid
(j) General and miscellaneous expenses of £1,000 were paid
(k) The proprietor withdrew £300 of stock for his own use
(l) £2,300 was spent on improvements/repairs to buildings. The repairs
     element amounted to about £600.

At 31 December 2001:

(a) £500 of debtors is believed unlikely to be received
(b) The following expenses are found to be unpaid:
  • Heat and Light £100
  • Administration £200
(c) Equipment and vehicles are to be depreciated at 25% p.a. on cost
(d) Closing stock is valued at £4,000.

Prepare a profit and loss account for the year ended 31 December 2001
and a balance sheet as at that date.

3 The following is the list of assets, drawings and expenses, on the one
   hand, and capital, liabilities and revenues, on the other, drawn up at
   the end of the year for a manufacturing business. From this list you
   are required to prepare a set of final accounts after incorporating the
   adjustments given below the list.

	£	£
Advertising	40,000	
Bank charges and interest	2,000	
Capital		500,000
Drawings	70,000	
Discount received		2,000
Discount allowed	5,000	

	£	£
Factory power	40,000	
Furniture	9,000	
General expenses – Factory	20,000	
– Office	60,000	
Insurance	10,000	
Heat and light	5,000	
Plant and machinery	150,000	
Purchases of materials	350,000	
Packing and transport	10,000	
Rent and rates	12,000	
Repairs to plant	15,000	
Office salaries	40,000	
Sales		800,000
Opening stock		
Raw materials	50,000	
Finished goods	70,000	
Work in progress	16,000	
Factory wages	200,000	
Debtors	100,000	
Creditors		60,000
Cash	88,000	
	1,362,000	1,362,000

The following adjustments are to be made:
Closing stock

Raw materials	60,000
Finished goods	75,000
Work in progress	18,000

The following amounts are outstanding

Factory power	7,200
Rent and rates	8,000
Heat and light	2,000
General expenses	
Factory	500
Office	800

Insurance paid in advance amounted to £2,000.
80% of the Rent and rates, Heat and light, and Insurance is to be allocated to the factory and the rest to the office.
Depreciation on furniture and plant and equipment is to be provided for at the rate of 10%.

Chapter 6

The measurement of profit – depreciation

<table>
<tr><td>

6.1
Introduction

</td><td>

This chapter aims to give further consideration to the problems of measuring profit (income), particularly in the area of depreciation.

</td></tr>
<tr><td>

6.2
Objectives

</td><td>

On completion of this chapter you should be able to:

- explain the concept of depreciation
- appreciate that there are substantial elements of subjectivity regarding depreciation and
- apply this concept in a practical way with regard to final accounts.

</td></tr>
<tr><td>

6.3
Problems of applying the matching convention

</td><td>

We have already seen that, in accounting, profit is measured following the matching convention.

</td></tr>
</table>

Activity 1
Can you remember what the matching convention says?
Jot down your answer on a sheet of paper.

You should have answered something like this.

The matching convention says that, in measuring profit, we should match expenses to the revenues which they help to generate, in the same accounting period. In order to gain anything useful from the profit and loss account we need to be able to see the net effect of the revenues for the period. Unless we are careful to set the expenses incurred in earning the revenues against those revenues we shall get a distorted view of trading.

In the examples which we have considered so far in this book, matching expenses to revenues has tended to be pretty straightforward. In practice, however, it is frequently problematical. This is because there are sometimes different views on what is the appropriate way to match. This leads to preparers of financial statements needing to make judgements on what is the most appropriate approach. In the next three chapters we are going to consider three areas where matching tends to raise problems. We shall see that, in practice, the profit figure which emerges from the profit and loss account is not, as you may previously have supposed, definite and unequivocal. The expenses set against the revenues for a period are the product of some factual information about transactions and some judgements about the application of the matching convention. As we shall see, the amounts involved can be very significant.

6.4 **Measurement problems – depreciation: general principles**	Assets have been broadly defined as expected future benefits, while expenses can be seen as benefits used up. When fixed assets are acquired they will be shown in the balance sheet as assets (at historic cost). However, the benefits inherent in fixed assets tend to be used up over time, with the result that after a period of time, the future benefit remaining will tend to be low, or even nil. Since the profit and loss account matches the expenses incurred in generating revenues to those revenues, some attempt needs to be made to calculate the amount of depreciation to be set against the revenues generated period by period.

Activity 2

Can you think of any fixed assets which do not depreciate?
Jot down your answer on a sheet of paper.

The obvious one which occurred to us is freehold land. Land is an asset which tends not to depreciate as a result either of usage or the mere passage of time. This is because land tends to hold its value. You may well have thought of some other answer which is equally correct.

It is clear that the amount of benefit which has actually been used up can only be ascertained at the end of a fixed asset's life. It is impossible to tell with complete accuracy how much benefit has been used up in each accounting period. All that can be done is to make an estimate of the amount of benefit used up in each year, on some *systematic and rational basis*. When a fixed asset is disposed of, the total *actual* depreciation over its life can be ascertained. This can be compared with the estimated depreciation, which has been treated as an expense over the life of the asset. If there is a difference between these two figures, the necessary adjustment can be made.

It is important to note that depreciation is not a process of valuation, but one of *allocation*. By way of example, suppose that a retail business paid £800 for a sign to be put up in front of one of its shops, with the name of the business on the sign. This is a fixed asset because it has likely future economic benefit and it is not bought for resale. Suppose also that the business has a policy of changing its signs for more up-to-date ones every four years. It seems pretty likely that the sign will have zero second-hand value, even when it is brand-new. No other person or business would be likely to want to buy it. If the annual depreciation expense were the fall in market value, the annual depreciation charges would be £800 in the year of purchase of the sign and zero for each of the next three years of the life of the sign. Since this asset has been purchased in the expectation that it will be kept for four years and that it will perform to the same level of efficiency for each of the four years of its life, with negligible charges for repairs and maintenance, the amount of the benefit expected to be obtained from the asset would be much the same for each year, and annual charges based upon the above figures would not appear appropriate. A more rational and systematic approach would be to charge depreciation evenly over the asset's life, namely £200 for each year.

Such an approach has the result that fixed assets will not be shown in balance sheets at their current value, but at cost less depreciation, the resulting figure being known as *net book value* or *written-down value*. Given the going concern convention (see Chapter 3) it is not necessary to show current values of fixed assets, since it is assumed that the business will not be sold. In interpreting accounts, however, it is important to recognize that potentially significant differences may exist between book and current market values.

The approach suggested above (namely £200 depreciation each year) is the result of *allocating* depreciation over the estimated life of the asset, in line with the benefits used up. It is based upon an assumption that the total expense of having the asset for the four years is £800, and this has been allocated equally to each year in line with the estimated benefit used up.

Depreciation can therefore be defined as a systematic and rational method of allocating that part of the cost of an asset, the benefit of which has been used up during an accounting period. It is important to remember that, in considering depreciation, the charge for each period will be dependent on factors, not all of which are known at the time that the charge is made. Depreciation is thus not a precise measurement process.

There are four main factors which need to be considered in arriving at an appropriate depreciation figure:

(a) The cost of the asset
(b) The disposal or salvage value of the asset.

These two are necessary to be able to ascertain the estimated total depreciation which is to be allocated, namely the difference between the two items.

(c) The useful life of the asset in the business.

Obviously some idea of the period over which the total is to be allocated is necessary.

(d) A method of depreciation which is both systematic and rational.

Each of these four factors will now be considered in detail.

The *cost of an asset* will include all costs incurred in acquiring an asset, in installing it, and generally making it ready for use. For example, part of the cost of a shop sign will be the cost of installing it in front of the shop. Similarly, in the purchase of an asset such as a building, legal costs would be treated as part of the cost. Since buildings cannot normally be bought without incurring legal expenses these must be seen as an integral part of their cost. Installation costs of machinery are frequently necessary. They are as necessary to the ability of the machine to carry out its purpose as are the costs of obtaining the machine, because without them the machine will lie idle. Costs such as installation and legal costs cannot reasonably be matched against the revenues of just the period during which they are incurred. In the balance sheet they are therefore added to the cost of obtaining the machine.

The *useful life of an asset* depends on two factors: deterioration and obsolescence. Most fixed assets suffer a deterioration in their physical condition, due either to usage or to the passage of time or perhaps both. In time they will deteriorate to such a condition that no further benefit can be obtained from them. The time that it takes to get to this condition represents their useful physical life. Given a guarantee of reasonable care it is usually fairly easy for a technical expert to make an estimate of the physical useful life of an asset. However, there is another factor to be taken into account in estimating the useful life of an asset to the business. This is the factor known as *obsolescence*, which relates to the fact that an asset may become out of date, and cease to be able to compete effectively with newer assets. The period of expected useful life with regard to competing effectively is known as the *economic life* of an asset.

It is quite possible that an asset may be purchased with a physical life well in excess of its economic life. For example, suppose that a business buys equipment which has a virtually guaranteed physical life of ten years, but that this business then finds that after three years new equipment is invented which does the same job as the old, at half the cost, so from the start of year 4 the equipment has no further use to the business. Under such circumstances it is highly likely that use of the old equipment would cease after three years. This would mean that the amounts charged for depreciation during the three years of useful life would not cover the actual depreciation over that period. This in turn means that the amount of depreciation matched against the revenues of those three years will be very much less than it should have been, but that in the year of disposal (year 4) the depreciation charge will be much higher. This will result in an overstatement of profit for each of the three years and an understatement for year 4. Clearly, therefore, a realistic attempt should be made to estimate the likely economic life of an asset, and not just its physical life, since the economic life may be the more important factor. Depreciation should be based upon the shorter of the two lives. Useful economic life may be influenced by such factors as technological progress, changes in consumer demand, and changes in supply due to greater competition. Such factors are difficult for the individual business to anticipate or control, but some attempt should be made if a sensible depreciation policy is to be achieved. As much objective evidence as is obtainable should be considered in arriving at the estimate.

Activity 3

Which type of fixed assets would tend to have economic lives shorter than their physical lives? For which types of fixed assets would the two lives tend to be the same?

Generally it is assets in areas where innovation and changing technology are important which tend to have economic lives which are shorter than the economic ones. Thus computers tend to have economic lives shorter than their physical lives. Many old computers still work as well as ever they did. Their economic life may well be over, however, because more recently developed hardware may be able to perform a much better job, perhaps at no great cost.

Generally assets in traditional, low-technology areas tend to have economic value for as long as they continue to do the job. An example is a hammer used by a carpenter.

The *disposal* or *salvage value* (also known as the *residual value*), which needs to be estimated in order to calculate the total expense to be allocated over the useful life of the asset, poses similar problems, and can often be little more than an informed guess. If the useful life is expected to be the physical life then it is likely that a technical expert could make a reasonable estimate of salvage value. Where the useful life is the economic life, any estimate made is unlikely to be very accurate. It is very difficult to estimate whether a change in economic factors will make an asset completely obsolete, or whether it will simply make it obsolete for one particular business (i.e. some other business may still be able to use it profitably). It is, therefore, difficult to tell whether the disposal value will be a fairly high second-hand value, or a very low scrap value. Any such judgement will be highly subjective. The convention of prudence (dealt with immediately below) means that a pessimistic view of disposal value is usually taken.

Depreciation provides us with our first real meeting with the prudence convention. This convention says that in preparing financial statements, we should err on the cautious side. Hence profits are usually only recognized when they have been realized (see realization convention), while losses are usually taken fully into account as soon as their likelihood is seen. Accounting has a number of areas, of which depreciation is just one, where more than one approach may be taken. This convention maintains that the more prudent approach should always be taken.

In the context of depreciation, the prudence convention encourages preparers of accounting statements to underestimate both the useful lives of assets and their likely disposal values, rather than to overestimate them.

In practice, deducing the depreciation expense for a period is somewhat unsatisfactory, in that objectivity can rarely be achieved, while prudence tends to encourage the use of pessimistic figures. Clearly the information necessary to calculate depreciation charges for a period is extremely difficult to estimate. Depreciation should be based on information which is as objective as possible. Nevertheless a high degree of subjectivity exists.

Activity 4

Define depreciation and outline the four main factors which are needed to ensure an appropriate depreciation charge in the profit and loss account?

   See if you can remember the answers without looking back.

We saw above that depreciation can be defined as a systematic and rational method of allocating that part of the cost of an asset, the benefit of which has been used up during an accounting period.

   The four main factors which need to be considered in arriving at an appropriate depreciation figure are:

(a) The cost of the asset
(b) The disposal or salvage value of the asset
(c) The useful life of the asset in the business
(d) A method of depreciation which is both systematic and rational.

**6.5
Methods of
depreciation**

This section deals with possible methods of allocating depreciation to each accounting period on a systematic and rational basis. Once the cost of the asset has been identified and the disposal proceeds (residual value) estimated, the estimated expense of owning the asset, over its useful life, is identifiable (i.e. cost less residual value). This total expense can be allocated in any way considered appropriate, and a number of variations can be found in practice. Nevertheless, most businesses appear to have adopted one of two methods, namely:

(a) straight-line depreciation and
(b) reducing-balance depreciation.

**Straight-line
depreciation**

The basis of this method is that the amount of benefit obtained (used up) during the useful life of an asset is spread evenly over the whole of that life. This can be summarized in the following:

$$\text{Annual depreciation} = \frac{\text{Original cost} - \text{disposal value}}{\text{Useful life}}$$

For example, consider an asset which costs £550, which has an estimated useful life of five years and scrap value of £50. The total cost which has to be allocated over the five years is £500, being the original cost less the scrap value. Using the straight-line method the assumption is made that benefit is obtained equally in each of the five years. The annual depreciation charge would therefore be £100, being the total cost to be allocated divided by the time over which it is to be allocated. This method is by far the most popular of those used in practice in the UK.

The reason that this method of depreciation is called straight-line depreciation is because, if the net book value (cost less depreciation) is graphed against time, the result is a straight line. Such a graph for the above example is shown in Figure 6.1.

Reducing-balance depreciation

This method leads to a relatively large annual depreciation expense in the first year of ownership of the asset, reducing year by year as the life of the asset increases. Figure 6.2 uses the same data as in Figure 6.1, except that the reducing-balance method of depreciation has been used.

There are two main justifications for taking this approach:

• prudence
• matching

By treating relatively large parts of the cost of assets as a depreciation expense in the early years, a prudent view is taken. This is justified by the difficult judgements which often need to be made in assessing the two unknown factors (economic life and residual value) which are not known when annual depreciation expenses are being assessed.

This approach also recognizes that with certain assets, it is necessary to pay an increasing sum for repairs and maintenance in order to preserve the same operating efficiency from year to year. The cost of the asset and the cost of repairs and maintenance are thus *both* integral parts of the preservation

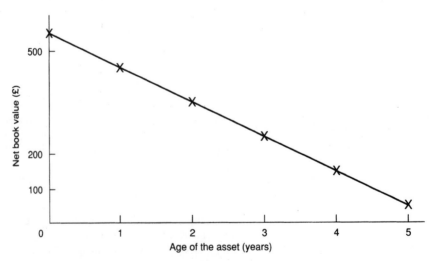

Figure 6.1. Graph of net book value against age, using the straight-line depreciation method

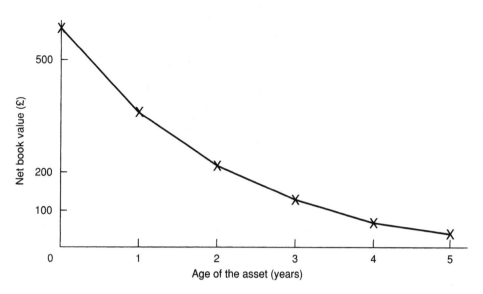

Figure 6.2. *Graph of net book value against age, using the reducing balance depreciation method*

of efficiency, and therefore a system should be devised which equates the total charge for the year. This will include both depreciation and repairs and maintenance charges. Since in the early years of an asset's life repairs and maintenance costs are likely to be low while in later years they rise, the amount of depreciation charged each year must decrease if the total charge for each accounting period is to be approximately the same. Where the asset concerned is helping to generate a fairly steady level of revenues over its life, it is appropriate that a fairly steady expense of operating the asset is matched against each year's revenues.

Activity 5

Consider an asset which cost £550, which is expected to have a residual value of £50 after a life of five years. Suppose now that the costs of repairs and maintenance are expected to be as shown in the table below.

Complete the following table assuming straight-line depreciation.

Year	Depreciation	Repairs and maintenance	Total
1	. . . .	NIL	. . . .
2	. . . .	50	. . . .
3	. . . .	100	. . . .
4	. . . .	150	. . . .
5	. . . .	200	. . . .

Your answer should look like this:

Year	Depreciation	Repairs and maintenance	Total
	£	£	£
1	100	nil	100
2	100	50	150
3	100	100	200
4	100	150	250
5	100	200	300

In respect of the above activity, let us assume that the repairs and maintenance costs have been incurred to preserve the same operating efficiency of the asset from year to year. Under this assumption it seems inappropriate to allocate depreciation on the straight-line basis, and thus to charge an increasing total amount from year to year. What is required is a system which allocates depreciation in such a way that a decrease in depreciation from year to year approximately equals the expected increase in repairs and maintenance over the same period, thus equating the total cost.

The usual method of reducing the depreciation charge each year is to take a fixed percentage of the written-down value at the beginning of the period. In other words, depreciation is charged as a percentage of a reducing balance. A formula exists which enables a percentage rate to be calculated which will spread the total depreciation expense over the expected life. This is:

$$D_p = (1 - \sqrt[n]{R/C}) \times 100\%$$

where D_p = fixed depreciation percentage
n = useful life of the asset in years
R = residual value of the asset
C = cost of the asset

In most examination questions the percentage is given.

Activity 6

Complete the following table for the asset referred to in Activity 5, using the reducing-balance method of depreciation at a rate of 40%.

Year	Depreciation	Repairs and maintenance	Total
1	Cost 550 × 40% = 220	nil	220
2	Book value 330 × 40% = ...	50	. . . .
3	Book value . . . . . × 40% = ...	100	. . . .
4	Book value . . . . . × 40% = ...	150	. . . .
5	Book value . . . . . × 40% = ...	200	. . . .
	Residual value approximately		

Your table should look something like this:

Year	Depreciation	Repairs and maintenance	Total
	£	£	£
1	550 × 40% = 220	nil	220
2	330 × 40% = 132	50	182
3	198 × 40% = 80	100	180
4	118 × 40% = 48	150	198
5	70 × 40% = 28	200	228
	Residual value = £42		

It can be seen from Activity 6 that the annual total charge is more appropriate than the total charge in Activity 5, given the assumptions made. The reducing-balance method would also be appropriate for assets where the benefits are expected to be greater in earlier years, so a greater portion needs to be matched to revenues in earlier years.

For assets where time is the chief factor, as far as using up assets is concerned, the straight-line method is more likely to be used. Where assets become less efficient with age and increases in repairs and maintenance result, the reducing-balance method is the more appropriate.

Activity 7

Can you think of any assets where the passage of time, rather than wear or obsolescence, is the only factor causing depreciation?

We believe that assets which involve the right to do something provide examples of such assets. A purchased lease, i.e. the right to occupy premises for some period of time, depreciates as the life of the lease moves towards its end. Provided that the premises are not physically deteriorating, or becoming obsolete in some way, passage of time is likely to be the only reason for the depreciation.

A variation on the reducing-balance method is the *sum of the digits method.* This method is so called because the number of years (the digits) of the asset's life are summed, and the depreciation allocated each year is expressed as a fraction of this figure. To make this clearer, consider an example.

Suppose an asset is expected to last for three years. The sum of the digits is one plus two plus three, the years of its life, giving a total of six. The depreciation allocated each year is then arrived at by expressing the digits as fractions of the total, six, putting them in descending order, to make the depreciation expense higher in the earlier years. In other words, in Year 1 the depreciation allocated would be 3/6, in Year 2 it would be 2/6 and in Year 3, 1/6. This again gives us a reducing amount of depreciation from year to year. This method has the not inconsiderable advantage of being easy to understand and to apply.

Activity 8

Using the same figures as in Activities 6 and 7, namely an asset which costs £550, with a disposal value of £50, and repairs and maintenance costs as shown, complete the table below, assuming depreciation has been calculated using the sum of the digits method.

Year	Depreciation	Repairs and maintenance	Total
	£	£	£
1	. . . .	Nil	. . . .
2	. . . .	50	. . . .
3	. . . .	100	. . . .
4	. . . .	150	. . . .
5	. . . .	200	. . . .

Is this method more or less suitable than that of Activity 7, given the assumptions made?

Your table should look something like this:

Year	Depreciation	Repairs and maintenance	Total
	£	£	£
1	$5/15 \times 500 = 167$	nil	167
2	$4/15 \times 500 = 133$	50	183
3	$3/15 \times 500 = 100$	100	200
4	$2/15 \times 500 = 67$	150	217
5	$1/15 \times 500 = 33$	200	233

The resulting figures suggest that this method is less suitable than the reducing-balance method used in Activity 6, given the assumptions made, since the total charge is less steady over the five years.

6.6 Accounting entries

Once the figure for annual depreciation has been calculated, appropriate entries must be made in the profit and loss account and balance sheet. You will recall that, when an expense is recognized, we:

- increase expenses (in effect, reduce capital)
- reduce an asset or increase a claim

by the amount of the expense.

As an example of dealing with the depreciation expense, let us consider the figures from Activity 8 (an asset which cost £550, has a disposal value of £50, which is expected to last five years) the entries would be as follows, assuming straight-line depreciation:

Year 1
- include depreciation expense in profit and loss account
- reduce the asset

by £100 (the depreciation expense for the year).

The asset will thus be shown in the balance sheet at £550 − £100 = £450 written-down (or book) value.

Year 2
- include depreciation expense in profit and loss account
- reduce the asset

by £100 (the depreciation expense for the year).
The asset will thus be shown in the balance sheet at £550 − £200 = £350 written-down (or book) value.

Year 3
- include depreciation expense in profit and loss account
- reduce the asset

by £100 (the depreciation expense for the year).
The asset will thus be shown in the balance sheet at £550 − £300 = £250 written-down (or book) value.

Year 4
- include the depreciation expense in profit and loss account
- reduce the asset

by £100 (the depreciation expense for the year).
The asset will thus be shown in the balance sheet at £550 − £400 = £150 written-down (or book) value.

Year 5
- include depreciation expense in profit and loss account
- reduce the asset

by £100 (the depreciation expense for the year).
The asset will thus be shown in the balance sheet at £550 − £500 = £50 written-down (or book) value, which is also (by design) the estimated disposal value.

This procedure results in an appropriate charge to the profit and loss account each year, and ensures that the asset in the balance sheet will be shown at its written-down value, namely cost less the *total* depreciation to date. For example, in Year 3 the written-down value of £250 reflects the cost figure, less the £300 total depreciation taken to that time.

This will be followed until the disposal of the asset. If the asset is kept in use for a period of time *after* Year 5, no further depreciation will be charged, since the total expense relating to the cost of the asset will already have been charged to profit and loss over the first five years.

If the asset is disposed of for £50, its estimated disposal value, the entries will be simply:

- increase cash by £50
- reduce asset by £50 (effectively eliminating it from the accounts)

If the asset is disposed of for a higher amount, say £75, the entries will be:

- increase cash by £75
- reduce asset by £50 (eliminating it)
- increase revenues (profit on disposal) by £25.

If the asset is disposed of for a lower amount, say £25, the entries will be:

- increase cash by £25
- reduce asset by £50 (eliminating it)
- increase expenses (loss on disposal) by £25.

Profits or losses on disposal are included in the profit and loss account for the year of disposal. They should be seen as an adjustment to bring depreciation taken to date (based on estimates) into line with *actual* depreciation. In fact, unless the magnitude of the profits or losses on disposals is large, the amounts are usually added to or subtracted from the normal depreciation expense for the accounting period, shown in the profit and loss account.

Irrespective of when the asset disposal takes place, the profit or loss on disposal is calculated by taking the difference between the sale proceeds and the written-down value of the asset at the time of disposal.

Activity 9

A vehicle costs £5,000. It is expected to be kept for five years, and then sold for £500. Depreciation is to be calculated using the sum of the digits method. In fact the vehicle is sold at the end of Year 3, for £1,500.

Show the accounting entries in the books for each of the three years, clearly identifying the expense included in the profit and loss statement each year, also the written down value at the end of each year.

You should have come up with something like this:

Total amount to be depreciated = cost less disposal value = £5,000 − £500 = £4,500. This is to be spread over five years using sum of the digits (i.e. $5 + 4 + 3 + 2 + 1 = 15$).

Depreciation would, therefore, be expected to be charged as follows:

Year 1 $5/15 \times 4,500 = £1,500$
Year 2 $4/15 \times 4,500 = £1,200$
Year 3 $3/15 \times 4,500 = £900$
Year 4 $2/15 \times 4,500 = £600$
Year 5 $1/15 \times 4,500 = £300$

Entries in the accounts:
Year 1

- *increase expense (depreciation) in the profit and loss account by £1,500*
- *reduce asset (vehicle) by £1,500*

Therefore written-down value = £5,000 − £1,500 = £3,500.

Year 2
- *increase expense (depreciation) in the profit and loss account by £1,200*
- *reduce asset (vehicle) by £1,200*

Therefore written-down value = £3,500 – £1,200 = £2,300.

Year 3
Sale of asset with written-down value of £2,300, for £1,500, gives a loss of £800. The accounting entries are:

- *increase cash by £1,500*
- *increase an expense (loss on disposal) by £800*
- *reduce asset (vehicle) by £2,300.*

Note that in Year 3, depreciation has not been taken in the usual way. This is because the asset is disposed of in the period (albeit at the end). The Year 3 depreciation expense must be the difference between the book value of the asset at the end of Year 2 and its disposal proceeds. It can be argued that depreciation should be calculated on a pro-rata basis for the period of use in the year of disposal. Depreciation in Year 3 would thus be taken at £900 (3/15 × £4,500), reducing the written-down value of the asset to £1,400. Disposal of the asset for £1,500 would then result in a profit on disposal of £100. The entries for Year 3 would be as follows:

- *increase expenses (depreciation) by £900*
- *reduce asset (vehicles) by £900*
- *increase cash by £1,500*
- *reduce asset (vehicles) by £1,400*
- *increase revenue (profit on disposal) by £100.*

The result of this more complex approach is effectively the same as that reached earlier, in that the total effective expense for Year 3 is £800. In the first treatment this was shown as a loss on disposal. In the second treatment this is reflected in depreciation of £900 and a profit on disposal of £100. Clearly calculating depreciation in the year of disposal is not necessary to arrive at the correct total charge for the year. Remember that so-called profits or losses on disposal are really final-year adjustments to depreciation, to bring estimated depreciation in line with actual depreciation.

In the treatment to date, the asset being depreciated is shown at its written-down value on the balance sheet. It is considered more informative to show the asset at cost, and deduct from it the related total depreciation taken to date. The end result, the written-down value, is the same, but the additional information provides useful insights into the business in terms of the expectations with regard to asset holding and asset replacement. The entries are slightly more complex, since inevitably the asset must remain in the accounts at cost. In fact what happens is that the reductions in the asset are shown under a separate heading, known as depreciation provision or aggregate depreciation, and that this is combined with the asset (at cost) in the balance sheet. A record of the depreciation provision is kept for each type of asset being depreciated.

Using the same example which we met earlier (namely an asset which costs £550, is expected to last five years, with an expected disposal value of £50, being depreciated using straight-line depreciation), this revised procedure would result in the following entries.

Year 1
- include depreciation expense in the profit and loss account – £100
- increase depreciation provision (aggregate depreciation) – £100

The balance sheet would thus show:

Asset–cost	£550
Less depreciation provision	£100
	£450

Year 2
- include depreciation expense in the profit and loss account – £100
- increase depreciation provision (aggregate depreciation) – £100

The balance sheet would thus show:

Asset–cost	£550
Less depreciation provision	£200
	£350

The remaining years will follow the same principles. In the year of disposal the sale proceeds will be compared with the written-down value as before, with the asset and its associated depreciation being eliminated. For example, assume that the asset was sold at the end of Year 3, for £300. The entries would be:

• Increase cash	£300		
• Reduce asset	£550	(eliminating it)	the written-
• Reduce depreciation provision	£200	(eliminating it)	down value
• Increase an expense – loss on disposal	£50		

Where assets are acquired part-way through a year it is common to calculate depreciation on a strict time basis. Sometimes, however, a less precise approach is adopted and depreciation is taken on the balance held at the year end, irrespective of the date of acquisition.

Self-assessment question 6.1

F.O. Leo purchases a lorry on 1 July 1997 for £20,000. He decided that the lorry should last for five years, after which it is likely to be sold for £4,000. Leo's accounting year is from 1 January to 31 December.

(a) Assuming straight-line depreciation show the entries relating to vehicles and depreciation for 1997 and 1998, clearly identifying the expense for depreciation for each year, and the balance sheet figures for vehicles. Assets are to be shown at cost and associated depreciation provisions.

(b) On 31 December 1999 the lorry was sold for £11,000. Show the 1999 entries.

(c) What other methods of depreciation could be used? Are they appropriate in this case?

6.7
Summary

This chapter has provided you with an introduction to the problems of profit measurement in the area of depreciation. The underlying principles of depreciation have been discussed, and a range of methods of calculating depreciation have been identified. The accounting entries have been explained. You should now be aware of the likely impact of depreciation and associated asset movements on the profit and loss account and balance sheet. You need to recognize that depreciation provides an example of judgement and subjectivity in accounting.

Exercises

1. Compare the effect of using the reducing-balance method of depreciation, the sum of the digits method, and the straight-line method, by completing the following table:

Year	Reducing balance using 40%		Sum of the digits		Straight line	
	Book value at year end £	Depreciation for year £	Book value at year end £	Depreciation for year £	Book value at year end £	Depreciation for year £
0	1500	–	1500	–	1500	–
1						
2						
3						
4						
5	0		0		0	

All calculations to be made to the nearest whole number. Any balances remaining to be written off in the fifth year.

2 What is the nature of obsolescence in relation to plant and machinery? How can it be provided for in the financial accounts of a business?

3 Assuming the data in Question 1, which method of depreciation would you use if repairs and maintenance costs were steady? If these costs were rising as follows which method would you use? Year 1 – £50, Year 2 – £150, Year 3 – £250, Year 4 – £350, Year 5 – £450.

4 A business with a year end at 31 December buys equipment on 1 January 1997 for £12,000. It buys further equipment on 1 July 1999 for £16,000. On 30 June 2000 the first set of equipment was sold for £5,500. Depreciation is to be charged at 25% on a reducing-balance basis.

   Show the relevant extracts from the profit and loss account, and the balance sheet, as they relate to the financial years 1997, 1998, 1999, and 2000. You should assume that depreciation will be calculated on a pro-rata basis for equipment purchased part-way through a year, but that no calculation of depreciation is made in the year of disposal.

5 Discuss the extent to which depreciation will provide the necessary funds to replace an asset when it ceases to be productive.

Chapter 7

Measurement problems – stock valuation

7.1 Introduction

This chapter aims to give further consideration to the problem of measuring profit, with a particular focus on stock valuation and the calculation of cost of sales.

7.2 Objectives

On completion of this chapter you should be able to:

- calculate cost of sales for a business in a variety of ways;
- explain the various approaches to stock valuation;
- use different methods of stock valuation to derive cost of sales and closing stock
- explain the lower of cost or market value rule
- illustrate how different stock valuation methods impact on the calculation of profit.

7.3 Background

We saw in Chapters 3-5 that cost of sales is an important expense, which is matched against sales revenue in the trading account, to arrive at a figure for gross profit. So far the cost of sales figure has usually been *given* in examples and exercises. In fact the calculation of cost of sales is rather more involved than this implies and the figure is usually arrived at in one of two ways:

(a) Add all purchases of stock to any opening balance on a stock account. As stock is used up a transfer needs to be made from the stock account to cost of sales. The resulting accounting entries will be to reduce stock and increase cost of sales. Note that this will require the identification (or at least an estimate) of the cost of the goods being sold.

(b) Keep track of all purchases and purchases returns over the year. At the end of the accounting period derive the cost of sales figure, using the trading account, as follows.

Opening stock		x
+ Purchases	x	
− Returns	$\underline{x}$	
		$\underline{x}$
		x
Less closing stock		$\underline{x}$
Therefore cost of sales		x

If anything was spent on transporting incoming goods (known as carriage in) it would be shown immediately below the purchases figure, since it is viewed as an integral part of the purchase price.

In fact both of the above methods require a process of stock valuation to occur, either when stock is sold, or at the year end. The point has already been made that assets should be shown at cost, so the question as to the value to be attached to stock would appear to be simple – stock is valued at cost. This cost should include all costs incurred in bringing the stock to its present location and condition. However, such an approach, while generally true, is not quite as simple as it appears to be, particularly in times of inflation or changing prices.

For example, a garden centre has in stock 100 bags of peat which had cost £1.50 each, when they were bought a few weeks ago. A further 500 bags were bought for £1.60 each. What is the cost (which should be matched against the sales revenue) of the next bag of peat sold?

Various approaches are possible, but (as with depreciation) a small number appear to be the most widely used, and three of these are given below.

7.4 Stock-valuation methods

First in, first out (FIFO)

The stock is valued *as if* the first item held in stock is the first item issued. On this assumption the next bag of peat sold would be costed out (i.e. treated as an expense) at £1.50. This method seems logical, in that the oldest stocks would normally be sold first. Of course, in some cases, e.g. petrol added to a fuel tank, even this logic fails. Use of FIFO does mean that the price at which goods are costed out will probably be insufficient to replace those goods in times of inflation. The result of this is that it may be argued that the cost of sales does not really represent the value leaving the business as a result of the sale. If we are to match an expense to the revenue, it seems illogical to match an old cost (£1.50) to a current revenue.

Activity 1

The garden centre in the above example decided to stock a new line of bags of fertilizer. Purchases and sales during the first few weeks of stocking the product were, in chronological order, as follows:

Bought   60 bags   @   £1 each
Sold   40 bags
Bought   60 bags   @   £1.10 each
Sold   70 bags

Try to work out the cost of the sales figure for the period and the value of the stock at the various points during the period, assuming that the stock usage is priced on a FIFO basis.

Your answer should be something like this:

				Cost of sales	Value of remaining stock
				£	£
Bought	60 bags	@	£1.00 each		60.00
Sold	40 bags			40.00 (i.e. 40 @ £1.00)	40.00
					20.00
Bought	60 bags	@	£1.10 each		66.00
					86.00
Sold	70 bags			75.00 (i.e. 20 @ £1.00 plus 50 @ £1.10)	75.00
					11.00

Last in, first out (LIFO)

In answer to the criticism made about FIFO, it may be seen as being preferable to value stock issues on the basis of last in, first out (LIFO). Note that this relates only to the *process of valuation*. Where possible, oldest stocks should normally be issued first, though in the case of non-perishable goods like peat, this may not be too important. Using LIFO, issues are simply valued at the most recent value of stock in hand. It is argued that this results in something much nearer to replacement cost being included in cost of sales figure in the trading account. It also means that the current cost (or close to it) is being matched to a current revenue.

Using LIFO, the transfer to cost of sales for the next bag of peat sold would be £1.60.

Activity 2
Can you say what will be the general effect on the value of the remaining stock of using LIFO to value stock issues, during a period of changing prices?

The answer is that it will reflect old costs of buying the stock.

Unfortunately, under LIFO it is possible for the balance sheet values of stock to become significantly out of line with the current cost of the stock in hand (because the value placed on the stock in hand would be as if it is old stock). LIFO is not currently permitted to be used for tax purposes in the UK, a fact which has tended to reduce its practical importance. Also the use of current cost accounting (discussed in Chapter 23) has meant that the advantages of LIFO, in terms of measuring profit, can be obtained without its balance sheet disadvantages.

Activity 3

Using exactly the same data as in Activity 1, try to work out the cost of the sales figure for the period and the value of the stock at the various points during the period, assuming that stock usages are priced on a LIFO basis.

Your answer should be something like this:

			Cost of sales	Value of remaining stock
			£	£
Bought	60 bags @ £1.00 each			60.00
Sold	40 bags		40.00 (i.e. 40 @ £1.00)	40.00
				20.00
Bought	60 bags @ £1.10 each			66.00
				86.00
Sold	70 bags		76.00 (i.e. 60 @ £1.10 plus 10 @ £1)	76.00
				10.00

The weighted average cost (AVCO)

Using this method the value of any existing stock is added to the value of new stock, and a weighted average is calculated. All subsequent stock issues are at this average cost, until such time as new receipts of goods require a further calculation. Using the above example the AVCO per bag of peat would be arrived at as follows:

$$((100 \times 1.50) + (500 \times 1.60))/600 = £1.583$$

The next bag issued would thus be costed at £1.583.

Activity 4

Using exactly the same data as Activity 1, try to work out the cost of sales figure for the period and the value of the stock at the various points during the period, assuming that stock usages are priced on an AVCO basis.

Your answer should be something like this:

			Cost of sales	Value of remaining stock
			£	£
Bought	60 bags @ £1.00 each			60.00
Sold	40 bags		40.00 (i.e. 40 @ £1.00)	40.00
				20.00

Bought	*60 bags* @ *£1.10 each*		*66.00*
			86.00
Sold	*70 bags*	*75.25 (i.e. 70 × £86/80)*	*75.25*
			10.75

Activity 5

A business is very careful about always using the oldest stock first. Which method of stock valuation would be most appropriate?

This is a bit of a trick question. The method of stock valuation used has absolutely nothing to do with the way in which the stock is actually handled. The choice between FIFO, LIFO and AVCO would depend on the attitudes of the managers of the business to how most logically to match expenses against revenues. Obviously you do not know what their attitude would be.

Self-assessment question 7.1

(a) Explain why the statement 'you value stock at historic cost' is not as simple as it appears.

(b) The Unibike Company started trading on 1 January 1997, to sell bicycles to students. During the first three years of business the FIFO method of stock valuation is used in the preparation of its annual accounts.

The following information relates to the first three years of business.

	1997	*1998*	*1999*
Sales	200 @ £80	250 @ £100	300 @ £120
Purchases	300 @ £50	300 @ £60	250 @ £80
Overheads (paid and incurred)	£4,000	£5,000	£6,000

All purchases may be assumed to have taken place on 1 January of the relevant year, before any sales for the year have occurred.

Using the layout given below show:

- the figure for closing stock at the end of each year, using FIFO, LIFO and AVCO
- the figure for cost of sales for each of the three years, using FIFO, LIFO and AVCO
- the profit figure for each of the three years under each of the three methods

FIFO method
Trading and profit and loss account

	1997	1998	1999
Sales			
Cost of sales			
Gross profit			
Overheads			
Net profit			

Stock account	Qty Price £	Qty Price £	Qty Price £
Opening balance			
Purchases			
Issues (cost of sales)			
Therefore Closing stock			

LIFO
Trading and profit and loss account

	1997	1998	1999
Sales			
Cost of sales			
Gross profit			
Overheads			
Net profit			

Stock account	Qty Price £	Qty Price £	Qty Price £
Opening balance			
Purchases			
Issues (cost of sales)			
Therefore Closing stock			

AVCO
Trading and profit and loss account

	1997	1998	1999
Sales			
Cost of sales			
Gross profit			
Overheads			
Net profit			

Stock account	Qty Price £	Qty Price £	Qty Price £
Opening balance			
Purchases			
Issues (cost of sales)			
Therefore Closing stock			

Clearly the calculation of an appropriate cost of sales figure, and the associated balance sheet figure for stock, is not quite as straightforward as it seems. The impact of the different approaches on the measurement of profit, and the statement of financial position (the balance sheet), must be clearly recognized.

In a time of cost inflation, the use of FIFO will result in the highest profit of the three methods, but the most current valuation figure for stock remaining in hand. The use of LIFO will result in the lowest figure for profit. Its use will also give the most out-of-date stock figure in the balance sheet. The use of AVCO gives a compromise solution to the two. Which is the most appropriate or useful figure for profit is a subject that will be returned to in later chapters, particularly in Chapter 23 which includes a more general discussion of the problems of accounting during periods of inflation. It is worth repeating the point that the method used (FIFO, LIFO or AVCO) has nothing to do with the actual order in which stock is used.

7.5 The 'lower of cost or net realizable value' rule

Certain exceptions arise to the rule that stock is valued at historic cost (however calculated). It should be remembered that an asset has been defined as expected future benefit. As long as there is an expectation that stock can be sold at a future date, at a price in excess of cost, there is no reason to show it at other than historic cost. In the event, however, of the expectations changing, so that future sale value is expected to be lower than cost, it would not be reasonable to include the asset in the balance sheet at cost, since this expected future benefit is less than the cost. Under such circumstances stock should be valued at the expected net realizable value. Net realizable value is arrived at by deducting any costs of disposal from the realizable value. In most cases cost would be the basis used. This is because businesses would normally be in the position where the disposal value of their stock is higher than the cost of the stock. Where this is not normally the case it would mean that the business would be constantly sustaining trading losses.

The choice of the lower of cost and net realizable value means that a more cautious view is taken of the value of stock remaining in hand. This is obviously another example of the prudence convention at work.

7.6 Stock valuation of manufactured goods

When a business is engaged in the manufacture of goods, the problems of stock valuation become greater, since stocks will include a variety of materials, work-in-progress, and finished goods. The identification of the cost of work-in-progress and finished goods is not always easy. Cost may be defined as the expenditure incurred in the normal course of business to bring a product to its current location and condition. For manufactured goods these normally include purchase costs, plus conversion costs. These latter costs include labour and expenses (e.g. subcontracted work) directly related to the stock concerned, and an appropriate share of overheads incurred to get the stock into its present location and condition. Not surprisingly, stock valuation under such circumstances can be a somewhat imprecise process.

It is generally true of accounting for stock that judgements need to be made by the preparers of accounting statements. These judgements can, in certain types of business, have profound effects on the figures shown in the accounting statements. In turn this can greatly affect the perceptions of users of the accounting statements of the trading and position of the business.

**7.7
Summary**

This chapter has provided you with an introduction to some of the problems of profit measurement that relate to stock valuation and calculation of cost of sales. As with depreciation, you should now be aware that even the calculation of cost of sales is not quite as straightforward as it might at first sight appear. Various stock valuation methods were examined and their consequences noted. You should note that the methods used in this chapter have nothing to do with physical issuing of stocks, but are purely assumptions for valuation purposes. Clearly any good business is likely to ensure that oldest stocks are used up first.

Exercises

1 Give three examples of methods of stock valuation, indicating the advantages and disadvantages of each.
2 The following information relates to your business:
Stock of goods on 1 January – 1000 units valued at £9.80 each
Purchases throughout the year:

1 January	1000 units at £10.20 each
1 March	1000 units at £10.60 each
1 May	1000 units at £10.90 each
1 July	1000 units at £11.40 each
1 September	1000 units at £11.60 each
1 November	1000 units at £11.90 each

Each month 500 units were sold.

Show clearly the cost of goods sold figure, and the closing stock valuation, assuming stock sold is valued at:

(a) Weighted average price
(b) FIFO
(c) LIFO

Assuming that the selling price is £15 per unit, calculate the gross profit under each of these methods.
3 A business has opening stock of £10,000 and closing stock at the year end of £15,000. Purchases during the year amounted to £100,000, with £2,000 being returned. Carriage on inward stocks cost £3,000. During the year the owner took stock which had cost £5,000.
    Calculate the cost of sales for the year.

Chapter 8

Profit measurement – bad and doubtful debts: the conventions

8.1 Introduction

This chapter deals with another important problem area in profit measurement in general, and matching in particular, namely bad and doubtful debts. The second part of the chapter reviews the accounting conventions and reinforces the work done in Chapters 6–8.

8.2 Objectives

On completion of this chapter you should be able to:

- explain what a bad debt is;
- explain the need for a bad debt provision, with particular emphasis on the matching principle;
- adjust the accounts to reflect bad debts and changes in the provision;
- identify and explain the main conventions which underpin accounting;
- develop examples which show that the profit calculation involves considerable subjectivity.

8.3 Debtors/bad and doubtful debts

Assets are expected future benefits. The asset of debtors represents expected future cash inflows for goods already sold (but not yet paid for). However, in almost every business there will be some debtors who will not pay their debts. This is in spite of the fact that most businesses take considerable care to try to ensure that all sales on credit result in a receipt of cash before too long. At the end of a year it is unlikely that the total debtors figure will represent expected future benefits, since the expected future benefit will be a lower figure. Some adjustment is therefore necessary to the debtors figure.

In deciding on the nature of this adjustment it is important to note that typically in practice there are a series of *individual* debtors records (referred to as accounts) kept, one for each debtor, and the total of these is the debtors figure which goes into the balance sheet. Any adjustments made in the accounts must therefore relate to *specific* debtors.

A first step in any adjustment needed to the debtors figure is to consider the degree of certainty there is that payment will (or will not) be received. This usually means that a business can look through its debtors accounts and tell with a reasonable degree of certainty that certain specific debtors are unlikely to pay their debts, for a variety of reasons. Such debts are known as *bad debts*. Under such circumstances the accounts of the *specific* debtors concerned will be reduced by the amount of the bad debt, and an expense – bad debts – will be increased and be included in the profit and loss statement.

In the context of a debtor becoming a bad debt, the appropriate entries are, in principle:

- reduce the debtor's figure
- increase expenses (bad debts written off)

by the amount of the debt which has gone bad.

Under the matching convention, it is important that the expense of a particular bad debt written off is as closely matched as possible, in the same accounting period, to the original revenue which gave rise to that debt. This is because the bad debt is an expense directly caused by the revenue.

Where the debt is judged to have gone bad during the same period as that in which the relevant sale was made, the accounting entries are exactly as specified above. Clearly this cannot happen with debtors outstanding at the period end as any future bad debts will arise in future periods. This is dealt with immediately after the next activity.

Activity 1
Why do we not simply cancel the sale when a debt goes bad?

The answer is that the sale has taken place and, therefore, it is correct to record it as such. The fact that the cash is never received is a separate issue. The ratio of gross profit to sales is a useful, and much-used, one. This and other useful ratios would be distorted and give a wrong impression if all the sales were not included.

Once the *identifiable* bad debts have been recorded, and the debtors figure accordingly reduced, the second step must be embarked upon. The problem with this step is slightly different. There will almost certainly be a doubtful area, where it is not possible to say with certainty which debtors will not pay. However, in practice it is often possible to estimate fairly accurately the total amount of the remaining debts which will turn out to be bad, even though it may be impossible to say which individual debtors will not pay. The problem is thus as follows:

- the total debtors figure is too high – by the amount estimated for doubtful debts – and therefore needs to be reduced
- the estimate for doubtful debts is an overall figure, not related to individual debtors accounts. It is thus impossible to achieve the reduction required by deducting the estimated doubtful debts from individual debtors accounts.

The problem is solved in a similar way to the problem of showing accumulated depreciation (depreciation provision). The estimate of doubtful debts is held in an account called a *bad (or doubtful) debts provision*. This is then deducted from the debtors figure in the balance sheet to give an effective reduction in the asset. The corresponding entry (remember the convention of duality) is an expense in the profit and loss account – referred to as the 'increase in bad debts provision'.

Example	Suppose that Wessex Enterprises had trade debtors on 31 December of £1,050, broken down as follows: debtor 1 – £30; debtor 2 – £100; debtor 3 – £20; debtor 4 – £200; debtor 5 – £50; debtor 6 – £150; debtor 7 – £200; debtor 8 – £125; debtor 9 – £75; debtor 10 – £75; debtor 11 – £25. On further analysis of the debts outstanding it was found that debtors 1 and 3 were unlikely to pay their debts. In addition it was decided that further debts of £50 were unlikely to be paid (based upon past experience, which indicated that typically about 5% of debtors would not pay), but it was uncertain which debtors would not pay.

The first stage is to deal with the bad debts which can be related to individual debtors (i.e. 1 and 3). The entries for this are:

- increase an expense – bad debts – £50
- reduce debtor 1 – £30
- reduce debtor 3 – £20

The second stage is to deal with the remaining estimated bad debts, which cannot be related to individual debtors. The entries are:

- increase an expense – increase in bad debts provision – £50
- increase bad debts provision – £50

The expense 'increase in bad debts provision' will be included in the profit and loss account. In the balance sheet debtors will appear as follows:

debtors	£1,000
less bad debts provision	£50
	£950

The net amount of £950 represents the expected future benefit associated with debtors.

The next stage in the process occurs when bad debts actually arise, which relate to the provision already made. Clearly when a bad debt arises the appropriate debtors must be written off. However, this still leaves the question of the appropriate double entry, with two possibilities.

The first of these is that bad debts relating to last year's provision may be set against that provision, with any remaining balance being included in the profit and loss account for the current year. (If too much were taken into the provision last year the excess would be included as a revenue for the current year. If too little were taken an additional expense would be needed.) Bad debts of the current year, and an estimate of doubtful debts of the current year, would then follow the same principles as set out above.

The above approach can only be used if the system of recording debtors is sufficiently detailed to relate debts to each particular financial period. It also means that at the end of each year a new provision will have to be set up, and this provision will have to be kept completely separate from any provisions outstanding from previous years. Such a system can be inconvenient, and is likely to cause more work than that described below, with no real advantages.

The second, and most widely used approach, is to show bad debts as an expense – bad debts – in the year in which they arise, and to adjust the bad debts provision from one year to the next, making it larger or smaller, as the estimate of bad debts increases or decreases.

Example	Picking up from the previous example, let us now assume that, at the end of the second year, total debtors, after writing off all known bad debts, amount to £1,200. At the end of the second year the bad debts provision brought forward from the first year would be £50 (assuming the second approach identified above). Past experience indicates that typically about 5% of debtors will not pay their debts. This implies that at the end of year 2 the bad debts provision needs to be 5% × £1,200, i.e. £60. Since a balance of £50 already exists it is only necessary to increase the provision by £10. The accounting entries are thus:

- expense – increase in bad debts provision £10
- increase bad debts provision £10

The expense 'increase in bad debts provision' will be included in the profit and loss account. In the balance sheet the asset debtors would appear as follows:

Debtors	£1,200
Less bad debts provision	£60
	£1,140

If the estimate for the provision indicates that a reduction is needed the accounting entries would be:

- reduce bad debts provision
- increase a revenue 'reduction in bad debts provision' by the amount of the reduction needed

It is important to note both the similarities with and differences from the depreciation provisions. Both bad debts provisions and depreciation provisions require adjustment every year, and any changes therein must be recorded in the profit and loss account as revenues or expenses. However, the expectation with depreciation provisions is that they will accumulate each year, until the net book value is the expected disposal value. No such expectation exists with regard to debtors. With these the expectation is more likely to be a set percentage of debtors, not an accumulating figure. As the total for debtors changes so will the tendency for the amount needed for the bad debts provision.

The final question which must be answered is 'why bother with a provision at all? Why not simply write off debts as they become bad?' The answer is provided by the *matching principle*, which states that revenues and expenses for a period should be matched. Since sales on credit are recognized in one period the expenses associated with these sales, including bad debts and bad debt provisions, should be charged in that period.

Activity 2

Wessex Enterprises had trade debtors on 31 December 2000, the end of its accounting year, totalling £21,500. All these debts arose from 2000 sales.

On consideration of the debts outstanding it was found that debtors with debts totalling £100 were unlikely to pay their debts and it was decided to write them off. In addition it was decided to create a provision for doubtful debts of 5% of the remaining debts, based on past experience which indicated that typically about 5% of debtors would not pay.

How would these be dealt with in the accounts?

The first stage is to deal with the bad debts which are to be written off to the 2000 profit and loss account. The entries are:

- *increase an expense (bad debts) by £100*
- *reduce debtors by £100*

The second stage is to deal with the remaining suspected bad debts. The amount of provision required is £1,070 [(£21,500 − 100) × 5%]. The entries are:

- *increase an expense (creation of doubtful debts provision) by £1,070*
- *increase bad debts provision by £1,070*

The expense 'creation of doubtful debts provision' will be included in the profit and loss account. In the balance sheet debtors will appear as follows:

	£
Debtors (£21,500 − 100)	*21,400*
Less bad debts provision	*1,070*
	20,330

The net amount of £20,330 represents the expected future benefit associated with debtors, taking a prudent view.

Self-assessment question 8.1

At 31 December 2001, Wessex Enterprises had debts outstanding of £23,400. When these were considered in detail it was decided that two of them totalling £300 were very doubtful and should be written off in full. Both related to sales made in 2001. In addition, a general doubtful debts provision of 5% of the remaining debts should be established.

During 2002, the business sold goods on credit for a total of £147,800 and received cash from debtors totalling £143,700. Debts totalling $1,800 were written off during the year, £910 of which related to sales made during 2001. By the end of 2002, there were no remaining debts relating to 2001 sales, either because the cash had been received or the debts had been written off. At 31 December 2002, it was decided to create a provision equal to 5% of the debts outstanding at that date.

Show the balance sheet figures for debtors (including the provision) at 31 December 2001 and 2002.

Show the expenses and revenues relating to bad and doubtful debts for each of the two years ended 31 December 2001 and 2002.

Activity 3

Can you remember why we create a doubtful debts provision?

The reason is to treat potential bad debts as expenses in the accounting period, during which the revenues with which they are associated are recognized. This is done in order to follow the matching convention. At the same time, the existence of the doubtful debt provision reduces the book value of the debtors. This is consistent with the prudence convention.

Nothing that has been said so far should leave the impression that businesses lightly accept the fact that an individual or organization which owes it money for goods or services bought on credit (or for any other reason) will not pay. In practice businesses which sell on credit typically have quite sophisticated systems of credit control, including debtor collection routines, the monitoring of debts and the issuing of reminders to late payers. Where payment cannot be obtained by normal methods the selling business may resort to the use of the law of contract to enforce payment. However, in some cases it will still prove impossible to collect the debts.

Activity 4
Do you know, or can you guess, the type of activities which a well-organized business would undertake in respect of making sales on credit?

The activities would include: .

- *Taking up references for new credit customers*
- *Making a judgement on how much credit to advance to new customers*
- *Reviewing the credit limits of existing customers*
- *Ensuring that no customer is allowed to exceed the established credit limit*
- *Ensuring that invoices, statements and reminders are sent to customers on a routine and prompt basis*
- *Taking steps to deal with customers who are exceeding the agreed credit period.*

Where payment cannot be obtained by normal methods the selling business may resort to the use of the law of contract to enforce payment. However, in some cases it will still prove impossible to collect the debts.

**8.4
The conventions
of accounting**

So far in this book a number of conventions have been introduced. These will now be briefly reviewed. They are as follows.

**Money
measurement**

Items in accounting statements are described in terms of money. Items or factors which are incapable of being described in this way must, therefore, be excluded from accounting statements.

Business entity

This convention simply says that, from an accounting point of view, the business is to be treated as a self-contained entity, separate from all who are connected with it.

Duality

This convention requires that each transaction affecting the business has two effects on the balance sheet.

Historic cost

This convention states that assets should normally be shown in accounts at their outlay cost to the business.

| **Stable monetary unit** | This assumes that the measurement unit in accounting, the unit of currency, retains a stable value relative to other assets over time. |

| **Going concern convention** | This convention holds that, unless there is reason to take a different view, the business should be treated as if it will continue for the foreseeable future. |

| **Realization** | The convention of realization maintains that revenues should be recognized when they are capable of objective measurement and the asset value receivable is reasonably certain. This is typically taken to be when the goods or service pass to, and are accepted by, the customer. |

| **Matching** | This convention holds that expenses should be matched to the revenues which they helped to generate such that the revenue and its associated expenses are set against one another in deducing the income of a business for a particular accounting period. |

| **Accruals** | This convention maintains that profit (or loss) for a period is the difference between revenues earned during the period and their related expenses, not the difference between cash receipts and payments for the period. |

| **Prudence (or conservatism)** | In preparing financial statements accountants err on the cautious side. Hence profits are usually only recognized when they have been realized (see realization convention), while losses are usually taken fully into account as soon as their likelihood is seen. Accounting has a number of areas where more than one approach may be taken. This convention maintains that the more prudent approach should always be taken. |

To these conventions must be added three more which have not expressly been discussed so far – consistency, materiality and objectivity.

| **Consistency** | As has been seen, numerous ways frequently exist for dealing with certain matters associated with accounting (e.g. depreciation, stock and debtors valuation). Complete freedom with regard to accounting policies would make manipulation and 'window dressing' of financial data fairly easy. It would also make comparison of commercial effectiveness, etc. between one period and another very difficult. In order to prevent this, the convention of consistency requires a consistent application of a particular policy from one accounting period to the next. When a change of accounting policy is considered necessary, the change should be made on a semipermanent basis. Activity 5 illustrates the extent to which changes in accounting policies have the potential to mislead a user of the accounts. |

Activity 5

The following final accounts relate to a business

Balance sheet as at 31 December

	1998 £	1999 £		1998 £	1999 £
Fixed assets			Capital		
Cost	20,000	20,000	Opening balance	25,000	30,000
Depreciation provision	–	4,000	Net profit	10,000	14,000
	20,000	16,000		35,000	44,000
			Less drawings	5,000	6,000
			Closing balance	30,000	38,000
Current assets			Current liabilities		
Stock	8,000	12,000			
Debtors	10,000	12,000	Creditors	10,000	8,000
Cash	2,000	6,000			
	40,000	46,000		40,000	46,000

Profit and loss account for the year ending 31 December 1999

	£		£
Opening stock	8,000	Sales	70,000
Purchases	48,000		
	56,000		
Less closing stock	12,000		
Cost of sales	44,000		
Gross profit	26,000		
	70,000		70,000
Depreciation	4,000	Gross profit	26,000
Other expenses	8,000		
Net profit	14,000		
	26,000		26,000

Notes

1 Depreciation of fixed assets has been taken at 20% per annum straight line
2 Stock has been valued assuming FIFO
3 No provision has been made for doubtful debts

Recalculate the profit figure for 1999 assuming:

1 Depreciation to be taken at 40% on a reducing-balance basis
2 Stock to be valued on a LIFO basis. Assume that this will result in a closing stock figure of £8,000 (and thus a cost of sales figure of £48,000)
3 A bad debt provision is to be set up at 5% of debtors

Revised accounts would be as follows:

Profit and loss account for the year ended 31 December 1999

	£		£
Opening stock	8,000	Sales	70,000
Purchases	48,000		
	56,000		
Less closing stock	8,000		
Cost of sales	48,000		
Gross profit	22,000		
	70,000		70,000
Depreciation	8,000	Gross profit	22,000
Other expenses	8,000		
Increase in DDP	600		
Net profit	5,400		
	22,000		22,000

Balance sheet as at 31 December 1999

	£	£	£		£
Fixed assets				**Capital**	
Cost			20,000	Opening balance	30,000
less depreciation			8,000	Net profit	5,400
provision			12,000		35,400
				less drawings	6,000
				Closing balance	29,400
Current assets				**Current liabilities**	
Stock		8,000			
Debtors	12,000			Creditors	8,000
less DDP	600	11,400			
Cash		6,000	25,400		
			37,400		37,400

Materiality

This convention recognizes that in preparing accounts the amount of detail given will need to be varied according to the size of the organization, and to the importance of particular items to the achievement of overall organizational goals. All important items must be shown in detail. Less important items may be included under more general headings, rather than be separately disclosed. (*Note:* All items *must* be included: this convention is concerned with the number of detailed headings under which items are included.) The convention is also concerned with the extent to which it is necessary strictly to follow the other conventions. When the amounts involved are trivial it may be judged that the cost of strictly following a particular convention is not justified by the greater accuracy which may result. For example, where a particular type of expense is trivial and difficult to relate to a particular revenue, the matching convention may be disregarded and the expense set against the revenues of the period in which the cash, relating to the expense, was actually paid.

Objectivity

This convention, which is effectively a facet of reliability, basically says that, in preparing financial reports, the preparer should try to use data which is as objective and reliable as possible. Objective data is data which can be independently verified, which is not based upon the opinion of any person within the organization or involved in preparing the accounting statements. It is free from personal bias. In other words, the accounts should be concerned, as far as possible, with facts and as little as possible with opinions.

Each of these conventions will be critically discussed in some detail in Chapter 22.

8.5 Summary

This chapter has provided you with an introduction to the problems of profit measurement in the area of bad and doubtful debts. Possible methods of dealing with these problems have been identified, which try to match expenses with appropriate revenues.

In considering the options set out in the last three chapters it should have become clear that the measurement of profit is rather less objective than might be expected. Different profit figures can be arrived at for individual accounting periods depending upon the methods chosen for dealing with the problems raised in this chapter. Over the entire life of a business the differences will even out. On a year by year basis this is not the case.

The chapter concludes with a brief consideration of the accounting conventions.

We have now completed our consideration of the basic elements of recording accounting data. In these first eight chapters we have concentrated on issues of principle, rather than on some of the more practical aspects of maintaining accounting records. The next three chapters will deal with practical accounting in more detail. These should be useful for all students of accounting and those non-specialists who wish to obtain a better understanding of the detailed process of accounting. Later sections of the book can be used without study of the next three chapters. Of course it is highly likely that study of these chapters will heighten the understanding of all students, including the non-specialist.

Exercises

1 The following debtors were outstanding at the end of 1998: debtor 1 – £100; debtor 2 – £50; debtor 3 – £50; debtor 4 – £100; debtor 5 – £50; debtor 6 – £25; debtor 7 – £75.

At the end of the year the credit controller examined the list and concluded that debtor 5 was not likely to pay his debt. It was therefore to be written off as bad. In addition he decided that an additional $12\frac{1}{2}$% of debtors (£50) were unlikely to pay, on the basis of past experience. A provision was to be established.

During 1999 debtors 3 and 6 went bankrupt and could not pay their debts. All others who were debtors at the beginning of the year paid their debts during the year. Also during the year sales to debtors 1 and 2 amounted to £300 and £200 respectively. Sales to debtors 8 to 20 totalled £5,000, and to debtor 21 totalled £50. All debts relating to debtors 1 and 2 were settled during the year. Cash received from debtors 8 to 20 amounted to £4,000. At the end of 1999 it was concluded that debtor 21 would probably not pay, and that a provision of 10% would be needed for the remaining debtors.

Use the layout set out below to show the debtors and their associated balances at the end of both 1998 and 1999, and the associated profit and loss account items for the two years.

Debtors balance	Balance as per question	1998 transactions +	−	Closing balance	1999 transactions +	−	Closing balance
1	100						
2	50						
3	50						
4	100						
5	50						
6	25						
7	75						
8–20							
21							
Total	450						

Profit and loss account	1998	1999
Bad debts expense		
Increase/decrease in bad debts provision		

Balance sheet

Debtors
Less bad debts provision

2 From the following information for a business show the relevant figures for bad debts, and changes in the bad debt provision, in the profit and loss account for 1998 and 1999, and the figures which would appear for debtors and bad debts provision in the balance sheets as at 31 December 1998 and 1999

1 January 1998	Debtors balance	£4,000
	Bad debts provision	£200
Year to 31 December 1998	Sales	£20,000
	Cash received	£18,000
	Sales returns	£600
	Bad debts	£100
Year to 31 December 1999	Sales	£25,000
	Cash received	£26,000

		(including a bad debt
		recovered of £40)
Sales returns		£1,000
Bad debts		£200

The bad debt provision is to be maintained at 5% of year-end debtors

3 'Profit is an elusive concept.' Discuss this statement, illustrating the difficulties confronting the accountant in his or her attempt to measure profit.

4 Comment on the suggestion that the measurement of financial accounting information of the type presently reported is as much based on subjective opinion as on objective evidence.

5 Discuss the importance of the following conventions.

(a) consistency
(b) prudence
(c) objectivity.

6 The following is the balance sheet of a business at the beginning of 2000 (i.e. 1 January)

	£	£		£	£
Fixed assets			*Capital*		54,000
Premises		30,000			
Fixtures and Fittings					
– cost	12,000				
– depreciation provision	2,000	10,000			
Equipment					
– cost	15,000				
– depreciation provision	5,000	10,000	*Loan (10% interest)*		10,000
		50,000			
Current assets			*Current liabilities*		
Stock	7,000		Creditors	8,000	
Prepaid insurance	100		Accrued wages	1,000	9,000
Debtors	10,000				
Cash	5,900				
		23,000			
		73,000			73,000

Notes:
The prepaid insurance relates to a premium which covers the 12 months to 31 March 2000.
The accrued wages relate to overtime worked in December 1999.

The following represents a *summary* of the transactions which took place during 2000.

(a) Stock was purchased on credit for £70,000.
(b) Stock was purchased for cash for £15,000.
(c) Cash sales amounted to £40,000.

(d) Credit sales amounted to £100,000.

(e) Wages of £25,000 were paid.

(f) Rent of £1,250 was paid. This covered the fifteen months to 31 March 2001.

(g) General expenses of £5,000 were paid.

(h) Rates and insurance of £1,200 were paid. This included a £500 insurance premium covering the period 1 April 2000 to 31 March 2001.

(i) Additional equipment was purchased on 1 January for £3,000. This was financed from a loan for the full amount, with interest payable at 20% per annum.

(j) Cash received from debtors amounted to £95,000, which was in satisfaction of debts of £97,000, the remainder being discount.

(k) Cash paid to creditors amounted to £71,000, which was in satisfaction of debts of £72,000, the remainder being discount.

(l) The owner withdrew £200 in stock and £6,000 in cash.

(m) £1,000 of credit sales were returned. £500 of credit purchases were returned.

(n) Some of the fittings – cost £2,000, depreciation provision £1,000 – were traded in part-exchange for new fittings. The total cost of the new fittings was £4,000, of which £1,500 was a part-exchange allowance, and £2,500 was paid in cash.

(o) The owner won £5,000 on the football pools. This was paid into the business.

(p) A bill for holidays for the owner – total £500 – was paid from the business bank account.

At the end of the year the following items of additional information are obtained:

(a) Bad debts amounting to £1,500 are to be written off.

(b) Depreciation is to be provided for as follows:
    – premises – none
    – equipment – 20% on cost
    – fixtures and fittings – 10% on cost
    Depreciation is to be taken on those assets still in use at the year end, not on those disposed of during the year.

(c) The two items of loan interest remain unpaid.

(d) Christmas overtime payments of £800 have not yet been paid.

(e) Closing stock is valued at £10,000.

Required

Prepare a trading and profit and loss account for the business for the year ending 31 December 2000 and a balance sheet as at that date.

Part Three

Practical Accounting

This part, which consists of three chapters, deals with accounting in practice. It is targeted at those of you who need a knowledge of double-entry book-keeping. On completion of these chapters you should be able to prepare a full set of accounts, using traditional ledger accounts.

The third chapter in this part (Chapter 11) aims to provide you with a broad explanation of more detailed accounting systems, including computerized systems.

This part can be excluded without affecting the flow of later chapters.

Chapter 9

Practical accounting – ledger accounts

**9.1
Introduction**

The aim of the book so far has been broadly to provide you with an understanding of the basic principles of accounting, particularly with regard to the balance sheet and the profit and loss account, and to enable you to prepare final accounts from a set of transactions. It will no doubt have become apparent, however, in working through activities and examples, that the system adopted becomes more of a problem as the number of transactions increases. In practice a business with a large number of transactions would need to use a system which is able to cope rather more effectively with increased amounts of data. The system of pluses and minuses, made on the face of a balance sheet and profit and loss account, will not do. In practice a business is likely to use one, or a combination, of the following:

(a) a system of *ledger accounts*, based upon the system of double-entry book-keeping
(b) a *computerized system* – typically based upon the principles used to date, but with a capability to handle large volumes of data.

This chapter aims to provide an introduction to the first of these two systems, while a later chapter will deal with computerized systems. This section of the book aims to provide an overview of systems found in practice, and to show that the *end product* of these systems is the same as that achieved so far in the book, and that the underlying principles are identical.

The emphasis of this chapter is primarily on accounting systems as they relate to the preparation of final accounts. However, information of an accounting nature may well be useful in a variety of other ways, e.g. stock control, credit control, assistance with planning and decision making, establishing how actual results compare with planned performance etc. The design of accounting systems should clearly reflect these needs. As will be seen, the use of the database concept, and the idea of management information systems, means that the typical computer system has considerable advantages over a manual system, particularly as regards flexibility of use of the information contained within it.

**9.2
Objectives**

On completion of this chapter you should be able to:

• explain the practical limitations of the system used so far in this book to record accounting transactions, and appreciate the need for a system able to cope rather better with a large volume of transactions;

- explain how the system of ledger accounts relates to the system of recording used so far in this book;
- explain the basic principles of double-entry book-keeping and apply these principles;
- appreciate the role of the trial balance and use the trial balance in the accounting process;
- explain the relationship between ledger accounts and final accounts;

**9.3
Ledger
accounts –
double-entry
book-keeping**

General principles

In preparing final accounts we have used the following basic equation

$$\text{Assets} = \text{Capital} + \text{Liabilities}$$

At the end of a period of trading this equation has been modified as follows:

Assets at = Capital at the beginning of the period
the end of   + Injections of new capital
a period   + Net profit/ − net loss
                  − Drawings
                  + External liabilities

Since Profit = Revenue − Expenses this can be modified as follows:

Assets = Opening capital
         + Injections
         + Revenue − expenses
         − Drawings
         + External liabilities

This can be rearranged as follows:

Assets   = Opening capital
+ Drawings   + Injections
+ Expenses   + External liabilities
                  + Revenues

This is an equality which must exist, unless mistakes have been made.

Clearly, if a list can be prepared which sets out the above components, it would be fairly straightforward to convert it into a set of final accounts. The procedure would be broadly as described in earlier chapters. Revenues and expenses would be summarized in a profit and loss account, from which the net profit or loss could be calculated. This figure would then be added to (or subtracted from) the capital, with drawings being deducted from the resulting figure.

The system of *ledger accounts* is based upon the equality shown above, and permits a system whereby assets, drawings and expenses may be effectively recorded on one side of the equation, while capital, liabilities and revenues may be recorded on the other side.

The basic record used in a system of ledger accounts is called an *account*. An account is a record of one or more items, relating to some person or thing, kept under an appropriate heading. The form of an account is:

Debit side		Title			Credit side
Date	Detail	Amount	Date	Detail	Amount
		£			£

In earlier times all of the accounts of a business were kept in a book (or books) known as the ledger(s). Hence the term ledger accounts.

Each transaction is recorded in accounts for the particular person or thing it affects. All transactions are entered in date order. The words debit and credit are used to denote the side of an account on which an entry is made. The word debit means to make an entry on the left-hand side, while the word credit means to make an entry on the right-hand side.

By convention, assets, expenses and drawings are recorded on the debit side, while capital, liabilities and revenues are recorded on the credit side. Reductions in assets, drawings or expenses are recorded on the credit side of these accounts, while reductions in capital, liabilities or revenues are recorded on the debit side. It is not surprising that increases in assets and expenses, on the one hand, and claims and revenues, on the other, are shown on the opposite sides of their respective accounts. They do, after all, appear on opposite sides of the balance sheet.

When using a system of ledger accounts the convention of duality results in a system whereby *every transaction has both a debit and a credit entry*, hence the phrase *double-entry book-keeping*. The 'detail' column in each ledger account provides a cross-reference facility, and shows the title of the account in which a corresponding double entry is being made.

Example

Record the following in ledger accounts:

(a) 1 January   J. Jones invests £10,000 in a business
(b) 5 January   The business buys stock for £5,000 cash
(c) 8 January   It buys a further £1,000 of stock on credit
(d) 15 January   It sells stock which had cost £1,000 for £1,500 cash
(e) 21 January   It acquires a new machine for £4,000 cash
(f) 28 January   It pays rent of £500 relating to January and February

You should note that other than item (f) above this example is the same as was used in Chapter 3.

The double-entry required is as follows:

(a) Increase an asset – cash
    Increase a liability – capital
    When recording this in ledger accounts the entries become:
    Debit Cash   £10,000
    Credit Capital   £10,000

(b) Increase an asset – stock
     Decrease an asset – cash
     When recording this in ledger accounts the entries become:
     Debit Stock   £5,000
     Credit Cash   £5,000
(c) Increase an asset – stock
     Increase a liability – creditors
     When recording this in ledger accounts the entries become:
     Debit Stock   £1,000
     Credit Creditors   £1,000
(d) Increase an asset – cash
     Increase a revenue – sales
     Increase an expense – cost of sales
     Reduce an asset – stock
     When recording this in ledger accounts the entries become:
     Debit Cash   £1,500
     Credit Sales   £1,500
     Debit Cost of Sales   £1,000
     Credit Stock   £1,000
(e) Increase an asset – machinery
     Reduce an asset – cash
     When recording this in ledger accounts the entries become:
     Debit Machinery   £4,000
     Credit Cash   £4,000
(f) Increase an expense – rent
     Reduce an asset – cash
     When recording this in ledger accounts the entries become:
     Debit Rent   £500
     Credit Cash   £500

At the end of a period each account can be *'balanced off'*. This is nothing more than comparing the sum of each of the two sides of the balance sheet and carrying the difference forward. The process of balancing off can be seen in the cash account and the stock account below, where debits exceed credits, with the excess being brought down as a debit balance.

The ledger accounts are shown below:

Capital

		£			£
			January 1	Cash	10,000

Cash

		£			£
January 1	Capital	10,000	January 5	Stock	5,000
15	Sales	1,500	21	Machinery	4,000
			28	Rent	500
			31	Balance	2,000
		11,500			11,500
January 31	Balance	2,000			

Stock

		£			£
January 5	Cash	5,000	January 15	Cost of Sales	1,000
8	Creditors	1,000	31	Balance	5,000
		6,000			6,000
January 31	Balance	5,000			

Creditors

		£			£
			January 8	Stock	1,000

Cost of Sales

		£			£
January 15	Stock	1,000			

Sales

		£			£
			January 15	Cash	1,500

Machinery

		£			£
January 21	Cash	4,000			

Rent

		£			£
January 28	Cash	500			

Activity 1
Show how the following transactions will be recorded in ledger accounts:

(a) Stock is purchased on credit for £500
(b) The owner withdraws £250
(c) The owner brings his own car into the business, for use solely by the business. The car is currently valued at £3,000
(d) Goods which cost £500 are sold for £600 cash
(e) Rent of £200 is paid
(f) Goods which cost £1,000 are sold for £1,250 on credit
(g) Bank interest of £50 is paid
(h) Receive £1,000 from debtors
(i) Purchase equipment for £4,000 with a loan from the bank for the full amount

Note that this activity was Activity 5 in Chapter 3.

(a) *Debit stock (or purchases)*
   Credit creditors
(b) *Debit drawings (or capital)*
   Credit cash
(c) *Debit motor vehicle*
   Credit capital (an injection)
(d) *Debit cost of sales (an expense)*
   Credit stock
   Debit cash
   Credit sales (a revenue)
(e) *Debit rent*
   Credit cash
(f) *Debit cost of sales (an expense)*
   Credit stock
   Debit debtors
   Credit sales (a revenue)
(g) *Debit interest (an expense)*
   Credit cash
(h) *Debit cash*
   Credit debtors
(i) *Debit equipment*
   Credit loan

Activity 2
Show the ledger entries for the following transactions:

(a) C. Mille invests cash of £15,000 in a business known as Polyprint & Co.
(b) The business borrows £3,000 from the bank.

(c) It purchases plant and equipment for £10,000 cash and a vehicle for £3,000 cash.
(d) It purchases £7,500 worth of stock on credit.
(e) It purchases £2,000 worth of stock for cash.
(f) It sells stock which had cost £6,500 for £11,000, on credit.
(g) It receives £8,000 cash from debtors.
(h) It pays £5,000 cash to creditors.
(i) It pays £500 in wages.
(j) It pays £250 rent.
(k) C. Mille withdraws £500 for his own use.

(a) Debit cash
Credit capital
(b) Debit cash
Credit loan
(c) Debit plant and equipment (with £10,000)
Credit cash (with £10,000)
Debit vehicle (with £3,000)
Credit cash (with £3,000)
(d) Debit stock
Credit creditors
(e) Debit stock
Credit cash
(f) Debit cost of sales (with £6,500) (an expense)
Credit stock (with £6,500)
Debit debtors (with £11,000)
Credit sales (with £11,000)
(g) Debit cash
Credit debtors
(h) Debit creditors
Credit cash
(i) Debit wages (an expense)
Credit cash
(j) Debit rent (an expense)
Credit cash
(k) Debit drawing (or capital)
Credit cash

Activity 3

The following transactions occur, all of which affect the debtors account:

(a) Sales on credit amounted to £10,000.
(b) Sales on credit amounted to £5,000.

(c) Cash received from debtors amounted to £7,800, which was in satisfaction of debts of £8,000, the remaining £200 being discount allowed.

(d) Bad debts of £500 were written off.

State the effect of these transactions in terms of double-entry book-keeping.
Enter the appropriate amounts in the debtors account and balance off the account.

(a) *Debit debtors*
   Credit sales
(b) *Debit debtors*
   Credit sales
(c) *Debit cash with £7,800*
   Debit discount allowed with £200
   Credit debtors with £8,000
(d) *Debit bad debts*
   Credit debtors

Debtors

	£			£
Sales	*10,000*		*Cash*	*7,800*
Sales	*5,000*		*Discount allowed*	*200*
			Bad debts	*500*
			Balance c/d	*6,500*
	15,000			*15,000*
Balance b/d	*6,500*			

The balance carried forward is calculated by adding each of the two sides (£15,000 and £8,500), and working out the difference. The balance carried down (also known as carried forward) is inserted on the smaller side, making it balance. The double entry is completed by inserting the balance brought down (also known as brought forward) on the other side of the account.

The trial balance

At this point every transaction has been recorded in ledger accounts, and each account has been totalled, and balances carried forward. It should thus be possible to extract a list of balances which gives the identity referred to earlier, namely:

$$\begin{array}{ll} \text{Assets} & \text{Capital} \\ +\,\text{Drawings} = & +\,\text{Liabilities} \\ +\,\text{Expenses} & +\,\text{Revenues} \end{array}$$

This list, when prepared from a set of ledger account balances, is known as a **trial balance**. The trial balance for the business of J. Jones would be as follows:

Trial balance as at 31 January

	Debit £	Credit £
Assets		
Cash	2,000	
Stock	5,000	
Machinery	4,000	
Expenses		
Cost of sales	1,000	
Rent	500	
Capital		10,000
Liabilities		
Creditors		1,000
Revenues		
Sales		1,500
	12,500	12,500

The figures which appear in a trial balance reflect the *cumulative effect* of the transactions recorded in the accounts. The trial balance represents an important stage in the process of internal checking. It acts as a partial check on the accuracy of the recording process. It does not guarantee that there are no errors, but a trial balance that does *not* agree provides clear evidence that there have been mistakes made in the recording process. Steps must be taken to identify these errors, and correct them, before moving on to the next stage of the process.

Activity 4

Which of the following errors will prevent the trial balance from agreeing, and which will not?

(a) A payment of rent which was incorrectly debited to rates.
(b) A payment for improvements to buildings which was debited to repairs.
(c) The receipt of cash which was debited to cash and debited to debtors.
(d) The payment of wages which was debited to wages as £10,100, and credited to cash as £11,000.
(e) The writing off of a bad debt which was debited to debtors and debited to bad debts.
(f) The situation in which two mistakes are made.
  – a receipt from a customer for £500 which was in satisfaction of a debt of £520, £20 being discount, which was debited cash £500, debited discount allowed £50, credit creditors £520, and
  – a payment of an electricity bill of £580, which was debited to Electricity as £550 and credited cash as £580.

(a) The first of these will not prevent the trial balance from agreeing.
(b) This will not prevent the trial balance from agreeing.
(c) This will stop the trial balance agreeing.

(d) *This will stop the trial balance agreeing.*
(e) *This will stop the trial balance agreeing.*
(f) *This will not stop the trial balance agreeing*

Some further comment on the last activity is useful.

- The first point of note is that not all these errors are equally important. For example, the first of the errors will not change the profit figure, but will simply alter the balance between the items of expense in the profit and loss account. Error (b), by comparison, will result in profits being understated by the amount of the error.
- The second point is that you should note that with errors such as (c) and (e), where both entries are on one side, that the effect will be a difference in the trial balance of twice the amount of the error.
- The third is that compensating errors are extremely difficult to find.

In a system of ledger accounts, the profit and loss account is a formal part of the ledger accounting system. Revenues and expenses are transferred to the profit and loss account. (Though the profit and loss account may be further subdivided into a manufacturing account, a trading account, and a profit and loss account, along the lines set out in Chapter 5.) The net profit or loss is subsequently transferred to the capital account, along with drawings. The balance sheet is nothing more than a list of balances in the ledger accounts, at a particular time, which must represent assets or claims. Any pre-payments, accruals and similar adjustments must therefore be shown as balances on an account. In the example used above–J. Jones–assuming that a profit and loss account was required for January, and a balance sheet as at 31 January, the only adjustment needed would be for rent, the payment for which relates to both January and February. Since £500 was paid covering these two months it is reasonable to suppose that £250 relates to January, and should be shown as an expense of January, while the remaining £250 represents a prepayment at the end of January, which should be carried forward as a balance, and thus be listed in the balance sheet.

A complete set of accounts for the business of J. Jones is given below; along with a balance sheet as at 31 January. The trading and profit and loss accounts could, of course, be presented in a variety of alternative formats, but the underlying principles hold in all cases.

Capital

		£			£
			January 1	Cash	10,000
January 31	Balance c/d	10,250	31	Net profit	250
		10,250			10,250
			January 31	Balance b/d	10,250

Cash

		£			£
January 1	Capital	10,000	January 5	Stock	5,000
15	Sales	1,500	21	Machinery	4,000
			28	Rent	500
			31	Balance c/d	2,000
		11,500			11,500
January 31	Balance b/d	2,000			

Stock

		£			£
January 5	Cash	5,000	January 15	Cost of Sales	1,000
8	Creditors	1,000	31	Balance c/d	5,000
		6,000			6,000
January 31	Balance b/d	5,000			

Creditors

		£			£
January 31	Balance c/d	1,000	January 8	Stock	1,000
		1,000			1,000
			January 31	Balance b/d	1,000

Cost of Sales

		£			£
January 15	Stock	1,000	January 31	Trading	1,000

Sales

		£			£
January 31	Trading	1,500	January 15	Cash	1,500

Machinery

		£			£
January 21	Cash	4,000	January 31	Balance c/d	4,000
		4,000			4,000
January 31	Balance b/d	4,000			

Rent

		£			£
January 28	Cash	500	January 31	Profit & loss	250
			31	Balance c/d	250
		500			500
January 31	Balance b/d	250			

Trading

		£			£
January 31	Cost of sales	1,000	January 31	Sales	1,500
31	Gross profit	500			
		1,500			1,500

Profit & Loss

		£			£
January 31	Rent	250	January 31	Gross profit	500
31	Net profit	250			
		500			500

In practice the trading and profit and loss account is likely to be *presented* in one of the ways shown earlier. The above represents the entries in the actual accounts.

The balance sheet, which is simply a list of account balances appropriately set out, is as follows:

Balance sheet as at 31 January

	£		£
Machinery	4,000	Capital	10,250
Stock	5,000	Creditors	1,000
Prepaid rent	250		
Cash	2,000		
	11,250		11,250

As with the profit and loss account, this would typically be *presented* in one of the ways set out earlier.

Several points emerge from the above example.

1 Using ledger accounts every transaction has a double entry, with a debit entry being matched by a corresponding credit entry.
   Increases in assets, expenses and drawings are debits
   Reductions in assets, expenses and drawings are credits
   Increases in capital, liabilities and revenues are credits
   Reductions in capital, liabilities and revenues are debits.
2 The question as to whether such things as rent are assets or expenses does not arise at the recording stage, since the entry is the same. The split into assets and expenses only needs to be made at the end of the period, when a profit and loss account is being prepared. Any prepayments or accruals (which appear as debit or credit balances b/d) will be dealt with automatically using a system of ledger accounts. The same is true of revenues, liabilities and related adjustments.

3 Ledger accounts can cope with quite large numbers of transactions neatly and effectively.

4 The end product of a system of ledger accounts is identical to that of the system used earlier in these units.

Activity 5

Record the following items in ledger accounts, draw up a trial balance, close off the appropriate accounts, and prepare a balance sheet as at 31 January.

(a) 1 January   D. Harvey puts in £10,000 to start a new business of his own, calling it Wight Enterprises.
(b) 1 January   Borrows £5,000 from P. Perks.
(c) 1 January   Buys equipment for £3,000 cash.
(d) 2 January   Buys stock for resale for £800 cash.
(e) 3 January   Buys further stock of £2,200 on credit.
(f) 4 January   Stock which cost £600 is sold for £600 cash.
(g) 5 January   Stock which cost £200 is sold for £200 on credit.
(h) 7 January   Cash of £800 is paid to creditor.
(i) 8 January   Cash of £200 is received from debtor
(j) 10 January   Harvey withdrew £500 cash from the business for his private use.
(k) 11 January   Harvey pays the creditor £400 from his personal funds
(l) 12 January   Goods which cost £600 are sold for £800 cash.
(m) 13 January   Goods which cost £100 are sold on credit for £90.
(n) 15 January   Stock to the value of £2,000 is bought on credit.
(o) 15 January   Rent of £30 is paid.
(p) 18 January   Stationery is bought for £100 cash.
(q) 20 January   Miscellaneous expenses of £50 are paid in cash.
(r) 28 January   Goods which cost £500 are sold for £750, £250 cash being received and £500 due at the end of February.

On 31 January it was discovered that only £80 of stationery was still in hand. These transactions formed the basis of exercise 4 in Chapter 3, and activity 5 of Chapter 4, so their treatment should not pose particular problems. The emphasis of this question is on the preparation of a separate profit and loss account.

The accounts prior to the adjustment for stationery should appear as follows:

Equipment

		£			£
January 1	Cash	3,000			

Capital

		£			£
			January 1	Cash	10,000
			11	Creditors	400
					10,400

Loan–P. Perks

		£			£
			January 1	Cash	5,000

Drawings

		£			£
January 10	Cash	500			

Cash

		£			£
January 1	Capital	10,000	January 1	Premises	3,000
1	P. Perks	5,000	2	Stock	800
4	Sales	600	7	Creditors	800
8	Debtors	200	10	Drawings	500
12	Sales	800	15	Rent	30
28	Sales	250	18	Stationery	100
			20	Misc. expenses	50
			31	Balance c/d	11,570
		16,850			16,850
January 31	Balance b/d	11,570			

Stock

		£			£
January 2	Cash	800	January 4	Cost of sales	600
3	Creditors	2,200	5	Cost of sales	200
15	Creditors	2,000	12	Cost of sales	600
			13	Cost of sales	100
			28	Cost of sales	500
			31	Balance c/d	3,000
		5,000			5,000
January 31	Balance	3,000			

Stationery

		£			£
January 18	Cash	100			

Creditors

		£			£
January 7	Cash	800	January 3	Stock	2,200
11	Capital	400	15	Stock	2,000
31	Balance c/d	3,000			
		4,200			4,200
			January 31	Balance b/d	3,000

Debtors

		£			£
January 5	Sales	200	January 8	Cash	200
13	Sales	90	31	Balance c/d	590
28	Sales	500			
		790			790
January 31	Balance b/d	590			

Sales

		£			£
			January 4	Cash	600
			5	Debtors	200
			12	Cash	800
			13	Debtors	90
			28	Cash	250
			28	Debtors	500
					2,440

Cost of sales

		£			£
January 4	Stock	600			
5	Stock	200			
12	Stock	600			
13	Stock	100			
28	Stock	500			
		2,000			

Rent

		£			£
January 15	Cash	30			

Miscellaneous expenses

		£			£
January 20	Cash	50			

The trial balance as at 31 January would appear as below:

	Debit	Credit
Premises	3,000	
Capital		10,400
Drawings	500	
Loan–Perks		5,000
Stock	3,000	

Stationery	100	
Debtors	590	
Creditors		3,000
Cash	11,570	
Sales		2,440
Cost of sales	2,000	
Rent	30	
Miscellaneous expenses	50	
	20,840	20,840

Once the trial balance agrees we can proceed to completion of the final accounts. The opening of a trading account and a profit and loss account can proceed with the appropriate revenue and expense accounts being closed to these two new accounts as follows:

Sales

		£			£
January 31	Trading	2,440	January 4	Cash	600
			5	Debtors	200
			12	Cash	800
			13	Debtors	90
			28	Cash	250
			28	Debtors	500
		2,440			2,440

Cost of sales

		£			£
January 4	Stock	600	January 31	Trading	2,000
5	Stock	200			
12	Stock	600			
13	Stock	100			
28	Stock	500			
		2,000			2,000

Rent

		£			£
January 15	Cash	30	January 31	Profit and loss	30

Miscellaneous expenses

		£			£
January 20	Cash	50	January 31	Profit and loss	50

Stationery

		£			£
January 18	Cash	100	January 31	Balance c/d	80
			31	Profit and loss	20
		100			100
January 31	Balance b/d	80			

Trading

		£			£
January 31	Cost of sales	2,000	January 31	Sales	2,440
31	Gross profit c/d	440			
		2,440			2,440

Profit and loss

		£			£
January 31	Rent	30	January 31	Gross profit b/d	440
31	Misc. expenses	50			
31	Stationery	20			
31	Net profit–to Capital	340			
		440			440

The adjustment to stationery arises when the account for stationery needs to be identified as an asset or an expense. Either we have to know what the stationery used up cost us, with the remainder being carried forward as an asset, or (more likely) we need to establish how much is left remaining as an asset, with the amount used up becoming an expense.

Drawings and the net profit are then closed to the capital account, as shown below:

Capital

		£			£
January 31	Drawings	500	January 1	Cash	10,000
31	Balance c/d	10,240	11	Creditors	400
			31	Net profit (from P & L)	340
		10,740			10,740
			January 31	Balance b/d	10,240

Drawings

		£			£
January 10	Cash	500	January 31	Capital	500

The balance sheet can then be drawn up simply by listing the account balances in an appropriate form:

Fixed assets

Premises		3,000
Current assets		
Stock	3,000	
Stationery	80	
Debtors	590	
Cash	11,570	
		15,240
		18,240
Capital	10,000	
Plus injection	400	
Net profit	340	
	10,740	
less drawings	500	
		10,240
Long-term liabilities		
Loan		5,000
Current liabilities		
Creditors		3,000
		18,240

Self-assessment question 9.1

The balance sheet of James and Co., a small retailing business, showed the following position at 31 October 1999.

Balance sheet as at 31 October 1999

	£	£		£
Fixed assets			Capital	35,000
Premises	35,000			
Fixtures and Fittings	5,000		Long-term loans	15,000
Vehicles	3,600			
		43,600	Current liabilities	
Current assets			Creditors	10,600
Stock	7,000			
Debtors	5,000			
Cash	5,000			
		17,000		
		60,600		60,600

The following transactions were recorded during the month of November:

(a) Cash received from debtors £3,000
(b) £2,000 was paid back on the loan
(c) Cash sales amounted to £7,000
(d) Credit sales amounted to £4,000
(e) Stock was purchased on credit, amounting to £3,200
(f) Cash was paid to creditors, amounting to £5,600
(g) The cost price of goods sold was £6,500
(h) Wages were paid for the month totalling £1,200
(i) Other expenses paid for the month totalled £1,800
(j) The vehicle shown in the balance sheet (book value £3,600) was sold for £3,000
(k) A new vehicle was purchased for £5,000. £2,500 was paid immediately, and a loan was taken out for the remainder
(l) Interest on the long-term loan for the month was paid; amounting to £250
(m) The owner withdrew £500 from the bank and £100 worth of stock for his own use
(n) In addition to the sales listed above, damaged stock costing £150 was sold for £100 cash

1 Open the accounts necessary to include the opening balance sheet.
2 Record the above transactions in ledger accounts.
3 Draw up a trial balance as at 30 November.
4 Prepare a trading and profit and loss account for November.
5 Prepare a balance sheet as at 30 November.

9.4 Summary

This chapter has shown how a detailed system of double-entry accounting (ledger accounts) operates. The nature of ledger accounts has been introduced, with duality effectively being implemented through double-entry book-keeping. The trial balance was introduced as a means of providing a check on the accuracy of the double-entry book-keeping process. Limitations of the trial balance were discussed. The final accounts were then prepared, incorporating a profit and loss account (possibly including a trading account as well) as part of the accounting system. The balance sheet is seen as simply a listing of account balances at the period end.

Exercises

1 Record the following transactions in ledger accounts, draw up a trial balance, and prepare a profit and loss account and balance sheet.

(a) C. Mille invests cash of £15,000 in a business known as Polyprint & Co.
(b) The business borrows £3,000 from the bank.
(c) It purchases plant and equipment for £10,000 cash and a van for £3,000 cash.
(d) It purchases £7,500 worth of stock on credit.

(e) It purchases £2,000 worth of stock for cash.
(f) It sells stock which had cost £6,500 for £11,000, on credit.
(g) It receives £8,000 cash from debtors.
(h) It pays £5,000 cash to creditors.
(i) It pays £500 in wages.
(j) It pays £250 rent.
(k) C. Mille withdraws £500 for his own use.

2 Milly commenced business as a florist on 1 January 1999. The following information has been collected concerning the business transactions over the first two months of trading.

January 1	Paid £60,000 cash into the business
	Borrowed £20,000 from her parents (interest free)
2	Purchased a property for £55,000 cash
3	Purchased a delivery van for £3,000 cash
	Paid road tax and insurance for the van for one year – ending 31 December 1999. Total amount £360
4	Purchased new till £500
5	Paid £2,000 cash for shop fittings
	Arranged with bank that overdraft facilities up to £5,000 would be available as required
6	Acquired stock costing £2,000 on credit

On 7 January the shop was opened for business and the following is a summary of the transactions up to the end of February:

(a) Further stock purchased on credit £4,200
(b) Cash sales £5,000 (cost of sales £2,900)
(c) Credit sales £2,000 (cost of sales £1,250)
(d) Shop assistant's wages £500
(e) Vehicle expenses £150
(f) Goods returned to suppliers at cost £150
(g) Paid to suppliers for goods supplied £3,500, in satisfaction of debts of £3,600, the difference being discount
(h) Received from debtors £1,800
(i) Paid rates on the shop for the period 2 January to 28 February, amounting to £300
(j) Paid an electricity bill for January, amounting to £75
(k) Milly withdrew £1,000 to cover her salary for the period

You are required to complete a set of ledger accounts to record the above transactions, draw up a trial balance and prepare a profit and loss account for the period 1 January to 28 February and a balance sheet as at 28 February.

Chapter 10

Ledger accounts – further complications

10.1 Introduction

This chapter deals with a number of complications, namely period-end adjustments including prepayments and accruals, and deferred revenues; asset purchases, disposals and depreciation; accounting for stock; and accounting for bad and doubtful debts.

10.2 Objectives

On completion of this chapter you should be able to:

- record prepayments and accruals in a system of ledger accounts;
- record deferred revenues in a system of ledger accounts;
- record the purchase and disposal of assets in ledger accounts, together with depreciation and depreciation provisions;
- record transactions relating to stock in ledger accounts;
- record bad and doubtful debts in ledger accounts

10.3 Period-end adjustments – prepayments, accruals and deferred revenues

The activities and self-assessment question of Chapter 9 only included relatively simple period-end adjustments. Chapter 5 dealt with some quite complicated period-end adjustments using the system of pluses and minuses. This section shows how these adjustments will be dealt with using a system of ledger accounts.

Let us consider the following example.

Example

The following items appear in the balance sheet of a business as at 31 December 1999

Current assets	£
Prepaid insurance	300
Prepaid heating	100

Current liabilities	
Accruals wages	1,000
Deferred revenue rent	500

During the year to 31 December 2000 the following cash receipts and payments were recorded:

Cash receipts
Rent (relating to the period 1 April 2000 to 30 September 2000) £1,000

Cash payments	£
Wages	25,000
Insurance	1,200
Heating	1,000

At the year end (31 December 2000) you ascertain that £500 of wages and £200 of heating bills remain outstanding, and that £400 of insurance has been prepaid.

You are required to prepare ledger accounts for 2000 showing the entries for rent receivable, insurance, heating, and wages, clearly showing the transfer that would be made to the profit and loss account.

What figures, if any, relating to these transactions, would be included in the balance sheet as at 31 December 2000, and under what heading would they appear?

The ledger account for wages would appear as follows:

Wages

		£			£
	Cash	25,000	January 1	Balance b/d	1,000
December 31	Balance c/d	500	December 31	Profit & loss	24,500
		25,500			25,500
			December 31	Balance b/d	500

The opening accrual is shown as a credit balance, reflecting a liability. This balance is brought down from the last period, having been included (under the accruals convention) as an expense for 1999. The cash paid for the year is debited to wages. This clears last year's accrual and £24,000 for wages relating to a time which is later than 31 December 1999. By the end of 2000, a further $500 is outstanding, so the amount of expense for the year must be $24,500. This 'accrual' is effectively included as an expense in the year (the debit) and carried forward as a liability at the year end (the credit).

Some students find it easier to keep a separate account at the period-end for prepayments and accruals. In the above example the amount brought forward would have been credited to an accrued wages account at the end of 1999. At the start of 2000, this entry would be 'reversed', which effectively cancels out the accrual and transfers it to the wages account for the year. At the end of the year any prepayments or accruals are transferred to a separate account, in this case to Accrued wages.

Accrued Wages

1999		£	1999		£
January 1	Wages	1,000	January 1	Balance b/d	1,000
			December 31	Wages	500

Wages

		£			£
	Cash	25,000	January 1	Accrued wages	1,000
					1,000
December 31	Accrued wages	500	December 31	Profit & loss	24,500
					24,500
		25,000			25,000

The net effect is the same as earlier.

The ledger account for insurance is given next.

Insurance

		£			£
January 1	Balance b/d	300	December 31	Balance c/d	400
	Cash	1,200	December 31	Profit & loss	1,100
		1,500			1,500
December 31	Balance b/d	400			

The prepaid insurance is brought down as a debit balance. The cash paid during the year for insurance is debited to the account. In all likelihood this will be an annual premium which will result in a prepayment at the end of 2000. At the end of the year you establish that there is in fact a prepayment of £400. This is carried down to the next year (effectively reducing the expense). The brought-down figure at the end of the year represents an asset – insurance prepaid. By a process of deduction the expense for the year must be £1,100 and this is transferred to the profit and loss account.

The ledger account for heating is given below:

Heating

		£			£
January 1	Balance b/d	100	December 31	Profit & loss	1,300
	Cash	1,000			
	Balance c/d	200			
		1,300			1,300
			December 31	Balance b/d	200

The prepayment was shown as an asset (a debit balance) at the end of 1999. This is brought down from last year and is effectively assumed to become an expense of the next year. Any further payments are debited to the heating account and credited to cash. At this stage the account shows expenses of £1,100. By the end of the year it is clear that £200 of heating expense for the year remains unpaid, so this amount is debited to the heating account for 2000 and effectively credited as a brought-down figure at the end of the year, representing a liability. Given that in this case the brought-down date is effectively the start of the next accounting period, the carried-down/brought-down figures can be seen as separating the amounts into two discrete accounting periods.

Of course, if you wish you could open separate prepayment and accruals accounts as shown below:

Prepaid heating

		£			£
January 1	Balance b/d	100	January 1	Heating	100

Heating

		£			£
January 1	Prepaid heating	100	December 31	Profit & loss	1,300
	Cash	1,000			
December 31	Accrued heating	200			
		1,300			1,300

Accrued heating

		£			£
			December 31	Heating	200

Turning to the revenue relating to rent receivable, the ledger account is shown below:

Rent receivable

		£			£
December 31	Profit & loss	2,000	January 1	Balance b/d	500
				Cash	1,000
			December 31	Balance c/d	500
		2,000			2,000
December 31	Balance b/d	500			

The opening liability – a deferred revenue – is effectively a prepayment *to the business*. Until such time as it falls due it remains a liability. By the end of March the payment in advance is no longer an advance, but is due, so it becomes a revenue. The cash received covers six months of the current year so is obviously credited to the revenue account. At the end of the year it is evident that the rent is now in arrears as nothing has been received relating to the period 1 October to 31 December. In the absence of any other information it is reasonable to assume that the three months outstanding will be at the same rate as earlier (i.e. £500 per quarter). This amount, which is due, needs to be added (i.e. credited) to the rent receivable and debited as an asset (rent owing at the year-end). Debiting rent receivable as shown does this. Alternatively the debit can be to a separate asset account with a subsequent reversal of entries in the new year.

Activity 1

Record the following in ledger accounts. Show clearly any transfers to the profit and loss account. You should assume that the financial year of the business concerned is 1 January to 31 December 1999.

(a) Stationery costing £500 was purchased on 1 January 1999. At 31 December 1999 £150 worth was left.
(b) Electricity bills were paid during the year ending 31 December 1999 amounting to £450. All these bills relate to the year ending 31 December 1999. One bill remains unpaid, covering the period 1 November 1999 to 31 January 2000, amounting to £150.
(c) Rates of £2,000 were paid on 31 December 1998. They relate to the period 1 October 1998 to 31 March 1999. A further £2,000 was paid at the end of May covering the period 1 April to 30 September. A further £2,000 was paid on 1 January 2000 relating to the period 1 October 1999 to 31 March 2000. Assume that the level of rates is constant over the years concerned.

The ledger accounts are as shown below:

Stationery

		£			£
January 1	Cash	500	December 31	Balance c/d	150
			December 31	Profit & loss	350
		500			500
December 31	Balance b/d	150			

Electricity

		£			£
	Cash	450	December 31	Profit & loss	550
December 31	Balance c/d	100			
		550			550
			December 31	Balance b/d	100

Rates

		£			£
January 1	Balance b/d	1,000	December 31	Profit & loss	4,000
May 31	Cash	2,000			
December 31	Balance c/d	1,000			
		4,000			4,000
			December 31	Balance b/d	1,000

Activity 2

The following items appear in the balance sheet of a business at 31 December 1998.

Under current assets	£	Under current liabilities	£
Debtors and prepayments		Creditors and accruals	
Rates	200	Rent	500
		Electricity	100
		Deferred revenue	
		Interest receivable	200

During the year to 31 December 1999 the following cash receipts and payments were recorded:

Receipts

Interest – covering the six months from 1 April to 30 September   £400

Payments

Rent – covering the quarter ending	31 December 1998	£500
	31 March 1999	£500
	30 June 1999	£500
	30 September 1999	£500
	31 December 1999	£500
	31 March 2000	£500
Electricity – covering the quarter ending	31 January 1999	£150
	30 April 1999	£120
	31 July 1999	£70
	31 October 1999	£120
Rates – covering the six months ending	30 September 1999	£450
	31 March 2000	£450

Show the relevant ledger accounts for the year ending 31 December 1999, clearly showing the transfer to the profit and loss account for the year.

This is the same content as Self-assessment question 4.4, but with the emphasis being on ledger accounts.

The ledger accounts are as follows:

Rent

		£			£
	Cash	500	January 1	Balance b/d	500
	Cash	500	December 31	Balance c/d	500
	Cash	500	December 31	Profit & loss	2,000
	Cash	500			
	Cash	500			
	Cash	500			
		3,000			3,000
December 31	Balance b/d	500			

Electricity

		£			£
	Cash	150	January 1	Balance b/d	100
	Cash	120	December 31	Profit & loss	460
	Cash	70			
	Cash	120			
December 31	Balance c/d*	100			
		560			560
			December 31	Balance b/d	100

*Two months based on last year's equivalent bill (i.e. 150 × 2/3)

Rates

		£			£
January 1	Balance b/d	200	December 31	Balance c/d	225
	Cash	450	December 31	Profit & loss	875
	Cash	450			
		1,100			1,100
December 31	Balance b/d	225			

Interest receivable

		£			£
December 31	Profit & loss	800	January 1	Balance b/d	200
				Cash	400
			December 31	Balance c/d	200
		800			800
December 31	Balance b/d	200			

Self-assessment question 10.1

Pat Trill rents a property from which he runs a retailing business. The annual rental payable is £4,000. The property has three floors, and Pat decides to sub-let one floor to a firm of solicitors who wish to open a small branch office in the town. The annual rent receivable is £1,500.

Pat's accounts are made up for the financial year ending 30 June.

The balance sheet prepared for Pat's business on 30 June 1997 showed, among other things, the following:

Debtors and prepayments
Rent receivable   £375
Prepaid rent   £1,000

During the following years the following *cash transactions* are made relating to rent payable and rent receivable

	Rent paid £	Rent received £
Year to 30 June 1998	4,000	1,875
Year to 30 June 1999	3,000	1,125
Year to 30 June 2000	3,000	2,250

Show the ledger accounts for 'rent receivable' and 'rent payable' for each of the three financial years ending 30 June 1998, 1999 and 2000.

10.4 Accounting for fixed assets and depreciation

Chapter 6 dealt with the general principles of depreciation and introduced you to the accounting entries based on the system of pluses and minuses. In this section we turn to how these accounting entries are handled using a system of ledger accounts.

Purchase of fixed asset

When a fixed asset is purchased for cash all that needs to be done is simply

- debit fixed asset
- credit cash

When the purchase is on credit the double-entry becomes:

- debit fixed asset
- credit creditors

It was noted in Chapter 6 that generally fixed assets are shown at cost, with a corresponding depreciation provision being set up. In the balance sheet the depreciation provision is shown together with the cost, to give a net written-down value.

Depreciation

Once the annual depreciation is calculated, the normal entries are:

- debit depreciation (expense)
- credit depreciation provision

The depreciation account will be closed off to the profit and loss account. The depreciation provision will remain on the books and so will appear on the balance sheet at the end of the period.

Example

Using the figures from section 6 of Chapter 6, namely an asset which had cost £550, had an expected residual value of £50, which is depreciated over five years using straight-line depreciation, the ledger accounts will be as follows:

On purchase
- debit fixed asset   550
- credit cash or creditors   .   550

End of year 1
- debit depreciation (expense)   100
- credit depreciation provision   100

- debit profit and loss   100
- credit depreciation expense   100
  (thus closing this account)

This means that balances will remain on the asset account and the depreciation provision. These will appear in the balance sheet as follows:

Fixed asset at cost   550
less Depreciation provision   100
                                   ———
                                   450

End of year 2
- debit depreciation (expense)   100
- credit depreciation provision   100
  (adding to the existing provision)

- debit profit and loss   100
- credit depreciation expense   100
  (thus closing this account)

This means that balances will remain on the asset account and the depreciation provision. These will appear in the balance sheet as follows:

Fixed asset at cost   550
less Depreciation provision   200
                                                        ───
                                                        450

In the event of the asset remaining in use for the entire planned life (i.e. 5 years) the same process will occur each year, with the result that the entire £500 will have been written off as an expense and the net book value shown on the balance sheet will be £50. For year 6 and beyond, should the asset still be in use, there will be no further depreciation, unless the residual value is revised downwards in the light of the extended use.

Asset disposal

Only when the asset is disposed of, and the sale price is known, can we know with precision the amount of the depreciation that has occurred over the asset's life. The difference between the cost and the disposal proceeds measures the actual depreciation over the actual life. Prior to this we have been making estimates of the depreciation. Any difference between depreciation recorded in the accounts and the actual depreciation must be reflected in the accounts (i.e. the profit and loss account). If actual depreciation exceeds that recorded in the books then we need to charge some additional depreciation to the profit (the so-called loss on disposal) and vice versa.

Fixed asset disposals are usually recorded through a disposal account, which is used as follows:

When the asset is disposed of

- debit cash (or debtors)
- credit the disposal account with the amount of the proceeds.

As the asset is no longer an asset the relevant accounts (i.e. asset account, depreciation provision) must be closed as follows:

- debit disposal with the cost of the asset
- credit the asset at (cost) account
- debit depreciation provision account
- credit the disposal account with the amount of the accumulated depreciation provision.

This means that the disposal account is effectively a profit and loss account relating to this particular transaction.

| **Example** | Suppose that (continuing the earlier example) the asset is sold at the end of two years for £250. The disposal account would appear as follows: |

Disposal

		£			£
December 31	Asset	550	December 31	Cash	250
			31	Depn provision	200
			31	Loss on disposal	100
		550			550

The loss on disposal will be transferred to the profit and loss. This means that the charge to profits will be £100 depreciation in year 1, and £100 depreciation in year 2 plus a further £100 loss on disposal, giving £300 in total, reflecting the actual fall in value (£550 – £250).

Activity 3

Show the disposal account if the sale proceeds were £400.

The account would appear as follows:

Disposal

		£			£
December 31	Asset	550	December 31	Cash	400
December 31	Profit on disposal	50	31	Depn provision	200
		600			600

Other complications

Sometimes an asset is purchased as part of a trade-in deal. Typically when this happens the purchase price is reduced by the amount of allowance given by the supplier in return for the asset being traded in, in part-exchange.

Example

The asset used in the preceding example is traded in for a new asset at the end of two years of use. The trade-in allowance is £375. The cost of the new asset is £1,000, which means that the cash payment will be £625.

The old asset will be effectively sold (traded in) for £375. The proceeds will be credited to the disposal account and debited to the (new) asset account. The balance of £675 will be credited to cash and debited to the (new) asset account.

The relevant accounts will be:

Asset

		£			£
January 1	Balance b/d	550	December 31	Disposal	550
December 31	Disposal (trade-in)	375	December 31	Balance c/d	1,000
31	Cash	625			
		1,000			1,000
December 31	Balance b/d	1,000			

Disposal

		£			£
December 31	Asset	550	December 31	Asset (traded in)	375
December 31	Profit on disposal	25	31	Depn provision	200
		575			575

When assets are purchased part-way through a year it is common (but not essential) for depreciation to be charged on a pro-rata basis. So for a business with a financial year of 1 January to 31 December which purchased a new fixed asset on 1 July, you might find that depreciation is charged at half the usual rate. Other businesses might decide to charge a full year's depreciation on all assets in use at the year-end. You should take care to read examination questions carefully and establish what is required.

Activity 4

A business with a year-end at 31 December buys equipment on 1 January 1997, for £12,000. It buys further equipment on 1 July 1999 for £16,000. On 30 June 2000 the first set of equipment was traded in for £5,500, as part allowance on a new asset costing £15,000. Depreciation is to be charged at 25% on a reducing-balance basis.

Show the relevant accounts for the financial years 1997, 1998, 1999, and 2000. You should assume that depreciation will be calculated on a pro-rata basis for equipment purchased part-way through a year, but that no calculation of depreciation is made in the year of disposal.

Show the extracts from the balance sheet relating to equipment.

Asset – cost

1997		£			£
January 1	Cash	12,000	December 31	Balance c/d	12,000
		12,000			12,000

1998					
January 1	Balance b/d	12,000	December 31	Balance c/d	12,000
		12,000			12,000
1999					
January 1	Balance b/d	12,000	December 31	Balance c/d	28,000
July 1	Cash	16,000			
		28,000			28,000
2000					
January 1	Balance b/d	28,000	June 30	Disposal	12,000
June 30	Disposal	5,500	December 31	Balance c/d	31,000
30	Cash	9,500			
		43,000			43,000
2001					
January 1	Balance b/d	31,000			

Disposal

2000		£			£
December 31	Asset	12,000	December 31	Asset (traded-in)	5,500
December 31	Profit on disposal	438	31	Depn provision	6,938
		12,438			12,438

Depreciation

1997		£			£
December 31	Depreciation prov.	3,000	December 31	Profit & loss	3,000
1998					
December 31	Depreciation prov.	2,250	December 31	Profit & loss	2,250
1999					
December 31	Depreciation prov.	3,688	December 31	Profit & loss	3,688
2000					
December 31	Depreciation prov.	5,375	December 31	Profit & loss	5,375

Profit & loss (extracts)

1997		£			£
December 31	Depreciation	3,000			
1998					
December 31	Depreciation	2,250			
1999					
December 31	Depreciation	3,688			
2000					
December 31	Depreciation	5,375	December 31	Profit on disposal	438

Workings

	Equipment 1 £	2 £	3 £	£
1997				
Cost	12,000			
Depreciation	3,000			
Written-down value (wdv)	9,000			
1998				
Depreciation (25% of wdv)	2,250			
wdv	6,750			
1999				
Cost		16,000		
Depreciation (25% of wdv)	1,688	2,000*		
wdv	5,062	14,000		
2000				
Cost – Trade-in			5,500	
Cash			9,500	
			15,000	
Depreciation		3,500	1,875**	
			13,125	

*25% = 4,000 but only for 1/2 year so 2,000
**25% = 3,750 but only for 1/2 year so 1,875

Balance sheet extracts	1997	1998	1999	2000
Equipment – cost	12,000	12,000	28,000	31,000
Depreciation provision	3,000	5,250	8,938	6,375
	9,000	6,750	19,062	24,625

**10.5
Accounting for
stock**

Chapter 7 explained the problems of stock valuation. This section is concerned with the ledger accounts that are involved.

**Dealing with cost
of sales through
the trading
account**

Many businesses do not keep detailed track of the cost of goods sold. We saw earlier that cost of sales can be calculated as follows:

Trading account

Opening stock		x
Plus purchases	x	
less purchases returns	x	
		x
		x
less closing stock		x
= Cost of sales		x

The procedure for arriving at this is given below:

- the opening stock is known;
- any purchases are added (debited) to a separate purchases account;
- any purchases returns are credited to a separate purchases returns account;
- these three accounts are closed by transfer to the trading account;
- at the end of the accounting period the stock is physically counted and valued, using one of the methods identified in Chapter 7;
- closing stock is debited to the stock account and effectively credited to the trading account;
- the resulting figure in the trading account represents the cost of sales figures for the period.

The above format is the one most commonly used for presentation purposes. When converted to a strict double-entry process the Trading account will appear in the ledger accounts as follows.

Trading account

	£		£
Opening stock		Purchases returns	
Purchases		Closing stock	

Activity 5

The opening stock for a business was £10,000. Purchases during the year amounted to £50,000, while purchases returns were £2,000. Closing stock was counted and valued at £12,000.

Show the accounts for stock, purchases, purchases returns and trading for the year.

Stock

		£			£
January 1	Opening stock	10,000	December 31	Trading (opening)	10,000
December 31	Trading (closing)	12,000			

Purchases

		£			£
	Cash/creditors	50,000	December 31	Trading	50,000

Purchases returns

		£			£
December 31	Trading	2,000		Creditors	2,000

Trading account

		£			£
December 31	Opening stock	10,000	December 31	Purchases returns	2,000
31	Purchases	50,000	31	Closing stock	12,000
			31	Balance c/d	46,000
		60,000			60,000
December 31	Balance b/d	46,000			

The trading account balance reflects the cost of sales.

You should note that sometimes owners withdraw stock for their own consumption. Under these circumstances the cost of sales as calculated above will be too high. It is necessary to reduce the effective cost of sales by the amount of the stock drawing. The double-entry is to debit drawings and credit trading.

A further point to note is that some purchases may require carriage to be paid (known as carriage in). This is seen as part of the cost of purchases and is added to them in the trading account.

Keeping track of cost of sales – continuous or perpetual method

Many businesses keep detailed control of their stocks, and maintain detailed stock records. Increasingly the use of barcoding provides a sophisticated means of stock control, e.g. see the large-scale supermarkets.

As a minimum, a company that wishes to maintain good stock control will require to keep detailed stock accounts along the following lines:

Stock

	Debit – goods received			Credit – goods issued			Balance		
Date	Quantity	Cost/unit	Total cost	Quantity	Cost/unit	Total cost	Quantity	Cost/unit	Total cost

This enables detailed records to be kept which clearly fit within the framework of double-entry book-keeping. This method facilitates the various systems of stock valuation identified in Chapter 7.

Activity 6

In the example used in Chapter 7, the garden centre decided to stock a new line of bags of fertilizer. Purchases and sales during the first few weeks of stocking the product were, in chronological order, as follows:

Bought   60 bags   @   £1 each
Sold   40 bags
Bought   60 bags   @   £1.10 each
Sold   70 bags

Use the above account to work out the cost of sales figures for the period and the value of the stock at the various points during the period, assuming that the stock usage are priced on a FIFO basis.

Stock

Date	Debit – goods received			Credit – goods issued			Balance		
	Quantity	*Cost/unit*	*Total cost*	*Quantity*	*Cost/unit*	*Total cost*	*Quantity*	*Cost/unit*	*Total cost*
	60	1	60				60	1	60
				40	1	40	20	1	20
	60	1.10	66				20	1	20
							60	1.10	66
				20	1	20			
				50	1.10	55	10	1.10	11

Self-assessment question 10.2

Re-do Activity 6 using LIFO and AVCO

**10.6
Accounting for bad debt and bad debt provisions**

The main problems in this area were identified in Chapter 8. These were:

• bad debts
• bad (or doubtful) debt provisions

Bad debts

When a debt is deemed to be uncollectable it is written off. The accounting entries are quite straightforward, as follows:

• debit bad debts account (an expense account)
• credit the appropriate debtor account

At the end of the accounting period the bad debts account will be closed to the profit and loss account as follows:

- debit profit and loss
- credit bad debts

Bad or doubtful debt provisions

When a *new provision* is set up the entries in the accounts are:

- debit an account called increase in bad debt provision
- credit bad (or doubtful) debt provision

The increase in bad debt provision account is then closed off to the profit and loss account at the period end. As an alternative, the first debit above can be made directly to the profit and loss account.

When a *provision is in existence* the amount of any necessary **increase** is:

- debited to an account called increase in bad debt provision (or directly to the profit and loss account)
- credited to the bad (or doubtful) debt provision.

If the existing provision needs to be reduced the entries are:

- debit the bad (or doubtful) debt provision.
- credit an account called decrease in bad debt provision (or the profit and loss account).

Self-assessment question 10.3

The following is the balance sheet of Shah & Co as at 31 December 1998:

Balance sheet as at 31 December 1998

	£	£		£
Fixed assets			Capital	20,000
Buildings		8,000		
Equipment		5,000		
Vehicles		3,000	Loan	5,000
		16,000		
Current assets			*Current liabilities*	
Stock	5,000		Creditors	3,500
Debtors	3,000			
Cash	4,500			
		12,500		
		28,500		28,500

Given below is a summary of the transactions which took place during the year to 31 December 1999. (*Note*: This list does not reflect the order in which transactions took place.)

(a) Stock purchased on credit £42,000.
(b) Sales for cash £10,000.
(c) Sales on credit £40,000.
(d) Cash received from debtors £36,000.
(e) Cash paid to creditors £35,000.
(f) Cash paid for wages (all relating to the year) £5,000.
(g) Cash paid for other expenses £3,000.
(h) Rent paid amounts to £1,500.
(i) Rates paid amount to £750.
(j) The owner withdrew £2,500 in cash.

At the end of the year you note the following:

(i) A rates demand has been received, relating to the period 1 October 1999 to 31 March 2000, amounting to £500;
(ii) Depreciation of equipment is to be taken, amounting to £1,000, together with depreciation of vehicles, amounting to £600.
(iii) Closing stock is valued at £20,000
(iv) You discover that the rent paid relates to the period 1 January 1999 to 31 March 2000.
(v) Rates covers the period 1 January 1999 to 30 September 1999.

Required
Record the opening balance and the transactions (a) to (j) in a set of ledger accounts. Then draw up a trial balance. Once you have achieved a trial balance which agrees, incorporate the adjustments (i) to (v) into the accounts. From your accounts prepare a profit and loss account and balance sheet for presentation purposes.
This is a modification of the first example in Chapter 5

10.7 Preparing a set of final accounts from a trial balance

Following on from earlier chapters it should be fairly easy to prepare a set of final accounts from such a list, subject to any adjustments which need to be made. All that is required is for the items included in the trial balance to be put into the profit and loss account or balance sheet, as appropriate, with adjustments being made where necessary. Any adjustments needed will require a double-entry to be made. That is not true of items in the trial balance, which reflect the results of double-entry already made.

Activity 7
From the following trial balance of W. Lamb draw up a trading and profit and loss account for the year ended 31 December 1999, and a balance sheet at that date.

Trial balance as at 31 December 1999

	Debit £	Credit £
Stock	34,000	
Capital		120,000
Purchases	126,000	
Sales returns	1,200	
Salaries and wages	37,500	
Motor vehicles (cost)	15,000	
Motor vehicles (depreciation provision)		3,000
Furniture & fittings (cost)	4,000	
Furniture & fittings (depreciation provision)		800
Debtors	36,000	
Creditors		16,000
Bad debts provision		2,200
Sales		195,200
Purchases returns		2,000
Rent and rates	3,500	
Insurance	800	
Motor expenses	6,500	
Office expenses	2,200	
Heating and Lighting	1,600	
General expenses	2,900	
Premises	50,000	
Cash	10,000	
Drawings	8,000	
	339,200	339,200

Notes to be taken into account at 31 December

(a) Stock in hand at the year-end is valued at £30,000
(b) Rates of £500 are owing
(c) Insurance prepaid amounts to £200
(d) The bad debts provision is to be adjusted to 5% of debtors
(e) Depreciation is to be provided at the rate of 20% on cost for vehicles and 10% on cost for furniture and fittings

This answer is based on a vertical format. A two-sided approach is clearly also acceptable.

Trading and profit and loss Account for the year ending 31 December 1999				Workings
	£	£	£	
Sales			195,200	
less returns			1,200	
			194,000	
Opening stock		34,000		
Purchases	126,000			
less returns	2,000			
		124,000		
		158,000		
less closing stock		30,000		
Cost of sales			128,000	
Gross profit			66,000	
Plus **other revenues**				
Decrease in BDP			400	
			66,400	
Less **other expenses**				
Salaries & wages		37,500		
Rent & rates		4,000		3,500 + 500
General expenses		2,900		
Heating & lighting		1,600		
Insurance		600		800 – 200
Motor expenses		6,500		
Office expenses		2,200		
Depreciation – fixtures & fittings		400		
Depreciation – vehicles		3,000		
			58,700	
Net profit			7,700	

Balance sheet as at 31 December 1999

	£	£	£	Workings
Fixed assets				
Premises			50,000	
Fixtures & fittings – cost		4,000		
less depreciation provision		1,200		800 + 400
			2,800	
Vehicles – cost		15,000		
less depreciation provision		6,000		3,000 + 3,000
			9,000	
			61,800	

Current assets			
Stock		30,000	
Debtors	36,000		
less BDP	1,800		2,200 − 400
		34,200	
Prepayments		200	
Cash		10,000	
		74,400	
Less **liabilities due within one** year			
Creditors	16,000		
Accruals	500		
		16,500	
Net current assets		57,900	
Net assets		119,700	
Financed by:			
Capital			
Opening balance		120,000	
Net profit		7,700	
		127,700	
Less drawings		8,000	
		119,700	

<table>
<tr><td>

10.8 Summary

</td><td>

This chapter has dealt with a number of areas of practical accounting that usually give students most trouble. The accruals convention requires a differentiation between revenues and receipts, and expenses and payments. The first section of this chapter dealt with the accounting treatment of this area. The next three sections dealt with the accounting treatment of depreciation, stock, and bad and doubtful debts. The final section provided an example of how easy it is to complete a set of final accounts from a trial balance. This section should complement and reinforce the material covered in Chapters 4 and 5.

You should now be in the position where you could maintain a basic set of accounts from which you could prepare a set of final accounts.

</td></tr>
</table>

Exercises

1 (a) One business lends £10,000 to another business on 1 January 1999, at an annual rate of interest of 15%. Its financial year is from 1 October to 30 September. Cash received relating to interest on the loan is as follows:

30 June 1999	£750
1 January 2000	£750

30 June 2000	£750
31 December 2000	£750

Show the rent receivable account for the years ending 30 September 1999 and 2000.

(b) A business rents a property to a tenant from 1 January 1998 at an agreed rental of £10,000 per annum. Its financial year runs from 1 January to 31 December.

Cash relating to the rental is received as follows:

1 January 1998	£5,000
30 June 1998	£5,000
31 December 1998	£5,000
1 July 1999	£5,000
1 January 2000	£5,000

The tenant was in financial difficulties from mid-2000, and it is agreed that any arrears of rent will be paid in 2001.

Show the rent receivable account for 1998, 1999 and 2000.

2 F.O. Leo purchases a lorry on 1 July 1997 for £20,000. He decided that the lorry should last for five years, after which it is likely to be sold for £4,000. Leo's accounting year is from 1 January to 31 December.

(a) Assuming straight-line depreciation show the accounts relating to vehicles and depreciation for 1997 and 1998, clearly identifying the expense for depreciation for each year, and the balance sheet figures for vehicles. Assets are to be shown at cost and associated depreciation provisions.

(b) On 31 December 1999 the lorry was sold for £11,000. Show the 1999 entries.

3 From the following information for a business show the accounts for bad debts, and changes in the bad debt provision, together with extracts from the profit and loss account, for 1998 and 1999.

1 January 1998	Debtors balance	£4,000
	Bad debts provision	£200
Year to 31 December 1998	Sales	£20,000
	Cash received	£18,000
	Sales returns	£600
	Bad debts	£100
Year to 31 December 1999	Sales	£25,000
	Cash received	£26,000
		(including a bad debt recovered of £40)
	Sales returns	£1,000
	Bad debts	£200

The bad debt provision is to be maintained at 5% of year end debtors.

4 The following is the trial balance of a sole trading business at the end of its financial year:

Trial balance as at 30 June 2000

	Debit £	Credit £
Stock-in-trade at 1 July 1999	27,500	
Capital		80,380
Purchases	103,700	
Sales		179,800
Rent and rates	2,760	
Insurance	700	
Motor expenses	5,780	
Office expenses	2,540	
Heating and lighting	1,820	
General expenses	2,840	
Freehold premises	45,000	
Cash	3,200	
Salaries and wages	24,600	
Motor vehicles (cost)	17,500	
Motor vehicles (depreciation provision)		5,300
Furniture & fittings (cost)	12,800	
Furniture & fittings (depreciation provision)		2,360
Debtors	28,400	
Creditors		13,100
Bad debts provision		3,400
Drawings	5,200	
	£284,340	£284,340

The following information is also available:

(a) Stock-in-trade at 30 June 2000 was physically counted and was valued at £26,300.
(b) Rates of £570 were owing at 30 June 2000.
(c) A motor vehicle repair carried out in June 2000 costing £220 was still unpaid at the end of the year.
(d) The bad debts provision is to be adjusted to 5% of debtors at 30 June 2000.
(e) Depreciation is to be provided at the rate of 25% p.a. on cost for vehicles and 15% p.a. on cost for furniture and fittings.

Prepare a trading and profit and loss account for the year ended 30 June 2000 and a balance sheet as at that date for the business.

5 Prepare manufacturing, trading and profit and loss statement for the year ending 31 December and a balance sheet at that date for D. King, a manufacturer, from the following trial balance and additional information.

Trial balance as at 31 December

	Debit	Credit
Advertising	50,000	
Bad debts	6,000	
Bad debts provision		4,000

Capital		400,000
Drawings	25,000	
Discount received		2,500
Discount allowed	3,000	
Furniture – cost	20,000	
Furniture		
– depreciation provision	6,000	
Equipment – cost	200,000	
Equipment		
– depreciation provision	40,000	
Factory power	40,000	
Factory expenses	60,000	
Premises	300,000	
Repairs to equipment	10,000	
Insurance	6,000	
Rent and rates	9,000	
Heat and light	15,000	
Purchases of raw materials	200,000	
Packing and distribution	30,000	
Factory wages	200,000	
Office salaries	50,000	
Stocks – January 1		
– Raw materials	50,000	
– Work in progress	40,000	
– Finished goods	50,000	
Bank charges	2,000	
General office expenses	15,000	
Salesmen's salaries	50,000	
Debtors	100,000	
Creditors		32,500
Cash	61,000	
Sales		927,000
Loans		200,000
Loan interest	20,000	
	1,612,000	1,612,000

Additional information available at the year-end:

(a) Stock on hand at 31 December was as follows:
    Raw materials   £60,000
    Work in progress   £30,000
    Finished goods   £60,000
(b) Amounts unpaid relate to:
    Factory expenses   £2,000

Rent and rates   £1,000
General office expenses £1,000
(c) Amounts prepaid relate to:
Insurance   £1,000
Factory wages   £4,000
(d) 80% of the expenses relating to insurance, heat and light, and rent and rates, should be charged as manufacturing expenses, with the remainder being attributable to administration.
(e) Depreciation of equipment is to be included at 20% per annum, on cost. All of the equipment relates to manufacture.
Depreciation of furniture is to be included at 10% per annum, on cost. All of this relates to administration.
(f) The bad debts provision is to be maintained at 5% of debtors.

6 This exercise is the same as Exercise 6 from Chapter 8. The difference is that you are required to set up ledger accounts and record the opening balances and the summary transactions, draw up a trial balance, incorporate the adjustments, prepare a trading and profit and loss account as part of the double-entry system. You are not required to prepare a set of final accounts in good style as you should have done this earlier. You should check that the net profit figure agrees with your earlier figure. You should also check that the balance sheet prepared in Chapter 8 reflects actual account balances at the end of the year. The following is the balance sheet of a business at the beginning of 2000 (i.e. 1 January):

	£	£		£	£
Fixed assets			*Capital*		54,000
Premises		30,000			
Fixtures and fittings					
– cost	12,000				
– depn provision	2,000	10,000			
Equipment					
– cost	15,000				
– depn provision	5,000	10,000	Loan (10% interest)		10,000
		50,000			
Current assets			*Current liabilities*		
Stock	7,000		Creditors	8,000	
Prepaid insurance	100		Accrued wages	1,000	9,000
Debtors	10,000				
Cash	5,900				
		23,000			
		73,000			73,000

Note
The prepaid insurance relates to a premium which covers the twelve months to 31 March 2000. The accrued wages relate to overtime worked in December 1999.

The following represents a *summary* of the transactions which took place during 2000.

(a) Stock was purchased on credit for £70,000
(b) Stock was purchased for cash for £15,000
(c) Cash sales amounted to £40,000
(d) Credit sales amounted to £100,000
(e) Wages of £25,000 were paid
(f) Rent of £1,250 was paid. This covered the fifteen months to 31 March 2001.
(g) General expenses of £5,000 were paid
(h) Rates and insurance of £1,200 were paid. This included a £500 insurance premium covering the period 1 April 2000 to 31 March 2001.
(i) Additional equipment was purchased on 1 January, for £3,000. This was financed from a loan for the full amount, with interest payable at 20% per annum.
(j) Cash received from debtors amounted to £95,000, which was in satisfaction of debts of £97,000, the remainder being discount.
(k) Cash paid to creditors amounted to £71,000, which was in satisfaction of debts of £72,000, the remainder being discount.
(l) The owner withdrew £200 in stock and £6,000 in cash.
(m) £1,000 of credit sales were returned £500 of credit purchases were returned.
(n) Some of the fittings – cost £2,000, depreciation provision £1,000 – were traded in part-exchange for new fittings. The total cost of the new fittings was £4,000, of which £1,500 was a part-exchange allowance, and £2,500 was paid in cash.
(o) The owner won £5,000 on the football pools. This was paid into the business.
(p) A bill for holidays for the owner – total £500 – was paid from the business bank account.

At the end of the year the following items of additional information are obtained:

(a) Bad debts amounting to £1,500 are to be written off.
(b) Depreciation is to be provided for as follows:
     – premises – none
     – equipment – 20% on cost
     – fixtures and fittings – 10% on cost
     Depreciation is to be taken on those assets still in use at the year-end, not on those disposed of during the year.
(c) The two items of loan interest remain unpaid.
(d) Christmas overtime payments of £800 have not yet been paid.
(e) Closing stock is valued at £10,000.

Chapter 11

Accounting systems

This chapter aims to provide a very broad understanding of the nature of accounting systems, both manual and computerized. In practice even the system of double-entry book-keeping rapidly becomes unwieldy as the volume of transactions increase. Ways need to be found of dealing with this volume/scale-oriented problem. In general, systems are devised which break down the recording process into subdivisions, to provide manageable parts, for which individuals or teams can be given responsibility.

Another important feature of good accounting systems is the need for good internal control systems, in which one part of the system acts as a check on another part.

A further extremely important aspect of accounting and information systems is the requirement to produce a whole host of documents necessary for the operation of the business. Invoices, credit notes, statements, receipts, wage slips etc. provide examples. Systems must ensure that these documents flow quite naturally as part of the process.

It is not our aim to provide a lot of detail in this area in this particular book. However, those of you who wish to go on to become accountants will undoubtedly need to get to grips with this subject, as it is essentially one of the basic functions of accounting.

On completion of this chapter you should be able to:

- identify the main elements of internal control and explain the need for sound internal control in accounting systems;
- explain the need for a detailed system of data collection;
- outline the main components of a computerized accounting system, and its relationship with the systems introduced to date.

In order to ensure that the accounting system delivers accurate records and reports it is important that the system is designed to ensure that transactions are properly handled, and that errors are discovered. Errors may be accidental or deliberate. Any good accounting system will include procedures and techniques which help to detect and prevent them. These are known collectively as *internal control*.

A number of key elements of internal control can be identified, the most important of which are probably those listed below:

- proper procedures for ensuring transactions are properly processed

- suitable documents and accounting records are produced so as to leave an audit trail
- clear delegation and separation of duties
- adequate physical control over assets
- honest and capable employees
- independent verification of performance

Typically these involve a range of detailed approaches which include the following:

- make sure that some sort of procedures manual is prepared
- ensure that an appropriate authorization process occurs
- number important documents
- develop comparative financial statements
- prepare a budget of expected results
- develop an organization chart and clear job descriptions
- separate record keeping from custodianship of assets (e.g. don't give the cashier access to the records)
- separate authorization of expenditure from the record keeping
- separate purchasing from receiving
- ensure that detailed records of assets are kept and limit access to these records
- have sound safeguards to protect documents and computer files with back-ups as appropriate
- deposit receipts intact so as to ensure a clear audit trail
- hire good people with good references
- require annual vacations to be taken
- set up a conflict of interest policy
- reconcile bank statements independently
- regularly check that your records of assets reflect the assets in your possession
- have an annual audit.

This list is illustrative rather than complete.

Activity 1

From an internal control standpoint:

(a) Why is it important that staff are required to take their annual leave?
(b) Why should a cashier not have access to the accounts?
(c) What problems can arise regarding conflicts of interest?
(d) Why is important to develop a clear job specification and ensure that there is a clear separation of duties?
(e) Why is it important that authorization of expenditure is carefully controlled?
(f) Why is an inventory of assets owned an important part of the system of internal control?

(a) *Perpetuation of fraud is easier when staff are continually present. Forcing staff to take leave means that other people are required to carry out their functions, with an increased likelihood of any fraud being detected.*

(b) *If a cashier had access to the accounts he would be able to adjust the accounting records to cover any missing cash. For example, he could take cash received from a debtor and write off the debtor as a bad debt, pocketing the cash himself.*

(c) *Bias in things such as tendering can be introduced if the employee has an interest in a tendering business.*

(d) *Employees need to know what is required of them. Separation of duties enables different parts of the process to be carried out by different people, with one acting as a check on the other.*

(e) *Unless expenditure is properly authorized the expenditure cannot be said to be under control, and the amount of waste and excess will increase.*

(f) *If a business does not know what it owns it can never know what has been stolen or lost.*

11.4 Subsidiary records – manual systems

Even using a system of ledger accounts the volume of transactions can become so great that ways of collecting and summarizing data through a system of records *subsidiary* to the accounts need to be devised. As with ledger accounts, those intending a career in accountancy will need to become conversant with subsidiary records. Others are seldom likely to become closely involved in subsidiary records. The remainder of this section therefore aims to provide a very broad review of the typical manual system.

As has already been pointed out, the sheer volume of transactions in most businesses prevents the systems used so far, both the system of pluses and minuses, and that of ledger accounts, being used in the way set out in this book. In practice it is necessary to devise a system which will satisfy the following criteria:

1 It can handle *large volumes of data*. This means that the accounting function must be split up in a way which permits a number of people to operate certain parts of it.

2 It must be designed in such a way that it can be effectively *checked and controlled*.

3 It can be closely linked to the systems devised to produce the *documentation and records* needed by the business in its routine transactions, e.g. invoices, credit notes, cheques, receipts etc.

In practice this is achieved by *subdividing the ledger* into several sections, and supporting the entries by a series of *subsidiary records* which together cover all feasible transactions. Responsibility for each subdivision of the ledger, and each subsidiary record, can then be given to designated individuals within the organization. These individuals can then complete the recording of *part* of the process. This should facilitate the smooth running of the system, and should enable checks to be built into it, to prevent (or at least identify) errors, omissions and fraud.

Typical *divisions of the ledger* are:

- the cash book, which contains the cash and bank accounts;
- the sales (or debtors) ledger, which contains the accounts of customers (debtors);
- the purchases (or creditors) ledger, which contains the accounts of suppliers (creditors);
- the nominal ledger, which contains the accounts which are to be closed off to the trading and profit and loss account;
- the general ledger, which contains any remaining accounts.

This is summarized in Figure 11.1.

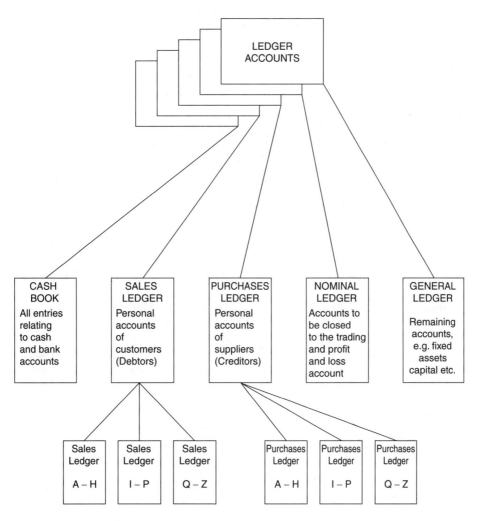

Figure 11.1. *A typical divisions of the ledger*

The reasons for these divisions are fairly clear. The largest volume of transactions will typically involve sales, debtors, cash, purchases and creditors. It may well be convenient for one person to be given responsibility for maintaining the sales (or debtors) ledger – the accounts of customers (debtors). This is made much easier if all these records or accounts are recorded in one place. Similar systems may be introduced for cash and creditors.

Clearly some sort of system is needed for organizing the ledger accounts. This is usually done by reference to a *chart of accounts*. This is effectively a listing of all the accounts in the ledger(s). The chart is usually associated with detailed folio references, if a manual system is in operation, or a detailed system of coding for a computerized system. A typical chart of accounts, with coding, might look like the following:

Asset accounts (100–199)

Fixed assets	*100–149*
Land	100
Buildings	110
Equipment – cost	120
Equipment – depreciation provision	122
Vehicles – cost	130
Vehicles – depreciation provision	132
Current assets	*150–199*
Stock (1)	150
Stock (2)	151
Debtors	160
Bad debts provision	161
Cash at bank	170
Cash in hand	180

Liability accounts (200–299)

Equity	*200–229*
Ordinary share capital	200
Preference share capital	210
Share premium	215
Net profit	220
Retained profits	225
Ordinary dividends	227
Preference dividends	228
Long-term liabilities	*230–249*
Debentures	230
Mortgages	240
Current liabilities	*230–299*
Creditors	230
Bank loan	240
Accruals	250

Expense accounts (300–399)

Purchases	300
Purchases returns	305
Carriage in	310
Discount allowed	320
Wages	330
Salaries	340
Rent	350
Rates	355
Insurance	360
Heating and lighting	365
Interest	370
Depreciation – equipment	375
Depreciation – vehicles	380
Bad debts	385

Revenue accounts (400–499)

Sales	400
Sales returns	420
Dividends receivable	460
Discount received	470
Interest	480

You should note that with a coding system like this that there is space to insert new codes, that subtotalling is relatively easy, and that a system of this type is comprehensive. A chart of accounts of this type can fit easily with the kind of subdivisions of the ledger identified earlier.

Even where a system of this sort occurs, other problems of recording data emerge, since different people may wish to have access to the same data. For this reason, and for purposes of improving internal control, it is usual for *all* transactions to be recorded in an appropriate form prior to recording in the ledger accounts. These initial recordings are made in what are known as *subsidiary records*.

Typically subsidiary records are kept for:

- sales and returns on credit;
- purchases and returns on credit;
- cash receipts;
- cash payments;
- petty cash items, e.g. postage, stationery etc.;
- a journal, for any remaining items.

For example, sales on credit might be recorded initially in a subsidiary record known as a sales book. This recording might be in the form of a listing of invoices sent out, or it might simply be a batch of invoices filed together for a particular day or week. In order to record correctly these items in the accounts it is necessary to increase (debit) a series of debtors, and to increase (credit) sales. The debtor accounts will need to have detailed entries made in them. The sales account will not, and an entry of the total sales figure will suffice. If the entries in the sales book (or the invoices in the batch) are totalled the appropriate entries can be made as follows:

- a set of detailed debit entries in the debtor accounts
- a single total credit entry in the sales account.

Figure 11.2 indicates diagramatically how such a process will work.

These entries can be made by *different people*, at *different times*, thus making easier the *separation of duties* and the problems of access to the same basic data. The use of total figures also has the advantage of providing a check on the accuracy of the detailed entries, since the trial balance will not balance unless both the detailed postings and the total postings agree.

In practice, in other than small organizations, it will be necessary to involve a number of people in the recording process, and a careful subdivision of duties will enable further checks and controls to be built in. For example, if one employee records entries relating to say, cash receipts in the cash book, while another records the equivalent entries in the individual debtor accounts, a cross-checking effectively occurs. The same principle typically applies to such things as discounts, bad debts etc. Such cross-checks should

Figure 11.2. *Sales and sales returns book*

help identify errors prior to preparation of the final accounts. It is also worth noting that the more such checks are used, the more difficult it becomes for fraud to take place without a considerable degree of collusion between record keepers.

Similar principles apply to all the other subsidiary records and ledgers. The purchases book lists purchases and associated creditors. The purchases are then recorded (posted) in the purchases account *in total*, while the creditors are posted in the creditors ledger *in detail*. The same principles apply to the purchases returns book. Cash receipts and cash payments journals list cash receipts and cash payments respectively, but usually do it in such a way that permits totals to be posted wherever possible. In all these subsidiary records the entry is sufficiently detailed to be able to ensure the correct double-entry is made. Many businesses keep a petty cash book, which deals with small cash items. All will keep a journal, which deals with anything not dealt with in any of the other subsidiary records. It is often used extensively for year-end adjustments and provides an opportunity to set out some quite complicated transactions in one place (initially) which can then be easily posted.

The overall aim of a manual system is to ensure that:

1 all items are recorded in a way which can effectively handle large volumes of data;
2 totals are used as a way of cutting down on detailed entries in the accounts, as well as providing a cross-check on the accuracy of the equivalent double-entries;
3 a sound system of internal control operates, in which the work of one individual provides a check on the work of another.

Self-assessment question 11.1

Paul is responsible for entries in the nominal ledger of a business. Matthew is responsible for the sales (debtors) ledger. A sales book is kept in which the total of each sales invoice is recorded, along with the name of the customer. Paul and Matthew complete their records on Monday and Tuesday respectively, on which days they have access to the sales book of the previous week.

(a) What recordings will Paul make in his ledger?
    What recordings will Matthew make in his ledger?
(b) If the sales book were to be incorrectly totalled, and overstated by £1,000, what would be the impact of this error on a trial balance drawn up?

Assume now that James is the cashier of the business. He collects the cash, and makes the necessary entries in the cash book.

(c) If he collected cash from a customer and put it in his pocket without recording it in the cash book, what is Matthew likely to do as a result?
(d) If you were in charge of the business would you give James authority to write off bad debts? Why/why not?
(e) Assume that Matthew was given authority to write off bad debts, how could he contrive to embezzle funds from the business?
(f) Would you give James and Matthew authority to write off bad debts, given their current responsibilities? Why/why not?

11.5 Computerized systems

Increasingly accounting records are maintained on a computer using accounting software. Systems vary considerably, but the end product must still include the profit and loss account and balance sheet. A computerized system is likely to be associated with larger numbers of transactions, particularly relating to such things as sales, purchases, stock issues, receipts and payments of cash (or cheques), payroll etc. It is also likely that a computerized system will offer other considerable advantages with regard to the printing of documents necessary to the efficient running of the business, and in the opportunity it provides to use information in a variety of ways. In designing a computerized system it is thus important to ensure:

1 That the system will cope with these *large amounts of data*;
2 That the variety of *documents necessary to the efficient running of the business* can be produced by the system;
3 That the data kept on computer can be *analysed and summarized in ways which will be of use to the decision-making process* within the firm. Among other things this should include a set of final accounts.

Activity 2

What sort of documents are likely to be required by a typical business?

A variety of documents are required by most businesses. These typically include: orders, sales invoices, credit notes, statements, delivery notes, stock records, cheques for payment, wages slips etc.

Activity 3

What kind of statements and reports are likely to be produced and used by the business for purposes of decision making?

Clearly profit and loss statements, cash flow statements and balance sheets are prepared and are useful. Many businesses produce budgets and monthly statements, together with comparisons of budget and actual performance. Ageing profiles of debtors can be really useful in terms of credit control. Records relating to stock levels and turnover (all in detail) can be useful, as can detailed analyses of revenues.

The essence of a computerized system is that a computer file will need to be maintained for each item to be found in a set of accounts. In many instances these files will need to be broken down into a more detailed set of records. For example, files are likely to be kept for debtors, creditors, stock and wages, all of which will almost certainly need to have more detailed records kept within them. Individual records will need to be maintained for each debtor and creditor, for each item of stock, and for each employee (for purposes of tax, National Insurance, etc.). These files will be updated to reflect such things as sales and purchases, returns, stock issues and returns, and weekly or monthly wages and salaries. Only the totals of such files would be needed for a set of final accounts, but the detailed records are a necessary part of day-to-day decision making and control. For example, the maintenance of detailed stock records should help in establishing, on the spot, stock availability or expected delivery time, as well as assisting with regard to decisions about such things as re-ordering, optimal stock levels, etc. Detailed debtors records are needed for purposes of cash collection and credit control. Detailed creditor records are necessary to ensure payment is made at an appropriate time, and that available discounts are taken. Individual wages records need to be maintained to ensure the correct deduction of such things as tax, National Insurance and pension contributions, and the payment of any bonuses, overtime, holiday pay etc.

In order to operate effectively a computerized system must be based on an adequate system of coding. This is nothing more than the identification of an appropriate code for each type of asset, liability, revenue or expense. The chart of accounts referred to earlier provides a very good starting point.

However, the system should not be constrained by this. The coding system must be sufficiently detailed to permit a range of analyses and printouts in as much detail as is considered necessary by the business. Information can then be fed into the computer, by keyboard, tape, scanning, mark sensing or other methods, to update the records and print out documents as required. The method used to update records is one of pluses and minuses, so the approach used in earlier chapters is essentially the same as that used in a computerized system.

Accounting packages typically operate by the use of menu-driven screens, in which the user can select the part of the routine he or she wishes to operate. It is not uncommon to find that the various parts of the routine correspond reasonably closely to the components of a manual system described earlier.

Activity 4

If you were using a menu driven computerized accounting a system what would you expect to find when selecting the following from a menu?

sales ledger
purchases ledger

The sales ledger includes the detailed debtors accounts arising from credit sales, while the purchases ledger contains creditors, associated with credit purchases.

In a properly designed computer system, while the concept of duality still applies, it is usual to find that the information which forms the basis of a double-entry is only put into the computer once. The system, which should be properly integrated, should then be designed to ensure that this basic information is recorded and analysed as needed. This is not to say that all the parts of the system need to be updated at the same time. Indeed, it is quite common to find that the two entries relating to a transaction take place at a different time. For example, one part of a system might be to print out sales invoices. The printing of the invoices is likely to be carried out in conjunction with a detailed updating of individual debtors accounts. However, the updating of the sales account may occur at a somewhat later date, and be entered in total. As long as the system is designed to ensure that the second entry is made, at some stage before the preparation of final accounts, this need cause no problems. It is in fact not different in principle to a detailed manual system of subsidiary records which might be designed in conjunction with a system of ledger accounts. What is important is that the system is designed in a way which can take a single input, and record and analyse it as needed.

In the final analysis a computerized system still follows the same basic principles as were set out earlier. It is likely to include a series of subroutines dealing with different aspects of the business, producing necessary documents and detailed records, which can then be integrated and analysed to produce a set of final accounts. However, it must also be recognized that the capability of modern computers has the potential to change the way we think about things, the way we analyse information and the way in which we make decisions.

In practice a computerized accounting system is likely to be part of a *management information system* (MIS). A MIS is one in which a variety of information is collected, analysed and communicated through the organization so as to help in its efficient management and functioning. Typically a MIS uses the database concept, in which data is stored in an appropriate way, and then accessed and analysed as needed, both routinely and on an *ad hoc* basis. Routine transactions may relate to sales, payments of customers accounts, wages etc. Less routine analysis may relate to forecasting and financial modelling, which will be introduced in Chapter 18.

A computerized accounting system is likely to have fewer errors than a manual system. Errors of addition, or errors which arise because the two aspects of a transaction are not both correctly recorded, should be eliminated. Nevertheless, computerized accounting systems can create additional security problems. For example, it is necessary to ensure that information is input correctly; it is necessary to ensure that both data and software are not corrupted by unauthorized users; and the amount of documentation is likely to be less, thus reducing the ability to check for errors/fraud etc. Computerized systems involve some considerable differences in internal control. The main differences are:

- many source documents are eliminated, as operators make an entry directly into the computer – this implies control of access is essential;
- sophisticated tampering can appear legitimate, with the presumption that as it's in the computer it has been authorized;
- programs require extensive checking for error and fraud;
- silly things can happen because the computer is not able to make judgements;
- separation of duties is more difficult, if not impossible, when all the activities occur within the computer;
- new and different errors occur, including hardware failures and system failures;
- complicated programs are often difficult to test fully;
- the operating systems may not be secure;
- audit trails are invisible, and have to be devised in very different ways – information can be changed without any physical evidence;
- if access to the system is obtained by an unauthorized individual, that individual probably has access to a lot of information;
- electronic information is easy to lose and back-ups are essential;
- users tend to believe that the computer is correct and don't check information provided;
- use of the telephone as part of the system can create problems, including breakdowns, opportunity for hackers to gain access to systems, introduction of errors through the communication process.

Activity 5
(a) How might the lack of an audit trail be dealt with?
(b) What additional back-up facilities are required with a computer system?

(a) Use of special programs, test data etc. to ensure that systems are operating as planned.
(b) Regular copying (backing-up) of records so that recovery from a 'crash' is not too difficult or time consuming. In the case of large systems access to other computers is probably a useful precaution.

Overall, computerized systems have advantages over manual systems where there are many transactions, where documents need printing, and where flexibility and speed of analysis is important.

11.6 Summary

This chapter has provided you with a brief review of accounting systems in practice. The system of ledger accounts, which was outlined and illustrated in earlier chapters, is recognized as being a necessary part of the system, but insufficient on its own. In practice it is clear that the volume of transactions which require recording, when coupled with the need to produce a variety of documents and other records, will necessitate further modifications and extensions to the systems of recording. The principles of manual and computerized systems were outlined, with emphasis on the need to develop effective control mechanisms. In practice most systems of accounting are now computerized, at least in part.

Since this book aims to provide an introduction to accounting for the non-specialist (the *users* of accounting information) this chapter is deliberately restricted in scope. It provides only a very broad overview of accounting systems in practice. Should you wish to pursue this area further you will need to study a more specialist accounting text, where you will find a number of descriptions of more fully developed systems. You should not be too surprised if the accounting systems you encounter in practice are rather more sophisticated than the system of pluses and minuses used in this book. What should be clear, however, is that any system used in practice will follow the principles adopted in this book, and the end product, in terms of final accounts, is identical.

Exercises

1 Explain the difference between the ledger and subsidiary records.
2 What are the underlying principles of subsidiary records?
3 Identify the key elements of internal control in a manual accounting system.
4 List as many issues as you can relating to internal control of computerized accounting systems.

Part Four

Accounting for Companies: The Regulatory Framework

This part consists of five chapters, and aims to introduce you to the important subject of the accounts of limited companies. Chapters 12 and 13 deal with the nature of limited companies and introduce company acounting.

Chapter 14 provides an introduction to the regulatory framework within which company accounting operates. This includes an introduction to company law, the Stock Exchange requirements and accounting standards. It is not intended that you should know the detailed provisions of the accounting regulations. Rather, it should provide you with sufficient understanding, when coupled with the knowledge derived from Chapters 12 and 13, to understand a set of company acounts.

Most published accounts relate to groups of companies and, as a result, include items not found in the accounts of individual companies. Chapters 15 and 16 aim to provide an understanding of groups, and the implications of group structures on published accounts.

Chapter 12

An introduction to the accounts of limited companies

12.1 Introduction	This chapter aims to provide a broad introduction to the nature of limited companies, and the particular accounting aspects associated with them.
12.2 Objectives	On completion of this chapter you should be able to:

On completion of this chapter you should be able to:

- identify the critical features of a company, notably its separate legal entity; the relationship between shareholders and directors; and limited liability;
- explain how companies are typically financed;
- identify the legal and practical restrictions which exist with regard to transferring funds to shareholders, including the payment of dividends;

12.3 Limited companies – importance and environment: an overview

There are three basic types of legal form which a UK business tends to take:

(a) *Sole proprietorships (sometimes known as sole trading businesses).* This is where one person owns and manages the business, perhaps employing other people to help. The legal and financial obligations of the business are borne entirely by the owner of the business, with the law making little or no distinction between the obligations of the sole proprietor, as a business person, and as a private individual. Thus, for example, the law would not view differently a loan taken out by the sole proprietor to pay for a business asset and money borrowed by the sole proprietor to pay for a holiday. Many small businesses, like corner shops, public houses and plumbers, are sole proprietorships. So far in this book, we have looked at the accounts of sole proprietors.

(b) *Partnerships.* These are businesses owned and managed by a group of people, usually a small group. As is the case with sole proprietorships, the law does not draw a real distinction between the obligations of partners, as business people, and as private individuals. Partnerships are very like sole trading businesses, but with more than one participant. Many small businesses, of the type which are often sole trading businesses, are owned and managed by more than one person. Thus where, as is often the case, a corner shop is owned and managed by a married couple, it is a partnership business. Most partnerships are very small, both in terms of the number of partners and the scale of the business. However, since the ethics of some professional bodies will not allow their members to practise except as sole proprietors and partners many professional partnerships are very large businesses.

(c) *Limited companies.* These are businesses usually owned by more than one person (shareholders) and managed by a committee (board of directors). Unlike sole proprietor and partnership businesses, the company is a distinct legal entity (separate legal person) separate from the owners and managers. As a result of the separateness of the company and its owners, the law *does* draw a real distinction between the obligations of the company and those of the owners. The private sector of the UK economy is dominated by limited companies.

The accounting peculiarities of limited companies arise directly from the particular legal status of the limited company. This chapter will, therefore, include a brief consideration of the *legal and administrative environment* in which limited companies operate. The aim here is not to provide a detailed legal examination of the limited company, but simply to outline its more significant aspects. More particularly the aim is to explain, in broad terms, those aspects which impinge on accounting.

In this context it is important to note that limited companies are regulated by a series of Companies Acts which were consolidated into the Companies Act 1985, and extended by the Companies Act of 1989. These Acts lay down a large number of rules which must be followed by those who manage a limited company. These rules have the objective of ensuring, as far as it is reasonable to do so, that those who deal with a limited company are not misled by its managers.

12.4 The nature of a limited company

Legal entity

A limited company is an artificially created legal person. It is an entity which is legally separate from all other persons, including those who own and manage it. It is quite possible for a limited company to take legal action, say for breach of contract, against any other legal person, again including those who own and manage it. Actions between limited companies and their shareholders or managers do occur from time to time.

Obviously an artificial person can only function through the intervention of human beings. In the case of a limited company it is the owners who ultimately control the company.

The separate legal status which limited companies have should not be confused with the accounting convention of business entity. The business entity convention applies to all businesses, whether or not they are limited companies.

Shares, shareholders and directors

A limited company may have a minimum of one owner although most have more than this. Capital must, therefore, be subdivided in a way which will enable the relative proportions of ownership to be ascertained. Capital (the owners' claim) is thus divided into shares. The shareholders (or members, as they are sometimes known) are the owners of the company; profits and gains accrue to them; losses are borne by them up to a maximum of the amount of their agreed investment in the company.

For a variety of sound practical reasons the day-to-day management of the company is delegated, by the shareholders, to directors who may themselves own some shares in the company. Shareholders elect directors in much the same way as citizens elect Members of Parliament in a parliamentary democracy. They also fail to re-elect them if the directors' performance is judged by shareholders to be unsatisfactory. Usually one-third of the directors retire from office each year, frequently offering themselves for re-election. Typically, each share carries one vote, thus each shareholder has as many votes as shares. Where a company has a large number of shareholders, a particular individual holding a large number of shares, even though not a majority of them, can wield tremendous power. This is because most shareholders of large companies tend not to use their votes. The board of directors is the business's top level of management, so to control its composition is substantially to control the company.

As a separate legal entity, the company does not depend on the identity of its shareholders for its existence. *Transfer of shares* by buying and selling or by gift is therefore possible. Thus a part – even all – of the company's ownership or equity can change hands without it necessarily having any effect on the business activities of the company. It should be noted that the price at which shares change hands is of no *direct* concern to the company, and will not affect the accounts of the company at all. Nevertheless, a low price is likely to indicate a relatively poor market perception of the business. This may lead to pressure for changes in the board, difficulties in raising further funds from the financial markets, and then threat of a takeover by another business. A high price is likely to help the current board retain its position, and may assist in achieving effective takeovers of other businesses.

Since the company can continue irrespective of precisely who the shareholders happen to be at any given moment, the company can theoretically have a perpetual life span.

Limited liability

One of the results of the peculiar position of the company as having its own separate legal identity is that the *financial liability of the owners (shareholders) is limited* to the amount which they have paid (or have pledged to pay) for their shares. If the company becomes insolvent (financial obligations exceed value of assets) its liability is, like that of a human person, limited only by the amount of its assets. It can be forced to pay over all of its assets to meet or partially to meet its liabilities, but no more. Since the company and the owners are legally separate, owners cannot be compelled to introduce further finance. The position of a shareholder in this regard does not depend upon whether the shares were acquired by buying them from an existing shareholder or whether they were bought direct from the company.

This contrasts dramatically with the position of sole proprietors and partners. The owners of these *unincorporated* businesses cannot, in law, separate personal obligations and assets from those of the business. Thus, for example, a sole proprietor or partner, whose business debts exceed business assets, will be required to introduce personal assets to meet the unpaid business debts. It is not legally possible for sole proprietors and partners to protect what they might like to think of as non-business assets from being used to meet unsatisfied business obligations. Shareholders in a limited company are, however, able to 'ring fence' their financial obligations to the company and keep their personal assets safe from any of the company's claimants.

Activity 1

It was mentioned above that some professional bodies will not allow their members to practise in the form of a limited company.

Can you think of the reason for this?

The reason for this is to stop professionals, who owe a duty of great care and expertise to their clients, avoiding the full implications of any action taken against those professionals for negligence, etc. as a result of trading through a limited company. The logic of this is that the professionals will tend to take their responsibilities more seriously, where they know that the effect of negligence, etc. could be that they lose everything, not just that part of their wealth which they think of as being involved in their professional business.

Activity 2

The tremendous growth in the economies of the Western world over the last two centuries has often been attributed (at least in part) to the advent of limited companies.

Jot down the features of limited companies which you consider likely to have been of most importance in the above phenomenon.

Most of the relevant points have been mentioned already in this chapter.

There are probably two main points here:

- *The ability to split capital into shares, enabling more investors to own part of a single enterprise. Given the high cost of assets since the Industrial Revolution, it is unlikely that many enterprises could have grown as rapidly as they have without this widening of ownership. Without this growth, mass production and its benefits would probably not have been possible.*
- *The separate legal identity of limited companies and the consequent effect of this, in terms of limited liability, provided further impetus to the growth of industry, since the maximum loss for an individual investor is limited and clearly specified.*

Types of company

Companies may be categorized into public companies and private companies. *Private limited companies* are companies with a limited number of shareholders, which generally have certain restrictions on the rights of owners to transfer their shares. Private companies tend to be smaller, family-held companies.

Private companies use the word *Limited (Ltd)* after their name in all formal documentation.

Public limited companies are companies whose shares have been offered to the public at large, and which have no restrictions on transferability of shares. Typically public companies are larger companies with more widespread share ownership. Public companies use the words *public limited company (Plc)* after their name in all formal documentation.

The number of private companies is many times greater than the number of public companies. However, the public companies are far more important in terms of output, assets and contribution to gross national product.

Many public companies are *listed on the Stock Exchange*. This means that a market exists on the Stock Exchange for their shares. There is thus a facility to buy and sell shares in such a company easily and conveniently. Inevitably, therefore, shares in listed companies are likely to be seen by many investors as being more attractive than those of unlisted companies.

Activity 3

Can you think of any reason why the price at which shares are transferred from one person to another may be different from the amount originally invested in the company?

(You may need to reconsider some of the basic accounting conventions referred to in earlier chapters in answering this question.)

A main reason is that, according to the historic cost convention, assets are shown in the books of a business at cost. The future earnings power of those assets will tend to determine the market value. Differences between book and market value of these assets is likely to make the ownership of shares in a company more or less attractive.

Retained profits are associated with increases in the net assets of a business, and thus with increases in the ownership equity. Other things being equal, the retention of profits should lead to increases in share price, provided that such retentions are put to good use.

Share prices reflect a variety of influences, some of which are worldwide (e.g. the 1987 crash), some are economy-wide, and some relate specifically to the prospects of an individual business (a prospective takeover, for example, may significantly affect the price of the shares of an individual company). In essence it is the supply/demand relationships for shares of a particular company which dictate price.

The share price is thus a reflection of a variety of factors, any of which may lead to share price being substantially different from the amount originally invested per share.

Formation of a limited company

Creating a new company is a very cheap and simple operation which can be carried out with little effort on the part of the promoters, for very little cost (less than £100 in total).

Formation basically requires the promoters to make an application to the Registrar of Companies (Department of Trade and Industry). The application must be accompanied by several documents, the most important of which is a proposed set of rules, or constitution, for the company defining how it will be administered. These rules are contained in two documents known as the Memorandum of Association and Articles of Association. Broadly speaking, the memorandum defines the company in relation to the outside world. It will thus include such things as:

- the name of the company, the area of the UK in which the registered office is situated;
- the objects for which the company was formed;
- a declaration that the liability of the members is to be limited;
- the amount of capital that the company takes power to acquire;
- the shares into which it is to be divided.

A public limited company will also have a clause stating that it is a public limited company.

The articles of a company are its internal regulations, and are subordinate to, and controlled by, the memorandum. They will show how the company is to be administered and will give particular reference to matters relating to the raising of capital, directors' powers, dividends and reserves, and accounts and audit.

All the documentation becomes public once the company has been formally registered. A file is opened at Companies House in Cardiff on which are placed the various documents. The file is constantly available for examination by any member of the public who wishes to see it. As we shall see later in the chapter, companies must also send the Registrar a copy of their annual accounts each year. These too are placed on the file and are, therefore, available for public scrutiny.

Activity 4

Can you guess why it is necessary for limited companies to include either 'Plc' or 'Ltd' in their names?

The reason is to warn people and organizations who might deal with a company in some way that the liability is limited to the extent of the company's assets (i.e. the personal assets of the shareholders are not included in the fund available to creditors, in the event of the company having insufficient assets to meet its obligations). It also advises people that they can find out various bits of information about the company from Companies House.

12.5 Ownership of companies

As we have already seen, companies are owned by the shareholders, with an individual's portion of the ownership of the company defined by the number of shares owned. When a company is first formed, the entire owners' claim will be represented by share capital. Once the company starts to trade, it is likely that the amount of the owners' claim will increase. This is because profits and gains might not be drawn by the shareholders, but left in the company. The law requires that the balance sheet value of the share capital cannot be expanded to reflect the increase in the owners' claim; the shares must be left in the balance sheet at the value at which they were issued. The additional owners' claim is put, in the balance sheet, under the separate heading of *reserves*. The sum of the share capital and the reserves, at any particular time, represents the entire claim of the shareholders against the company.

12.6 Share capital

The share capital of a limited company may be subdivided into different categories. In practice, the two most important of these are:

- Ordinary share capital
- Preference share capital.

Each of these types of share capital is made up of a number of shares, normally with an agreed nominal or par value. In other words, a company with ordinary share capital of, say, £1 million, may make up this capital in the form of 1 million shares of £1 each, 2 million shares of 50p each, or any other variation deemed appropriate.

Activity 5

Eight friends decide to form a company to start a business. They agree to supply £5,000 each to provide the original share capital. They are thinking of having a share capital of eight shares of £5,000 each. Their accountant has advised them to have 40,000 shares of £1 each.

Can you think why the accountant gave this advice?

The reasons we could think of are as follows:

- *It will not be practical for the shareholders to sell part of their investment. They will either have to sell all of it or nothing. If there are £1 shares, the shareholders can sell virtually any portion of their total investment.*
- *A similar point is that, if the company wishes to raise additional share capital in the future, it will be saddled with having to raise it in very large amounts per investor. This may well make it impossible to raise additional share capital.*

In fact, it is possible to subdivide existing shares into smaller denominations, but it is easier to establish smaller nominal share values from the outset.

Shares may be issued in such a way that the agreed price can be payable in instalments. This would usually be where a company does not need the full amount of the cash immediately and it is felt that investors might find the issue more attractive if payment is by instalment. For reasons which were raised in respect of Activity 3, it is also quite common for shares to be issued at a price which is in excess of the nominal price.

It might be useful to distinguish a number of terms with regard to capital.

Authorized capital is the maximum amount of share capital which the company is empowered to issue under its Memorandum of Association. This figure can be increased, provided that certain procedures are followed, and approvals obtained, but this may take some time.

Issued capital is the amount of capital which the company has specifically asked shareholders to subscribe.

Partly paid shares arise where shares are being issued on an instalment basis. Until such time as the total amount has been asked for by the company such shares will be *partly* paid. A shareholder holding a partly paid share is liable for payment of the unpaid part of the share on the agreed date, or, if no date is agreed, by a date to be fixed by the company. Failure to make such a payment could lead to the shares being forfeited. Once a share has become fully paid, the shareholders cannot be required to make any further payment to the company. Liability is limited to payment of the agreed amount.

Share premium is the difference between the agreed total price for a share and its nominal value. In the accounts of a limited company, share capital must be shown at the par value or, in the event of partly paid shares at the part called up, less any agreed portion for a share premium. Any premium paid to the company must be shown separately in the balance sheet.

The share premium account is an example of a reserve, i.e. part of the owners' claim over and above the nominal share capital. In many countries, the law does not require that a distinction be drawn between nominal share values and share premium; all the proceeds of a share issue are treated as share capital. It is not clear why UK law makes the distinction, particularly when UK law requires that share premium is treated almost identically to share capital.

Example	A company with an authorized capital of 100,000 shares with a nominal value of £1 each issues 50,000 shares at their nominal value. The effect on the balance sheet would be as shown below.

Assets   *Claims*
Cash   +   £50,000   Issued capital   +   £50,000
                                              (50,000 £1 shares fully paid)

Activity 6

See if you can show the effect on the balance sheet of a company of the following transactions, by filling in the blank spaces below.

A company with an authorized capital of 100,000 shares with a nominal value of £1 each issues:

(a) 50,000 £1 shares payable 50p immediately, and the remaining 50p at some future date.
   Assets   *Claims*
   Cash   . . . .   Capital   . . . .

(b) 50,000 shares payable in full, at a premium of 50p

Assets		Claims	
Cash	. . . .	Capital	. . . .
		Share premium	. . . .

You should have come up with the following:

		£		£
(a)	Assets		Claims	
	Cash	+25,000	Share capital	+25,000
(b)	Assets		Claims	
	Cash	+75,000	Share capital	+50,000
			Share premium	+25,000

Where shares are issued on an instalment basis, and a premium is to be included in the price, it is usual for the premium to be taken as part of the first instalment. For example, if 50,000 £1 shares were issued at a premium of 50p, payable £1 immediately, and 50p a year from now, the effect on the balance sheet would be as follows:

Assets		Claims	
Cash	+£50,000	Share capital (partly paid)	£25,000
		Share premium	£25,000

Ordinary shares

These are issued by the company to investors who are prepared to expose themselves to risk in order also to expose themselves to the expectation of high investment returns, which both intuition and evidence tell us are associated with risk. Ordinary shareholders of successful companies usually receive cash dividends on an annual or more frequent basis. Dividends to shareholders are the equivalent of drawings by a sole proprietor. The funds available for payment of dividends is what remains after all expenses, including interest on long-term loans and any dividends on preference shares, have been met. Dividends may be further restricted at the discretion of the directors. Dividends are therefore uncertain; prior claims may exhaust the available funds or the directors may decide to plough back profits at the expense of ordinary share dividends. The maximum amount of dividend which a company may pay at any particular time is restricted by law. Why this restriction exists, and how it is applied, will be discussed later in the chapter.

In principle, where funds are retained rather than distributed they remain the property of the ordinary shareholders who are the ultimate owners or equity holders. In that sense, retained profits are as much part of the ordinary shareholder's return as are the dividends, since profits retained should have a direct effect on the value of the shares. In fact, retained profits represent a major source of long-term finance for UK companies. Other things being equal, the retention of profits, and their subsequent reinvestment in profitable ventures, should lead to an expectation of increased earnings in the future, which is likely to lead to an increase in share price. In considering the adequacy of earnings for a company, it is thus important to bear in mind these two components, namely dividends and growth in share price. Historically, in the UK, increases in the value of equities have tended to represent a larger element than have dividends in returns to shareholder, i.e. dividends have tended to be less important to shareholders than have capital gains.

Not surprisingly, given the above comments, there is no reason why shares, when traded between investors, should be priced according to the original issue price or their face value (nominal or par value). Perceptions of the value of a share in any particular company will change with varying economic circumstances, so that share prices will shift over time. It might be helpful to repeat that shareholders selling their shares in a particular company for some price has no direct effect on that company. The company will simply pay future dividends and give future voting rights to the new shareholder.

It is the ordinary shareholders who normally have the voting power within the company. It is thus the ordinary shareholders who effectively control the company. Each ordinary share confers equal rights on its owner in terms of dividend entitlement, voting power and a distribution of the company's assets, should the company be closed down (liquidated). Two shares carry exactly twice as much of these rights as does one share. The law forbids the directors from discriminating between the rights of different shareholders, other than on the basis of the number of shares owned (assuming that the shares owned are of the same class). Miss X owning 100 shares in Z Plc should have equal rights in respect of her shareholding as Mr Y who owns a similar number of shares in the same company. The Stock Exchange and other non-statutory agencies also seek to promote this equality.

Preference shares

These represent part of the risk-bearing ownership of the company, though they usually confer on their holders a right to receive the first slice of any dividend which is paid. There is an upper limit on the preference dividend per share, which is usually defined as a percentage of the nominal value of the share. Preference share dividends are usually paid in full, provided that sufficient profit (and cash) exists. Preference shares give more sure returns than equities (ordinary shares) do, though they by no means provide certain returns. Preference shares do not usually confer voting rights. They do not automatically give the same preference in repayment in a liquidation as they do in payment of dividends, though in some companies such preference does exist.

Preference shares of many public companies are traded in the capital market. As with equities, prices of preference shares will vary with investors' perceptions of future prospects. Generally preference share prices are less volatile than those of equities, as dividends tend to be fairly stable and usually have an upper limit.

In terms of the amount of funds raised, preference shares are not a very important source of funds.

Raising share capital

Share capital can be raised in a variety of ways, ranging from funds provided by a small group of individuals (like a family), merchant bankers and other institutional backers, to funds raised directly from the public. A detailed examination of the advantages and disadvantages of the various sources of finance is beyond the scope of this book.

Shares are not always issued for cash. Issuing shares in exchange for other assets, including the shares of another company, is not uncommon. For example, most takeovers are effected by the purchasing company issuing its own shares to the shareholders of the target company, in exchange for the shares held by those shareholders. In many cases, the takeover offer may also include an element of cash and/or loan stocks. More detail on how takeovers occur is given in Chapter 15.

Shares issued at a premium

As we have seen, it is not uncommon for companies to issue shares at above their nominal or face value.

For example, suppose that a business which has 100,000 shares of £1 each continues in business successfully for several years, retaining some of its profits (£100,000 in total) to help fund an expansion programme. This results in a balance sheet which appears as follows (summary form only):

	£		£
Assets		*Claims*	
Net assets	200,000	Ordinary share capital (100,000 shares of £1 each fully paid)	100,000
		Reserves (retained profit)	100,000
	200,000		200,000

If share prices reflected book values each share would be worth £2 (£200,000/100,000). If a further 100,000 £1 shares were issued at par (£1 each), the resulting balance sheet would be:

Assets		*Claims*	
Net assets	300,000	Ordinary share capital (200,000 shares of £1 each fully paid)	200,000
		Reserves	100,000
	300,000		300,000

If share prices continue to reflect book values, the above issue would result in a share price of £1.50 (£300,000/100,000). Existing shareholders would effectively lose part of their claim, to the advantage of the new shareholders. This is because all shareholders of a particular category have equal rights, irrespective of when such shares were issued.

Activity 7

In the above example, at what price would the new shares need to be issued to preserve the existing shareholders' effective wealth, assuming that book value reflects share price?
    Show the revised balance sheet after the issue of new shares at that price.

You should have come up with the fact that the shares would need to be issued at £2, the current market price. The resulting balance sheet would appear as follows:

Assets	£	Claims	£
Net assets	400,000	Ordinary share capital	
		(200,000 shares of £1 each	
		fully paid)	200,000
		Reserves	100,000
		Share premium account	100,000
	400,000		400,000

This should leave the share price at £2 per share.

In practice, the share price is unlikely to be as closely related to book value as is implied above. However, the current market price per share is likely to provide a good guide to an appropriate issue price for any new shares, provided that expectations about the earnings associated with the new capital are similar to those associated with the existing business. In the final analysis, the price agreed will reflect a balance between the need for the new capital and the likely demand from investors for the new shares at various prices. Likely demand levels will in turn reflect expected future earnings.

Self-assessment question 12.1

A company, with the balance sheet given below, intends to issue 100,000 £1 ordinary shares at a price of £2.50 per share, which is the market price of existing shares.

Assets	£000	Claims	£000
Net assets	200	Ordinary share capital	100
		(100,000 shares of £1 each	
		fully paid)	
		Reserves	100
	200		200

(a) What is the book value per share?
(b) Show the balance sheet after the new issue.

(c) What is the book value per share after the new issue?
(d) What reasons may exist for the book value per share to differ from market price per share?

Rights issues

Sometimes a new issue will be made to people, or organizations, which were not previously shareholders. It is more common, however, for new issues by existing companies to be offered, in the first instance, to existing shareholders. Such an issue is known as a rights issue. A rights issue is an offer to existing shareholders of a *right to acquire further shares in proportion to the shareholders' existing holdings*. When the rights are taken up cash is actually paid into the business by the shareholders. The price at which shares are offered in a rights issue is usually below the current share price. Rights to acquire shares at a preferential rate can be sold, so shareholders who do not wish to take up the offer (or who cannot afford to) may sell their rights to others who might wish to do so. Such an approach virtually guarantees the success of a rights issue.

Example

A company with 1 million shares of £1 each, with a market value of £5 each, makes a rights issue on a one-for-five basis (all shareholders will be offered one new share for every five which they already hold), at a price of £3 per share. The value put on the company before the rights issue is thus £5 million. Since the rights issue will be 200,000 new shares at a price of £3, the proceeds will be £600,000. *After* the issue, other things being equal, the market is likely to value the company at £5.6 million. Since there will now be 1.2 million shares the market price per share should settle at around £4.67 (i.e. 5.6 million/1.2 million). The new shares can be obtained for £3 each, so it would be worth paying up to £1.67 to obtain a right.

If the rights were traded at £1.67 each, the position of two shareholders taking different approaches to the issue can be seen to be effectively identical. For a shareholder owning five shares before the rights issue, the total value of the investment will be £25 (5 × £5).

A shareholder who takes up the right will pay a further £3, making the total investment £28. After the issue this will be reflected in a holding of six shares, each priced at £4.67.

A shareholder who does not take up the right, but sells it for £1.67, will thus own five shares at £4.67 per share (£23.33) and will have cash of £1.67, making a total of £25. Clearly, if the rights are traded at £1.67 there is no change in the relative wealth of shareholders who take up the rights and those who do not. In practice, of course, it is unlikely that prices will change with the precision implied above, but the general principles remain valid. If a rights issue is associated with expansion, or an improvement in prospects, the value of the shares after the rights issue may well be higher than would be suggested using the above approach.

> The advantages of rights issues to a company are threefold:
>
> - they are a relatively cheap form of finance, since there are no advertising costs and administrative costs are low;
> - since rights are issued in proportion to existing shareholdings, control may be retained by existing shareholders;
> - the price at which the rights issue is set will not affect existing shareholders' wealth, provided that they either take up the rights or sell them. The example which precedes Activity 7 shows that this is not true with issues made to the general public.

12.7 Reserves

Amounts of shareholders' capital (owners' claim) over and above the share capital are known as reserves. Reserves are in essence retained profits and gains. They may arise in a number of ways, the most common of which are given below.

Revenue reserves

Profits should arise in the normal course of trading. From these dividends may be paid, along with any tax bills associated with the profits made (corporation tax). Any profits remaining are accumulated in various revenue reserve accounts. Typically, revenue reserves are shown under one or a combination of the following headings:

- revenue reserves
- profit and loss
- general reserve
- fixed asset replacement reserve

There is no legal difference between these, and the precise title used is a matter of preference. The reason for making the distinction between the various revenue reserves is normally to give some indication of the purpose of retaining the profit.

Capital reserves

Capital reserves are retained gains which have arisen from transactions *not related to trading* as such. The most common are:

(a) *Share premium.* The difference between the nominal or par value of a share (or the part called) and the agreed issue price, or that part of the nominal value which has been 'called'. We have discussed this reserve already.

(b) *Revaluation reserve.* This reflects the unrealized increase in value of an asset which has been revalued in the balance sheet. For example, suppose that a company which owned property shown in the books at £1 million wished to revalue it to £2 million. The property would be increased to £2 million in the fixed assets area of the balance sheet, and a corresponding increase in owners' claim would be needed. Since the share capital of a company must be shown at its nominal value, the increase in value will need to be shown elsewhere. It is, therefore, recorded in a revaluation reserve. It is important to note that the revaluation reserve reflects unrealized profits. This fact can have an important bearing on the payment of dividends, as will be seen later in this chapter.

Activity 8

Which accounting conventions are breached by reflecting market value of fixed assets in the balance sheet?

The breached conventions are:

- *Historic cost.*
- *Realization.*

These conventions are not infrequently breached by companies whose fixed assets have a market value greater than their cost. This departure from the accepted rule is tolerated by company law. Such deviations can be confusing to users of accounting information, however.

(c) *Capital redemption reserve.* This is a special reserve which is associated with the repayment of share capital, and will be dealt with in more detail shortly.

Companies are not legally required to distinguish between capital and revenue reserves in their balance sheets. Separate disclosure is required by law for certain capital reserves, namely the share premium and capital redemption reserve. Any other reserves should be classified under headings which are appropriate to a particular company's business.

12.8 Transferring funds to shareholders

Company law lays down strict rules surrounding the extent to which companies may transfer assets to their owners (i.e. their shareholders). This contrasts dramatically with the total absence of restriction surrounding the rights of sole proprietors and partners to take assets from their businesses.

Activity 9

Why do you think this contrast exists?

The contrast exists because of the separate legal status of companies and, springing from this, the limited liability of shareholders. If business assets are transferred to become personal assets of sole proprietors and partners, the accessibility of these assets to claimants against the business remains the same. Assets transferred by a company to its shareholders change their status in terms of their accessibility to claimants against the company.

> As a result, company law restricts the right of companies to transfer assets to shareholders.

A buffer for creditors

The aim of company law, in this context, is to safeguard the interests of creditors and lenders. If capital could be paid out to shareholders, without restriction, it would be possible for unscrupulous shareholders to make large payments to themselves, leaving the creditors to salvage what they can. Company law seeks to establish that all existing and potential creditors or lenders know that the shareholders' interests in the company cannot be reduced below the amount of *effective fixed capital*, as a result of making payments to themselves out of the company's assets.

Example

Consider the balance sheet of Mario Ltd.

Fixed assets	£	Claims	£
Fixed assets	800	Ordinary share capital	2,000
Investments	1,200	(1,000 shares of £1 each	
Current assets		fully paid)	
Stock	500	Share premium	1,000
Debtors	500	Profit and loss account	400
Cash	1,200	Creditors	800
	4,200		4,200

Suppose that no rules about capital maintenance exist.

The company sold the investments and stock, at their balance sheet values, and collected the cash owing from the debtors in full. All the owners' claims were then settled in cash.

The balance sheet after these transactions would appear as follows:

Fixed assets	£	Claims	£
Fixed assets	800	Ordinary share capital	–
Investments	–	(1,000 shares of £1 each	–
Current assets		fully paid)	
Stock	–	Share premium	–
Debtors	–	Profit and loss account	–
Cash	–	Creditors	800
	800		800

The creditors are in a very much less secure position after these transactions than they were before. Before the transactions, there were assets with book value totalling £4,200 available to meet the creditors' claim, including £1,200 in cash. As a result of the transactions it will mean that, unless the fixed assets realize at least their book value, the assets of the company will be unable to meet the claim of the creditors. Since the other assets

> are now in the hands of the shareholders, whose liability is limited, the creditors can do no more than hope that the fixed assets will realize at least £800 so that their claim can be met in full.

Clearly, people and organizations will be reluctant to work for, trade with or lend money to a company which can suddenly erode the security of external claimants in this way. This would make the limited company useless as a device for encouraging enterprise and commerce. As a result, company law has established that transfers of company assets to shareholders are restricted.

The purpose of the law is, therefore, to provide a buffer for the creditors and lenders. Creditors and lenders should be able to be confident that a certain part of the shareholders' equity cannot be taken out of the business. The law seeks to ensure that this buffer cannot be reduced below the amount of *effective fixed capital* (i.e. share capital + non-distributable reserves). The situation outlined in the above example could thus not arise. In fact, the effective capital could not normally be reduced below £3,000 as a result of payments being made to shareholders. Why it is this figure will be explained shortly.

It is worth noting that the conditions identified above do not ensure that effective fixed capital cannot be reduced under any circumstances. If the company were to sustain trading losses this could eat into the effective fixed capital.

It is also worth noting that company law does not set a minimum level of effective fixed capital. The law merely demands that whatever level of effective fixed capital has been set by the company cannot normally be reduced as a result of payments to shareholders.

Funds may be transferred from the company to shareholders as a result of three types of transaction:

(a) the payment of dividends
(b) the redemption of capital
(c) liquidation of the company

Very clear rules, set out in the 1985 Companies Act, exist in these areas.

Dividends

In essence dividends can only be paid out of realized profits. The total available will reflect the profits accumulated over the years, net of any losses. The total available will include trading profits and profits on disposal of fixed assets. Surpluses arising from revaluing fixed assets, however, cannot be distributed as a dividend.

Activity 10
Bubbly Ltd started trading in 1999 when it made a loss for the year of £100,000. In 2000 it made a profit of £80,000. What is the maximum dividend which the company could legally pay at the end of 2000?

The answer is zero; there is still a cumulative net loss overall of £20,000.

Activity 11

Photo Ltd started trading in 1999 when it made a profit of £100,000. In 2000 it sustained a loss of £80,000. What is the maximum dividend which the company could pay at the end of 2000, assuming that no dividends were paid in 1999?

The answer is £20,000, i.e. the cumulative net retained profit.

Activity 12

As well as the trading results given in Activity 11 you find that during 2000 Photo Ltd sold a plot of land which had cost £100,000 for £150,000 and had revalued another similar plot which had also cost £100,000 to £150,000. What is the maximum dividend which the company could pay at the end of 2000?

Your answer should be £70,000 – the £50,000 profit on disposal plus the £20,000 from cumulative profits. The revaluation reserve of £50,000 could not be distributed as a dividend.

In paying dividends, it is important to note that preference shareholders will take priority over ordinary shareholders. An ordinary dividend cannot be paid until the due preference dividend has been paid. The directors are not obliged to declare dividends, either preference or ordinary, but in practice preference dividends are seldom missed.

In practice, the amount of dividend which is actually paid to ordinary shareholders usually falls well short of the legal maximum. Several reasons may be given for this.

(a) It has already been noted that capital and reserves together must equal net assets (the balance sheet equation). However, there is no direct link between reserves and cash. A shortage of liquid funds is likely to lead to dividend payments which are a relatively small part of the distributable reserves. Legally, it is possible to borrow cash to pay dividends.

(b) Retained profits, as has already been mentioned, represent the major source of funds for new investments by companies. Low dividends leave more funds for growth.

(c) Differences in the basis of taxation may attract certain shareholders to companies associated with low dividends, high growth and thus increasing share price.

It is important to note that reserves are not cash balances, despite the fact that people talk about 'paying dividends out of reserves'. For example, consider the following balance sheet, relating to Andros Ltd, as at 31 December 2000.

Assets	£	Claims	£
Net assets	173,000	Share capital (100,000 ordinary shares of £1 each)	100,000
		Revaluation reserve	20,000
		Profit and loss account	53,000
	173,000		173,000

(Note that in this example retained profits (revenue reserves) are shown simply under the heading 'profit and loss account'.)

If the directors of Andros Ltd decide to pay a dividend they will take part of the net assets (presumably cash, though dividends can, and very occasionally do, take other forms) and give it to the shareholders in accordance with the number of shares owned by each one. Suppose that a dividend of £25,000 is decided upon. This will have the effect of reducing the net assets to £148,000 (i.e. £173,000 − £25,000). The other aspect of this transaction is that the shareholders' claim against the company will be reduced by £25,000, thus reducing the profit and loss account balance from £53,000 to £28,000.

Reserves are part of the claim of the shareholders on the net assets of a business. The existence of reserves implies nothing about the availability of cash to pay out such reserves as dividends. It is perfectly possible to have substantial reserves and limited cash, indeed even an overdraft. Under such circumstances, while it may be legally possible to pay dividends, the liquidity position of the company may make this commercially imprudent. There is no legal reason why a company should not use borrowed funds to finance a dividend, provided that there are sufficient revenue reserves to cover the dividend. There may be good commercial reasons why such a policy should not be used. On the other hand, a company could quite feasibly have plenty of cash but no distributable reserves (see Activity 10), making a dividend illegal.

Redemption of shares and share repurchase

Subject to certain restrictions companies are allowed to reduce share capital, either by redeeming share capital or by buying some of their own shares, from the shareholders, and cancelling those shares. These are very similar activities, in terms of their overall effect on the company, so we shall refer to them both as share redemptions. Such redemptions occur relatively infrequently. One reason for redemptions is that sometimes companies find that they have more capital than they can effectively use. Another reason is that shares are sometimes issued on the understanding that they will be redeemed at some point.

We have already seen that, in the context of transferring funds to shareholders, the guiding principle is that the interests of creditors and lenders take priority over those of shareholders.

In order to preserve the relative position of the creditors and lenders, a redemption can only occur if certain rules are followed. In broad terms, a company may only redeem (repay) share capital where the total effective fixed capital is not reduced as a result of the redemption. Effective fixed capital means share capital plus non-distributable reserves.

Example

Suppose that the balance sheet of Crete Ltd is as follows:

Assets	£	Claims	£
Net assets	153,000	Ordinary share capital (100,000 shares of £1 each fully paid)	100,000
		Redeemable preference shares (20,000 shares of £1 each fully paid)	20,000
		Profit and loss account	33,000
	153,000		153,000

The company wishes to redeem the preference shares. In the above balance sheet the total effective fixed capital is £120,000 before redemption of the preference shares. This figure must be preserved *after* the redemption of the preference shares.

This can be effected in one (or a combination) of two ways:

(a) by issuing new shares to replace those redeemed;
(b) by converting an appropriate amount of distributable reserves into share capital (by the use of a bonus issue), or into a separate undistributable reserve which may be seen as being effectively the same as share capital.

It is worth noting that the overall effect of a share redemption is, in essence, much the same as the payment of a dividend. This is to say that the effective capital stays the same; distributable reserves go down by the same amount as the cash which is paid to the shareholders.

A bonus issue arises when a company converts part of its reserves into share capital. We shall consider bonus issues, and the reason for them, shortly.

If the redeemable preference shares were to be replaced by a new issue of 20,000 £1 ordinary shares at par the effect would be as follows:

Assets	£	Claims	£
Net assets	153,000	Ordinary share capital (120,000 shares of £1 each fully paid)	120,000
		Profit and loss account	33,000
	153,000		153,000

Since the total capital remains the same (£120,000) after the redemption of the preference shares, the legal provisions with regard to redemption have been satisfied.

Suppose now that the preference shares were to be redeemed at par, without a new issue of shares to replace them. The initial impact of redemption would be to change the balance sheet as follows:

Assets	£	Claims	£
Net assets	133,000	Ordinary share capital	100,000
		(100,000 shares of £1 each fully paid)	
		Profit and loss account	33,000
	133,000		133,000

However, this balance sheet reflects a reduction in effective fixed capital, by £20,000. This is illegal. Under such circumstances, therefore, an amount equivalent to the effective reduction (i.e. the nominal value of the shares redeemed) must be transferred from distributable reserves to share capital or undistributable reserves, so as to maintain the effective fixed capital. This transfer may be done in a number of ways:

(a) by opening a new capital (i.e. undistributable) reserve known as the capital redemption reserve, and transferring the appropriate amount to it, from distributable reserves;
(b) by converting distributable reserves into share capital by a bonus issue;
(c) by a combination of (a) and (b) totalling £20,000.

If the first of these is done the balance sheet of Crete Ltd would appear as follows:

Assets	£	Claims	£
Net assets	133,000	Ordinary share capital	100,000
		(100,000 ordinary shares of £1 each)	
		Capital redemption reserve	20,000
		Profit and loss account	13,000
	133,000		133,000

It should be noted that the capital redemption reserve is to be treated as if it is share capital, and thus may not be distributed as a dividend or reduced, other than by a court order. It may, however, be used to issue bonus shares, since this does not involve a reduction in effective fixed capital. In the balance sheet after the redemption the effective fixed capital is thus £120,000 (share capital plus the capital redemption reserve), thus maintaining it at the required level.

If a bonus issue on a one-for-five basis was made from distributable reserves the balance sheet would appear as follows:

Assets	£	Claims	£
Net assets	133,000	Ordinary share capital (100,000 shares of £1 each fully paid)	120,000
		Profit and loss account	13,000
	133,000		133,000

In this case the bonus issue must come from distributable reserves, to satisfy the legal conditions. As before, the capital after the redemption is £120,000, satisfying the legal requirements.

Activity 13

The balance sheet of Leonidas Ltd is as follows:

Assets	£	Claims	£
Net assets	200,000	Ordinary share capital (120,000 shares of £1 each fully paid)	120,000
		Redeemable preference share capital (30,000 shares of £1 each fully paid)	30,000
		Profit and loss account	50,000
	200,000		200,000

The directors decide to redeem all the preference share capital at par.
This is to be partially replaced by a new issue of 20,000 ordinary shares of £1 each, at par.
   Show the balance sheet after the redemption and new issue.

The balance sheet should look something like this:

Assets	£	Claims	£
Net assets	190,000	Ordinary share capital (140,000 shares of £1 each fully paid)	140,000
		Capital redemption reserve	10,000
		Profit and loss account	40,000
	190,000		190,000

Activity 14

The balance sheet of Hopeful Ltd is as follows:

Assets	£	Claims	£
Net assets	170,000	Ordinary share capital (120,000 shares of £1 each fully paid)	120,000
		Redeemable preference share capital (30,000 shares of £1 each fully paid)	30,000
		Profit and loss account	20,000
	200,000		200,000

The directors decide to redeem all of the preference share capital at par.

They do not intend to issue any new shares because the company has plenty of cash available for the redemption.

   Show the balance sheet after the redemption and new issue.

This is a bit of a trick question. It would be illegal to redeem more than 20,000 of the preference shares because there are only distributable reserves available to that extent. The availability of cash is not the only important factor here.

| **Liquidation** |

A limited company, because it has separate existence from its shareholders, does not die when they do. The only way in which the company's demise can be brought about is by following the statutorily defined steps to liquidate the company. Liquidation involves appointing a liquidator to realize the company's assets, pay the claimants and formally to lay the company to rest.

   The initiative to liquidate the company usually comes either from:

(a) the shareholders, perhaps because the purpose for which the company was formed has been served; or
(b) the company's creditors (including loan creditors), where the company is failing to pay its debts. In these circumstances the objective is to stop the company from trading and to ensure that non-cash assets are realized, the proceeds being used, along with any cash assets, to meet (perhaps only partially) the claims of the creditors. This type of liquidation is sometimes referred to colloquially as bankruptcy.

| **Order of paying claimants** |

Irrespective of which type of liquidation is involved, the liquidator, having realized all of the non-cash assets, must take great care as to the order in which the claimants are paid. Broadly speaking the order is:

(a) *Secured creditors*, where the security is on a specified asset or group of assets. The proceeds of disposal of the asset are to be applied to meeting the specific claim. If the proceeds are insufficient the creditor must stand with the unsecured creditors for the shortfall. If the proceeds exceed the amount of the claim, the excess goes into the fund available to unsecured creditors.

(b) *Unsecured creditors*. This would usually include most trade creditors. It would also include any unsecured loan creditors.

Only after the creditors have been paid in full will the balance of the funds be paid out to the shareholders. If the preference shares carry no right to priority of payment, each share (ordinary and preference) will be entitled to an equal portion of the residue of funds. Where preference shares bestow the right to payment before ordinary shareholders, each ordinary share will command an equal slice of the funds remaining after the creditors and preference shareholders have had their full entitlement.

The order of payment of creditors will be of little consequence except where there are insufficient funds to meet all claims. Where this is the case, each class of claim must be met in full before the next class may participate.

Activity 15

Failure Ltd has been trading unprofitably for several years and has recently experienced a cash shortage so severe that it has not been able to pay its debts. The creditors have successfully initiated a winding-up by the court. At the date of the winding-up order the balance sheet was as follows:

	£000	£000	£000
Fixed assets (at cost less depreciation)			
Land & buildings		80	
Plant & machinery		10	
Motor vehicles		5	
			95
Current assets			
Stock		10	
Trade debtors		12	
		22	
Creditors: amounts falling due within 1 year			
Bank overdraft	26		
Trade creditors	14		
		40	
		(18)	
Creditors: amounts falling due more than 1 year from now			
Loan stock (secured on land & buildings)		50	
			(68)
Net assets			27

Financed by
Share capital   60
less *accumulated losses*   33
                                                         ——
                                                         27
                                                         ══

When the liquidator realized the assets, the following amounts were received:

	£000
Land & buildings	70
Plant & machinery	2
Motor vehicles	3
Stock	9
Trade debtors	12

You are required to show how the available funds should be deployed by the liquidator.

Your answer should look something like this:

	£000
Proceeds from liquidation	*96*
Cost of assets disposed of	*117*
Therefore loss on disposal	*21*

The loss would be borne by the shareholders, thus reducing their claim to £6,000. The available funds would be distributed as follows:

		£000
1	*Loan stock*	*50*
2	*Creditors and overdraft*	*40*
3	*Shareholders*	*6*
		96

Note that the accumulated losses in the balance sheet of Failure Ltd are, in effect, a negative reserve.

12.9 Bonus shares

A bonus share is a share which is given to shareholders 'free', with no cash being required by the company. It is not an increase in the shareholders' claim. It is not a transfer of company funds to the shareholders. This is why we are dealing with bonus issues in a separate section.

Bonus shares are issued in proportion to existing holdings of shares. Very little in life is really free, and bonus shares are no exception to this. If bonus shares are issued, and share capital is increased by the amount of the new shares issued, there must be a corresponding adjustment somewhere else in the balance sheet. Since no cash is received the adjustment cannot be to increase cash. In fact, all that happens with a bonus issue is that certain reserves are converted into paid-up share capital. The adjustment for a bonus issue is thus to increase share capital and to decrease reserves. A bonus issue does not therefore increase the owners' claims on the company (which is the sum of share capital and reserves), but simply shifts part of the claim from reserves to share capital. The directors may convert reserves into share capital by the use of bonus shares at any time. Any reserves, including capital redemption reserve and share premium, can legally be converted into bonus shares. The issue of bonus shares is also referred to as a *scrip* or *capitalization issue*.

Example

The balance sheet of Andros Ltd is as follows:

Assets	£	Claims	£
Net assets	173,000	Ordinary share capital	100,000
		(100,000 shares of £1 each fully paid)	
		Revaluation reserve	20,000
		Profit and loss account	53,000
	173,000		173,000

The directors decide to convert the revaluation reserve, and £30,000 of the profit and loss account balance, into share capital, by making a one-for-two bonus issue to existing shareholders, i.e. giving each shareholder one additional new share in respect of every two shares already held.
The balance sheet immediately following the issue would be:

Assets	£	Claims	£
Net assets	173,000	Ordinary share capital	150,000
		(150,000 shares of £1 each fully paid)	
		Profit and loss account	23,000
	173,000		173,000

Activity 16
(a) Do you think that the shareholders will be more wealthy after the bonus issue than they were before it?
(b) What do you believe to be the effect of the bonus issue on the reserves which are available for dividend?

Your answers should have been along the following lines:

(a) *The bonus issue should not make any difference to shareholder wealth, since the ownership claim remains at £173,000.*
(b) *Distributable reserves fall from £53,000 to £23,000.*

It should be clear from this activity that bonus issues do not, of themselves, lead to increased shareholder wealth. They are certainly not free. Indeed, in the above example not only does the total claim of the shareholders remain the same, but the amount available for distribution as a dividend has fallen. Under such circumstances it is difficult to see much point in an issue of bonus shares. However, several reasons for their use may be given.

(a) In spite of the points made above many shareholders like receiving bonus issues, and may feel better off.
(b) For many well-established businesses the chance of a significant portion of reserves actually being distributed is minimal. Under such circumstances a movement from reserves into capital reflects the realities of the situation, that the reserves concerned are considered by the company to be part of the effective fixed capital.
(c) Where a company is seeking a loan, the potential lender may prefer that the ability of the company to make cash payments in the form of dividends to its shareholders be restricted. It may therefore set as a condition of any loan that revenue reserves are wholly or partly converted into shares.
(d) It is frequently anticipated that after the bonus issue the company will continue to pay the same dividend per share. Since each shareholder will then own more shares, the dividend paid will be higher. If shareholders prefer dividends this may be to their advantage.
(e) If the price per share becomes high it is sometimes the case that the shares become less easy to trade on the Stock Exchange, leading to a lessening of interest in the shares on the part of the investing public. Research studies have suggested that there are certain ranges of share price which are better than others, in terms of generating activity on the market. Under such circumstances a bonus issue, while leading to a fall in share price, may not result in as large a fall as might be expected, leaving shareholders slightly better off. This is because the increased marketability of the shares may have a beneficial effect on the share price.

Example

Kos Ltd has the following balance sheet:

Assets	£	Claims	£
Net assets	1,000,000	Ordinary share capital (100,000 shares of £1 each fully paid)	100,000
		Reserves	900,000
	1,000,000		1,000,000

The current share price on the Stock Exchange if £12. This means that the current market value of the company is £1.2 million. Suppose now that a bonus issue on a five-for-one basis was made. The resulting balance sheet would be:

Assets	£	Claims	£
Net assets	1,000,000	Ordinary share capital (600,000 shares of £1 each fully paid)	600,000
		Reserves	400,000
	1,000,000		1,000,000

Only the capital structure of the business has changed. The net assets remain the same. It may reasonably be presumed that the future prospects of the business are unchanged by the bonus issue. Under such circumstances, the market value of the company should remain at £1.2 million, which should in turn lead to a price of £2 per share. At this price shareholders are no better off, and no worse off. A holder of one share valued at £12 before the bonus issue now has six shares valued at £2 each. However, the implication of the argument put forward in (e) above is that there would be more interest from potential investors for shares with a price of £2 each than for shares with a price of £12. The result of an increase in investor interest may be that the new share price settles at a higher figure than £2 (say £2.10). In these circumstances, greater wealth may result from the bonus issue. The holder of one share, valued at £12, would now have six shares valued at £2.10, i.e. a total value of £12.60, giving an increase of 5% on the holding. Despite the possible reasons for bonus shares which are given here, it is still not clear why they exist. They occur, however, and their implications in terms of accounts need to be recognized.

Where a choice exists as to which reserves should be capitalized (i.e. converted into share capital), it is sensible to convert first those reserves which are not available for dividends, thus preserving maximum flexibility in the future with regard to cash dividends. Of course, where the bonus issue occurs for the reasons set out in (c) above this flexibility is precisely what a potential lender is trying to limit.

Activity 17

Spiros Ltd has the following balance sheet:

Assets	£	Claims	£
Net assets	850,000	Ordinary share capital (400,000 shares of £1 each fully paid)	400,000
		Share Premium	150,000
		Revaluation reserve	150,000
		Revenue reserves	150,000
	850,000		850,000

Have a try at showing the effect on the balance sheet of a bonus issue:

(a) on a one-for-four basis
(b) on a one-for-two basis
(c) on a one-for-one basis

Explain *why* you have done what you have done. You should assume that the company wishes to retain the maximum dividend payment potential.

Your balance sheets should look something like this:

(a)

Assets	£	Claims	£
Net assets	850,000	Ordinary share capital (500,000 shares of £1 each fully paid)	500,000
		Share premium account	50,000
		Revaluation reserve	150,000
		Revenue reserves	150,000
	850,000		850,000

(b)

	£		£
Net assets	850,000	Ordinary share capital (600,000 shares of £1 each fully paid)	600,000
		Revaluation reserve	100,000
		Revenue reserves	150,000
	850,000		850,000

(c)

	£		£
Net assets	850,000	Ordinary share capital (800,000 shares of £1 each fully paid)	800,000
		Revenue reserves	50,000
	850,000		850,000

In order to preserve flexibility with regard to the availability of reserves for distribution as cash dividends it would be prudent to convert reserves in the order:

(a) *share premium – since this has very limited uses,*
(b) *revaluation reserve – not distributable unless the profit is actually realized,*
(c) *revenue reserves.*

Self-assessment question 12.2

The balance sheet of Corfu Ltd is as follows:

Assets	£	Claims	£
Net assets	800,000	Ordinary share capital	400,000
		(400,000 shares of £1 each fully paid)	
		Share Premium	100,000
		Revaluation reserve	200,000
		Revenue reserves	100,000
	800,000		800,000

The company decides to make a bonus issue on a one-for-four basis, followed by a rights issue on a one-for-five basis, at a premium of 50p.
   Show the balance sheet after these issues.
   Explain the movements in reserves fully.

**12.10
Long-term loans**

Most companies borrow funds on a long-term, occasionally on a perpetual, basis. Lenders enter into a contractual relationship, with the company with the rate of interest, its date of payment, the redemption date and amount all being terms of the contract. Many long-term lenders require rather more by way of security for their loan than the rights conferred on any lender under the law of contract. Typically they insist that the principal and sometimes the interest as well are secured on some specific asset of the borrowing company, frequently land. Such security might confer on lenders a right to seize the asset and sell it to satisfy their claims where repayment of principal or interest payment is overdue.

A particular form of long-term loan which is associated with companies is the *debenture*. This is essentially a loan evidenced by a deed. Debentures can be broken down into small parts, each for an agreed amount (say, £10 for each unit). Holders of the debentures are then entitled to interest and repayment as set out in the overall loan agreement associated with the debenture issue. The debentures of many companies are traded on the Stock Exchange. It is thus possible for someone owed £100 by company X to sell this debt to another investor who, from the date of the sale, will become entitled to receive interest and repayment of the principal, in due course. Such payment amounts and dates are contractual obligations, so there is less doubt surrounding them than applies to returns from shares, more particularly where the loan is secured. For this reason, loan stocks tend not to fluctuate very much in their market value. To a lesser extent this is also true of preference shares.

In passing, it is worth noting that loan interest is regarded as a business expense, and is thus generally deducted from profits in assessing liability to tax.

Activity 18
Can you suggest reasons why companies typically raise some of their long-term finance from borrowing, instead of obtaining it from existing or new shareholders?

We came up with the following points:

- *To fund expansion without any loss of control. Since lenders do not have any voting rights in a company, they cannot normally participate in management/decision making.*
- *To fund expansion which could not otherwise take place, since the resources of the owners are limited.*
- *To obtain larger returns on projects by borrowing at a rate which is lower than the expected return on the project. The additional returns all accrue to the owners. This approach, and its associated risks, is dealt with more fully in later chapters.*
- *Interest on loans is a tax-deductible expense, making it quite a cheap form of finance.*

12.11 Summary

This chapter has provided you with an introduction to the nature and accounts of limited companies. The various types of share capital were introduced, as were reserves (various types of retained profits). The rules which surround the transfer of funds to shareholders (dividends, redemptions and liquidations) were considered. The nature of loan stock was examined.

Exercises

1 Show the effect on the balance sheet of a company of the following transactions.

A company with an authorized capital of 100,000 ordinary shares of £1 each and 50,000 preference shares of £1 each issues:

(a) 50,000 ordinary shares of £1 each, at a premium of 25p, payable 75p immediately, and the remainder at some future date.

Assets   *Claims*
Cash £..........   .... £..........
              .... £..........
              .... £..........

(b) 100,000 ordinary shares of £1 each, at a premium of 50p, payable in full immediately, and 25,000 preference shares of £1 each, at par, also payable in full immediately.

Assets   *Claims*
Cash £..........   .... £..........
              .... £..........
              .... £..........

2 The balance sheet of XYZ Plc is presently as follows:

	£ millions	£ millions
Fixed assets at cost, less accumulated depreciation		210
Current assets		
Stock	158	
Debtors	68	
Cash	42	
	268	
Current liabilities		
Trade creditors	60	
		208
		418
Capital and reserves		
Ordinary shares of £1 each, fully paid		200
Profit and loss account (retained profit)		218
		418

The company's shares are traded on the Stock Exchange at a price which reflects the balance sheet value of the assets and claims.

The company wishes to make a one-for-two rights issue to ordinary shareholders at an issue price of £1.50 per share.

Required
(a) What is the current market price of the shares?
(b) How much will each ordinary share be worth after the rights issue?
(c) How much would a right to buy one new share be worth?
(d) Show the balance sheet immediately after the rights issue was completed, assuming that all of the shares are successfully issued.

3 The balance sheet of Abacus Ltd is currently as follows:

	£	£
Fixed assets at valuation and cost, less accumulated depreciation		350,000
Current assets		
Stock	75,000	
Debtors	43,000	
Cash	176,000	
	294,000	
Current liabilities		
Trade creditors	29,000	
		265,000
		615,000

Capital and reserves	
Ordinary shares of £1 each, fully paid	350,000
Preference shares of £1 each, fully paid	150,000
Revaluation reserve	50,000
Profit and loss account (retained profit)	65,000
	615,000

The directors wish to use most of the cash to redeem the whole of the preference shares at par. They are adamant that they do not wish to raise any new share capital. They have expressed a willingness to raise more cash by way of a debenture issue, if absolutely necessary.

Advise the directors of their best course of action in this.

4 The balance sheet of ABC Plc is as follows:

	£ millions	£ millions
Fixed assets at cost and valuation, less accumulated depreciation		34
Current assets		
Stock	26	
Debtors	23	
Cash	16	
	65	
Current liabilities		
Trade creditors	13	
		52
		86
Capital and reserves		
Ordinary shares of £1 each, fully paid		50
Shares premium account		10
Capital redemption reserve		10
Revaluation reserve		9
Profit and loss account (retained profit)		7
		86

The directors wish to make a one-for-two bonus issue to ordinary shareholders.

Advise the directors of the most practical way to do this and show the 'capital and reserves' area of the balance sheet after the bonus issue, assuming that the directors take your advice.

5 The balance sheet of Aristo Ltd is as follows:

	£	£
Fixed assets at cost		425,000
less accumulated depreciation		227,000
		198,000

Current assets		
Stock	87,000	
Cash	77,000	
	12,000	
	176,000	
Current liabilities		
Trade creditors	69,000	
		107,000
		305,000
Capital and reserves		
Ordinary shares of £1 each, fully paid		150,000
Preference shares of £1 each, fully paid		
(redeemable at par)		100,000
Profit and loss account (retained profit)		55,000
		305,000

The directors of the company have made a few suggestions relating to the shares and reserves of the company and have asked the company's accountant to redraft the balance sheet as it would appear if the suggestions are acted upon. The accountant has checked that all of the suggestions are legally possible. The redrafted balance sheet is as follows:

	£	£
Fixed assets at cost and valuation		505,000
less accumulated depreciation		227,000
		278,000
Current assets		
Stock	87,000	
Debtors	77,000	
Cash	12,000	
	176,000	
Current liabilities		
Trade creditors	69,000	
		107,000
		385,000
		£
Capital and reserves		
Ordinary shares of £1 each, fully paid		200,000
Capital redemption reserve		50,000

Share premium	50,000
Revaluation reserve	80,000
Profit and loss account (retained profit)	5,000
	385,000

What do you think that the directors' proposals were? Explain your answer. How would the proposals, if implemented, affect the maximum legally permitted dividend?

Chapter 13

Accounting for companies

13.1 Introduction	This chapter provides an overview of the major differences between accounting for limited companies and accounting for sole traders. In doing this it provides a clear framework for accounting for companies.
13.2 Objectives	On completion of this chapter you should be able to: • explain the accountability requirements imposed on directors; • identify the main differences in accounting for companies as compared with accounting for sole traders; • prepare a set of final accounts including an appropriation account.
13.3 Accountability of directors/ published accounts	The law imposes a *duty on directors*: • to keep accounting records sufficient to show and explain the company's transactions and sufficient to enable a balance sheet and a profit and loss account to be prepared, • to report annually both to the shareholders, and to some extent to the world at large, on the performance of the company's trading.

With regard to this latter duty directors are required to prepare annually (or to have prepared) a *report for the shareholders*. The minimum contents of the report are prescribed by law, though in practice this minimum is often exceeded. Principally the report consists of a profit and loss account, a balance sheet and a cash flow statement, though a directors' report is also required. These accounting statements, which are required to show a true and fair view of the trading results, financial position and cash flows of the company, are generally subject to audit by an independent firm of accountants, though there are exceptions for small companies.

A copy of the annual report must be sent to each shareholder and debenture holder. A copy must also be sent to the Registrar of Companies to be placed on the company's file, which is available for inspection by anyone wishing to do so. In practice, large companies also send copies of the report to financial analysts and journalists. Such companies will usually comply with a request from any private individual for a copy.

The annual report is a major, but not the only, source of information to interested parties, including existing and prospective shareholders, on the progress of the company. Companies whose shares are listed on the Stock Exchange are required by its rules to publish summarized accounting statements on a half-yearly basis. In practice, most large companies, from time to time, issue information over and above that which is contained in the annual and half-yearly reports.

The form and content of published accounts will be dealt with in more detail in the next chapter, on the regulatory framework of accounting.

It is worth emphasizing at this point that the accounting records kept by companies are basically the same as those of a sole proprietor, and follow the same principles as have been set out in earlier chapters. Similarly, the final accounts are much the same. It should be noted that at this stage the emphasis is on the broad principles of company financial reporting. A whole range of requirements exists with regard to the *publication* of accounting information relating to companies. These will be dealt with in Chapter 14, on the regulatory framework of accounting.

The profit and loss account

In essence, the various items included so far under revenues and expenses, in the trading and profit and loss accounts, are all likely to be found in the accounts of a limited company. With a company there will be additional expenses listed, covering the following items

- Auditors remuneration – the expenses associated with the auditing (checking by an appropriately qualified accountant) of accounts.
- Directors salaries – directors are employees of the company so their pay is deemed to be an expense. For a sole trader the drawings, even if effectively in lieu of salary, remain a drawing and not an expense.
- Debenture interest – debentures are a form of financing usually associated with companies.

The profit and loss appropriation account

With a sole trading business it is clear that the net profit is the entitlement of the owner, and it is accordingly added to capital. Any drawings are deducted from capital. With a limited company there is a need for an appropriation account, in which the net profit is allocated. Part of the profit will almost certainly need to be set aside in order to pay corporation tax. (Corporation tax is, as its name implies, a tax levied on the profits and gains of companies.) The net profit after tax is all the entitlement of the shareholders, but some sharing out will be necessary if more than one category of shareholder exists. Dividends may be paid, while transfers may also be made to appropriate reserves (e.g. general reserve).

To deal with this need to share out, or appropriate, profits, an appropriation account is needed. The same approach is used for a partnership, where profits need to be shared out. The appropriation account would typically appear as follows:

Net profit for the year	*x*
Less: corporation tax	*x*
After-tax profit	*x*
Add profit and loss account balance brought forward	*x*

Total unappropriated profit · *x*
Less: Transfers to reserves · · · · · · · · · · · · *x*
Less: Dividends · *x* · · *x*
Profit and loss account balance
   carried forward · *x*

Activity 1

A company has a net profit of £50,000. It also has a balance of £10,000 in its profit and loss account from previous years. Corporation tax is expected to be £20,000. £5,000 is to be transferred to a general reserve. £16,000 is to be paid as an ordinary dividend, and £5,000 as a preference dividend.

   Using the model shown above, draft the appropriation account.

Your appropriation account should look something like this:

	£ 000	£ 000
Net profit for the year		50
Less Corporation tax		20
After tax profit		30
Add profit and loss account balance brought forward		10
Total unappropriated profit		40
Less		
Transfers to General reserve	5	
Dividends: Preference	5	
Ordinary	16	
		26
Profit and loss account balance carried forward		14

It should be noted that the appropriation account forms part of the accounting system, so the concept of duality applies to it. A corresponding entry is necessary for all the items in the appropriation account, with a resultant effect on the balance sheet. The corresponding entries are as follows:

- The net profit will be the figure entered in the profit and loss account.
- A claim for the estimated corporation tax (known as a corporation tax provision) will need to be set up.
- Dividends paid will typically result in a reduction in cash. Dividends proposed at the year end, but as yet unpaid, will need to be reflected in a current liability.
- Transfers to reserves will be added to any existing amounts in these reserve accounts, resulting in an increased total being shown.

- Any unappropriated profit will be carried forward as a balance on the profit and loss account. It will thus appear in the balance sheet at the end of the period, as a part of reserves, and will be carried forward as the opening balance on the appropriation account for the next period.

The balance sheet

The balance sheet of a company follows the same principles as the balance sheet of a sole proprietor, and the same general headings are used. The main differences arise in the area of capital and reserves, although a small number of differences elsewhere in the balance sheet may be noted.

Fixed assets
These must be disclosed at cost less aggregate depreciation provision, with totals for both cost and aggregate depreciation provisions being shown.

Current assets
No differences.

Current liabilities (i.e. liabilities payable within a year)
Additional items will be included to cover dividends unpaid and corporation tax.

Liabilities payable more than a year from the balance sheet date
These may include debentures and other loan stocks.

Capital and reserves
The share capital and reserves of a company are shown under separate headings.

Share capital
This will include the various categories of share capital which have been issued, at their nominal or par value.

Reserves
This section will include the various reserve accounts, normally with separate disclosure of the share premium, revaluation reserves, capital redemption reserves, and the distributable revenue reserves. The revenue reserves may be subdivided further, to include such things as general reserve, profit and loss account, etc.

Activity 2

A limited company has an authorized share capital of £1 million, divided into 250,000 preference shares (7%) of £1 each and 750,000 ordinary shares of £1 each.

All the preference shares have been issued and fully paid, together with 500,000 ordinary shares, again fully paid. Both categories of share were issued at par.

At the beginning of the current financial year (1 January) the balance on general reserve was £150,000, while the profit and loss account balance was £15,000.

At the year end (31 December) the following claims and assets were found to exist:

- creditors £125,000
- fixed assets (at cost) £600,000
- fixed assets (depreciation provision) £120,000
- current assets £660,000

The net profit for the current year was £100,000. A corporation tax provision of £30,000 is to be set up, being the estimated liability on profits, being payable on 30 September of the following year. The directors also recommend that:

- the preference dividend is paid;
- £15,000 is transfered to the general reserve;
- a dividend of 10% of the nominal value of the shares is paid to ordinary shareholders.

Have a try at preparing a profit and loss appropriation account for the year and a balance sheet as at 31 December.

Your answer should look something like this:

Profit and loss appropriation account for the year ended 31 December

	£	£
Net profit for the year		100,000
Less: Corporation tax		30,000
Net profit after tax		70,000
Profit and loss account balance brought forward		15,000
Total available for appropriation		85,000
Less:		
Transfer to general reserve	15,000	
Preference dividends	17,500	
Ordinary dividends	50,000	
		82,500
Unappropriated profit carried forward		2,500

Balance sheet as at 31 December

	£	£	£
Fixed assets			
– cost			600,000
– depreciation provision			120,000
			480,000
Current assets		660,000	
Less: **Creditors payable within a year**			
Creditors	125,000		
Corporation tax	30,000		

Preference dividend	*17,500*	
Ordinary dividend	*50,000*	
	222,500	
		437,500
Net assets		*917,500*
Financed by:		
Capital		
Ordinary share capital		*500,000*
Preference share capital		*250,000*
		750,000
Reserves		
General reserve	*165,000*	
Profit and loss	*2,500*	
		167,500
		917,500

You should note that many companies pay an interim dividend, usually half-way through the year, in anticipation of profits. The double entry is to credit cash and to debit an interim dividend account. This debit will remain on the books until the end of the year and hence will appear in the trial balance. At the end of the year, when the appropriation account is being prepared, the interim dividend will be credited (thus closing the account) and the appropriation account will be debited with the amount of the interim dividend.

When the final dividend is paid the appropriation account will be debited with the amount of the final dividend and a current liability credited – proposed dividends.

Self-assessment question 13.1

The trial balance* of RAC Ltd as at 31 December 2000 was as follows:

	£	£
Ordinary share capital		200,000
Preference share capital (10%)		50,000
Land & Buildings	200,000	
Equipment – cost	50,000	
Equipment – depreciation provision		20,000
Fittings – cost	50,000	
Fittings – depreciation provision		25,000
Stock	30,000	
Discount received		2,000
Discount allowed	3,000	

Directors' remuneration	30,000	
Sales		530,000
Debtors	50,000	
Creditors		30,000
Purchases	300,000	
Selling & distribution expenses	30,000	
Loan (10%)		40,000
Loan interest	2,000	
Administration expenses	40,000	
Profit & loss account balance brought forward		25,000
Wages & salaries	50,000	
Cash	100,000	
Bad debts	2,000	
General reserve		15,000
	937,000	937,000

You are given the following additional information relating to the year end:

(a) Closing stock is valued at £35,000.
(b) Loan interest of £2,000 is due.
(c) £2,000 of administration expenses are outstanding.
(d) £1,000 of the selling and distribution expenses have been prepaid.
(e) depreciation is to be taken in 2000 on the basis of 10% on cost for equipment and fittings. No depreciation is to be calculated for land and buildings.
(f) The directors have recommended that the preference share dividend is to be paid, along with an ordinary dividend of 20% of the nominal value of the shares.
(g) £25,000 is to be transferred to general reserve.

Required
Prepare trading, profit and loss and appropriation accounts for RAC Ltd for the year ending 31 December 2000, and a balance sheet as at that date. *If you omitted study of Chapters 9-11 all you need to know is that a trial balance is a list of balances. The figures in the left-hand column are assets, drawings or expenses, while the right-hand column include revenues, equity and liabilities.

13.4
Summary

The chapter has provided you with an introduction to the final accounts of limited companies.

The next chapter considers the rules with which companies must comply in respect of their financial reporting to shareholders and to the world at large.

Exercises

1 As at 1 January 1999 a company has a (credit) balance on its profit and loss account of £50,000. Net profit for the year ending 31 December 1999 was £290,000. During the year a half-year's dividend was paid on the £500,000 (6%) preference shares, and the directors now propose that the balance available for distribution should be appropriated as follows:

(a) £100,000 to be provided for corporation tax.
(b) The second half of the preference dividend to be paid early in 2000.
(c) An ordinary dividend of 10% on the 1,000,000 £1 ordinary shares to be paid early in 2000.
(d) £20,000 to be transferred to the general reserve.

Show the appropriation account for the year.

2 X Ltd commenced business on 1 January 1999, with an authorized share capital of 200,000 ordinary shares of £1 each, and 200,000 (5%) preference shares of £1 each. It issued all of the ordinary shares and 100,000 of the preference shares on 1 January 1999, and the remaining preference shares on 1 January 2000. All issues were fully paid and at par.

In the year ending 31 December 1999 the profit was £40,000, and in 2000 was £60,000. Transfers to general reserve were to be £20,000 in each year, and dividends of 5% were declared on ordinary shares in 1999, and of 10% in 2000.

Prepare appropriation accounts for each of the years ending 31 December 1999 and 2000.

3 The following balances remain in the records of the South Devon Engineering Company Ltd after the preparation of trading and profit and loss accounts for the year ending 31 December 1999:

	£
180,000 £1 ordinary shares (fully paid)	180,000
9% Loan stock	100,000
Machinery (cost)	300,000
Motor vehicles (cost)	20,000
Furniture and fittings (cost)	25,000
General reserve	30,000
Profit and loss account	
balance brought forward	20,000
Net profit for year	50,000
Depreciation provisions:	
machinery	60,000
motor vehicles	5,000
furniture and fittings	5,000
Debtors	30,000
Creditors	15,000
Stocks	45,000
Cash	45,000

Prepare a profit and loss appropriation account for the year ended 31 December 1999, and a balance sheet as at that date. The directors decide to recommend that £15,000 be transferred to general reserve, and that a dividend of 15% be paid on the ordinary shares.

4 The following is a list of the items which appeared in the accounting records of Caterers Ltd as at 31 December 2000. These figures, which are classified as either assets and expenses or as claims and revenues, reflect all of the transactions for the year, except those which are specified towards the end of the question. The authorized capital was 500,000 ordinary shares of £1 each and 200,000 preference shares (6%) of £1 each.

	Assets/ expenses £	Claims/ revenues £
Ordinary share capital		500,000
Preference share capital (100,000 fully paid)		100,000
Properties at cost	400,000	
Motor vehicles at cost	80,000	
Motor vehicles depreciation provision		20,000
Investments (cost)	50,000	
Investment income		5,000
Profit and loss balance 1 January 2000		40,000
Debtors	150,000	
Creditors		120,000
Directors' remuneration	50,000	
Sales		800,000
Purchases	500,000	
Wages and salaries	100,000	
Transport expenses	30,000	
Bad debts written off	5,000	
Bad debts provision		5,000
Administration expenses	40,000	
Advertising	20,000	
Stock	120,000	
Cash	45,000	
	1,590,000	1,590,000

Prepare trading, profit and loss and appropriation accounts for the year ending 31 December 2000 and a balance sheet as at that date, incorporating the following adjustments:

(a) Depreciation on vehicles at the rate of 25% per annum on cost.
(b) £2,000 of the administration expenses have been prepaid at the year-end.

(c) Wages of £3,000 are owing at the year end.
(d) The bad debts provision is to be maintained at 5% of debtors.
(e) Closing stock is valued at £150,000.
(f) £20,000 is to be transferred to the general reserve.
(g) A dividend of 12% on the ordinary shares is recommended.

Chapter 14

The regulatory framework

14.1 Introduction

This chapter is concerned with the framework of regulations, legal and otherwise, which prescribe the way in which the accounts of limited companies are prepared and presented.

14.2 Objectives

On completion of this chapter you should be able to:

- discuss the influence of law in determining the form and content of corporate financial reports;
- discuss the influence of Stock Exchange requirements on the form and content of the accounts of listed companies.
- explain the need for accounting standards in financial reporting;
- discuss the advantages and disadvantages of setting accounting standards.

14.3 The regulatory framework

In the UK, it has long been accepted that limited liability companies require a framework of regulations to govern their financial accounting and reporting activities. At present, this regulatory framework consists of two main elements – statute law and non-statutorily determined accounting standards. Broadly, the law sets out the general framework and accounting standards are designed to support the legal requirements. Where companies are listed on the Stock Exchange, or have shares traded on the Unlisted Securities Market, there are certain Stock Exchange regulations to be adhered to. These represent a third element of financial reporting regulation.

14.4 The legislative framework

An important feature of limited liability companies is the separation of ownership from control. Shareholders appoint directors who then become responsible for the day-to-day running of the business. Such an arrangement, however, leads to a requirement for accountability. The directors, who act for and on behalf of the shareholders, have to account to the shareholders for their stewardship of the business. Since the mid-nineteenth century, the law has been concerned with protecting the shareholder by trying to ensure appropriate accountability. The law has also been concerned with protecting creditors who lend to companies with limited liability status. Thus, to protect the interests of both investors and creditors it has been considered necessary to regulate, through statutory means, the form and content of company financial reports.

Activity 1

Can you think why the law concerns itself with protecting shareholders and creditors in this way?

We think that the answer is that it is generally considered to be beneficial to society to have a healthy private sector economy. This requires that businesses are able to raise capital from investors. In attracting investors, it helps if the business has limited liability. Unfortunately, limited liability tends to weaken the position of creditors. It is cumbersome to run a business without using credit. All this tends to imply that the best interests of society are served by a legal environment in which the interests of both shareholders and creditors are protected. The provision of accounting information to shareholders, and to anyone else who wishes to see it, goes some part of the way to creating an environment in which people are prepared to invest in, or to trade with, limited companies.

The current law, which is set out in the Companies Acts 1985 and 1989, requires company directors to keep accounting records sufficient to show and explain the company's transactions and to enable a balance sheet and profit and loss account to be prepared. The directors must produce a profit and loss account on an annual basis with a balance sheet as at the last day of each accounting year. Both of these statements are required to show a true and fair view of that which they purport to indicate. The directors must also produce a 'directors' report' which provides further financial information. The published accounts must include these three statements together with an auditors' report which expresses the opinion of the independent auditors, concerning the statements. A copy of these accounts must be sent to each shareholder and debenture holder and must be laid before the annual general meeting of the company. (However, the shareholders of private companies may decide to dispense with this requirement if they feel such a formality is unnecessary, e.g. where the shareholders already have access to the company's financial reports.) A copy of the accounts must also be filed with the Registrar of Companies and this copy is made available for public scrutiny. In practice, large companies also send copies of their accounts to financial analysts and journalists. They will also usually comply with a request from any private individual for a copy of the accounts.

Over the years successive Companies Acts have sought to increase the extent of regulation concerning the preparation, form and content of company financial reports. Thus, statutory requirements now cover such areas as the accounting principles to be adopted, the financial items to be disclosed and the format of the financial statements. The requirements are now fairly comprehensive and try to ensure that, from a shareholders' perspective, the accounts provide a useful basis for investment decision making in addition to fulfilling a stewardship role, i.e. the honest reporting by directors of what has been done with shareholder funds. It should be noted, however, that small and medium-sized companies are exempt from many of the disclosure requirements set out in the Companies Acts.

Activity 2

Is it really necessary for laws to be enacted to protect the interests of shareholders? Would it not be acceptable for shareholders to agree with the directors the kind of financial information they require?

Many would object to this idea. It may well be possible for shareholders to agree a suitable set of financial information with the directors. However, shareholders are not the only users of accounting information and therefore this could pose problems for other users. It could also lead to small shareholders being disadvantaged.

This approach to disclosure would almost certainly lead to significant variations in disclosure between companies. This, in turn, may create problems for potential investors.

Activity 3

Can you think of any reason why smaller companies are exempt from certain accounting provisions of the Companies Acts?

We could think of two reasons which are, to some extent, linked. These are:

- *Compliance with accounting requirements costs money, at least in terms of accountants' time. In some cases, this cost will be much the same for all companies, irrespective of their size. This means that the burden of compliance falls proportionately more heavily on smaller companies.*
- *It is likely to be the case that users of the accounts of small companies have other means of obtaining information about the company. For example, in very many small companies the shareholders are fairly close to the directors; indeed all the shareholders may be directors. In these circumstances, information about the company will probably be freely available to all the shareholders. Creditors often do not rely on the accounts of small companies in making their credit decisions. Such decisions are more frequently made on the view of the creditors of the reliability of the directors. It is quite common for the directors of small companies personally to guarantee loans and credit given to the company. This has the effect of making a loan to a company much the same, in terms of limited liability, as a loan to a human individual.*

The law tends to take the view that it is not necessary for smaller companies to bear the burden of full compliance.

The balance sheet and profit and loss account

Company law, in an effort to standardize the presentation of financial reports, prescribes that the published balance sheet and profit and loss account should adhere to certain formats. The law permits a choice of two formats for the balance sheet and a choice of four formats for the profit and loss account. These formats are shown in Appendix 1 to this chapter. With regard to the balance sheet formats, it appears that format 1 is the more widely used in the UK. You may have noticed that the vertical balance sheets used in previous chapters were based on this format. The formats for published profit and loss accounts indicate that a substantial amount of information must be disclosed. However, expenses are typically grouped under very broad headings and the published version of the profit and loss account is thus likely to be far less informative than that produced for internal management purposes.

As a substantial amount of information has to be disclosed it is not always possible to contain the information within the financial statements themselves, and recourse is often taken to the use of supporting notes. Thus, in looking at a set of published accounts, it is important to read the notes in conjunction with the main financial statements. A more detailed set of items which must be disclosed is included in Appendix 2 to this chapter. It is important to recognize that the law prescribes the minimum information to be disclosed. In practice, this minimum is often exceeded.

In addition to setting out the items to be disclosed and the format of the main financial statements, the law also states the accounting principles which must be adopted in preparing these statements. These principles are as follows:

(a) the company is presumed to be carrying on business as a going concern;
(b) accounting principles will be applied consistently between years;
(c) the amount of a particular item will be determined on a prudent (conservative) basis;
(d) the accruals concept will be applied in determining profits;
(e) each component of asset or liability will be separately determined in determining the aggregate figure to be shown in the accounts.

These principles have been widely applied in the preparation of accounts by companies for many years, but have only been incorporated into statute law in fairly recent times.

As we saw earlier, the profit and loss account and balance sheet must show a true and fair view of the trading results and financial position of the company. This is an overriding requirement, so much so that the Companies Acts permit the directors to depart from any of the other requirements concerning these financial statements, if they consider that this is necessary, to ensure that a true and fair view is shown. However, the directors must provide details of any departure along with the reasons for them.

The directors' report

In addition to the requirements concerning publication of a balance sheet and profit and loss account, there is also a legal requirement for a company to publish a directors' report. This report must set out, in respect of the financial year in question, a review of the development of the business of the company (and its subsidiaries) during the year and their position at the end of it. The report should contain details of the following:

- names of directors at any time in the period
- proposed dividends
- proposed transfers to reserves
- principal activities of the company (and its subsidiaries) and of any changes
- significant changes in fixed assets
- an indication of the difference between book and market values of land and buildings
- details of directors' shareholdings and debentures in the company at the start and close of the year.
- details of UK political and charitable donations where the average number of employees is over 250, details of employment and training of disabled people, health, safety and welfare at work of the company's employees and the involvement of employees in the affairs, policy and performance of the company
- important post-balance-sheet events
- the company's likely future developments
- the company's research and development activities
- the company's acquisition of its own shares.

The Companies Acts do not specify a particular format for the directors' report.

The auditors' report

Most companies are required to appoint an independent firm of auditors. The auditors make a report to the shareholders which expresses their opinion as to whether:

(a) the balance sheet gives a true and fair view of the state of affairs at the balance sheet date:
(b) the profit and loss account gives a true and fair view of the profit or loss for the period;
(c) the accounts have been prepared in accordance with the Companies Act 1985.

To help them to form an opinion of the accounts, the auditors have the right of access to the company's underlying financial records at all times. They are also entitled to expect to be able to obtain information and explanations from the company's officers. If the auditors are not satisfied in any of the areas mentioned above they have a duty to qualify their report and set out the reason for this qualification. They must also qualify their report if they believe that the contents of the directors' report is inconsistent with the published accounts.

It is important to be clear that the auditors report their *opinion* on the truth and fairness of the accounts. They do not certify that the accounts are correct. The opinion is reached as a result of close examination of the balance sheet and the profit and loss account and by examining a sample of the documents and records on which those accounting statements are based.

Small companies are exempt from the legal requirement to appoint auditors.

Activity 4
Can you suggest why the law requires the audit of the published accounts of limited companies?

The answer really picks up the point made by Activity 1, namely that it is in the best interests of society for the position of creditors and shareholders to be protected. Part of this protection is in the form of information, supplied by the directors, on various aspects of the company's recent past activities and position. Clearly the directors have a vested interest in this information painting as rosy a picture of the company's fortunes as possible. In order that users of the information have a reasonable level of confidence in the accounting statements, they are subjected to audit. The auditors are required by law to be professionally qualified accountants. This should mean that the auditors will be skilled, experienced, independent and objective. The auditors have been seen as watchdogs of the shareholders, watching over the reporting activities of the directors.

**14.5
Stock Exchange
requirements**

The requirements of the Stock Exchange are broadly concerned with the provision of more detailed information than is required by law. These requirements must be complied with by all companies listed on the Stock Exchange. (A company is said to be 'listed' if its shares are traded on the Stock Exchange.) The main requirements are as follows:

- the annual accounts must be published within six months of the relevant year-end;
- the annual accounts must include a geographical analysis of turnover, the principal country in which each subsidiary operates, details of borrowings falling within certain time categories, details of companies in which 20% or more of the equity is held, and the amount of interest capitalized by the company;
- the accounts must include explanations concerning any significant departures from accounting standards or any significant variation between actual trading results and published forecast results;
- publication of a half-yearly or interim report setting out details concerning turnover, profit, taxation and dividends.

Any company which fails to adhere to these regulations could be removed from the Stock Exchange list. This would mean the company's shares could not be traded on the market.

Activity 5
Why is removal from the Stock Exchange list of any importance to the company and its directors?
You may not have come across this point before, but you should be able to think through the answer.

In general, potential investors will only be prepared to buy shares in a company where they know that the opportunity to sell these shares, in an orderly market, exists. Removal of a company's shares from the Stock Exchange list is likely to mean, therefore, that the company would find it extremely difficult to raise new money from a share issue. Perhaps more importantly, in the short term, existing shareholders are likely to become very unhappy about their inability to sell their shares. This could well have repercussions for the directors, whose right to be directors depends on being elected by the shareholders.

Activity 6

Obtain a copy of the published accounts of a limited company. Examine them so as to satisfy yourself that you are aware of their contents.

Self-assessment question 14.1

The following information was extracted from the accounts of Marina Plc as as 31 December 2000.

	£000
Preference share capital – £1 shares fully paid (10%)	500
Ordinary share capital – 50p shares fully paid	1,000
General reserve	200
Share premium	200
Profit and loss account balance as at 1 January	50
Sales	5,000
Sales returns	50
Purchases	3,000
Purchases return	100
Carriage in	50
Wages and salaries	
– production/warehousing	200
– administration	200
– selling and distribution	400
Motor expenses	
– administration	20
– distribution	80
General distribution expenses	350
General administration expenses	150
Debenture interest	28
Directors remuneration	200
Bad debts	120
Discount allowed	50

Discount received	20
Debentures (redeemable in 2002) 7%	400
Loans repayable within one year	100
Bank overdraft	43
Debtors	600
Creditors	200
Stock	250
Premises (cost)	2,000
Plant and Machinery (cost)	120
Vehicles (cost)	200
Depreciation provision (plant and machinery)	30
Depreciation provision (vehicles)	50
Interim preference dividend paid	25

Notes: the following are not incorporated into the figures above:

(a) Stock at 31 December was valued at £300,000
(b) Depreciation of vehicles is to be apportioned 20% administration 80% distribution
(c) Depreciation of plant and machinery is to be regarded as an expense of distribution
(d) Plant and machinery is to be depreciated at the rate of 20% on cost. Vehicles are to be depreciated at 25% on cost
(e) Corporation tax on profits for the year is estimated to be £58,000, payable in nine months time
(f) £20,000 is to be transferred to the general reserve
(g) The final preference dividend is to be paid, along with an ordinary dividend of 6%

Required
(a) A trading and profit and loss account for the year ending 31 December 2000, for internal use.
(b) A profit and loss statement for the year ending 31 December, and a balance sheet as at 31 December in a format suitable for publication.

14.6 Accounting standards

The need for standards

It has been made clear in previous chapters that accounting is not an exact science. There are several areas where subjective judgement is required in determining the appropriate accounting policy to be followed. In particular, judgement is required when allocating certain costs and revenues between accounting periods and when valuing assets. Depreciation, stock valuation and the treatment of doubtful debts (see Chapters 6-8) provide examples of the need for subjective judgement in cost allocation and asset valuation decisions. The problem of employing subjective judgement in preparing accounts is that different judgements concerning what is appropriate can lead to quite different views of financial position and performance.

In order to illustrate this point consider the following example:

Example

Dee Ltd and Gee Ltd operate in the same industry. Both companies commenced trading on 1 January. During the year to 31 December they have the following financial data:

	Dee Ltd £	Gee Ltd £
Sales	180,000	180,000
Expenses (excluding depreciation)	15,000	15,000
Purchases	90,000	90,000
Land purchased, at cost	100,000	100,000
Plant and machinery purchased, at cost	40,000	40,000
Debtors	50,000	50,000
Cash	50,000	50,000
Share capital	160,000	160,000

Both companies believed that the plant and machinery would last for five years, with no residual value. Dee Ltd uses the sum-of-the-digits method to depreciate the assets, Gee Ltd uses the straight-line method. Dee Ltd uses the LIFO method of stock valuation, which values closing stock at £18,000, whereas Gee Ltd uses the FIFO method of stock valuation, which values closing stock at £25,000 (assume that both companies have identical stock levels).

The profit and loss account for the year ended 31 December and the balance sheet as at 31 December, for each company, would appear as follows:

Profit and loss accounts for the year ended 31 December

	Dee Ltd £	Gee Ltd £
Sales	180,000	180,000
Less: Cost of sales		
(purchases, less closing stock)	(72,000)	(65,000)
Gross profit	108,000	115,000
Expenses	(15,000)	(15,000)
Depreciation*	(13,333)	(8,000)
Net profit	79,667	92,000

*Depreciation was calculated as follows:
Dee Ltd £40,000/5 = £8,000.
Gee Ltd $(£40,000 \times 5)/(5 + 4 + 3 + 2 + 1) = £13,333$

Balance sheets as at 31 December

Fixed assets	£	£
Land	100,000	100,000
Plant and machinery, at cost	40,000	40,000
less: Depreciation	(13,333)	(8,000)
	126,667	132,000
Current assets		
Stock	18,000	25,000
Debtors	50,000	50,000
Cash	45,000	45,000
	239,667	252,000
Represented by:		
Share capital	160,000	160,000
Profit retained	79,667	92,000
	239,667	252,000

As we shall see in later chapters, a popular means of assessing the performance of a business is to compare the profit for a period with the investment of the owners (return on capital employed). The measures for these two companies are:

Dee Ltd $79,667/239,667 = 33\%$

Gee Ltd $92,000/252,000 = 37\%$

It should be particularly noted that the judgements made in preparing the accounts of these two companies were not at all unreasonable or extreme.

This example illustrates that, despite each company having the same basic financial data, different judgements concerning the most appropriate accounting policies to be followed lead to quite different results for the year. This means, of course, that the more the preparation of accounts can be influenced by the subjective judgement of the preparers, the more difficult it becomes to make proper comparisons between different companies.

Subjective judgement is an unavoidable and important part of preparing financial accounts. However, many users do not appear fully to appreciate the role, or extent, of subjectivity in accounting. For some users, it does not seem possible for there to be a number of acceptable ways of preparing accounts or that preparers can determine what is acceptable for a particular company.

In the late 1960s, a series of mergers between companies highlighted the problems of permitting discretion in preparing financial statements. In particular, the takeover of AEI Ltd by GEC Ltd aroused considerable concern among users at the time. Briefly, the facts were that, following an agreed takeover by GEC Ltd, the management of AEI Ltd published a profit forecast for the accounting year which was near to completion. The forecast profit was £10 million. However, after the takeover the actual results for AEI Ltd as reported by GEC Ltd, was a £4.5 million loss. The difference of £14.5 million between the forecast and actual result was attributed, in part, to matters of fact (£5 million) but the remainder was attributed to matters of judgement (£9.5 million), i.e. applying different accounting policies to the basic financial data.

Following this and other accounting 'scandals' resulting from merger activities, the financial press, through its letter columns and articles, criticized the accountancy profession for permitting too much discretion to preparers. It was argued that comparability of financial results between companies was being seriously undermined because of the excessive 'licence' given to preparers and that, as a result, users could be seriously misled.

Activity 7
Can you think of any arguments which justify preparers of accounting information retaining discretion over the way in which financial reports are prepared?

The arguments, which have been put forward by various people, include:

- *Discretion might facilitate the reflection of a corporate personality, with risk-averse companies adopting very conservative accounting policies, and risk-seeking companies doing the opposite. This reflection might provide users of accounts with further information about the company.*
- *Use of discretion would permit a company to adopt accounting procedures considered to be most appropriate to its particular needs and circumstances. Since no two companies' needs and circumstances are identical, a 'horses for courses' approach to making accounting judgements, might be useful.*
- *Accounting standards may ossify accounting procedures, and inhibit development. Rule makers tend often not to be great innovators.*

The response of the accountancy profession

In December 1969, the public debate and criticism of the accounting profession led the Institute of Chartered Accountants in England and Wales (the largest of the UK professional accountancy bodies) to publish a *Statement of Intent on Accounting Standards in the 1970s*. In this document the Institute undertook to 'narrow the areas of difference and variety in accounting practice by publishing authoritative statements on best accounting practice which will, wherever possible, be definitive.'

The structure within which accounting standards have been created and enforced has developed over the years since 1969. The present institutional arrangements are now briefly described.

A body known as the Financial Reporting Council (FRC) is concerned with broad policy issues. Its membership is drawn from various interest groups including accounting practices, local and central government, industry and banking. The aims of this body are:

- to establish the overall direction of standard setting by providing the standard-setting body with guidance on its work programme
- to promote good financial reporting practice by preparing reports on financial reporting standards and exerting influence on government for legislative change where appropriate.

The FRC acts through two subsidiary bodies. One of these is the Accounting Standards Board (ASB). The ASB is charged with implementing the programme of standard-setting drawn up by the FRC. Its aim is to establish and improve standards of financial accounting and reporting, for the benefit of users, preparers, and auditors of financial information.

The ASB has an offshoot which is known as the Urgent Issues Task Force. The purpose of the task force is to consider and deal with an emerging issue quickly. It is able to provide guidance on certain issues which require a rapid solution without the necessity of undertaking widespread consultation with various interest groups.

The other body through which the FRC acts is the Financial Reporting Review Panel. The panel's role is to identify important departures from accounting standards, in the published accounts of companies, which could result in the accounts not showing a true and fair view of their financial position and/or performance. Where a particular departure is considered to be unacceptable, the directors of the company will be expected to amend the accounts. Failure to do so could result in the Review Panel (or the Secretary of State or the Stock Exchange) applying to the courts to require the directors of the company to comply with the legal requirement that the accounts show a true and fair view.

Activity 8

Should the setting of standards be the sole responsibility of accountants? Do you believe that non-accountants should be involved in the standard-setting process? Give reasons for your position.

Although accountants, as a profession, have considerable technical expertise, accounting reports are probably too important to leave to the profession alone. Accounting reports are for users, not accountants. Users and preparers can both bring different perspectives to the standard-setting process.

Setting accounting standards

In formulating an accounting standard on a particular topic the ASB undertakes considerable deliberation and consultation. The final outcome of these deliberations and consultations is a Financial Reporting Standard (FRS), often referred to as an 'accounting standard'. This is a document which sets out rules prescribing the way in which accounting reports should be prepared and/or presented. Generally, FRSs are meant to be adhered to in respect of all financial reports designed to give a true and fair view of profits earned and of financial position. However, there are some standards which apply only to larger companies. FRSs used to be known as Statements of Standard Accounting Practice (SSAP).

The preparation of a standard involves various stages. The major stages are often as follows:

1 identifying a suitable topic;
2 commissioning a research study on the topic;
3 preparing a draft FRS which is then published as an exposure draft (FRED);
4 allowing an exposure period of usually six months to give interested parties the opportunity to comment;
5 summarizing and reviewing the comments received and producing a final draft of the FRS.

On the whole, the system of developing FRSs, based on the publication of exposure drafts, has been successful. However, things do not always run smoothly. Occasionally, an exposure draft will provoke such controversy that it has to be withdrawn and a new exposure draft published or, in the extreme, the ASB may feel that the comments received on the exposure draft indicate that it is impossible to proceed with a standard. In some cases a published standard has been revised or withdrawn following criticism of its operation in practice. A list of accounting standards currently in place is given in Appendix 3 to this chapter.

Accounting standards are, in effect, legally binding on companies. This is because accounting standards define what is meant by 'a true and fair view' in particular contexts. Companies are required by law to produce accounts which show such a view. In 1997 a Financial Reporting Standard for Smaller Enterprises (FRSSE) was developed in recognition that the accounting requirements and disclosures for larger entities are not necessarily appropriate for smaller entities. FRSSE is an optional standard that may be applied by companies that would qualify as small under the 1985 Companies Act rules, and other entities that would have qualified as 'small' had they been incorporated.

Activity 9

Accounting standards, in effect, have legal force. Can you think of any good reasons why they are not actually part of the statutes of company law?

We feel that the strongest argument is that there could well be a loss of flexibility if standards are placed on the statute book. At present it is possible to withdraw, and perhaps amend, a particular standard if it is found that the standard is flawed in some way. If, however, the standard were embedded in law this would not be so easy to do. It would be necessary to ask parliament to repeal the relevant law and this may take a considerable amount of time and/or may be resisted by government. It would, for example, be difficult to persuade Members of Parliament that they should devote time to what they may consider to be a fairly obscure issue of financial reporting instead of using that time to discuss, say, the plight of the homeless.

Where a company fails to comply with a particular standard the auditors have a duty to qualify their audit report.

Types of standards

It has been said that accounting standards can be grouped into four main categories. These are as follows:

1 *Description.* These standards require that principles and methods applied in preparing the accounts be described. An example of this type of standard is FRS 15 which is concerned with accounting for tangible fixed assets. This contains no detailed recommendations on the method of depreciation to be adopted for such assets but does require, among other things, that the method of depreciation employed should reflect the pattern of economic benefits from the asset.
2 *Presentation.* These standards prescribe how information should be presented in the accounts. An example of this type of standard is FRS 1. This aims to standardize the way in which various items are presented in the accounts.
3 *Disclosure.* These standards are concerned with how and what information should be disclosed. An example of this type of standard is FRS 1. This standard requires that, for all but the smallest companies, a cash flow statement (see Chapter 17) be included in the financial reports.
4 *Valuation and profit measurement.* These standards are concerned with setting out rules concerning the valuation of assets and the calculation of profit. An example of this type of standard is SSAP 9 which lays down principles concerning the valuation of stocks and work-in-progress.

Some of the standards produced could be assigned to more than one of the categories listed above. Nevertheless, the categories do provide an insight to the issues addressed by the ASB.

14.7 Summary

In this chapter the regulatory framework of accounting has been examined. It has been seen that there are two main sources of regulation – the law and accounting standards. Accounting standards are designed to complement the law and, in effect, have statutory backing. For companies which are listed on the Stock Exchange there are additional regulations emanating from this body. The amount of regulation relating to companies has increased significantly over the years and there is no sign that this trend towards greater regulation is likely to change.

Useful web addresses	Financial Reporting Council www.frc.org.uk Accounting Standards Board www.asb.org.uk

Exercises

1 As a result of the development of the regulatory framework, companies are now required to disclose a great deal of information about their financial affairs. What do you think are the advantages and disadvantages of greater disclosure?

2 The following information has been extracted from the books of Simat Plc, after all the normal transactions of the year ended 31 March 2000 had been recorded:

	£
General distribution expenses	14,580
General administration expenses	17,350
Directors' remuneration	65,900
Debenture interest payable	11,200
Sales	748,850
Purchases	378,650
Wages and salaries	
Administrative	85,390
Distribution	67,400
Depreciation	
Plant and machinery	21,600
Motor vehicles	16,400
Interest receivable	4,200
Bad debts written off	6,380
Profit and loss account balance as at 1 April 1999	87,740
Stock at 1 April 1999	65,100
Auditors' remuneration	6,000

Notes

(a) Stock at 31 March 2000 was valued at £68,000.
(b) Corporation tax on profits for the year is estimated at £19,800.
(c) Ordinary dividend proposed is £20,000.
(d) £21,000 is to be appropriated to fixed asset replacement reserve.
(e) Depreciation of plant and machinery should be apportioned two-thirds administration and one-third distribution. Depreciation of motor vehicles should be divided equally between administration and distribution.

Required
(a) A trading and profit and loss account for internal purposes.
(b) A trading and profit and loss account for publication, using format 1.

Appendix 1: Companies Act 1985: formats for accounts

Balance sheet formats

Format 1

A Called-up share capital not paid
B Fixed assets
  I Intangible assets
    (i) Development costs
    (ii) Concessions, patents, licences, trade marks and similar rights and assets
    (iii) Goodwill
    (iv) Payments on account
  II Tangible assets
    (i) Land and buildings
    (ii) Plant and machinery
    (iii) Fixtures, fittings, tools and equipment
    (iv) Payments on account and assets in course of construction
  III Investments
    (i) Shares in group companies
    (ii) Loans to group companies
    (iii) Shares in related companies
    (iv) Loans to related companies
    (v) Other investments other than loans
    (vi) Other loans
    (vii) Own shares
C Current assets
  I Stocks
    (i) Raw materials and consumables
    (ii) Work-in-progress
    (iii) Finished goods and goods for resale
    (iv) Payments on account
  II Debtors
    (i) Trade debtors
    (ii) Amounts owed by group companies
    (iii) Amounts owed by related companies
    (iv) Other debtors
    (v) Called-up share capital not paid
    (vi) Prepayments and accrued income
  III Investments
    (i) Shares in group companies
    (ii) Own shares
    (iii) Other investments
  IV Cash at bank and in hand
D Prepayments and accrued income
E Creditors: amounts falling due within 1 year
    (i) Debenture loans
    (ii) Bank loans and overdrafts
    (iii) Payments received on account

(iv) Trade creditors
(v) Bills of exchange payable
(vi) Amounts owed to group companies
(vii) Amounts owed to related companies
(viii) Other creditors including taxation and social security
(ix) Accruals and deferred income
F Net current assets (liabilities)
G Total assets less current liabilities
H Creditors: amounts falling due after more than 1 year
(i) Debenture loans
(ii) Bank loans and overdrafts
(iii) Payments received on account
(iv) Trade creditors
(v) Bills of exchange payable
(vi) Amounts owed to group companies
(vii) Amounts owed to related companies
(viii) Other creditors, including taxation and social security
(ix) Accruals and deferred income
I Provisions for liabilities and charges
(i) Pensions and similar obligations
(ii) Taxation, including deferred taxation
(iii) Other provisions
J Accruals and deferred income
K Capital and reserves
I Called-up share capital
II Share premium account
III Revaluation reserve
IV Other reserves
(i) Capital redemption reserve
(ii) Reserve for own shares
(iii) Reserves provided for by the articles of association
(iv) Other reserves
V Profit and loss account

Format 2

Assets
A Called-up share capital not paid
B Fixed assets
I Intangible assets
(i) Development costs
(ii) Concessions, patents, licences, trade marks and similar rights and assets
(iii) Goodwill
(iv) Payments on account

II Tangible assets
    (i) Land and buildings
    (ii) Plant and machinery
    (iii) Fixtures, fittings, tools and equipment
    (iv) Payments on account and assets in course of construction
III Investments
    (i) Shares in group companies
    (ii) Loans to group companies
    (iii) Shares in related companies
    (iv) Loans to related companies
    (v) Other investments other than loans
    (vi) Other loans
    (vii) Own shares
C Current assets
  I Stocks
    (i) Raw materials and consumables
    (ii) Work-in-progress
    (iii) Finished goods and goods for resale
    (iv) Payments on account
  II Debtors
    (i) Trade debtors
    (ii) Amounts owed by group companies
    (iii) Amounts owed by related companies
    (iv) Other debtors
    (v) Called-up share capital not paid
    (vi) Prepayments and accrued income
  III Investments
    (i) Shares in group companies
    (ii) Own shares
    (iii) Other investments
  IV Cash at bank and in hand
D Prepayments and accrued income

Liabilities
A Capital and reserves
  I Called-up share capital
  II Share premium account
  III Revaluation reserve
  IV Other reserves
    (i) Capital redemption reserve
    (ii) Reserve for own shares
    (iii) Reserves provided for by the articles of association
    (iv) Other reserves
  V Profit and loss account

B Provisions for liabilities and charges
  (i) Pensions and similar obligations
  (ii) Taxation including deferred taxation
  (iii) Other provisions
C Creditors
  (i) Debenture loans
  (ii) Bank loans and overdrafts
  (iii) Payments received on account
  (iv) Trade creditors
  (v) Bills of exchange payable
  (vi) Amounts owed to group companies
  (vii) Amounts owed to related companies
  (viii) Other creditors including taxation and social security
  (ix) Accruals and deferred income
D Accruals and deferred income

Profit and loss account formats

Format 1

1 Turnover
2 Cost of sales
3 Gross profit or loss
4 Distribution costs
5 Administrative expenses
6 Other operating income
7 Income from shares in group companies
8 Income from shares in related companies
9 Income from other fixed asset investments
10 Other interest receivable and similar income
11 Amounts written off investments
12 Interest payable and similar charges
13 Tax on profit or loss on ordinary activities
14 Profit or loss on ordinary activities after taxation
15 Extraordinary income
16 Extraordinary charges
17 Extraordinary profit or loss
18 Tax on extraordinary profit or loss
19 Other taxes not shown under the above items
20 Profit or loss for the financial year

Format 2

1 Turnover
2 Change in stocks of finished goods and in work-in-progress
3 Own work capitalized
4 Other operating income
5 (a) Raw materials and consumables
  (b) Other external charges

6 Staff costs
   (a) Wages and salaries
   (b) Social security costs
   (c) Other pension costs
7 (a) Depreciation and other amounts written off tangible and intangible fixed assets
   (b) Exceptional amounts written off current assets
8 Other operating charges
9 Income from shares in group companies
10 Income from shares in group companies
11 Income from other fixed-asset investments
12 Other interest receivable and similar income
13 Amounts written off investments
14 Interest payable and similar charges
15 Tax on profit or loss on ordinary activities
16 Profit or loss on ordinary activities after taxation
17 Extraordinary income
18 Extraordinary charges
19 Extraordinary profit or loss
20 Tax on extraordinary profit or loss
21 Other taxes not shown under the above items
22 Profit or loss for the financial year

Format 3

A Charges
     (i) Cost of sales
    (ii) Distribution costs
   (iii) Administration expenses
   (iv) Amounts written off investments
    (v) Interest payable and similar charges
   (vi) Tax on profit or loss on ordinary activities
  (vii) Profit or loss on ordinary activities after taxation
 (viii) Extraordinary charges
   (ix) Tax on extraordinary profit or loss
    (x) Other taxes not shown under the above items
   (xi) Profit or loss for the financial year
B Income
     (i) Turnover
    (ii) Other operating income
   (iii) Income from shares in group companies
   (iv) Income from shares in related companies
    (v) Income from other fixed-asset investments
   (vi) Other interest receivable and similar income
  (vii) Profit or loss on ordinary activities after taxation
 (viii) Extraordinary income
   (ix) Profit or loss for the financial year

Format 4

A Charges
- (i) Reduction in stocks of finished goods and in work-in-progress
- (ii) (a) Raw materials and consumables
  - (b) Other external charges
- (iii) Staff costs
  - (a) Wages and salaries
  - (b) Social security costs
  - (c) Other pension costs
- (iv) (a) Depreciation and other amounts written off tangible and intangible fixed assets
  - (b) Exceptional amounts written off current assets
- (v) Other operating charges
- (vi) Amounts written off investments
- (vii) Interest payable and similar charges
- (viii) Tax on profit or loss on ordinary activities
- (ix) Profit or loss on ordinary activities after taxation
- (x) Extraordinary charges
- (xi) Tax on extraordinary profit or loss
- (xii) Other taxes not shown under the above items
- (xiii) Profit or loss for the financial year

B Income
- (i) Turnover
- (ii) Increase in stocks of finished goods and in work-in-progress
- (iii) Own work capitalized
- (iv) Other operating income
- (v) Income from shares in group companies
- (vi) Income from shares in related companies
- (vii) Income from other fixed-asset investments
- (viii) Other interest receivable and similar income
- (ix) Profit or loss on ordinary activities after taxation
- (x) Extraordinary income
- (xi) Profit or loss for the financial year

Appendix 2: Items which must be disclosed	The Companies Act 1985 includes a number of specific disclosure requirements. The more important of these are given below, but it must be recognized that this list is not intended to be exhaustive. Disclosure may be within the formats provided and/or by way of notes to the accounts.
General requirements	(a) Accounting policies (b) Corresponding figures for the preceding year, for every item in the profit and loss account or balance sheet.

Disclosure requirements relating to the balance sheet

(a) Share capital and debentures – including the authorized capital, the number and aggregate value of shares of each class, information about redeemable preference shares, and details of any share or debenture issues.

(b) Fixed assets – showing associated depreciation provisions.

(c) Investments – broken down into listed and other, showing the aggregate market value if different to the amount stated.

(d) Movements in reserves and provisions.

(e) Taxation, including the basis on which the charge for UK corporation tax is computed.

(f) Details of indebtedness – divided into that which is due within five years and beyond five years. Terms of repayment and interest, details of any security given, and the amounts of any cumulative dividends in arrears must all be given.

(g) Guarantees and other financial commitments, including such items as details of contracts for capital expenditure and pension commitments.

(h) Aggregate dividends.

Disclosure requirements relating to the profit and loss account

(a) The amount of the company's profit and loss on ordinary activities before taxation.

(b) Certain kinds of income and expense must be separately stated. These include interest on bank loans, interest on other loans, income from listed investments, rent from land, payments for the hire of plant and machinery and auditors' remuneration.

(c) Prior-year adjustments. These are amounts reported in the preceding financial statements as retained earnings which have been materially altered because of a change in accounting policies or the discovery of a fundamental error.

(d) Extraordinary income or expenses. These are amounts derived from transactions outside the ordinary activities of the company.

(e) The effect of any transactions that are exceptional by virtue of size or incidence, even though they fall within the ordinary activities of the company.

(f) Particulars of turnover, broken down by class of business and geographical markets.

(g) Particulars of staff, including the average number of persons employed in the year, the aggregate remuneration, social security costs and pension costs.

(h) The basis of any foreign-currency translation.

(i) Transfers to and from reserves and the aggregate amount of any dividends paid or proposed.

Other miscellaneous points

Schedule 5 of the Companies Act 1985 identifies a number of additional matters which must be disclosed in the annual accounts, either within the accounts or in a note to these accounts. Schedule 5 covers a number of areas, the most important of which relate to the following:

(a) the disclosure of particulars of the company's subsidiaries (i.e. companies which are partly or fully owned to such an extent that they can be effectively controlled) and of its other shareholdings;
(b) the disclosure of financial information relating to subsidiaries;
(c) the emoluments of directors (including emoluments waived), pensions of directors and past directors and compensation for loss of office to directors and past directors;
(d) the disclosure of the number of the company's employees who are remunerated at higher rates;
(e) particulars of loans and other transactions favouring directors and officers.

Appendix 3: UK accounting standards currently in force

SSAP 2 Disclosure of accounting policies
SSAP 4 Accounting for government grants
SSAP 5 Accounting for value added tax
SSAP 8 The treatment of taxation under the imputation system in the accounts of companies
SSAP 9 Stocks and long-term contracts
SSAP 13 Accounting for research and development
SSAP 15 Accounting for deferred tax
SSAP 17 Accounting for post-balance-sheet events
SSAP 19 Accounting for investment properties
SSAP 20 Foreign-currency translation
SSAP 21 Accounting for leases and hire purchase contracts
SSAP 24 Accounting for pension costs
SSAP 25 Segmental accounting
　FRS 1 Cash flow statements
　FRS 2 Accounting for subsidiary undertakings
　FRS 3 Reporting financial performance
　FRS 4 Capital instruments
　FRS 5 Reporting the substance of transactions
　FRS 6 Acquisitions and mergers
　FRS 7 Fair values in acquisition accounting
　FRS 9 Related party disclosures
FRS 10 Goodwill and intangible assets
FRS 11 Impairment of fixed assets and goodwill
FRS 12 Provisions, contingent liabilities and contingent assets
FRS 13 Derivatives and other financial instruments: disclosures
FRS 14 Earnings per share
FRS 15 Tangible fixed assets

Chapter 15

The accounts of groups of companies: 1

15.1 Introduction

The treatment of company accounts so far has dealt with single companies. In fact many companies form into groups, for a variety of reasons. Indeed, most large, well-known 'companies' are, in fact, groups. Accounting for groups of companies has its own particular aspects. The next two chapters aim to provide you with an appreciation of these aspects, so as to enable you to be able to understand a set of published accounts for a group of companies, and to apply the principles dealt with in subsequent chapters to groups as well as to individual companies. This chapter deals with general issues and the balance sheet, while Chapter 16 deals with the group profit and loss account.

15.2 Objectives

On completion of this chapter you should be able to:

- state the reasons why companies buy shares in the ownership of other companies;
- explain the nature of a holding company/subsidiary relationship;
- explain the rationale underlying the preparation of a set of group accounts;
- prepare a simple group balance sheet.

15.3 Shareholdings in other companies

One company can become a shareholder of another company in a number of ways, and for a variety of reasons. The accounting treatment of such transactions will vary depending upon the size and nature of the investment, and can be divided into the following broad types.

(a) A company may have liquid resources in excess of those which it needs immediately to finance its normal commercial activities. Rather than placing cash in a bank deposit account or in some other fixed-interest-bearing deposit, the company's treasurer may decide to make an investment in the share of another company. This will probably expose the investor company to a higher level of risk than would an investment in a deposit account. It will also, however, expose the investor company to the possibility that the returns, in terms of dividends and capital gains, could be very much higher than those normally associated with fixed-interest deposits. In such circumstances, the investment would probably represent a *relatively small portion of the total ownership of the other company*. From an accounting point of view, such an investment is easily dealt with in the final accounts of the investor company. The investment will be shown as an asset, valued at cost. Any dividends from the investment would appear in the profit and loss account as income.

(b) A company may own a *substantial, but not a controlling, portion of another company*. Here the objective of the investor company might be to exert influence over the other company. In practice, to own 20% of a company's shares may easily be sufficient to be able to exercise considerable influence. This might be because the remainder of the shares are owned by a relatively large group of unconnected shareholders, possibly many of whom take little interest in the company, except as a fairly remote investment. The way in which the investor company deals with the investment, and with the income from that investment, when it holds a substantial but not a controlling interest in another company, will be considered in the next chapter under the heading Associated Companies.

(c) A company may own a *majority of the shares of another company and therefore be in a position to control that company*. This may have arisen from purchasing shares of an existing previously unconnected company or perhaps from forming a new company to undertake a new activity into which the company is expanding. This establishes a group. Most of the rest of this chapter will consider how the final accounting requirements of the investor company are affected by the group situation. Before considering group accounts, however, it may be useful briefly to consider the reasons for the existence of groups of companies.

15.4 **Reasons for the existence of groups**	Most businesses wish to expand or grow.

Activity 1

Can you think of reasons why businesses seek to expand? Even if you have never formally studied this you should be able to make some guesses using your common sense.

The reasons we came up with are:

- *The elimination or at least reduction in competition.*
- *Safeguarding sources of supply or sales outlets.*
- *Access to the economies of scale available to larger businesses.*
- *Risk reduction through diversification.*

Organic expansion by taking on more staff, developing new sources of supply, products, processes and markets can be a time-consuming way of achieving expansion. It may be easier, and more appropriate, to buy an existing business. In these circumstances three main possibilities exist:

1 Assets can be purchased from an existing business, with the purchase consideration being cash, debentures or shares. The selling business is then wound up. This process is typically referred to as *acquisition* or *absorption*. Since only one company remains after the acquisition, the final accounts of that company follow the normal pattern.

2 Assets of two or more businesses can be sold to a new company, and the existing businesses wound up. This process is typically referred to as *amalgamation*. Again, since only one company remains, the final accounts raise no new questions.

3 Shares may be purchased in another company. Clearly, if enough shares in another company are purchased, the activities of that company can be effectively controlled by the investor company. There is no winding up of either business. Where effective control is achieved, a parent/subsidiary relationship arises. This is usually known as a *takeover* or *merger*. In practice, probably the most popular means of acquiring an existing business is to buy enough shares to control it. The purchase consideration for the shares of the potential subsidiary may be cash, i.e. the shareholders of what will become the subsidiary company receive cash from the potential parent company for their shares. More common, however, is the exchange of shares or the issuing of potential parent company loan stock to satisfy at least part of the purchase consideration. Here the potential parent company issues new shares and/or loan stocks which are transferred to the shareholders of the subsidiary. Thus, those who were shareholders of the subsidiary become share and/or loan stockholders of the parent company and the parent company takes their place as shareholders of the subsidiary. Share exchanges tend to be quite popular with potential parent companies since they involve no cash payment. Quite frequently, however, the takeover involves some combination of shares and/or loan stocks and/or cash, in satisfaction of the purchase consideration.

Clearly a company which acquires sufficient shares in another company to control it effectively can wind it up and use the assets as it wishes. However, there are advantages in not doing so.

Activity 2

Can you think of any reasons for keeping a subsidiary in existence as a separate company, even where it is wholly owned by the parent?

The reasons which occurred to us were:

- **Market identity.** *The directors of the parent company may feel that customers may prefer to deal with what they see as being a small company rather than with a large group.*

- **Administrative convenience.** *It may be felt that the staff of the subsidiary will have a greater feeling of independence and autonomy if it retains its identity as much as possible. This might be seen as likely to lead to a better-motivated staff.*
- **Limited liability.** *The directors of the parent company may prefer to retain the limited liability status of each company individually, rather than all parts of the group being one legal entity.*

Expansion by takeover is not necessarily the only factor leading to the creation of a group. A company may decide that it wishes, for limited liability or other reasons, to have the various parts of the business established as separate companies, all under the umbrella of the original company, which now becomes the parent.

15.5 **The definition of** **a group**	A group consists of two or more companies between which there is a parent/subsidiary relationship. A parent company is also known as a *holding company*. The 1989 Companies Act sets out a number of criteria which need to be satisfied for a company to be classified as a holding company. These typically relate to some aspect of control, as exercised by one company over another. Probably the most obvious form of control, and the one which will be assumed for the remainder of this chapter, relates to control of the voting rights. A holding company can thus be defined as one which controls another by holding a majority of the voting rights of that company. For effective control to exist there must be a right to appoint or remove directors having a majority of voting rights at board meetings. A subsidiary is thus a company which is effectively controlled by another company.

For the remainder of this chapter it will be assumed that to own more than 50% of the ordinary shares gives control and a group, therefore, exists. In practice, this is the basis of most group relationships.

15.6 **Types of group**	This arises where one holding company has control directly over one or more others, as follows:

Direct group	Holding company H Plc Subsidiaries S1 Ltd S2 Ltd S3 Ltd S4 Ltd

Here H Plc owns a majority of the ordinary shares of each of the four subsidiaries. The investment in the shares of each of the subsidiaries will appear as assets in the balance sheet of H Plc.

Vertical group	This arises where the holding company has a subsidiary with its own subsidiary, as follows:

Holding company   H ↓ Plc
Subsidiaries   S1 ↓ Ltd
                     S2 ↓ Ltd

Here the investment in the shares of S1 Ltd will appear in the balance sheet of H Plc and the investment in the shares of S2 Ltd will appear in the balance sheet of S1 Ltd. Both S1 Ltd and S2 Ltd are subsidiaries of H Plc. This will still be true if H Plc owns only slightly over half of the ordinary shares of S1 Ltd which in turn owns just over half of the shares in S2 Ltd. In these circumstances H Plc would only own just over a quarter of the shares of S2 Ltd. However, H Plc will control S1 Ltd, which in turn controls S2 Ltd. So the three companies form a group under the control of H Plc. A company like S2 Ltd in this context would usually be referred to as a sub-subsidiary.

Mixed group

This is where the holding company has two or more subsidiaries and at least one sub-subsidiary.

Holding company   /H Plc \
Subsidiaries   S1 Ltd   S2 Ltd
                   S3 Ltd

Some very complicated relationships can arise. Given the aim of this chapter, which is to provide an *appreciation* of group accounts, it will be restricted to direct groups. The principles remain the same in more complex groups. Implementation just becomes rather more laborious.

15.7 Group accounts: the legal framework

No matter what the strict legal position of a subsidiary may be, the practical, economic reality is that it is wholly under the control of the parent company. This is just as true irrespective of whether the parent owns just 50% of the shares or all of them. A group can quite logically be seen as one single business which is all under the control of the shareholders, acting through the directors, of the holding or parent company. In effect, the holding company controls the entire group. Accounting tends to try to reflect economic reality, rather than the strict legal position. This explains why all the subsidiary's assets and external claims are incorporated in the group balance sheet, even where the subsidiary is less than 100% owned by the parent.

The existence of a group of companies typically requires the presentation of a set of group accounts. The main objective of a set of group accounts is to disclose the results and state of affairs of the group as if it were a single company. The 1989 Companies Act provides the most recent update on the preparation of group accounts and effectively implements the European Community (EC) Seventh Directive on the subject.

In effect, UK company law requires that the holding company prepares and publishes a balance sheet and a profit and loss account for the entire group, in each case showing a true and fair view and viewed from the perspective of the shareholders of the holding company. These accounts are known as *group* or *consolidated accounts*. Small or medium-sized companies, or companies which are wholly owned or majority-owned subsidiaries of an EC parent, are exempt.

15.8 Preparation of a set of group accounts

The aim of a set of group accounts is to disclose the state of affairs and the results of the group in such a way as would be appropriate if the assets and liabilities, revenues and expenses of the group were those of a single legal entity. In order to achieve this the assets and claims of the subsidiaries are effectively added to those in the holding company's balance sheet, and the revenues and expenses of the subsidiaries are effectively added to those in the holding company's profit and loss account, subject to certain adjustments.

Before going on to consider group accounts in more detail there are several points which you should be clear about. These are:

(a) The holding company and the subsidiaries need to produce their own final accounts (profit and loss account and balance sheet). From these the group accounts will be prepared. The group accounts do not form part of the formal accounting system of the holding company or any of its subsidiaries.

(b) The only mention of the group relationship in the final accounts of the holding company is an asset *investment in subsidiary*, which will appear on its balance sheet, typically valued at cost to the holding company.

(c) In the final accounts of the subsidiary company, there is no explicit reference to the fact that it is a subsidiary of another company. Company balance sheets do not show who own each of the shares issued; the share capital is simply shown as one total, or at least, one total for each class of shares (ordinary, preference, etc.).

(d) The fact that companies may be members of a group may well affect their behaviour to one another. For example, trading may take place between them to an extent which might not be the case were they not related. Indeed the very reason for the existence of many groups is to promote, or perhaps to force, closer trading links. Where one member of a group has some commercial relationship with another (e.g. buying from, selling to, borrowing from, lending to), these relationships are reflected in the final accounts of the individual companies in very much the same way as if the other company concerned is not a member of that group. As will be seen later in this chapter, when group accounts are prepared, the effect of some of these relationships may well cancel each other out.

15.9 The group balance sheet

This explanation of the preparation of a group balance sheet will restrict itself to consideration of a group containing the holding company and just one subsidiary. In fact, the principles involved are essentially the same in more complex groups. The explanation will start with the most straightforward group situation. After that, consideration will be given to the factors which make things a bit more complicated.

Example

The following balance sheets relate to H Ltd, and S Ltd as at 1 January 1999, immediately after H Ltd had acquired all the share capital of S Ltd for £3 million.

	H Ltd £000	S Ltd £000
Fixed assets	4,500	2,500
Investments in S Ltd	3,000	–
Working capital	1,000	500
	8,500	3,000
Ordinary share capital (£1 shares fully paid)	6,000	2,000
Reserves	2,500	1,000
	8,500	3,000

To prepare a group balance sheet simply involves adding like items in the two balance sheets, except for the investment in S Ltd in the balance sheet of H Ltd and the shares and reserves at the date of acquisition of S Ltd. Since these two are equal in amount and one is an asset while the other is a claim, they completely cancel one another.

The group balance sheet would appear as follows:

Balance sheet as at 1 January 1999

	£000	Workings
Fixed assets	7,000	(4,500 + 2,500)
Working capital	1,500	(1,000 + 500)
	8,500	
Ordinary share capital	6,000	(H Ltd share capital)
Reserves	2,500	(H Ltd share capital)
	8,500	

This example shows the logic of the group balance sheet, bearing in mind that it is meant to show the situation from the viewpoint of the holding company shareholders. The balance sheet shows that these shareholders have a total claim against the group of £8.5 million and that this is presently deployed in financing £7 million of fixed assets and £1.5 million of working capital.

The reason why the investment in S Ltd cancels exactly with the shares and reserves of S Ltd is because H Ltd acquired *all* the shares of S Ltd for the balance sheet value of that company's net assets (£3 million in total, or

£3 per share). As we shall see later, this is a relatively unusual situation. In practice, for one reason and/or another, the two items will not exactly cancel each other.

This example relates to the particular situation which arises at the time of acquisition. In subsequent years, the position is slightly different.

Example

The following balance sheets relate to H Ltd and S Ltd, as at 31 December 2000.

	H Ltd £000	S Ltd £000
Fixed assets	5,500	3,000
Investments in S Ltd	3,000	–
Working capital	2,000	1,000
	10,500	4,000
Ordinary share capital (£1 shares fully paid)	6,000	2,000
Reserves	4,500	2,000
	10,500	4,000

H Ltd acquired all of S Ltd's capital on 1 January 1999 for £3 million when S Ltd's reserves stood at £1 million.

The group balance sheet would appear as follows:

Balance sheet as at 31 December 2000

	£000
Fixed assets	8,500
Working capital	3,000
	11,500
Share capital	6,000
Reserves	5,500
	11,500

In this case it is necessary to distinguish between pre- and post-acquisition reserves of the subsidiary. As was seen in the first example, the cost of the investment in S Ltd cancels out with the share capital and reserves at the time of acquisition, and these represent the net assets obtained at the acquisition. Since that time the net assets of the subsidiary have increased, since profits have been made and (some at least) retained in the reserves. Any profits made and retained by a subsidiary since it became a member of the group will be profits of that group, and as such will be added to group reserves. As we have seen, where pre-acquisition reserves exist they will be cancelled out (together with the share capital) with the investment in the subsidiary.

Activity 3

The following balance sheets relate to H Ltd and S Ltd, as at 31 December 2000

	H Ltd	S Ltd
	£000	£000
Net assets	5,000	4,500
Investments in S Ltd	3,500	–
	8,500	4,500
Ordinary share capital (£1 shares fully paid)	6,000	3,000
Reserves	2,500	1,500
	8,500	4,500

H Ltd acquired all of S Ltd's capital on 1 January 1999, for £3.5 million, when reserves in S Ltd were £500,000.
Prepare a group balance sheet as at 31 December 2000.

Your balance sheet should look something like this:

Balance sheet as at 31 December 2000

	£000	
Net assets	9,500	
Ordinary share capital	6,000	
Reserves	3,500	*£2.5 million in H Ltd and £1 million*
	9,500	*post-acquisition reserves in S Ltd*

Goodwill (or capital reserve) arising on consolidation

In practice, there will be very few cases where the cost of the holding company's investments in a subsidiary will be the same as the book value of net assets acquired. Typically, the amount paid for the investments in the subsidiary will exceed the balance sheet value of the net assets obtained.

Activity 4

Why will the cost of the investment in the subsidiary probably be more than the balance sheet value of that investment?

The reasons which occurred to us were:

- *The various conventions of accounting, particularly the prudence convention, tend to lead to the balance sheet value of assets being understated relative to their market value.*
- *Certain assets, like goodwill, tend not to appear on the balance sheet at all. Again, this is caused by the effect of the accounting conventions, particularly the historic cost convention.*

Under such circumstances, the investment in the subsidiary in the balance sheet of the holding company will not cancel with the shares and reserves of the subsidiary at the date of the acquisition.

Example

The following balance sheets relate to H Ltd and S Ltd as at 31 December 2000:

	H Ltd	S Ltd
	£000	£000
Fixed assets	3,500	3,800
Investments in S Ltd	4,000	–
Working capital	1,000	700
	8,500	4,500
Ordinary share capital	6,000	3,000
(£1 shares fully paid)		
Reserves	2,500	1,500
	8,500	4,500

H Ltd acquired all of S Ltd's capital on 1 January 1999, for £4 million in cash, when the reserves in S Ltd were £500,000.

Clearly the investment in S Ltd (£4 million) does not cancel out with the share capital and reserves at the time of acquisition (£3.5 million). There must be an amount of £500,000 which will need to be incorporated in some way into the group balance sheet. This is entirely logical, since if £4 million was paid for net assets with a balance sheet value of £3.5 million, there must be some undisclosed or undervalued asset involved. This asset is usually known as *goodwill on consolidation* or sometimes *cost of control*. The principle underlying goodwill on consolidation is the same as that underlying goodwill (in an accounting sense) generally, namely the amount paid for a complete business in excess of the total value placed on the individual assets (net of the liabilities).

Goodwill on consolidation can be calculated by comparing:

- what has been paid for the subsidiary (or part of it), with
- what has been obtained for it, i.e. the net assets at the time of acquisition (or part of them). The balance sheet value of the net assets at any point

in time can be calculated, either by adding the balance sheet values of the individual assets of the subsidiary and deducting the sum of the liabilities or by adding the capital and reserves of the subsidiary. (The *balance sheet equation* ensures that you should get the same answer by either method.)

The reserves of S Ltd can be split £500,000 pre-acquisition and £1,000,000 post-acquisition. Thus, what the parent bought for its £4 million was £3,500,000 of balance sheet assets plus £500,000 of goodwill.

The group balance sheet would thus appear as follows:

Balance sheet as at 31 December 2000

	£000
Fixed assets	7,300
Goodwill on consolidation	1,500
Working capital	1,700
	9,500
Share capital	6,000
Reserves	3,500
	9,500

Sometimes, the amount paid for the investments in the subsidiary is less than the net assets associated with the investment. Under such circumstances the difference will appear as a *capital reserve on consolidation* on the claims side of the balance sheet.

Activity 5

The following balance sheets relate to H Ltd, and S Ltd, as at 31 December 2000

	H Ltd	S Ltd
	£000	£000
Net assets	5,100	4,500
Investments in S Ltd	3,400	–
	8,500	4,500
Ordinary share capital	6,000	3,000
(£1 shares fully paid)		
Reserves	2,500	1,500
	8,500	4,500

H Ltd acquired all of S Ltd's capital on 1 January 1999, for £3.4 million, when reserves in S Ltd were £500,000.

Prepare a group balance sheet as at 31 December 2000.

Your answer should be along the following lines:

Capital reserve on consolidation *arrived at as follows:*
Pay £3.4 million
Get £3.5 million
Therefore £0.1 million capital reserve

Balance sheet as at 31 December 2000

	£000	
Net assets	9,600	
Ordinary share capital	6,000	
Capital reserve on consolidation	100	
Reserves	3,500	*£2.5 million in H Ltd and*
		£1 million in S Ltd
	9,600	

In practice, the calculation of goodwill is slightly more complicated than implied above, since the amount to be attributed to any purchased goodwill should be the difference between the *fair value* of the consideration given and the aggregate of the *fair value* of the net assets (valued separately). This means that the net assets are frequently revalued *in the group accounts*, at market value (but not necessarily in the accounts of the subsidiary). The effect will usually be to increase the net assets figures and decrease the amount of goodwill on consolidation.

This still leaves the question as to what should be done with goodwill when it is calculated. It has been shown above as an intangible asset, on the balance sheet. Like other fixed assets, goodwill should be written off to the profit and loss account over time when it is regarded as having a limited useful economic life. The relevant accounting standard on goodwill contains a rebuttable presumption that the useful economic life of goodwill will not exceed twenty years. In some cases, however, the useful economic life may be longer than twenty years in which case it is permissible to write off goodwill over a longer time period. In other cases, the current value of goodwill may not fall below the balance sheet value and so it would be appropriate not to write off any amounts. Where goodwill is written off over more than twenty years, or is not written off at all, the company must carry out regular reviews to ensure the balance sheet value of goodwill is not overstated.

Minority interests

So far it has been assumed that the holding company acquired 100% of the share capital of the subsidiary. From what was said earlier about effective control it is clear that this need not be the case. Other people or organizations may also own some shares in the subsidiary. This means that when group accounts are prepared these *minority interests* must be recognized. Minority interests in a group represent the claims of shareholders, other than members of the holding company, in the subsidiary. They represent the claim of these outside shareholders on the net assets appearing in the group balance sheet.

It must be remembered that the object of group accounts is to show the financial position of the group as a whole, as nearly as possible, in the way in which it would be shown if the holding company itself undertook all the activities of the members of the group, and all assets and liabilities of the group were attributable to a single company. This concept dismisses any suggestion that only the group's attributable proportion of assets and liabilities should be included in the group balance sheet. Conceptually, it is clear that all assets and liabilities of all group members should be included. It should be borne in mind that the parent company controls all aspects of its subsidiaries, not just the proportion of each of them which it owns, to the extent that shareholders other than shareholders of the holding company have a claim against these group net assets.

As we shall see later in the chapter, a similar approach is taken to minority interests in the group balance sheet.

Example

The following balance sheets relate to H Ltd and S Ltd as at 1 January 1999;

	H Ltd	S Ltd
	£000	£000
Net assets	20,000	5,000
Investment in S Ltd	3,000	–
	23,000	5,000
Share capital (£1 shares fully paid)	23,000	5,000

H Ltd acquired 60% of the shares of S Ltd, on formation of both companies on 1 January 1999.

When preparing the group balance sheet, it should be remembered that the parent company effectively controls all the net assets. There is thus little point in including only 60% of the net assets of the subsidiary. It is more logical to include all of the assets controlled by the group and show the proportion funded by minorities, as follows:

Group balance sheet as at 1 January 1999

	£000	
Net assets	25,000	
Share capital	23,000	
Minority interests	2,000	(i.e. 40% of net assets of subsidiary)
	25,000	

Where the subsidiary has traded either before or since the takeover, the calculation of minority interests is slightly more complex than this, since the minority share of net assets is arrived at by taking an appropriate proportion of the share capital and reserves (both pre- and post-acquisition) of the subsidiary.

The logic of the group balance sheet, where there are minority shareholders in the subsidiary, is fairly easy to follow. The group in the example has net assets of £25 million, all of which are under the control of the holding company's shareholders. This is financed mainly by those shareholders (£23 million), but partly by the minority shareholders of the subsidiary company.

Example

The following balance sheets relate to H Ltd and S Ltd at 31 December 2000:

	H Ltd	S Ltd
	£000	£000
Net assets	5,500	4,500
Investments in S Ltd	3,000	–
	8,500	4,500
Ordinary share capital	6,000	3,000
(£1 shares fully paid)		
Reserves	2,500	1,500
	8,500	4,500

The investments in S Ltd had cost £3 million, for 2 million £1 shares, at a time when S Ltd's reserves stood at £900,000.

The *goodwill on consolidation* can be calculated as follows:

What was paid	£3.0 million
What was obtained	£2.6 million
(Net assets = capital + reserves	
at the time of acquisition, i.e. £3.9	
million; H Ltd is entitled	
to two-thirds of this)	
Goodwill on consolidation	£0.4 million

The minority interests will be one-third of the net assets (capital + reserves) at the balance sheet date, namely £1.5 million. It should be noted that any distinction between pre- and post-acquisition profits is irrelevant as far as the minority shareholders are concerned.

The post-acquisition reserves in S Ltd are £600,000, two-thirds of which can be added to group reserves.

The **group balance sheet as at 31 December 2000** is as follows:

	£000
Net assets	10,000
Goodwill on consolidation	400
	10,400

Ordinary share capital	6,000	
Reserves	2,900	(£2.5 million from H Ltd + £0.4 million from S Ltd)
Minority interests	1,500	
	10,400	

As was discussed above, the goodwill would not normally be retained on the balance sheet but written off in one way or another.

Activity 6

The following balance sheets relate to H Ltd and S Ltd at 31 December 1999

	H Ltd	S Ltd
	£000	£000
Net assets	5,100	3,700
Investments in S Ltd	2,200	–
	7,300	3,700
Ordinary share capital (£1 shares fully paid)	5,000	2,500
Reserves	2,300	1,200
	7,300	3,700

The investments in S Ltd had cost 2.2 million, for 2 million £1 shares, at a time when S Ltd's reserves stood at £500,000.

Prepare a group balance sheet as at 31 December 1999.

You should have written something like the following:

Capital reserve on consolidation

Pay   £2.2 million
Get   £2.4 million
Therefore £0.2 million capital reserve

Reserves	£	
H Ltd	2,300,000	
S Ltd	560,000	80% of post-acquisition reserves of £700,000
	2,860,000	

Minority interests
20% of the capital and reserves (2.5 m + 1.2 m) = £740,000

Balance sheet as at 31 December 1999

	£000
Net assets	8,800
Ordinary share capital	5,000
Capital reserve on consolidation	200
Reserves	2,860
Minority interests	740
	8,800

Self-assessment question 15.1

The summarized balance sheets of Matt Ltd and James Ltd as at 31 December 2000 are as follows:

	Matt Ltd £000	James Ltd £000
Fixed assets	800	24,000
Investments in James Ltd (12,000 shares at cost)	29,000	
Current assets	400	2,000
	30,200	26,000
Current liabilities	(200)	(1,000)
	30,000	25,000
Ordinary share capital	20,000	15,000
Reserves	10,000	10,000
	30,000	25,000

The following information is also available:

1 Matt Ltd acquired the shares in James Ltd on 31 December 1999 when the reserves of James Ltd were £5 million.
2 At 31 December 2000 James Ltd owed Matt Ltd £100,000. This amount had been included in the current assets and current liabilities of Matt Ltd and James Ltd respectively.

Prepare a group balance sheet for the group as at 31 December 2000.

15.10 Summary	In this chapter you have been introduced to the nature and special accounting requirements of groups of companies. A group of companies is formed when one company has control, usually through owning a majority of the shares, of another company or companies. Groups can take various forms, some of them quite complex.

Groups of companies are formed for a variety of reasons, of which a desire for expansion through acquisition is an important one. There are other ways for one company to acquire another than by buying sufficient shares to control it, but the formation of groups is a popular approach in practice. Groups of companies are required to prepare a balance sheet and a profit and loss account for the group as a whole, as well as for the individual companies which it comprises.

In essence, the preparation of the group accounts is simply a process of incorporating most of the assets, claims, revenues and expenses of the group members into the balance sheet of the parent company, adding like items together. The remaining items which will be related to the owners' claim of the subsidiary and the amount of the investment in subsidiaries of the parent will be set off against one another. If these two do not exactly cancel one another, it will be for one or both of two reasons:

- The amount paid by the parent for its investment in the subsidiary is greater than or less than the value of the net assets acquired, in which case the difference will appear on the group balance sheet either as 'goodwill on consolidation' or as 'capital reserve on consolidation'.
- The parent does not acquire all the shares of the subsidiary. In this case the claim of the minority shareholders against the net assets of the group and the entitlement of those shareholders to share in the profits of the group must be recognized in the group balance sheet and profit and loss account respectively.

The overall objective of group accounts is to show the position and effectiveness of the entire group as if the assets, claims, revenues and expenses of all group members were actually those of the parent company. This chapter focused on the balance sheet while the next chapter focuses on the group profit and loss account.

Exercises

1 The balance sheets of H Ltd and S Ltd as at 31 December 2000 are as follows:

	H Ltd £000	S Ltd £000
Net assets	80,000	25,000
Investments in S Ltd	20,000	–
	100,000	25,000
Ordinary share capital (£1 shares fully paid)	50,000	15,000
Reserves	50,000	10,000
	100,000	25,000

H Ltd acquired all the shares of S Ltd when reserves of S Ltd were £5 million.

Prepare a group balance sheet as at 31 December 2000.

2 Take the same balance sheets as in question 1, but assume that H Ltd acquired all the shares of S Ltd when reserves of S Ltd were £3 million. Prepare a group balance sheet as at 31 December 2000.

3 Take the same balance sheets as in question 1, but assume that H Ltd acquired all the shares of S Ltd when reserves of S Ltd were £7 million. Prepare a group balance sheet as at 31 December 2000.

4 The balance sheets of H Ltd and S Ltd as at 31 December 2000 are as follows:

	H Ltd	S Ltd
	£000	£000
Net assets	80,000	25,000
Investments in S Ltd	20,000	–
	100,000	25,000
Ordinary share capital (£1 shares fully paid)	50,000	25,000
Reserves	50,000	–
	100,000	25,000

H Ltd acquired 20 million of the shares of S Ltd when reserves of S Ltd were nil.

Prepare a group balance sheet as at 31 December 2000.

5 The balance sheets of H Ltd and S Ltd as at 31 December 2000 are as follows:

	H Ltd	S Ltd
	£000	£000
Net assets	80,000	35,000
Investments in S Ltd	20,000	
	100,000	35,000
Ordinary share capital (£1 shares fully paid)	50,000	25,000
Reserves	50,000	10,000
	100,000	35,000

H Ltd acquired 15 million of the shares of S Ltd when reserves of S Ltd were £5 million.

Prepare a group balance sheet as at 31 December 2000.

Chapter 16

The accounts of groups of companies: 2

16.1 Introduction

This chapter introduces the problems of inter-company transactions, in particular, where transactions occur between companies within the group. Since the aim of a set of group accounts is to summarize the accounts of the group as if it were a single entity, such transactions need to be eliminated.

The second part of the chapter provides an understanding of the principles which underpin a group profit and loss account.

16.2 Objectives

On completion of this chapter you should be able to:

- identify the main areas of inter-company transactions which require adjustment in the group accounts;
- reflect these adjustments in a set of final accounts;
- explain the underlying principles involved in the preparation of a group profit and loss account;
- prepare a simple group profit and loss account.

16.3 Inter-company transactions

Most inter-company transactions present no problems, since in most cases one merely cancels out the other. Such a situation would arise if one company in a group makes a loan to another company in the group. As far as the group is concerned there is no external asset or liability. However, problems can arise in two other areas.

(a) Dividends paid by a subsidiary

When dividends are paid or proposed by a subsidiary the holding company should incorporate its share of these into its own accounts (i.e. increase cash or debtor (the subsidiary), increase profit). In the group balance sheet any obligation shown in the subsidiary company accounts can then be set against the current asset in the holding company accounts and effectively eliminated.

Example

H Ltd owns 80% of the ordinary share capital of S Ltd. S Ltd declares an ordinary share dividend of £10,000, which appears as a current liability on its balance sheet. H Ltd should increase its profit by £8,000, and set up a current asset; debtors S Ltd (dividends receivable) £8,000 (i.e. 80% of the dividends proposed by S Ltd).

> In the group accounts the £8,000 shown as a current asset in the accounts of H Ltd should cancel out with £8,000 of the proposed dividends shown in the current liabilities of S Ltd. This leaves uncancelled £2,000 proposed dividends in the accounts of S Ltd, which appears in the group balance sheet as a current liability (minority interest dividends).

(b) Transactions between one company in the group and another company in the group, at a profit

These are transactions of a type where one group member sells goods to another group member and these items, or a portion of them, are still in stock at the balance sheet date. Problems can also arise where one company sells to another member of the group fixed assets which the purchasing company deals with in its accounts as a fixed asset and the selling company as a normal trading transaction within its profit and loss account.

The difficulty arises from the basic idea that one cannot make profit simply by trading with oneself. The realization convention of accounting maintains that the revenue, and therefore any profit arising from it, normally should not be recognized until the goods pass to the customer. From the point of view of the group as a whole, transfers of assets from one member to another are in effect trading with oneself. No problem arises where the item has been subsequently sold to another party outside the group, within the financial year, since the profit will then have been realized. However, if this is not the case then unrealized profits must be eliminated from the accounts of the group. The effect of eliminating unrealized profit on the group balance sheet is to reduce the appropriate asset and to reduce profit (reserves).

Example

H Ltd owns 75% of the share capital of S Ltd. During its financial year it sells goods to S Ltd for £100,000, which had cost it £60,000. At the end of the financial year S Ltd still had £10,000 of those goods in hand (note that this is at cost to S Ltd).

The total profit on the transactions is £40,000, of which £36,000 has been fully realized by the group. However, the profit on the stock remaining within the group remains unrealized, as the stock has not yet been sold outside of the group. This amounts to £4,000. In the group balance sheet the stock would be reduced by £4,000, as would the group reserves.

It can be argued that if a holding company sells to a partly owned subsidiary then the profit on sales to the minority shareholders has actually been realized. If this approach were taken in the above example the unrealized profit would be reduced to £3,000 (i.e. 75% of £4,000). The most prudent treatment is probably to eliminate all unrealized profits, but the existence of alternative viewpoints needs to be recognized.

Activity 1 (a modification of self-assessment question 15.1)

The summarized balance sheets of Matt Ltd and James Ltd as at 31 December 2000 are as follows:

	Matt Ltd £000	James Ltd £000
Fixed assets	800	24,000
Investments in James Ltd (12,000 shares at cost)	29,000	
Current assets	400	2,000
	30,200	26,000
Current liabilities	(200)	(1,000)
	30,000	25,000
Ordinary share capital	20,000	15,000
Reserves	10,000	10,000
	30,000	25,000

The following information is also available:

1 Matt Ltd acquired the shares in James Ltd on 31 December 1999 when the reserves of James Ltd were £5 million.
2 During 2000 Matt Ltd sold goods which had cost £150,000 to produce to James Ltd for £200,000. At 31 December 2000 James Ltd still has half of these goods in stock, valued at cost to James Ltd and included in current assets.
3 At 31 December 2000 James Ltd owed Matt Ltd £100,000. This amount had been included in the current assets and current liabilities of Matt Ltd and James Ltd respectively.
4 No dividends had been paid by either company in 1999 or 2000, and none is proposed.

Prepare a group balance sheet for the group as at 31 December 2000.

Goodwill on consolidation

Pay	£29 m	
Get	£16 m	(£12 m ordinary share capital + £4 m reserves {80% at time of acquisition})
Goodwill	£13 m	

Inter-company transactions

Profit on goods sold by Matt to James amounts to £50,000.
Of this half is still unrealized from a group perspective
Hence reserves need to be reduced by £25,000
and current assets (stock) also need to be reduced by £25,000

Reserves

Matt	£10 m	
James	£4 m	(80% of post acquisition reserves)
	£14 m	
less unrealized profits	0.025	
	£13.975 m	

Minority interests

Capital James	£15 m
Reserves James	£10 m
	£25 m
	x 20%
	£5 m

Balance sheet as at 31 December 2000

	£000	£000
Fixed assets		24,800
Goodwill on consolidation		13,000
Current assets (i.e. less unrealized profit)	2,275	
Current liabilities	1,100	
		1,175
		38,975
Ordinary share capital		20,000
Reserves		13,975
Minority interests		5,000
		38,975

Typically the goodwill will be written off against the reserves.

16.4
The group profit and loss account

The objective of the group profit and loss account is to show a true and fair view of the earnings of the entire group for the particular period, distinguishing between that which is attributable to the shareholders of the holding company and that attributable to the minority shareholders of the subsidiary.

The procedure is to incorporate the whole of the subsidiaries' profit and loss accounts into that of the holding company, adding like items to one another. The portion of the resultant after-tax profit of the group which relates to any minority shareholders of subsidiaries is then deducted to arrive at the group profit attributable to the holding company's shareholders. This approach is consistent with that used in preparing a group balance sheet, of showing all the subsidiaries' net assets and the minority interest in them.

It has the advantage of showing the totals for revenues, expenses and profit of all the activities under the control of the group. This is necessary if meaningful conclusions are to be drawn about the group's success in trading operations.

The formats for published profit and loss accounts set out in the previous chapter need some modification for a group. Given below is an example of format 1, modified for a group.

Group profit and loss account for the year ended———

	£	Notes
Turnover	x	1
Cost of sales	(x)	1
Gross profit	x	1
Administration expenses	(x)	1
Distribution expenses	(x)	1
Other income	(x)	
Profit before tax	x	
Taxation	x	1
Profit after tax	x	1
Minority interest	x	2
Group profit for year	x	3
Appropriations		
Dividends	(x)	4
Reserves	(x)	4
Group retained profits for the year	x	
Retained profit brought forward	x	5
Retained profit carried forward	x	

Notes:

1 Normally the group profit and loss account will reflect the total of the equivalent figures in the holding and subsidiary company profit and loss accounts.
2 The minority interest is calculated as the share of *after-tax profits* in the subsidiary.
3 The group profit will be that of the holding company plus the share of *after-tax profits* of the subsidiary, less any unrealized profits.
4 Dividends will be those of the holding company only. Other appropriations, such as transfers to reserves, will be the holding company figures plus the appropriate share of any transfers to reserves made in the accounts of the subsidiaries.
5 The retained profits brought forward will be those relating to the group, which will be the sum of the retained profits brought forward in the holding company accounts plus the appropriate shares of post-acquisition profits in the subsidiary at the beginning of the period.

Example

The following profit and loss accounts relate to H Ltd and S Ltd for the year ended 31 December 2000:

	H Ltd	S Ltd
	£000	£000
Turnover	10,000	5,000
Cost of sales	(5,000)	(2,500)
Gross profit	5,000	2,500
Administration	(1,000)	(500)
Distribution	(1,000)	(500)
Profit before tax	3,000	1,500
Taxation	(1,000)	(500)
Profit after tax	2,000	1,000

H Ltd owns 80% of the share capital of S Ltd. No dividends were paid or proposed by either company.

The *group profit and loss account* would appear as follows:

	£000	Workings
Turnover	15,000	(10,000 + 5,000)
Cost of sales	(7,500)	(5,000 + 2,500)
Gross profit	7,500	
Administration	(1,500)	(1,000 + 500)
Distribution	(1,500)	(1,000 + 500)
Profit before tax	4,500	
Taxation	(1,500)	(1,000 + 500)
Profit after tax	3,000	
Minority interests	(200)	(20% × 1,000)
Profit after tax attributable to the group	2,800	

Dividends

When the subsidiary pays a dividend, most of it will go to the parent company, because the parent company is the majority shareholder. From the point of view of the subsidiary company, such a dividend represents an appropriation of profit and must be recorded in the profit and loss account as such. From the parent company's point of view, the dividend from the subsidiary is a revenue and must be recorded as such. From a group point of view, however, a dividend paid by one member to another is simply a transfer of cash within the group. There is neither an appropriation of profit, nor a revenue. In the group profit and loss account the two aspects of these intragroup dividends must be cancelled.

Example

The following profit and loss accounts relate to H Ltd and S Ltd for the year ended 31 December 2000:

	H Ltd	S Ltd
	£000	£000
Turnover	10,000	5,000
Cost of sales	(5,000)	(2,500)
Gross profit	5,000	2,500
Administration	(1,000)	(500)
Distribution	(1,000)	(500)
Income – dividends receivable	400	–
Profit before tax	3,400	1,500
Taxation	(1,000)	(500)
Profit after tax	2,400	1,000
Dividend paid	(1,000)	(500)
Profit and loss account balance c/f	1,400	900

H Ltd owns 80% of the share capital of S Ltd.

It should be clear that the dividends paid by S Ltd came *from* profits made by S Ltd. A total of 80% of these dividends are received by H Ltd and recorded in its accounts, reflecting the proportion of the shares owned. If the profits are included as shown in the preceding example, *and* the dividends receivable by H Ltd are added to them, a double counting would occur. The group profit and loss account would thus appear as follows:

	£000	*Workings*
Turnover	15,000	(10,000 + 5,000)
Cost of sales	(7,500)	(5,000 + 2,500)
Gross profit	7,500	
Administration	(1,500)	(1,000 + 500)
Distribution	(1,500)	(1,000 + 500)
Profit before tax	4,500	
Taxation	(1,500)	(1,000 + 500)
Profit after tax	3,000	
Minority interests	(200)	(20% × 1,000)
Profit after tax attributable to the group less dividends	2,800	
	(1,000)	
Group retained profit for the year	1,800	

Only dividends of the holding company will appear in the group profit and loss account. In effect, the dividend due to H Ltd from S Ltd is cancelled. The dividend due from S Ltd to the minority shareholders is included in minority interests.

Activity 2

The following profit and loss accounts relate to H Ltd and S Ltd for the year ended 31 December 2000:

	H Ltd	S Ltd
	£000	£000
Turnover	10,000	5,000
Cost of sales	(5,000)	(2,500)
Gross profit	5,000	2,500
Administration	(1,000)	(500)
Distribution	(1,000)	(500)
Income – dividends receivable	400	–
Profit before tax	3,400	1,500
Taxation	(1,000)	(500)
After-tax profit	2,400	1,000
Dividends		
Preference	–	(400)
Ordinary	(1,000)	(250)
Profit and loss account balance c/f	1,400	100

H Ltd owns 80% of the ordinary share capital of S Ltd
    Prepare a group profit and loss account for the year ended 31 December 2000.

Your profit and loss account should look something like this:

Group profit and loss account for the year ended 31 December 2000

	£000	*Workings*
Turnover	15,000	(10m + 5m)
Cost of sales	(7,500)	(5m + 2.5m)
Gross profit	7,500	
Administration	(1,500)	(1m + 0.5m)
Distribution	(1,500)	(1m + 0.5m)
Profit before tax	4,500	
Taxation	(1,500)	(1m + 0.5m)
Profit after tax	3,000	
Minority interests	520	((20% × 0.6m) + 0.4m
Profit after tax attributable to the group	2,480	*preference dividend)*
Dividends	1,000	
Added to group reserves	1,480	

Reserves

Following on from the treatment of reserves in the group balance sheet, it should be clear that any balances brought forward on the group profit and loss account should include only those of the holding company and the post-acquisition element of those of the subsidiary.

Example

H Ltd acquired 80% of the ordinary share capital of S Ltd on 31 December 1999. The companies' outline profit and loss accounts for the year ended 31 December 2000 were as follows:

	H Ltd	S Ltd
	£000	£000
Profit after tax	2,000	1,000
Profit and loss balance b/f	1,000	1,000
	3,000	2,000
Dividends	(1,000)	(500)
Profit and loss balance c/f	2,000	1,500

This would result in a **group profit and loss account** for the year as follows:

	£000	
Profit after tax	3,000	
Minority interests	(200)	(20% × £1m)
Profit attributable to the group	2,800	
Dividends	(1,000)	(H Ltd only)
Profit retained for the year	1,800	
Profit and loss account balance b/f	1,000	(see below)
Profit and loss account balance of group c/f	2,800	

The profit and loss balance brought forward is made up of the balance brought forward in H Ltd (£1m), plus the post-acquisition share of the profit and loss account balance in S Ltd. Since the profit and loss account balance brought forward in S Ltd must represent the balance as at 31 December 1999, it must all be pre-acquisition. None of it is included in the balance brought forward in the group profit and loss account.

Activity 3

The following information is available for the year ended 31 December 2000:

	H Ltd	S Ltd	T Ltd
	£000	£000	£000
Profit after tax	20,000	4,000	5,000
Profit and loss balance b/f	15,000	3,000	8,000
Profit and loss balance c/f	35,000	7,000	13,000

H Ltd acquired 75% of the ordinary share capital of S Ltd on 31 December 1998, when the balance on the profit and loss account of S Ltd was £1m.

H Ltd acquired 80% of the ordinary share capital of T Ltd on 31 December 1999.

Show how this information would be reflected in the group profit and loss account for the year ended 31 December 2000.

Your profit and loss account should look something like this:

Group profit and loss account for the year ended 31 December 2000

	£000	*Workings*
Profit after tax	29,000	$(20m + 4m + 5m)$
Minority interests	2,000	$(25\% \times 4m) + (20\% \times 5m)$
	27,000	
Profit and loss balance b/f	16,500	$(15m + \{75\% \times [3m - 1m]\})$
	43,500	

**16.5
Disclosure in
group accounts**

The requirement to publish group accounts does not relieve each individual company in the group from its statutory obligation to keep its own records and to disclose its trading results and position. This means that, in practice, when accounts are published in the form of an annual report, they include not just a group profit and loss account and balance sheet but a holding company profit and loss account and balance sheet as well. Exemptions to the requirement to publish group accounts are obtainable for small and medium-sized groups and by parent companies which are subsidiaries of EC parents.

In practice some variation is found in the formats used. It should be remembered that, for purposes of disclosure, there are two approved balance sheet formats and four profit and loss account formats. The profit and loss account format used in this chapter is based upon format 1. Clearly any of the other three formats may be found, but the underlying principles of group accounts remain the same. Also it is worth noting that the profit and loss account formats set out in the legislation do not include appropriations or balances brought forward. Again slight variations are possible, but the same basic information must be included.

A further variation regarding the profit and loss account is permitted by the companies legislation. A holding company may dispense with publishing its own profit and loss account, provided that the group profit and loss account is rearranged to show how much of the group-retained profit is accounted for in the books of the holding company itself, as compared with the amounts retained in subsidiaries. Where this facility is used the published accounts will thus include a balance sheet for the holding company itself, a group balance sheet for the group, and a profit and loss account for the group.

16.6 Associated companies

At the beginning of this chapter the point was made that companies sometimes invest in the shares of another company without necessarily obtaining control of that company. Under such circumstances no group accounts are legally required. Nor would the preparation of a set of group accounts be logical. Basically the effect on the final accounts of the investor company is that the investment in the other company would be shown, typically at cost, and any dividends received would be included as income in the investor company's profit and loss account, with a consequent increase in cash.

This is the normal treatment for an investment which constitutes a relatively small part of the share capital of the company whose shares are being purchased. Such a treatment can be quite misleading, however.

Example

Suppose that H Ltd acquired 10% of the shares of Y Ltd on formation of Y Ltd for £1 million. During the first year of its trading, Y Ltd made a profit after tax of £2 million, and paid out a dividend of £500,000. H Ltd would show in its balance sheet:

Investment in Y Ltd	£1 million
and in its profit and loss account:	
Investment income: dividends from Y Ltd	£50,000

In fact, H Ltd's *share of earnings* in Y Ltd is £200,000 (10% × £2 million). The recording of the dividends only, while following both the realization convention and the convention of prudence, does not adequately reflect the earnings of the investment in Y Ltd. This point needs to be recognized when dealing with investments of this type.

Where enough shares of a company are held for the investing company to exert a significant influence over the other company, the accounting treatment is modified to reflect the investing company's share of earnings, as opposed to its share of dividends. A company which is not controlled, but where the ownership is sufficient to exert a significant influence, is known as an associated company of the investor company. An associated company is one in which there is an investment which is long-term and substantial, but not controlling, or where the investing company interest in the shares makes it effectively a partner in a joint venture or consortium, or where the investing company actively participates in the commercial or policy decisions. Typically, associates are those where the investment covers 20-50% of the voting capital.

Where an associate company exists there will be amendments made to the consolidated accounts of the investing group (but not to the individual accounts of the investing company). In the group profit and loss account there will be lines relating to:

- the share of profits or losses before tax of the associate company;
- the share of tax attributable to the associate company;
- the share of retained profit in the associate company.

The *consolidated profit and loss account* is thus likely to appear, broadly, as follows:

		£
Net profit before tax (holding company plus subsidiaries)		x
Share of profit before tax of associates		x
		x
Less: Corporation tax		
Holding company and subsidiaries	x	
Associates	x	
		x
Profit after tax		x
Minority interests		x
Profit attributable to the group		x
Less dividends		x
Net profit of year retained in group		x

Normally the amounts retained in the various companies (holding company, subsidiaries and associates) are also shown. In some formats the profit and loss balance brought forward from previous years will be added to give a profit and loss balance carried forward.

In the *consolidated balance sheet*, the investment in the associate company will need to be increased to reflect the inclusion of the share of net assets of the associate, together with any goodwill on acquisition.

If the investing company has no subsidiaries the share of associated company profits and retentions should be shown by way of a series of supplementary notes. You should note that the treatment of associate companies is different from a conventional consolidation. The individual items in the profit and loss account are not consolidated. Only the group share of the associate's net profit before tax is brought in, together with the share of tax and retained profit for the year. Similarly, in the balance sheet the assets and liabilities are not consolidated. Effectively the investment in the subsidiary is enhanced to reflect the increase attributable to post-acquisition earnings which are retained in the associate. This may be increased by any goodwill on the acquisition of the associate. Reserves are increased to match this.

Example

X Ltd acquired 25% of the ordinary shares of Y Ltd on the formation of Y Ltd. During Y Ltd's first year of trading the company generated pre-tax profits of £1.4 million. Tax was estimated at £600,000 leaving an after-tax profit of £800,000. A dividend totalling £200,000 was paid by Y Ltd, leaving £600,000 in reserves.

If Y Ltd were not to be treated as an associated company of X Ltd, all that would appear in the profit and loss account of X Ltd in respect of its investment would be its dividend of £50,000 (i.e. 25% of £200,000).

When treated as an associate company, the adjustments to the group profit and loss account are:

- Eliminate the dividend as income in the profit and loss account (take out the £50,000 dividend in the example);
- Add to the pre-tax profit of the investor company its share (£350,000) of the pre-tax profit of the associated company (i.e. 25% of £1.4 million);
- Add to the tax charge of the investor company its share (£150,000) of the associated company's tax charge (i.e. 25% of £600,000).

In practice, it will normally be necessary to add to the retained profits brought forward of the investor company, its share of those of the associated company. In this example there were no associated company-retained profits brought forward because it was the first year of trading.

In the group balance sheet X Ltd's investment in Y Ltd will need to be increased to reflect its share of retained profits in Y Ltd. Basically, the retained profit of Y Ltd will have increased by £150,000 (£200,000 less the £50,000 dividend previously included). The value of the investment in the shares of Y Ltd in the group balance sheet will thus need to be increased by the same amount. This is to reflect the fact that the investment has grown over the year as a result of undistributed profits.

Activity 4

The summarized profit and loss accounts of X Ltd and of Y Ltd for the year ending 31 December 2000 are as follows:

	X Ltd	Y Ltd
	£000	£000
Turnover	55,000	23,000
Cost of sales	32,000	12,000
Gross profit	23,000	11,000
Distribution costs	(9,000)	(5,000)
Administrative costs	(9,000)	(4,000)
	5,000	2,000

Dividends receivable from Y Ltd	100	–
Net profit	5,100	2,000
Corporation tax	2,000	800
After-tax profit for the year	3,100	1,200
Retained profit from last year	8,300	800
	11,400	2,000
Dividend paid	1,500	400
Retained profit carried to next year	9,900	1,600

X Ltd had paid £1.2 million for 25% of the ordinary share capital of Y Ltd on 1 January 1999, on formation of Y Ltd. Y Ltd had £4 million of ordinary share capital.

Have a try at revising the profit and loss account of X Ltd to incorporate the results of its associated company Y Ltd.

Also show the amounts which would be shown in the revised balance sheet of X Ltd for

• Retained profit (reserve); and
• Investment in Y Ltd

Your profit and loss account should look something like this:

Profit and loss account for the year ended 31 December 2000

		£000	Workings
Turnover		55,000	
Cost of sales		(32,000)	
Gross profit		23,000	
Administration		(9,000)	
Distribution		(9,000)	
Profit before tax		5,000	
Share of profits in associate		500	25% × 2m
		5,500	
Taxation: X Ltd	2,000		
Taxation: A Ltd	200		25% × 0.8m
		(2,200)	
Profit after tax		(3,300)	
Dividends		(1,500)	
Added to reserves		1,800	
Profit and loss account			
Balance b/f X Ltd	8,300		
Balance b/f Y Ltd	200		25% × 0.8m
		8,500	
		10,300	

The balance sheet would thus show £10.3 million under reserves.

The investment would increase by £0.4 million, to reflect the share of profits retained in Y Ltd, namely £0.2m from 1999 and £0.3m from 2000 (share of profits less tax as shown above) less the dividend paid to X Ltd.

Self-assessment question 16.1

The following are the group profit and loss accounts for A Ltd and B Ltd for the year ended 31 December 2000:

	A Ltd £000	B Ltd £000
Turnover	6,000	3,000
Cost of sales	(3,000)	(1,000)
Gross profit	3,000	2,000
Administration	(800)	(400)
Distribution	(1,000)	(400)
Investment Income	1,000	–
Profit before tax	2,200	1,200
Taxation	(700)	(300)
After-tax profit	1,500	900
Appropriated as follows:		
Dividends		
Preference	(300)	(100)
Ordinary	(600)	(500)
General reserve transfer	(400)	(200)
Retained profits for year	200	100
Profit and loss account balance b/f	500	500
Profit and loss account balance c/f	700	600

A Ltd purchased 80% of the ordinary share capital of B Ltd when the profit and loss account balance of B Ltd was £100,000. A Ltd owns none of B Ltd's preference shares.

The turnover figure for A Ltd includes profit on the sale of plant to B Ltd, amounting to £50,000.

A Ltd's investment income includes the dividend from B Ltd.

Prepare a group profit and loss account for the year ended 31 December 2000.

16.7 Summary

The chapter discussed the problems that arise with regard to intra-group transactions, and illustrated the consequences for preparation of the final accounts of a group. It also dealt with preparation of a group profit and loss account. Finally it dealt with the problem of investing in other companies, where the investment does not give a controlling interest. Where a company owns shares in another company, though not enough to control it, yet despite this is able to *exercise significant influence over it*, the latter company is known as an associated company. In these circumstances the investor company's share of the trading results of the associated company are incorporated in the investor company's final accounts, albeit in summarized form.

Exercises

1 The balance sheets of Great Ltd and its subsidiary Small Ltd at 31 December 1999 are as follows:

	Great Ltd £000	Small Ltd £000
Fixed assets		
Freehold land	2,000	1,500
Plant and equipment	1,500	1,200
Shares in Small Ltd (at cost)	3,300	
Current assets		
Stock	1,200	500
Debtors: Great Ltd		850
Others	600	300
Cash	1,000	150
	9,600	4,500
Current liabilities		
Creditors: Great Ltd	(850)	
Others	(400)	(100)
Debentures		(500)
	8,350	3,900
Ordinary share capital	6,000	3,000
(£1 shares fully paid)		
Share premium	250	
General reserve	1,100	400
Profit and loss account	1,000	500
	8,350	3,900

The following information is available:

(a) Great Ltd acquired its holding of 2.25 million shares in Small Ltd when the latter had balances of £300,000 on its general reserve and of £200,000 on its profit and loss account.

(b) In calculating the price payable by Great Ltd for its shares in Small Ltd the land owned by Small Ltd was professionally valued at £2 million.

Prepare a group balance sheet as at 31 December 1999.

2 X Ltd owns 100% of the share capital of Y Ltd. Its accounting year runs from 1 January to 31 December. During the year it sells stock which had cost it £400,000, to Y Ltd, for £500,000. Closing stock is currently shown (in Y Ltd's accounts) at cost to Y Ltd at £ 100,000.
How much profit has X Ltd made on the sales to Y Ltd?
How much of this is realized by the group?
What is the figure that would appear in the group balance sheet relating to this stock figure?

3 H Ltd owns 75% of the shares of S Ltd. During the year ending 30 June 2000 S Ltd sold goods costing £800,000 to H Ltd for £1 million. At the end of the year H Ltd still had half of these goods in stock.
Three alternative solutions are possible of dealing with the unrealized profit from the intra-group sale.
Complete the table below to show the alternatives, explaining your assumptions. Which do you think is the best?

Method	Effect on consolidated stock £	Effect on consolidated reserves £	Effect on minority interests £
1			
2			
3			

4 The profit and loss accounts below relate to Groucho Ltd and Marx Ltd for the year ending 31 December 2000.

	£000	£000
Turnover	120,000	20,000
Cost of sales	70,000	8,000
Gross profit	50,000	12,000
Distribution costs	(13,000)	(5,000)
Administrative costs	(6,000)	(3,000)
Income – dividends receivable	750	–
Profit after tax	31,750	4,000
Taxation	(10,000)	(1,500)
After-tax profit	21,750	2,500
Dividends	(10,000)	(1,000)
Added to reserves	11,750	1,500
Profit and loss b/f	50,000	8,000
Profit and loss c/f	61,750	9,500

Groucho Ltd bought 75% of the shares of Marx Ltd at a time when the profit and loss balance was £4 million.
Prepare a group profit and loss account.

5 H Ltd acquired 80% of the shares of S Ltd, and 30% of the shares of A Ltd. At the time of acquisition the reserves of S Ltd were £20 million and of A Ltd were £10 million.
The final accounts of the three businesses are given below:

Profit and loss account

	H Ltd £000	S Ltd £000	A Ltd £000
Trading profits for the year	120	80	50
Dividends receivable – S Ltd	20		
– A Ltd	6		
	146	80	50
Corporation tax	40	28	18
Profit after tax	106	52	32
Dividends	70	25	20
Retained profit for the year	36	27	12
Profit and loss b/f	64	40	20
Profit and loss c/f	100	67	32

Balance sheet

	H Ltd	S Ltd	A Ltd
Fixed assets	200	140	100
Investments in S Ltd	120		
Investments in A Ltd	50		
Current assets	170	100	70
Current liabilities			
Creditors	(30)	(20)	(10)
Tax	(40)	(28)	(18)
Dividends	(70)	(25)	(20)
	400	167	122
Capital	300	100	90
Reserves	100	67	32
	400	167	122

Prepare group final accounts incorporating the associate.

Part Five
The Analysis and Interpretation of Accounts

This part comprises seven chapters and provides a framework for using accounting information to help assess performance, and to make decisions about the future.

The first chapter of this part of the book (Chapter 17) deals with the cash flow statement. This statement reveals the flow of liquid funds through the business, and provides a valuable insight into the financing and investing activities for a particular period. The chapter shows how the cash flow statement is prepared and how the contents can be interpreted.

The next chapter (Chapter 18) is concerned with the future. It aims to change your perspective on accounting from one concerned with historic events to one concerned with future, albeit less certain, events. The chapter shows how the basic financial accounting framework, comprising the three statements (balance sheet, profit and loss account and cash flow statement) can be used either to assess future plans or as the basis of a corporate financial model of the future. Nowadays, computers play a key role in the preparation and alteration of financial plans. Financial planning requires a clear understanding of the interrelationships between the three accounting statements and this chapter should reinforce your understanding of accounting principles.

The following three chapters deal with various techniques which can be used to analyse the position and performance of a business as revealed by the financial statements. The techniques are used to evaluate the strengths and weaknesses of the business and to provide a basis for future decisions.

The final two chapters are concerned with the quality of information revealed in the financial statements. It is important to bear in mind that the quality of the analysis and interpretation will depend on the quality of the underlying information. In the first of these two chapters (Chapter 22), the accounting conventions underpinning the financial statements are reviewed and their advantages, problems and limitations are identified. Linked with this is a discussion on the work that has taken place to develop an agreed conceptual framework. The final chapter re-examines the problems of measurement of profit, with a particular focus on times of changing prices, and examines ways of dealing with them. Clearly such factors are also important in assessing performance.

Chapter 17

The cash flow statement

17.1
Introduction

This chapter explains the nature and purpose of the cash flow statement and how it is prepared. It also discusses how the cash flow statement may be used as a basis for decision making.

17.2
Objectives

On completion of this chapter you should be able to:

- discuss the purpose of the cash flow statement;
- identify the main sources and uses of liquid funds;
- prepare a cash flow statement;
- interpret the significance of the information revealed in this statement.

17.3
Nature and purpose of the cash flow statement

The cash flow statement sets out the sources and uses of cash (and near cash) over a period. It is important to recognize that, while profitability is an essential ingredient of success, it is by no means sufficient. Even though profits may be high, a business must still retain enough liquid assets to meet its obligations as and when they arise. A lack of liquidity can lead to major problems for a business. Indeed, many business failures stem from an inability to manage liquidity. Liquidity is also an important consideration when funding new projects.

The cash flow statement provides a useful tool for analysing management decisions and strategy. It can reveal such things as:

- the amount of liquid funds generated from operating activities;
- the ways in which financing occurred;
- investment (and disinvestment) activities during a period.

This kind of information can help users to assess whether liquid funds generated are sufficient and whether they have been raised and applied in an appropriate way.

The importance of liquidity to a business is difficult to overstate. It is not uncommon for a profitable business to be forced to cease trading because it does not have enough liquid funds to meet its maturing liabilities.

Activity 1
How do you think this situation can occur? Consider the case of a young, expanding business and the problems it could face.

A young, expanding business is particularly prone to liquidity problems. A business may start with little capital and borrow heavily in order to finance fixed assets and stock. Any profits made may be ploughed back in order to finance more fixed assets and stock, with insufficient consideration being given to the liquid assets necessary to continue operations. The result may be that, when the liabilities mature, there are insufficient liquid funds to pay the amounts due. The creditors may, therefore, seek to wind up the business in order that assets may be sold to pay the amounts owing. This may occur despite the fact that the business is making good profits. Thus, the business must be concerned with liquidity as well as profitability.

Activity 2

It has been stated above that making profits will not necessarily ensure that there will be sufficient liquid funds to meet maturing obligations. Profits made over a period will not usually equate with liquid funds generated during that period. To demonstrate this point consider the effect (i.e. increase/decrease/no effect) of the following transactions on both profitability and liquidity (i.e. cash):

Transaction	**Effect on profit**	**Effect on cash**
(a) Issue of shares		
(b) Sale of goods on credit		
(c) Purchase of fixed assets for cash		
(d) Depreciation of fixed assets		
(e) Repayment of a loan		
(f) Payment of a dividend		
(g) The settlement of a tax provision		
(h) The sale of a fixed asset for cash		

The solutions are as follows:

Transaction	*Effect on profits*	*Effect on cash*
Issue of share	*no effect*	*increase*
Sale of goods on credit	*increase*	*no effect*
Purchases of fixed assets for cash	*no effect*	*decrease*
Depreciation of fixed assets	*decrease*	*no effect*
Repayment of a loan	*no effect*	*decrease*
Payment of a dividend	*no effect*	*decrease*
The settlement of a tax provision	*no effect*	*decrease*
The sale of a fixed asset for cash	*increase/decrease by amount of profit or loss*	*increase by amount of sale proceeds*

17.4 Relationship with other financial statements

The cash flow statement is an integral part of the annual financial report of limited companies. Its importance, therefore, as a financial statement is clearly recognized. However, the statement does not normally provide information additional to that already given to users. Rather, it normally provides a selection, reclassification and summarization of information already shown on the profit and loss account and balance sheet. The statement is, nevertheless, very useful as it clearly identifies the changes in assets, capital and liabilities that occurred during the period and the effect of such changes on liquidity. Hence, the statement helps to provide a more complete picture of the business and the changes that have occurred.

17.5 What is meant by 'cash'?

Before we look at the preparation of the cash flow statement in detail it is necessary to be clear as to what is meant by the term 'cash' in this context. In order to adhere to the relevant accounting standard on this topic, cash is defined in rather broader terms than simply cash in hand and in the bank. The term also includes deposits repayable on demand with any qualifying financial institution, less overdrafts payable on demand.

17.6 The main elements of the cash flow statement

In order to adhere to the relevant accounting standard, the cash flow statement must be presented in a format which contains a number of major elements. Each element represents a particular source of cash inflow or outflow for the business during a period. The elements are as follows:

- *Operating activities*. This shows the cash flows arising from business operations.
- *Returns on investments and servicing of finance*. This sets out the interest and dividends both received and paid during the period.
- *Taxation*. This element sets out the taxation paid and any tax rebates that have been received.
- *Capital expenditure and financial investment*. This sets out the payments made for the purchase of fixed assets and the proceeds from the sale of any fixed assets. Fixed assets under this heading exclude acquisitions and disposals (see below).
- *Acquisitions and disposals*. This relates to acquisitions and disposals of businesses.
- *Equity dividends paid*. Dividends paid by the company or in a group by the parent.
- *Management of liquid resources*. This includes cash inflows and outflows relating to such things as short-term deposits.
- *Financing*. This shows the amounts received from the issue of shares and loans and the amounts paid to purchase or redeem shares and to repay loans.

The relevant accounting standard requires that each element be separately identified and that the sequence shown above (for at least the first six items) should be adhered to when preparing the cash flow statement.

In addition to the above the standard requires disclosure of a statement or note reconciling the operating cash flows with the operating profit.

For groups cash flows which represent internal transfers need to be eliminated. For associated companies the cash flows are confined to those cash flows that actually occur between the associate and the group.

Most small businesses are exempt from the requirement to include a cash flow statement as part of their financial statements. However, voluntary disclosure is encouraged in the Financial Reporting Standard for Smaller Entities.

17.7 The cash flow statement format

An example of the format for a cash flow statement is shown below. This reveals the net cash inflow (outflow) figure for each of the elements of cash flow. By adding together the net figures for each of the various elements, we derive a total of the net cash flows for the period.

Angles Ltd
Cash flow statement for the year ended 31 March 2000

	£000	£000
Net cash inflow from operating activities		18,000
Returns on investments and servicing of finance		
Interest received	2,000	
Interest paid	(3,000)	
Net cash inflow (outflow) from returns on investments and servicing of finance		(1,000)
Taxation		
Corporation tax paid		(4,000)
Capital expenditure		
Payments to acquire fixed assets	(8,000)	
Receipts from sales of fixed assets	3,000	
Net cash inflow (outflow) from investing activities		(5,000)
		8,000
Equity dividends		
Dividends paid		(5,000)
		3,000
Management of liquid resources		–
Financing activities		
Issue of ordinary shares	(10,000)	
Repayment of loan capital	(12,000)	
Net cash outflow from financing		(2,000)
Increase in cash		1,000

<table>
<tr><td>**17.8 Preparing the cash flow statement – a worked example**</td><td>In order to understand the way in which a cash flow statement is prepared, it is probably a good idea to work through an example. Consider the balance sheet and profit and loss account of Pentagon Ltd below:</td></tr>
</table>

Pentagon Ltd

Balance sheet as at 31 December	1999				2000	
	£	£	£	£	£	£
Fixed assets						
Cost		86,000				92,000
Less: Accumulated depreciation		22,000				31,000
		64,000				61,000
Current assets						
Stock	25,000				30,000	
Debtors	28,000				36,000	
Short-term investments	–				2,000	
Cash	4,000				6,000	
	57,000				74,000	
Less: Creditors falling due within 1 year						
Trade creditors	14,000			12,000		
Dividends proposed	4,000			3,000		
Corporation tax due	5,000			4,000		
	(23,000)			(19,000)		
		34,000				55,000
		98,000				116,000
Less: Creditors not due within 1 year						
10% Debentures		20,000				10,000
Net assets		78,000				106,000
Financed by:						
Share capital and reserves						
£1 Ordinary shares		40,000				60,000
Share premium account		1,000				3,000
Profit and loss account		37,000				43,000
		78,000				106,000

Profit and loss account for the year ended 31 December 2000

	£	£
Sales		96,000
Less: Cost of sales		64,000
Gross profit		32,000

Wages	7,000	
Administration expenses	1,000	
Depreciation	9,000	
		17,000
Net profit before interest and taxation		15,000
Interest payments		2,000
Net profit before taxation		13,000
Corporation tax		4,000
Net profit after tax		9,000
Appropriated as follows:		
Dividends proposed		3,000
Retained profit for the year profit		6,000
Add: Retained profit brought forward		37,000
Retained profit carried forward		43,000

Note: There was no sale of fixed assets during the year.

In order to prepare a cash flow statement for the year, we must identify the cash flows from each of the five elements discussed earlier. Let us now see how the cash flows from each element are calculated.

Net cash flows from operating activities

There are two ways in which the net cash flow from operating activities may be calculated:

- the direct method
- the indirect method

The *direct method* uses information which is gleaned from the underlying accounting records maintained by the business. These records should provide information concerning cash sales and cash received from trade debtors and cash paid out for goods and services for the period. The net cash flows from operating activities can be derived from this information as follows:

	£	£
Cash sales and amounts received from trade debtors		x
Less: Cash purchases and amounts paid to trade creditors	(x)	
Cash expenses and amounts paid to suppliers of other goods and services	(x)	
		(x)
Net cash inflow (outflow) from operating activities		x/(x)

We can see that the calculations required only use cash-based figures and should, therefore, be verifiable and free from any bias.

Activity 3

Calculate the net cash flow from operations for Pentagon Ltd for the year ended 31 December 2000 using the direct method.

Cash received from debtors *can be calculated as follows:*

Opening balance of debtors	28,000
Plus sales	96,000
	124,000
Less closing debtors	36,000
Receipts from debtors	88,000

Payments to creditors *can be calculated as follows:*

Opening balance of creditors	14,000
Plus purchases	x *see below*
	$14,000 + x$
Less closing creditors	12,000
Payments to creditors	$2,000 + x$

Purchases *can be derived as follows:*

Opening stock	25,000
Plus purchases	x
	$25,000 + x$
Less closing stock	30,000
Equals cost of sales	64,000

Solving for $25,000 + x - 30,000 = 64,000$ $x = 94,000 - 25,000 = 69,000$

Substituting in the second section above Payments to creditors = £71,000

Other cash expenses *would be payments for wages and administration (£7,000 + £1,000 = £8,000)*

Operating cash flows *must be:*

Receipts from debtors	188,000
Payments to creditors	(71,000)
Other expenses	(8,000)
Net cash flow from operations	9,000

Of course, should there be prepayments or accruals relating to the other expenses further adjustment to calculate the cash outflows will be necessary.

The *indirect method* uses the information contained in the profit and loss account and balance sheet of the business to derive the net cash flow from operating activities. The starting point is the net profit before taxation. This accrual-based figure, however, requires a number of adjustments in order to derive the net cash flow from operating activities.

The net cash flow from operating activities can be derived from the accrual-based information as follows:

	£	£
Net profit from operating activities		x
Add: Interest payable	x	
Depreciation for the year	x	
Loss on sale of fixed assets	$\underline{x}$	
		$\underline{x}$
		x
Less interest receivable	(x)	
Profit on sale of fixed assets	$\underline{(x)}$	
		$\underline{(x)}$
		x
(Increase)/decrease in stock held	$(x)/x$	
(Increase)/decrease in debtors	$(x)/x$	
Increase/(decrease) in creditors	$\underline{x/(x)}$	
		$\underline{(x)/x}$
Net cash flow from operating activities		$\underline{\underline{x}}$

Activity 4

Can you explain the reason for each adjustment shown above?

Interest payable and receivable is likely to involve cash movements during the period – although the timing of interest payments and receipts must be identified. However, these are dealt with in another part of the cash flow statement and so interest payable must be added back and interest receivable must be deducted in arriving at the net cash flow from operations.

The remaining adjustments are necessary to convert the accrual-based figure of profit into an operating cash flow figure.

Depreciation and any profits or losses on the sale of fixed assets will appear in the profit and loss account of a business. However, they do not involve cash movements and are simply book entries. Thus, depreciation and any losses on sale should be added back to arrive at the cash flow from operations and any profits on sale of fixed assets should be deducted. (Although cash may be generated on the sale of a fixed asset, this will be dealt with in another part of the cash flow statement.)

An increase in **stocks and debtors** will involve a reduction in cash and a decrease in these current assets will mean an increase in cash. Similarly, a decrease in **creditors** will mean a reduction in cash and an increase will increase the cash available.

To illustrate this point let us take a simple example. We know that, where sales are on credit, the sales figure for an accounting period is unlikely to represent the cash received from sales for the period. The cash received from sales can be calculated from information contained in the profit and loss account and balance sheet as follows:

	£
Debtors at beginning of period	x
Plus sales during the period	x
Minus debtors at the end of the period	(x)
Equals cash received from sales during the period	x

If sales during a period were £100,000, debtors at the beginning of the period were £10,000 and debtors at the end of the period were £20,000, the cash received from sales for the period would be £10,000 + £100,000 − £20,000 = £90,000. Thus, the increase in debtors (from £10,000 to £20,000) over the period has led to a lower figure of cash generated. If the debtors had stayed constant over the period, the cash generated would have been £100,000. By a similar logic, we can show that increasing stocks will result in a decrease in cash and increasing creditors will result in an increase in cash.

Whether the direct or indirect method is used, you should arrive at the same figure for net cash flow from operating activities.

Activity 5

Calculate the net cash flow from operations for Pentagon Ltd for the year ended 31 December 2000 using the indirect method.

Your answer should be as follows:

	£	£
Net profit before tax		13,000
Add: Interest charges	2,000	
Depreciation	9,000	
		11,000
		24,000
Less: Increase in stocks held (30,000 − 25,000)	(5,000)	
Increase in debtors (36,000 − 28,000)	(8,000)	
Decrease in creditors (12,000 − 14,000)	(2,000)	
		(15,000)
Net cash flow from operating activities		9,000

The *indirect method* has the advantage that it focuses attention on the implications for liquidity of four different factors:

- the cash flow from profits
- the implications for liquidity of the management of stock
- the implications for liquidity of the management of debtors
- the implications for liquidity of the management of creditors

For example, it is perfectly possible for a profit to be acceptable, with the implication that liquid funds should increase by the amount of the profit plus any non-cash expenses. However, if this is accompanied by substantial increases in stock or debtors, it is not necessarily the case that the net cash flow will be positive. The contribution to liquid funds from substantial improvements in profitability may be completely cancelled out by the inefficient management of stock, debtors or creditors. The approach used above enables the separate components to be analysed. By way of illustration, consider the fact that in the above example not only have stock and debtors increased over the period (a factor which might be reasonable if sales are higher than they were in previous periods) but creditors have decreased. Such a situation is unusual. In practice, it is more usual for increases in stock and debtors to be partly financed by increases in creditors. A decrease in creditors at the same time as increases in stock and debtors occur should normally be investigated by management.

The accounting standard permits presentation of operating cash flow by either the direct method (showing the relevant constituent parts) or the indirect method (calculating operating cash flows by adjustment to the operating profit reported in the profit and loss account).

A reconciliation between the operating profit reported in the profit and loss account and the net cash flow from operations should be given, either adjoining the cash flow statement or as a note. This means that even if the direct method of calculating operating flows is used, the reconciliation effectively requires the indirect method to be disclosed.

Returns on investments and servicing of finance

We saw above that this element of the cash flow statement identifies interest paid and received during the period, together with any other receipts (e.g. dividends) resulting from ownership of an investment.

Activity 6

Calculate the net cash inflow (outflow) on returns on investments and servicing of finance for the year ended 31 December 2000 for Pentagon Ltd.

Your answer should be as follows:

	£	£
Interest paid	(2,000)	
Net cash outflow from returns on investments and servicing of finance		(2,000)

Taxation	This element of the cash flow statement will show the corporation tax which has been actually paid during the year. In the UK, corporation tax is often paid nine months after the relevant year-end. Therefore the corporation tax provision appearing in the profit and loss account for the year will normally be paid in the following year.

Activity 7

What is the taxation paid for the year ended 31 December 2000 for Pentagon Ltd?

The figure is the corporation tax owing at the end of the year ended 31 December 1999, which is £5,000.

Capital expenditure	This element reveals the acquisition and disposal of fixed assets during the period.

Activity 8

Calculate the net cash inflow (outflow) relating to capital expenditure for the year ended 31 December 2000 for Pentagon Ltd.

We are told in the question that there are no sales of fixed assets during the period and so any change in the cost of fixed assets held must be due to acquisitions. From the balance sheets we can see that the fixed assets at cost at the beginning of the period was £86,000 and the balance at cost at the end of the period was £92,000, so the acquisitions during the period must have cost £6,000 (£92,000 – £86,000). Where there are also disposals of fixed assets during the period things can be more complex. However, we will deal with this situation later.

Acquisitions and disposals	These cash flows relate to any acquisition or disposal of any trade or business. There are no such transactions in this example.

| **Dividends** | It is common for final dividends to be announced (and shown in the appropriation account) in one accounting period and paid in the following one. The dividend figure for the cash flow statement will be the dividend actually paid during the period rather than the dividend announced in that period. |

Activity 9
Show the net cash flow relating to dividends for the year ended 31 December 2000 for Pentagon Ltd.

The dividends paid amount to £4,000. This was the amount outstanding at the end of the previous year. The amount of dividend appropriated in the year is still shown as outstanding at the year-end so cannot have been paid.

In the case of an interim dividend, it is likely that it will be both announced and paid within the same period. It will, therefore, be shown in the cash flow statement for that period.

Suppose, for example, that the £3,000 dividend appropriated for the year was paid half as an interim dividend and half as a final dividend. In this case the dividends paid during the year would be the £4,000 from last year plus the interim dividend of £1,500. In the closing balance sheet dividends outstanding would be £1,500.

| **Management of liquid resources** | This section includes cash flows in respect of liquid resources. Liquid resources are defined as current asset investments held as readily disposable investment. Such assets require ready conversion and an active market. |

In the example £2,000 was spent on short-term investments.

| **Financing** | This element shows the receipts and payments arising from share and loan transactions. The amounts received or paid during the year can often be deduced by simply comparing the balances on the share account or loan account at the beginning and end of the relevant period. However, where shares are issued at a premium, the total cash generated from the issue will be represented by the increase in both the share account and the share premium account. |

Activity 10
Calculate the net cash inflow (outflow) from financing for the year ended 31 December 2000 for Pentagon Ltd.

The answer to this activity is as follows:

Financing	£	£
Issue of ordinary shares {(60,000 – 40,000) + (3,000 – 1,000)]	22,000	
Repayment of debenture loan (10,000 – 20,000)	(10,000)	
Net cash inflow from financing		12,000

We have now calculated all the elements of cash flow for the period and are in a position to prepare the cash flow statement.

Activity 11
Prepare a cash flow statement for the year ended 31 December 2000 for Pentagon Ltd.

Your answer should be as follows:

Pentagon Ltd
Cash flow statement for the year ended 31 December 2000

	£	£
Net cash inflow from operating activities		9,000
Returns on investments and servicing of finance		
Interest paid	(2,000)	
Net cash inflow (outflow) from returns on investments and servicing of finance		(2,000)
Taxation		
Corporation tax paid		(5,000)
Capital expenditure		
Payments to acquire fixed assets	(6,000)	
Net cash inflow (outflow) from investing activities		(6,000)
		(4,000)
Dividends paid		(4,000)
		(8,000)
Management of liquid resources		
Short-term deposits		(2,000)
Financing activities		
Issue of ordinary shares	22,000	
Repayment of debenture loan	(10,000)	
Net cash outflow from financing		12,000
Increase in cash and cash equivalents		2,000

17.9 Analysis of changes in cash and cash equivalents during the year

The £4,000 increase in cash and cash equivalents which is revealed in the above statement can be reconciled with the changes in the balance sheet as follows:

Analysis of changes in cash and cash equivalents for the year

	£
Balance as at 1 January 2000	4,000
Net cash inflow during the year	2,000
Balance as at 31 December 2000	6,000

This reconciliation, of course, provides us with a useful check on the accuracy of our workings. It is also a requirement of the relevant accounting standard that this reconciliation be shown as a note to the cash flow statement prepared by companies.

17.10 Some further issues about preparing a cash flow statement

The above example involved the preparation of a fairly simple cash flow statement. There are, however, a few points concerning the preparation of cash flow statements which can cause difficulties. When preparing such statements, therefore, it is important to bear in mind the following:

- When using the indirect method, the profit figure to be used in calculating the net cash flows from operations is the net profit before tax and other appropriations. Increases in reserves arising from appropriations during the period should be ignored. Since the net profit before tax and appropriations is regarded as a source of cash flows, any increases in reserves arising from appropriations should not be included as it would represent double counting.
- Share issues represent a source of cash with one exception, the bonus or scrip issue. A bonus issue represents a capitalization of reserves, i.e. a book entry, and does not result in an inflow of funds. As a result, bonus issues should be ignored when preparing the cash flow statement. However, all other share issues will result in additional cash being generated.
- Movements in fixed assets may involve both the disposal of existing assets, and the acquisition of new assets. Where depreciation provisions are kept for each type of fixed asset, it may be useful to tabulate fixed asset movements as follows:

	Cost	Depreciation provision	Net	Notes
	£	£	£	
Opening balance	x	x	x	
Less: disposals	−x	−x	−x	(a)
	x	x	x	
Plus: new acquisitions at cost	x	–	x	
	x	x	x	

Less: depreciation for the year	–	+x	–x	(b)
Closing balance	x	x	x	

(a) Deduct the cost of any asset disposed of from the cost figure, deduct the depreciation figure on the asset being disposed of from the overall depreciation provision, and deduct the net book value of the asset from the net figure.

(b) The amount of depreciation taken in the year will increase the depreciation provision, which will, in turn, reduce the net book value of the asset.

- It is the cash received on the sale of fixed assets that must be included in the cash flow statement as an inflow of cash and not the profit arising on sales. Any profit (or loss) on sales is simply a book entry and usually represents over- (or under-) depreciation of the asset. Hence, it does not represent an inflow of funds and must not be included as such. Profits (or losses) on the sale of fixed assets which appear in the profit and loss account should be deducted (or added) to net profit before tax in order to derive the net cash flow from operations.

Activity 12

From the following balance sheet information relating to Octagon Ltd prepare a cash flow statement for the year ended 31 December 2000.

Balance sheet as at 31 December	1999		2000	
	£000	£000	£000	£000
Fixed assets				
Cost		1,800		2,700
Depreciation provision		400		600
		1,400		2,100
Current assets				
Stock	500		400	
Debtors	400		600	
Cash	300		700	
	1,200		1,700	
Less *Liabilities due within a year*				
Creditors	300		200	
Dividends proposed	100		150	
Corporation Tax	300		500	
	(700)		(850)	
Net current assets		500		850
		1,900		2,950

Capital and reserves		
Issued ordinary share capital	1,000	1,200
Preference share capital	500	600
Reserves	400	1,150
	1,900	2,950

Profit and loss account for the year ending 31 December 2000

	£000	£000
Sales		4,000
Cost of sales		1,300
Gross profit		2,700
Depreciation	500	
Loss on sale of fixed asset	100	
Other expenses	500	
		1,100
Net profit before tax		1,600
Corporation tax		500
Net profit after tax		1,100
less dividends proposed		150
Added to reserves		950

Additional information

1 During the year fixed assets were sold for £100,000. These had cost £500,000 and had been depreciated by £300,000.
2 There was a bonus issue to ordinary shareholders during the year on a one- for-five basis.

The solution is given below, together with workings.

Cash flow statement for the year ended 31 December 2000

	£000	£000	Note
Net cash inflow from operating activities		1,900	1
Returns on investments and servicing of finance			
Interest received	100		
Net cash inflow (outflow) from returns on investments and servicing of finance		100	
Taxation			
Corporation tax paid		(300)	
Capital expenditure			
Payments to acquire fixed assets	(1,400)		2
Receipts from sales of fixed assets	100		
Net cash inflow (outflow) from capital expenditure activities		(1,300)	
		400	

Dividends paid		(100)	3
		300	

Financing

Issue of preference capital	100		4
Net cash inflow (outflow) from financing		100	

Increase (decrease) in cash and cash equivalents	400

Analysis of changes in cash and cash equivalents during the year

Cash at beginning of period	300
Net cash inflow during the year	400
Cash at end of period	700

Notes

1 Net cash inflow (outflow) from operations

	£000	£000
Net profit before taxation		1,600
Add: Depreciation for the year	500	
Loss on sale of fixed assets	100	
		600
		2,200
Less: Interest receivable		100
		2,100
(Increase)/decrease in stock held	100	
(Increase)/decrease in debtors	(200)	
Increase/(decrease) in creditors	(100)	
		(200)
Net cash flow from operating activities		1,900

2 The fixed assets movements can be seen as follows:

	Cost	Depreciation provision	Net
	£000	£000	£000
Opening balance	1,800	400	1,400
Less: Disposals	−500	−300	−200
	1,300	100	1,200
Plus: New acquisitions at cost	1,400*	–	x
	2,700	100	x
Less: Depreciation for the year	–	500	−500
Closing balance	2,700	600	2,100

*Missing figure.
The sale proceeds of £100,000 are shown as an inflow.

3 The 1999 final dividends are assumed to have been paid in 2000.

4 The increase in ordinary share capital over the year was £200,000. All of this was attributable to a bonus issue. The increase in preference share capital, £100,000, is the result of a cash issue.

Self-assessment question 17.1

From the information provided below you are required to prepare a cash flow statement (using the indirect method) for the year ending 28 February 2001. Also prepare an analysis of changes in cash and cash equivalents during the year.

Balance sheets as at 28 February	2000 £	£	2001 £	£
Fixed assets				
Plant & equipment – cost	60,000		81,000	
Less depreciation provision	30,000		42,000	
		30,000		39,000
Motor vans – cost	14,000		17,000	
Less depreciation provision	6,000		9,000	
		8,000		8,000
		38,000		47,000
Current assets				
Stock	12,000		15,000	
Debtors	10,000		12,000	
Bank	3,000		1,000	
	25,000		28,000	
Less Creditors due within one year				
Trade creditors	18,000		15,000	
		7,000		13,000
		45,000		60,000
Less Creditors due in more than one year				
12% Debentures		–		10,000
		45,000		50,000
Represented by:				
Capital and reserves				
Ordinary £1 shares		30,000		30,000
Reserves		15,000		20,000
		45,000		50,000

Profit and Loss Account for the year ending 28 February 2001		
	£	£
Sales		120,000
Cost of sales	70,000	
Depreciation	15,000	
Other expenses	30,000	
		115,000
Net profit before tax		5,000
Add retained profit b/f		15,000
Profit and Loss Account balance at 28 February 2001		20,000

17.11 Interpreting the cash flow statement

The cash flow statement identifies the cash flow from operations and provides a useful insight into the financing and investing activities of management. Using the information provided, investors and other interested parties can decide whether the funding mix was appropriate given the financial policy and structure of the business and whether the funds generated were applied in the best possible way. A cash flow statement helps focus attention on the resources which are available for capital expenditure, and may provide useful insights into the best ways of financing such expenditure. For example, a choice may exist between leasing a new asset, or buying it, possibly using borrowed funds. The implications of the different financing methods need to be carefully considered, and the cash flow framework is particularly useful in this regard. A cash flow statement, or series of statements built up over time, may provide a useful indicator of security for lenders and creditors, and to likely profit distributions to owners. Such a statement may well suggest ways in which the working capital position may be improved.

While the emphasis of this chapter is on the preparation of a historic cash flow statement, forecast statements can be extremely useful to managers, investors and lenders in assessing the implications of potential future activities. This idea will be dealt with in more detail in the next chapter.

Activity 13

Outline the most significant factors revealed by the cash flow statement prepared in the self-assessment question above.

Your answer may be along the following lines:

- *The statement reveals that a significant proportion of the cash inflows were from operating activities. The remainder was generated through the issue of debentures.*

This shows that the business relied largely on the re-investment of profit to finance the expansion of the business. Shareholders were not called upon to provide additional funds during the period.

- *The funds raised (and more) were used for the purchase of more fixed assets. Hence, over the period there has been a decline in cash, which may give rise to concern.*
- *Using the indirect method, the impact of inappropriate working capital management can be seen. Increases in stock and debtors have an unfavourable effect on liquid funds, as has a reduction in creditors. Under normal circumstances, we would not expect changes in all three of these to result in a reduction in cash. Increases in sales might reasonably be expected to lead to increases in stock and debtors, but some of the resulting expenditure can usually be funded from increases in creditors. While there may be good reasons for the pattern revealed, some questions need to be asked about the reason for, and the consequences of, the reduction in cash.*

Self-assessment question 17.2

The following information relates to the activities of Hexagon Ltd:

Balance sheets as at 31 March	2000		2001	
	£	£	£	£
Fixed assets				
Freehold land at cost		700,000		780,000
Plant & equipment – cost	560,000		660,000	
Less depreciation provision	230,000		296,000	
		330,000		364,000
		1,030,000		1,144,000
Current assets				
Stock	356,000		498,000	
Debtors	330,000		344,000	
Bank	30,000		–	
		716,000		842,000
Total assets		1,746,000		1,986,000
Less Creditors due within one year				
Trade creditors	240,000		280,000	
Corporation Tax	120,000		150,000	
Proposed dividend	40,000		50,000	
Bank overdraft	–		56,000	
		400,000		536,000
		1,346,000		1,450,000

Represented by:		
Capital and reserves		
Ordinary £1 shares	400,000	600,000
Share premium	160,000	160,000
General reserve	450,000	250,000
Profit & Loss	336,000	440,000
	1,346,000	1,450,000

Summarized **Profit and Loss Account for the year ending 31 March 2001**

	£	£
Sales		4,520,000
Cost of sales	3,420,000	
Depreciation of plant	124,000	
Loss on sale of plant	8,000	
Other expenses	634,000	
		4,186,000
Net profit before tax		334,000
Corporation Tax		150,000
Net profit after tax		184,000
Less: Interim dividend paid	30,000	
Final dividend proposed	50,000	
		80,000
		104,000
Profit and loss account		
balance at 31 March 2000		336,000
Profit and loss account		
balance at 31 March 2000		440,000

You are informed that:

(a) In September 2000 a bonus issue of one share for every two held was made out of the general reserve.
(b) Plant which originally cost £80,000 was sold for cash. Accumulated depreciation relating to the plant sold amounted to £58,000.

Required
Prepare a cash flow statement and an analysis of changes in cash and cash equivalents for the year ended 31 March 2001. Comment on the information provided.

17.12 **Summary**

The cash flow statement, the profit and loss account and the balance sheet represent the principal financial statements presented to external users. The cash flow statement is similar to the profit and loss account in that both are concerned with flows over a period. It is concerned with the flow of liquid funds in and out of the business over a period while the income statement is concerned with the flow of profits over a period. Both the cash flow statement and income statement are dynamic statements, i.e. they are concerned with changes occurring over time. This contrasts with the balance sheet which provides a static picture of financial position. The cash flow statement, however, provides a useful link between the balance sheets at the beginning and end of each year. By showing the changes in assets, liabilities and capital which occur during the year, the cash flow statement helps explain how the business arrived at its current financial position. It is therefore a very useful tool of analysis.

Exercises

1 Are the following items added to or subtracted from the net profit before tax when deriving the net cash flow from operations? Mark your response with a cross under the appropriate heading.

	Added	Subtracted
Increase in stock		
Increase in debtors		
Increase in creditors		
Depreciation for the year		
Interest received		
Loss on sale of fixed asset		

2 Calculate the net cash inflows (outflows) from operating activities for the year using the direct method from the following information relating to H&S Ltd:

	£
Cash sales	280,000
Cash payments to trade creditors	323,000
Payments made to acquire fixed assets	75,000
Cash received from debtors	197,000
Cash expenses	54,000
Interest paid	22,000
Cash at bank at beginning of year	12,000
Cash at bank at the end of year	13,000
Dividends paid during year	26,000
Loan repaid	120,000

3 From the following information prepare a cash flow statement for 2000:

Balance sheet as at 31 December	1999		2000	
	£000	£000	£000	£000
Fixed assets				
Cost		1,800		2,700
Less accumulated depreciation		400		600
		1,400		2,100
Current assets				
Stock	500		400	
Debtors	400		600	
Cash	300		700	
	1,200		1,700	
Less: *Creditors falling due within one year*				
Creditors	(300)		(200)	
Dividends proposed	(100)		(150)	
Corporation tax	(300)		(500)	
	(700)		(850)	
Net current assets		500		850
Total assets less current liabilities		1,900		2,950
Capital and reserves				
Issued ordinary share capital		1,000		1,200
Preference share capital		500		600
Reserves		400		1,150
		1,900		2,950

Profit and Loss Account for 2000

	£	£
Sales		4,000
Cost of sales		1,500
Gross profit		2,500
Expenses	500	
Depreciation	500	
Loss on disposal of fixed assets	100	
		1,100
Net profit		1,400
Less appropriations		
Corporation tax	500	
Dividends proposed	150	
		650
Added to reserves		750

During the fixed year assets were sold for £100,000. These had cost £500,000 and had been depreciated by £300,000.

4 The management of your company is perplexed as to why its bank balance has gone down in the last year, even though profits have been satisfactory. From the following information prepare a cash flow statement to show how the cash has decreased during the year.

Balance sheet as at	1 January		31 December	
	£	£	£	£
Fixed assets				
Premises		60,000		70,000
Plant – cost	25,000		35,000	
Less: Accumulated depreciation	15,000		16,000	
		10,000		19,000
Vehicles – cost	15,000		18,000	
Less: Accumulated depreciation	8,000		6,000	
		7,000		12,000
		77,000		101,000
Investments at cost		40,000		50,000
Current assets				
Stock	30,000		50,000	
Debtors	40,000		70,000	
Cash	49,000		9,000	
	119,000		129,000	
Less: *Creditors falling due within one year*				
Creditors	50,000		30,000	
Dividends proposed	6,000		10,000	
Corporation tax	10,000		12,000	
	(66,000)		(42,000)	
Net current assets		53,000		77,000
Total assets less current liabilities		170,000		228,000
Less: *Creditors falling due in more than one year*				
Debentures		10,000		40,000
		160,000		188,000
Capital and reserves				
Issued ordinary share capital		100,000		120,000
Reserves		60,000		68,000
		160,000		188,000

During the year vehicles costing £6,000, which had been depreciated by £5,000, were sold for £2,000. Total depreciation charges for the year were £4,000, debenture interest was £3,000 and net profit before tax was £30,000.

5 From the following balance sheet information relating to Squares Ltd prepare a cash flow statement for the year ended 31 December 2000. Also prepare an analysis of changes in cash and cash equivalents for the year.

Balance sheet as at 31 December	1999 £	1999 £	2000 £	2000 £
Fixed assets				
Freehold land at cost		80,000		95,000
Plant – cost	75,000		85,000	
Less depreciation provision	30,000		40,000	
		45,000		45,000
		125,000		140,000
Current assets				
Stock	21,000		24,000	
Debtors	18,000		22,000	
Cash	4,000		1,000	
	43,000		47,000	
Less: *Creditors due within one year*				
Creditors	(20,000)		(18,000)	
Dividends proposed	(8,000)		(10,000)	
Corporation tax	(6,000)		(9,000)	
	(34,000)		(37,000)	
Net current assets		9,000		10,000
		134,000		150,000
Capital and reserves				
Issued ordinary share capital		70,000		80,000
Profit and loss account		44,000		46,000
General reserve		20,000		24,000
		134,000		150,000

The profit before tax for 2000 was £25,000.

(*Hint:* In this question a profit and loss account is not provided. It is therefore necessary to derive the figures you require from the balance sheets. To calculate the net cash flows from operations look at the changes between the balance sheets in order to derive the depreciation charge for the period.)

Chapter 18

The use of financial statements for planning and decision making

18.1 Introduction

This chapter aims to show how the three basic financial statements (balance sheet, profit and loss account and cash flow statement) can be used on a forecast basis, rather than on a historic basis, and to identify the contribution that such forecast statements can make to planning and decision making. The potential of computerized spreadsheets in this area will be illustrated.

18.2 Objectives

On completion of this chapter you should be able to:

- appreciate the need to formulate forecasts and plan in financial terms;
- recognize the integrated nature of the three financial statements, and appreciate their potential as the basis of a financial planning model;
- prepare forecast profit and loss accounts, forecast balance sheets and forecast cash flow statements from basic planning data and appreciate how the use of those statements can aid planning;
- explain the advantages of using spreadsheets to formulate a planning model.

18.3 Financial statements as a basis for forecasting

So far in this book we have considered three major financial statements (namely the balance sheet, the profit and loss account and the cash flow statement) which provide a completely integrated financial picture of an organization. In effect, these three statements are a financial model of the organization.

In considering plans for the future, there is no reason why the same three statements (or models) should not be used to provide a financial framework for assessing the financial implications, including the financial viability, of such plans. Eventually, after the end of the period to which the plans relate, accounting statements will be prepared to cover that period. At that time, it would seem sensible to assess the success of the plans by comparing the actual outcome for the period with that which was planned.

Activity 1

What are the advantages of the approach described in the previous paragraph?

If the forecast statements indicate that profits will not be satisfactory, or that the financial position will have weaknesses, the plans may need to be modified. In fact, the preparation of forecasts is likely to be particularly useful in deciding upon the best methods of financing the business, or of financing any new projects forming part of that business.

The major difference between forecast and historical financial statements is that historical accounting statements are based upon actual events and objective evidence, whereas forecasts are based on expected events and rather more subjective evidence or opinions. Of course, in preparing forecasts as much objective evidence as can be obtained should be used.

Financial statements for the current year generally represent a good starting point, and provide an objective base position for the development of an integrated financial planning model. In order to illustrate the principles of forecasting using the three financial statements, consider the following example.

Example

The directors of Green Ltd are reviewing the company's financial requirements for the year to 31 December 2001. The summarized balance sheet of Green Ltd as at 31 December 2000 was as follows:

	£	£	£
Fixed assets			
Freehold warehouse			32,000
Fittings and equipment – cost		20,000	
Depreciation provision		8,500	
			11,500
			43,500
Current assets			
Stock		23,000	
Debtors		32,500	
		55,500	
Creditors due within 1 year			
Creditors	19,800		
Bank overdraft	3,000		
		22,800	
			32,700
			76,200
Capital and reserves			
Ordinary share capital			40,000
Reserves			36,200
			76,200

The company's plans are based upon the following expectations for the year to 31 December 2001:

(a) The issue for cash of 10,000 £1 ordinary shares at a premium of 50p per share.
(b) The purchase of new equipment for £7,000 cash on 1 January.
(c) No dividends.
(d) Stock at the year end will be £29,000.
(e) The following trading transactions will occur at an even rate throughout the year:

Sales	£240,000
Purchases	£186,000
General expenses	£35,000
Directors' salaries	£8,000

(f) The period of credit allowed to customers will be 2 calendar months and the period of credit taken from suppliers will be $1\frac{1}{2}$ calendar months. All amounts (including debtors and creditors outstanding at 31 December 2000) will be paid in full at the end of the credit periods. No amounts for general expenses or directors' salaries will be outstanding, i.e. there will be no accruals or prepayments at the end of the year.
(g) Depreciation on all equipment held at the end of the year will be provided for at the rate of 10% per annum on cost.

The forecast statements for 2001 should appear as follows (workings as shown below):

Forecast profit and loss account for the year ending 31 December 2001

	£	£
Sales		240,000
Opening stock	23,000	
Purchases	186,000	
	209,000	
Less closing stock	29,000	
Cost of sales		180,000
Gross profit		60,000
Less: General expenses	35,000	
Wages and salaries	8,000	
Depreciation	2,700	
		45,700
Net profit		14,300

Forecast balance sheet as at 31 December 2001

Fixed assets	£	£
Freehold warehouse		32,000
Fittings and equipment – cost	27,000	
Depreciation provision	11,200	
		15,800
		47,800
Current assets		
Stock	29,000	
Debtors	40,000	
Cash	11,950	
	80,950	
Creditors due within a year		
Creditors	(23,250)	
		57,700
		105,500
Capital and reserves		
Capital		50,000
Share premium		5,000
Reserves		50,500
		105,500

Cash flow statement for the year ending 31 December 2001

	£	£
Operating activities		
Net profit before tax	14,300	
Depreciation/loss on cash	2,700	
Increase/decrease in stock	(6,000)	
Increase/decrease in debtors	(7,500)	
Increase in creditors	3,450	
Net cash inflow from operating activities		6,950
Capital expenditure		
Purchase of fixed assets	(7,000)	
Net cash outflow from capital expenditure activities		(7,000)
		(50)
Financing activities		
Shares issued	15,000	
Net cash inflow from financing activities		15,000
Increase in cash and cash equivalents		14,950

(The indirect method of preparing the cash flow statement is used in this case as it highlights the relationship between profit and cash, while also focusing on issues relating to working capital management.)

Workings

1 The items in the profit and loss account are provided by notes (e) and (g). The depreciation is taken as 10% on the cost of fittings and equipment owned at the end of the year.
2 With regard to the balance sheet, changes are arrived at as follows:

- Fittings and equipment (at cost) increase by £7,000 (the amount purchased during the year) to £27,000, with annual depreciation being 10% of this (£2,700). This in turn increases the amount of the depreciation provision at the year-end to £11,200.
- The closing stock figure is a directors' estimate (note (d)).
- The debtors figure represents 2 months' credit, i.e. one-sixth of sales.
- The cash figure reflects the opening overdraft and the increase in liquid funds expected for the year, which is in turn the figure resulting from the funds flow statement.
- The creditors figure represents $1\frac{1}{2}$ months' credit on the purchases $[(£186,000/12) \times 1.5)]$.
- The capital is increased by the new issue at its nominal value.
- The premium reflects the premium of 50p per share on the new issue.
- The reserves reflect the opening balance plus the profit for the year.

3 When preparing forecast cash flow statements, it is appropriate (and usually more convenient) to make assumptions or plans about levels of stock, debtors and creditors, and to see the impact of such plans on the liquid funds, in this case cash. The resulting change in liquid funds will clearly need to be incorporated into the balance sheet, as was shown above. The figures in the cash flow statement were arrived at as follows:

- Operating activities – net profit (from the profit and loss account) adjusted for depreciation and changes in working capital – the difference between the balance sheet figure at the end of 2000 and 2001.
- Financing activities (capital) – the new issue at a premium.
- Investing activities – the new equipment purchased.

It is important to recognize the interrelationships between the three statements, and to be able to assess the impact of changes in certain variables on all three statements.

Activity 2

Show the effect of the following alternative assumptions on the three financial statements:

	Profit and loss	Balance sheet	Cash flow
(a) dividends of £10,000 being proposed			
(b) the period of credit allowed to customers being reduced to $1\frac{1}{2}$ months			
(c) the period of credit taken from suppliers being reduced to 1 month			
(d) the period of credit allowed to customers being increased to 3 months			
(e) depreciation being taken at 20% per annum on cost			
(f) closing stock being valued at £35,000			
(g) an increase in sales of £20,000			
(h) an increase in general expenses of £5,000			

The solutions are:

	Profit and loss	*Balance sheet*	*Cash flow*
(a) Dividends of £10,000 being proposed	appropriation of £10,000	increase liability dividends proposed	none
(b) The period of credit allowed to customers being reduced to $1\frac{1}{2}$ months	none	reduction in debtors to £30,000	reduction in debtors £2,500 – effective source
(c) The period of credit taken from suppliers being reduced to 1 month	none	reduction in creditors to £15,500	reduction in creditors £4,300 – effective outflow
(d) The period of credit allowed to customers being increased to three months	none	increase in debtors to £60,000	increase in debtors £27,500 – effective outflow
(e) Depreciation being taken at 20% per annum on cost	reduce by further £2,700	reduce net assets by £2,700	adjustment to profit increased by £2,700
(f) Closing stock being valued at £35,000	increase profit by £6,000	increase stock £12,000	increase in stock £12,000 – effective outflow
(g) An increase in sales of £20,000	increase	increase in associated debtors/cash/reserves	increase in profit
(h) An increase in general expenses of £5,000	reduce	reduce reserves	reduce profit

18.4
Likely
information
needed for
forecast
statements

It is clear from the example given in the previous section that a substantial number of assumptions, estimates and decisions need to be made about the future direction of the business before a set of financial forecasts can be completed. In the example decisions were made about the acquisition of new plant, the new share issue, and not to pay dividends. Explicit decisions may have been made about such things as the desired level of stock, debtors and creditors. On the other hand, the level of these items may have been viewed more as an assumption, based upon previous trends. This still reflects an *implicit* planning decision. Given the importance of sound working capital management, it is suggested that these variables should reflect positive thinking, rather than be taken as something over which the business has little control. Some kind of estimates were made of expected revenues and associated costs. In practice, such estimates are likely to be rather more difficult than may have been implied by the above example.

Clearly the example given above was very simple, and in reality many more assumptions, estimates and decisions need to be made before a set of financial plans can be drawn up. The purpose of this section is to identify the kind of factors which are likely to arise in most businesses, so as to provide a more detailed framework in which to operate.

Estimates/assumptions/decisions relating to the profit and loss account

Sales

Sales estimates will need to be made to cover the range of products or services supplied by the business. It will probably be useful to separate existing products from new products, since a range of historic (and therefore objective) information is likely to exist for the former, which may well provide a sound base for estimates of future sales. Estimates of sales of new products are more likely to be supported by such things as market research studies. In both cases it will usually be necessary to estimate both sales quantity and sales price, and to establish likely *changes in sales volume* (i.e. changes due to the sale of a different number of products) and *changes in selling price* for future periods. Important factors relating to changes in sales revenue include: the state of the economy; changes in demand due to fashion and other factors; levels of inflation; product quality; after-sales service; and advertising. Some of these are capable of being influenced by an individual business: others are not.

Cost of sales and associated expenses

It is important in making estimates of expenses to distinguish between fixed and variable elements of cost. *Variable costs*, which frequently include things such as materials, wages and certain kinds of other expenses, are costs which vary in proportion to the level of output. As sales double, so variable costs double. *Fixed costs*, on the other hand, are costs which remain constant, or fixed, irrespective of the level of production. Of course, in practice many costs do not fall precisely into either category, and it may be necessary to make estimates of likely variations in costs over a range of output, using some kind of statistical cost analysis. In making estimates of future expenses, the split between variable and fixed elements is important since changes may be attributable to changes in the volume of output, and to changes in individual costs. Changes in the former should relate to sales (or changes in productivity), while changes in the latter may be unaffected by changes in volume, but be caused by factors outside of the control of an individual business. (The converse may, of course, be true.)

Activity 3

A business has sales of existing products as follows:

Product	Price per unit	Quantity	Sales revenue
A	£10	1,000	£10,000
B	£20	2,000	£40,000

Associated costs are as follows:

Product	Variable cost per unit	Fixed costs	Total costs
A	£5	£3,000	£8,000
B	£12	£6,000	£30,000

In the following year sales volume is expected to increase by 20% for product A, and 10% for product B. Selling price per unit will be held steady for product A, but will increase by 5% for product B. Costs are expected to increase by the expected rate of inflation for the next year, which is 7%.

Show the expected sales revenues and associated costs for products A and B for the next year.

The figures are as follows:

Sales	*Quantity*	*Price/cost*	*Total*
A	1,200 (1,000 + 20%)	£10	£12,000
B	2,200 (2,000 + 10%)	£21 (£20 + 5%)	£46,200
Variable costs			
A	1,200	£5.35 (£5 + 7%)	£6,420
B	2,200	£12.84 (£12 + 7%)	£28,248
Fixed costs			
A		£3,210 (£3,000 + 7%)	£3,210
B		£6,420 (£6,000 + 7%)	£6,420

Activity 4

How realistic is the assumption in Activity 1 that costs are expected to increase by the expected rate of inflation for the year?

The rate of inflation reflects a kind of average, and individual types of costs may well behave in a variety of ways. In practice, estimates will need to be made of changes for each major type. Some costs may be fixed in money terms, and will not rise at all.

In making forecasts of fixed costs for the future, it may also be necessary to distinguish clearly between those costs which involve a cash outflow, and those which do not (e.g. depreciation). Costs not involving a cash outflow will clearly not be subject to cost inflation as such. It will also be necessary to identify separately any costs which are specified in money terms, since these are also not subject to cost inflation. New ventures may well lead to increases in fixed costs over and above any incurred in previous years.

Activity 5

A business has total fixed costs in a particular year of £500,000, comprising £200,000 depreciation (based upon straight-line depreciation of fixed assets costing £1 million), £100,000 interest (based upon a fixed interest rate loan of £1 million), and cash costs (e.g. labour, materials, power costs etc.) of £200,000.
Estimate the total for fixed costs in the next year if cost inflation is expected to be 10%.

The fixed costs of £500,000 may be broken down as follows:

	£
Depreciation	*200,000*
Interest	*100,000*
Cash costs	*200,000*

If the total of fixed assets remains the same (£1m), as does the method of depreciation, there is no reason to suppose that the depreciation charge in the next year will change. Similarly, interest is not subject to an inflationary adjustment. Only the cash costs will be subject to the 10% inflation. Expected fixed costs for the next year are thus:

	£
Depreciation	*200,000*
Interest	*100,000*
Cash costs	*220,000*
Total fixed costs	*£520,000*

Depreciation and related costs

In order to make estimates of depreciation in future periods it is necessary to establish expected fixed asset movements, and to make the necessary calculations from these. Projected depreciation figures should be based upon current fixed assets plus any projected new purchases of fixed assets, less any projected disposals of fixed assets. Since accounting policies with regard to depreciation are likely to be well established, it should be possible to ascertain the implications of all expected transactions related to fixed assets by reference to a table along the lines shown below.

	Cost	Depreciation provision	Net
	£	£	£
Balance at the beginning of the year	x	x	x
Less disposals	(x)	(x)	(x)
Plus new assets acquired	x	–	x
Depreciation	–	x	x
Balance at the end of the year	x	x	x

In fact this approach will enable all fixed asset movements to be calculated, and relevant figures can then be put into each financial statement. The balances at the year-end reflect the figures needed for the balance sheet. The depreciation figure will form part of the profit and loss account. When the proceeds from the sale of fixed assets are compared with the net book value of disposals, any profit or loss on disposal can be calculated and be put into the profit and loss account. The sale proceeds will be reflected in the cash flow statement as a source, while the depreciation and profit/loss on disposal will be shown as adjustments to profit. The new assets acquired will show as an outflow in the investing activities section of the cash flow statement.

Activity 6

A business has equipment shown in its accounts at £500,000 cost, and £200,000 depreciation provision. It uses straight-line depreciation, based on 20% per annum, with depreciation being calculated on all assets held at a year-end. In the next year it expects to spend £200,000 and in the following year £100,000 on new equipment. In the next year it also expects to dispose of equipment (cost £50,000, depreciation £40,000) for £5,000. Using the tables below show the expected movements in fixed assets, and the relevant figures in the three major financial statements.

Balance sheet

Year 1

Equipment	Cost £	Depreciation provision £	Net £
Balance at the beginning of the year			
Less disposals			
Plus new assets acquired			
Depreciation			
Balance at the end of the year			

Year 2

Equipment	Cost £	Depreciation provision £	Net £
Balance at the beginning of the year			
Less disposals			
Plus new assets acquired			
Depreciation			
Balance at the end of the year			

Profit and loss account entries	Year 1 £	Year 2 £
Depreciation		
Profit/loss on disposal		
Cash flow statement entries	Year 1 £	Year 2 £
Operating flows		
Adjustment for depreciation/Loss on disposal		
Capital expenditure		
New equipment		
Proceeds from disposal of asset		

The solution is as follows:

Balance sheet

Year 1

Equipment	Cost £	Depreciation provision £	Net £
Balance at the beginning of the year	500,000	200,000	300,000
Less disposals	50,000	40,000	10,000
	450,000	160,000	290,000
Plus new assets acquired	200,000		200,000
Depreciation		130,000	(130,000)
Balance at the end of the year	650,000	290,000	360,000

Year 2

Balance at the beginning of the year	650,000	290,000	360,000
Plus new assets acquired	100,000		100,000
Depreciation		150,000	(150,000)
Balance at the end of the year	750,000	440,000	310,000

Profit and loss account entries	Year 1 £	Year 2 £
Depreciation	130,000	150,000
Loss on disposal	5,000	

Cash flow statement entries	Year 1 £	Year 2 £
Operating flows		
Adjustment for depreciation/ loss on disposal	130,000 5,000	150,000

Capital expenditure		
New equipment	*(200,000)*	*(100,000)*
Proceeds from disposal of asset	*5,000*	

Appropriations of profit	In making forecasts it will be necessary to make assumptions about tax rates, decisions about taxation planning (i.e. planned decisions which help reduce the tax burden), and decisions about dividends and transfers to reserves. Decisions with regard to preference share dividends are likely to be straightforward, since companies rarely pay less than the maximum amount. Decisions about ordinary dividends in large public companies also appear to follow fairly well-defined patterns, with dividends seldom being reduced, even in periods of quite poor trading results. Patterns in smaller companies are more variable.
Estimates/assumptions/decisions relating to the balance sheet	As has been made clear, decisions need to be made about the future acquisition and disposal of fixed assets and associated depreciation policies. Some consideration will need to be given to methods of financing new fixed assets, a point which will be returned to later.
Fixed assets	
Working capital	It is not the purpose of this chapter to explore working capital management in detail. Nevertheless, it should be clear from the earlier example that decisions should be made about the level of stock, debtors and creditors. The potential for problems in this area is enormous, and the analysis of working capital and liquidity will form an important part of the next chapter. Slack working capital management may result in large amounts of funds being tied up unnecessarily, with no increase in profits resulting. The link between the balance sheet and the cash flow statement should be clear.
Loans	It would be foolish to embark on a set of plans without some ideas on how plans are to be financed. Some decisions or assumptions in this area are required.
Capital	New capital issues occur infrequently. Where they do occur, detailed planning is appropriate. Retained earnings represent an important source of funds, and assumptions/decisions about levels of retentions are an important part of the planning process.
Estimates/assumptions/decisions about the cash flow statement	In fact, the items identified to date will frequently impact on any projections with regard to cash flow. These are: (a) profit (b) adjustments for depreciation (c) fixed asset acquisitions

(d) levels of working capital
(e) loans raised and repaid
(f) taxation and dividends
(g) capital raised or redeemed

Self-assessment question 18.1

The management of G. O. Ahead & Co Ltd are planning a vigorous expansion policy for the forthcoming year (2001), and have asked you to look at the financial implications of their plans to date. The following assumptions and estimates have been made in order to provide a basis for the planning.

Market position
(i) The total estimated market (based on the most current information available) for 2000 is £60 million.
(ii) Sales during 2000 are expected to be £3 million, based on a market share of 5%. However, the company expects to be able to achieve an increased market share in 2001, due to more aggressive marketing, with a 20% increase in sales volume being anticipated. It is expected that selling price will have to be held at current levels in 2001 since product demand tends to be elastic.

The economic environment
(i) The rate of inflation is assumed to continue at 5% per annum. This may be assumed to be an appropriate rate to inflate the costs of the company.
(ii) The rate of corporation tax is assumed to be 25% during the forthcoming year.

Dividend policy
(i) The dividend to be recommended in 2000 is 10%
(ii) It is planned that dividends should grow to 12% per annum in 2001 to cover inflation and to share in the hoped-for increased prosperity of the company.

Financial structure of the company
(i) Share capital consists of 1 million shares of £1 each, fully paid.
(ii) Reserves at the end of 2000 are expected to be £390,000.
(iii) Working capital has been controlled at levels considered to be optimal, and it is estimated that at the end of 2000 its proportions will be as follows:

Stock	12% of sales for the year
Debtors	20% of sales for the year
Cash	5% of sales for the year
Creditors	10% of sales for the year

Other current liabilities at the end of 2000 are expected to be:
- a provision for taxation on the profits for 2000 amounting to £120,000
- the estimated dividend for the year

(iv) It is intended to maintain the same working capital structure through 2001.

(v) Variable costs in 2000 are likely to be 50% of sales revenue.

(vi) Fixed costs, including depreciation of £100,000 computed at 10% on a straight-line basis, are expected to be £1 million in 2000. It is expected that a further £150,000 will have to be spent on advertising in 2001 in order to capture the increased share of the market, in addition to increased costs due to inflation.

Capital expenditure/fixed assets

(i) The company currently has fixed assets which cost £1 million, with an associated depreciation provision which is expected to stand at £200,000 at the end of 2000. Depreciation is 10% straight line.

(ii) To sustain the expansion programme the company plans to spend £350,000 on new fixed assets which will be purchased and set in use at the beginning of 2001. Depreciation will be on the same basis as existing assets. Some existing fixed assets will be sold to make way for the new assets. The cost of the assets being disposed of is £50,000, with associated depreciation being £40,000. It is expected to be sold in early 2001 for £5,000.

Required

(i) Make the necessary computations to reflect these plans.

(ii) Comment on the feasibility of the plans, particularly in the light of the desire of management that cash at the end of 2001 should equal 5% of sales for the year. Suggest any courses of action that management might take.

18.5 Using forecasts to help in decision making

Self-assessment question 18.1 was concerned with setting out the financial implications of a set of specific plans and assumptions. In reality planning and decision making is usually an iterative (trial-and-error) process, where modifications are constantly made to the plans until they reflect an acceptable outcome. Management would hope that such plans will be at or near an optimum, but frequently the process will cease once an acceptable outcome has been achieved. In Self-assessment question 18.1 it would seem reasonable to suppose that the management would react to the forecasts prepared in one of several ways:

(a) it would accept that its assumptions and decisions would lead to the fall in liquidity forecast, and implement the plans;

(b) it would find alternative ways of financing the plans, to ensure that the projected decrease in liquidity could be overcome;

(c) it would re-examine its plans to see if any changes could be made which would improve performance, probably with particular emphasis on liquidity.

Financial planning of the type described above is particularly amenable to any of these approaches. It undoubtedly identifies the financial implications of a set of plans. Hence, using Self-assessment question 18.1 as an illustration, *if actual events coincide with forecasts*, a measure of the cash shortage can be obtained, and the necessary arrangements made in good time. Without a forecast of funds flow the potential liquidity problem may not have been anticipated, since expected profits will enable the desired level of dividends to be paid.

However, where planning of the above type is most useful is with regard to modifications in plans. For example, suppose that the reaction of management to the figures shown in the solution to Self-assessment question 18.1 was to consider various ways of financing the new capital expenditure, so as to eliminate the liquidity problem. Such modifications can be made relatively easily, since the interrelationships are fairly clear.

Activity 7

Indicate the likely impact on both profitability and liquidity of G. O. Ahead & Co. Ltd. of the following alternative approaches to the new capital expenditure:

(a) The capital expenditure to be 60% financed from a bank loan carrying an interest rate of 15% per annum. The loan is to be repaid in equal annual instalments over the next four years, commencing on 31 December 2001.

(b) The new fixed assets to be leased on a six-year basis, at an annual charge of £60,000.

The solution is:

(a) *60% financing – £210,000, carrying an interest rate of 15%, would result in a decrease in profits before tax of £31,500. It would affect liquidity by reducing the source from profits by £31,500, but increase the inflow under financing activities – 'loans raised' – by £210,000, giving an overall increase in liquid funds of £178,500.*

(b) *Leasing at an annual charge of £90,000 would reduce profits by £55,000 (£90,000 less the depreciation which would have been charged on the new assets – £35,000). The impact on liquid funds would be to reduce the inflow from profits by £90,000, and to eliminate the application for fixed assets of £350,000.*

Either approach would solve the liquidity problem. Both reduce profits. The final decision reflects a balancing of concerns with profitability and liquidity.

It is suggested that the three forecast financial statements should be seen as an integrated financial model of the business, where the variables (i.e. the assumptions/decisions/estimates) can be changed to assess the implications of changes in the different variables on the expected future financial statements.

Sensitivity analysis is a particularly useful technique in this context. Sensitivity analysis essentially takes one variable and examines the effect of changes in that variable on the overall performance. It is thus particularly useful in identifying those variables which are most critical to the success or failure of the plans. Sensitivity analysis does not make any assumptions about the probability of occurrence of change in any one variable, but merely identifies the impact of such a change. Management must make its own interpretation of the probability of occurrence in reaching a decision.

Where a number of variables are to be changed at once, *scenario analysis* may be a useful technique to use. Essentially, scenario analysis is the analysis of likely results under a range of different assumptions about future events. Again, little is said about the likelihood of occurrence of the various scenarios, but the implications of different scenarios are at least worked out, and hopefully recognized.

Activity 8

Some businesses work out financial plans on a *doomsday* scenario.

What do you think this means?

What possible lessons do you think might be gleaned from such an approach, even if its probability of occurrence is low?

A doomsday scenario is one in which everything which can go wrong does go wrong. It is particularly useful in identifying all possible problem areas, so that their impact on results may be ascertained, and appropriate alternative approaches examined.

18.6 The use of spreadsheets in financial planning

An electronic spreadsheet is a computer package which is, in essence, nothing more than a grid on which various text, figures, equations and relationships can be inserted, under a specific set of assumptions.

As we have seen, the three basic accounting statements are a financial model of a business. Figures in one of the statements are linked to at least one other figure in the same statement, or in one of the other statements. Frequently this link is a particular policy of the management. For example, the debtors figure in the balance sheet is linked directly to the sales figure, in the profit and loss account, by the policy of the business on how long to allow debtors to pay their debts. The debtors figure is also linked to the cash flow statement by the same policy; the shorter the time allowed to debtors, the more cash will be in the bank.

A spreadsheet is ideal for developing forecast accounting statements, mainly because it will, if correctly specified, be able instantly to carry through all the effects of changing some variable. So, for example, if management wishes to see the effect on cash of shortening the debtors' collection period by, say, a week, this variable can be altered and the effect instantaneously reflected in all three statements.

Interrelationships between the various boxes on the grid need to be clearly established, with equations being used for all variables, i.e. those factors which could change. Absolute figures should only be inserted in the spreadsheet model for factors which are constants, i.e. there is little or no chance of them changing.

Provided that relationships have been properly defined and established on the spreadsheet, when changes in the variables are to be analysed, to assess the robustness of the plans, only these variables will need to be changed. Plans may thus be modified very easily simply by changing a small number of variables, with the result that a far better 'feel' can be obtained of the implications of changes in any of the constituent parts of the plan than could otherwise be obtained.

The following example might be helpful in developing an understanding of the use of spreadsheets.

Example

Mike, a friend of yours, is considering buying a small workshop in which to carry out a variety of work to do with the manufacture and repair of agricultural equipment. He knows that you are doing an accounting course as part of your studies, and asks you to help him develop some 'proper' figures to help him in his negotiations with his bank manager. In discussions with him you identify the following facts.

(a) The workshop will cost £25,000, including related legal fees, and equipment is expected to cost a further £5,000. The equipment is expected to last for ten years.

(b) The initial stocks of materials needed for manufacture and repair of equipment are likely to cost approximately £2,000. It is expected that a regular holding of this amount would avoid any problems with regard to delivery times. Material costs are expected to amount to approximately 25% of total revenue for the year.

(c) Mike has £5,000 of his own money to put into the business. He is currently thinking of asking his bank manager if he can borrow a further £30,000 from the bank. If he is successful interest will be at 15% per annum, and the debt will be repaid over ten years in equal annual instalments. Mike will also bring his van, valued at £2,000, into the business. The van is expected to last another five years.

(d) On average revenue will be received one month after the work has been carried out. This revenue will be the result of work by Mike and his assistant John, and is based upon an assumed 40-hour week, 48-week year, and an hourly charge rate of £10, for both of them.

(e) Mike expects to make cash drawings based upon an hourly rate of £5. John will be paid £3.50 an hour. Both will be paid for 52 weeks, to include four weeks' holiday pay.

(f) Other annual expenses are estimated as follows:

- rates   £1,000
- heat and light   £600
- telephone   £1,000
- vehicle expenses   £1,500
- insurance   £600
- other materials   £500

(g) Mike intends to operate the business as a sole trader, not as a limited company.

This example, which is based upon an actual business, encapsulates the essence of most planning and decision making. The problem may be broken down into the following components and related questions.

1 What assumptions can be made about the business, in terms of assets needed, likely levels of activity, and associated revenues and expenses?
2 Will a satisfactory profit be made, and what are likely profit levels in future years?
3 If the business plans are viable in terms of profitability, what are the working capital/liquidity needs of the business, how should the business be financed, and are there any potential liquidity problems which might arise in the future?
4 What might go wrong? How soundly based is the business? Can the business survive unfavourable events?

In this case, Mike has already made most of the critical assumptions. He has a very good idea of what the workshop will cost. (Indeed, cost of fixed assets is likely to be known fairly accurately, since it is probably based on actual prices and an estimate of inflation.) He has made assumptions, albeit implicitly in some cases, about working capital levels, revenue, expenses and workload. He has implicitly assumed that there will be enough work to keep himself and John working full-time (i.e. 40 hours per week for 48 weeks per year). This may be a questionable assumption, and it is one that will be reviewed later, but it is Mike's starting point. Given these assumptions, it should be possible to make an initial assessment of the likely financial performance of the business in its first year of operation.

In approaching a problem using a spreadsheet it is important to do a number of things:

1 Clarify all assumptions, and identify those factors which are to be treated as variables. In this example the variables chosen are: number of weeks' work for both Mike and John; the number of hours' work per week; the charge rate per hour; the rate of pay per hour; and the interest rate. Clearly other factors (e.g. the period of credit, the relationship between sales and variable costs, the period of repayment of the loan, the impact

of inflation on revenues and expenses) could, in real life, also change. To try to keep matters simple, we shall treat these factors as constants, i.e. we shall assume that there will not be any changes in these. The distinction between variables and constants is important in building the spreadsheet model. This is because we need to build into the model the facility to alter variables and for the full effect of those alterations to be reflected in all three statements. For constants, we need not go to the trouble of stating formulae, we can just insert the figure in £s.

2 Set out the spreadsheet so that figures can be calculated using some kind of formula relating to the variables which are to be examined in detail. This is likely to be more time-consuming than preparing a single forecast manually, but tremendous advantages accrue in terms of the potential for using sensitivity and scenario analysis.

3 Change the variables to identify the impact of such changes on the financial statements.

4 Using the results of the sensitivity analysis, identify the critical variables in terms of success or failure, assess the likelihood of their occurrence, establish whether they are within the control or influence of the company, and examine possible alterations in the plans which may improve the performance or position.

Given in Table 18.1 is a spreadsheet for Mike, setting out the forecast results for the first three years of business, under his initial assumptions. The assumptions are clearly identified in rows 1–10. Some of the figures in the financial statements have been inserted as actual figures, because they are constants. The variables have been put in using formulae. For example, the figure for revenue generated by John (C42) of £19,200 is calculated by multiplying the number of weeks worked by the number of hours per week worked, by the charge rate per hour. In effect, the instruction given to fill the box C4 is: insert in this box the result of multiplying the figure in C2 by the figure in C3, by the figure in C4. Any changes in any of the figures in rows 2–4, column C will thus *automatically* be reflected in changes in the figures in the profit and loss account. A similar approach is used to cover rows 43 (revenue generated by Mike), 48 (cost of sales; a function of sales), 49 (John's wages; a function of his hours worked) and 63 (Mike's wages; a function of his hours worked). All totals are based on formulae. Other links which are built in relate to the net profit and depreciation in the cash flow statement, both of which are picked up as formulae from the profit and loss account. Changes in working capital in the funds statement are also automatically calculated from the balance sheets, with closing figures for debtors reflecting sales for the year. The end result is, therefore, an integrated model which will respond correctly to changes in the underlying assumptions/variables.

The plans reveal that, on the assumptions set out, Mike can make sufficient profits to pay himself the intended wage (drawings). However, the plans do also reveal a problem of cash flow, with an overdraft being likely at the end of the year. This suggests that further thought needs to be given to the amount of loan, and the period over which it is to be repaid. Further

Table 18.1

	A	B	C	D	E
1	**Assumptions**		Year 1	Year 2	Year 3
2	John – weeks		48	48	48
3	John – hours per week		40	40	40
4	John – charge rate per hour	10	10	10	
5	Mike – weeks		48	48	48
6	Mike – hours per week		40	40	40
7	Mike – charge rate per hour	10	10	10	
8	John – rate of pay per hour	3.5	3.5	3.5	
9	Mike – rate of pay per hour	5	5	5	
10	Interest rate		0.15	0.15	0.15
11					
12					
13	**Balance sheet**	Start	End year 1	End year 2	End year 3
14					
15	*Fixed assets*				
16	Buildings	25,000	25,000	25,000	25,000
17	Equipment	5,000	4,500	4,000	3,500
18	Van	2,000	1,600	1,200	800
19					
20	*Current assets*				
21	Stock	2,000	2,000	2,000	2,000
22	Debtors	0	3,200	3,200	3,200
23	Cash	3,000	– 1,780	– 2,910	– 3,590
24					
25	Total assets	37,000	34,520	32,490	30,910
26					
27					
28	*Capital*	7,000	7,000	7,520	8,490
29	Net profit	0	10,920	11,370	11,820
30	Drawings	0	– 10,400	– 10,400	– 10,400
31					
32	*Debt outstanding*	30,000	27,000	24,000	21,000
33					
34	*Current liabilities*				
35	Creditors	0	0	0	0
36					
37	Total liabilities	37,000	34,520	32,490	30,910
38					
39					
40	**Profit and loss account**		Year 1	Year 2	Year 3
41	*Revenues*				
42	John		19,200	19,200	19,200

Table 18.1   *continued*

	A	B	C	D	E
43	Mike		19,200	19,200	19,200
44					
45	Total revenues		38,400	38,400	38,400
46					
47	*Expenses*				
48	Cost of sales		9,600	9,600	9,600
49	John – wages		7,280	7,280	7,280
50	Rates		1,000	1,000	1,000
51	Heat and light		600	600	600
52	Telephone		1,000	1,000	1,000
53	Vehicle expenses		1,500	1,500	1,500
54	Insurance		600	600	600
55	Other materials		500	500	500
56	Depreciation – equipment		500	500	500
57	Depreciation – truck		400	400	400
58	Interest		4,500	4,050	3,600
59					
60	Total expenses		27,480	27,030	26,580
61					
62	*Net profit*		10,920	11,370	11,820
63	*Drawings*		10,400	10,400	10,400
64					
65					
66	**Cash flow statement**				
67					
68	*Operating activities*				
69	Net profit		10,920	11,370	11,820
70	Adjusted for depreciation		900	900	900
71	Changes in stock		0	0	0
72	Changes in debtors		– 3,200	0	0
73	Changes in creditors		0	0	0
74					
75	*Capital expenditure*				
76	Sale of fixed assets		0	0	0
77	New assets		0	0	0
78					
79	*Drawings*		– 10,400	– 10,400	– 10,400
80					
81	*Financing activities*				
82	Loans repaid		– 3,000	– 3,000	– 3,000

Table 18.1

	A	B	C	D	E
83	Loans raised		0	0	0
84	New capital		0	0	0
85					
86	Net increase/decrease in cash		−4,780	−1,130	−680
87	Opening balance		3,000	−1,780	−2,910
88	Closing balance		−1,780	−2,910	−3,590

thought should also be given to the validity of the assumptions made, and the impact of changes therein.

It is clear from the solution that if the plans succeed, and the assumptions are correct, enough profit (£10,920) will be generated to enable Mike to cover his drawings (£10,400) for his own wages. However, the forecast cash flow statement shows a decrease in cash of £4,780 over the first year, with the result that the business would have an overdraft at the year-end. Such a position might be somewhat disconcerting for both Mike and his bank manager. Given the assumptions about the work rates of both Mike and John, it would seem appropriate to have a rather larger cushion of cash. It might be possible to arrange further funding from the bank (probably with extra security being needed, e.g. a second mortgage on Mike's house) to cover working capital needs, or to arrange a different repayment profile for the loan, which would require lower repayments of principal (as compared with interest) in the early years of the business.

In practice, it is likely that both Mike and his bank manager are likely to want to probe further with regard to the business. The bank manager is, after all, being asked to provide in excess of £30,000 funding. He will presumably want to know what the chances of repayment are, without having to resort to such drastic actions as foreclosing on a mortgage. The bank manager is, thus, likely to want to see forecasts for more than one year. Mike is likely to want to do the same, to ascertain how his wealth may be affected through trading at a profit or a loss. Both Mike and the bank manager are likely to ask what happens if the work rate is not as assumed, either because demand is lower than expected, or because of such things as illness. The impact of such changes on profit levels and liquidity need to be ascertained, as does the potential impact of changes in the interest rate on the loan.

On the basis of the results shown in Table 18.1, the business appears to be capable of achieving results which are acceptable to Mike, subject to the earlier (significant) reservations on funding, and the possibility of taking out a slightly larger loan, provided that the assumptions made are correct. In order to assess the impact of unfavourable events, it is necessary to change the assumptions/variables on which the figures are based. By way of illustration, assume that the charge rate per hour proves to be unrealistic, and that only £8 per hour can be achieved. For a new business, this is not an unrealistic assumption. If the new charge rate is now put into column C of rows 4 and 7 new results can be obtained immediately. These are shown in Table 18.2.

Table 18.2

	A	B	C	D	E
1	Assumptions		Year 1	Year 2	Year 3
2	John – weeks		48	48	48
3	John – hours per week		40	40	40
4	John – charge rate per hour		8	8	8
5	Mike – weeks		48	48	48
6	Mike – hours per week		40	40	40
7	Mike – charge rate per hour		8	8	8
8	John – rate of pay per hour		3.5	3.5	3.5
9	Mike – rate of pay per hour		5	5	5
10	Interest rate		0.15	0.15	0.15
11					
12					
13	**Balance sheet**	Start	End year 1	End year 2	End year 3
14					
15	*Fixed assets*				
16	Buildings	25,000	25,000	25,000	25,000
17	Equipment	5,000	4,500	4,000	3,500
18	Van	2,000	1,600	1,200	800
19					
20	*Current assets*				
21	Stock	2,000	2,000	2,000	2,000
22	Debtors	0	2,560	2,560	2,560
23	Cash	3,000	– 6,900	– 13,790	– 20,230
24					
25	Total assets	37,000	28,760	20,970	13,630
26					
27					
28	*Capital*	7,000	7,000	1,760	– 3,030
29	Net profit	0	5,160	5,610	6,060
30	Drawings	0	– 10,400	– 10,400	– 10,400
31					
32	*Debt outstanding*	30,000	27,000	24,000	21,000
33					
34	*Current liabilities*				
35	Creditors	0	0	0	0
36					
37	Total liabilities	37,000	28,760	20,970	13,630
38					
39					
40	**Profit and loss account**		Year 1	Year 2	Year 3
41	*Revenues*				

Table 18.2

	A	B	C	D	E
42	John		15,360	15,360	15,360
43	Mike		15,360	15,360	15,360
44					
45	Total revenues		30,720	30,720	30,720
46					
47	*Expenses*				
48	Cost of sales		7,680	7,680	7,680
49	John – wages		7,280	7,280	7,280
50	Rates		1,000	1,000	1,000
51	Heat and light		600	600	600
52	Telephone		1,000	1,000	1,000
53	Vehicles expenses		1,500	1,500	1,500
54	Insurance		600	600	600
55	Other materials		500	500	500
56	Depreciation – equipment		500	500	500
57	Depreciation – truck		400	400	400
58	Interest		4,500	4,050	3,600
59					
60	Total expenses		25,560	25,110	24,660
61					
62	*Net profit*		5,160	5,610	6,060
63	*Drawings*		10,400	10,400	10,400
64					
65					
66	**Cash flow statement**				
67					
68	*Operating activities*				
69	Net profit		5,160	5,610	6,060
70	Adjusted for depreciation		900	900	900
71	Changes in stock		0	0	0
72	Changes in debtors		– 2,560	0	0
73	Changes in creditors		0	0	0
74					
75	*Capital expenditure*				
76	Sale of fixed assets		0	0	0
77	New assets		0	0	0
78					
79	*Drawings*		– 10,400	– 10,400	– 10,400
80					
81	*Financing activities*				
82	Loans repaid		– 3,000	– 3,000	– 3,000

Table 18.2   *continued*

	A	B	C	D	E
83	Loans raised		0	0	0
84	New capital		0	0	0
85					
86	*Net increase/decrease in cash*		− 9,900	− 6,890	− 6,440
87	Opening balance		3,000	− 6,900	− 13,790
88	*Closing balance*		− 6,900	− 13,790	− 20,230

The result is that the profit (£5,160) is insufficient to pay Mike's wages, and that the cash flow pattern is disastrous. If a low charge rate is reasonably likely the business looks to be a shaky venture.

Suppose now that Mike, knowing that John has been somewhat unwell recently, also wishes to know what would happen if John were ill for a reasonable time. A change in the expected number of weeks worked could be inserted into the assumptions section of the spreadsheet, and the impact examined.

Clearly the spreadsheet offers opportunities for the analysis of the sensitivity of a range of variables, with changes being made in individual variables or a collection of variables. Care is needed, however, in setting up a spreadsheet in such a way that all important variables can be changed easily and conveniently.

18.7 Other uses of spreadsheets/ relationship with other methods of appraisal

The kind of approach to spreadsheets which has been used above may be used in a variety of other areas of appraisal and analysis. Later chapters cover the analysis and interpretation of accounts, with a variety of ratios being calculated and relationships examined. Spreadsheets can be used fairly easily to identify such relationships. There is no reason, for example, why the spreadsheet for Mike should not include the automatic calculation of various ratios relating to the forecasts. Considerable opportunities exist elsewhere.

It is important to recognize that the kind of planning and forecasting dealt with in this chapter typically represents only part of the overall process. Plans of this type are particularly effective in assessing future performance for a company as a whole. They will not provide an effective analysis for an individual project. Individual project appraisal, using techniques such as discounted cash flow, are likely to be dealt with in other parts of your studies. However, there is no reason why individual project appraisal and the kind of analysis carried out in this chapter should not both be carried out, and interrelated.

It is also important to note that the emphasis of the above plans is on a year-by-year basis. However, cyclical and seasonal variations may mean that more planning needs to be carried out on a shorter-term basis, say weekly or monthly. Exactly the same methodology could be used to deal with shorter periods. In practice, however, it is common to find that cash forecasting or cash budgeting on a short-term basis takes a slightly different form, identifying cash receipts and cash payments in rather more detail. Hence, instead of showing operating sources as net profit adjusted for depreciation, it is more common to identify cash received from sales, from debtors, from other revenues, and cash paid to creditors, paid for other expenses, etc. Such an approach should enable a much clearer picture to emerge of short-term cash fluctuations. Cash budgets are also likely to be dealt with in other parts of your studies.

18.8 Summary

This chapter has attempted to illustrate that the basic financial accounting statements can be used for planning and decision-making purposes. This is particularly important for business people, since the perspective on accounting is changed from one which is broadly historic to one which is rather more decision-oriented. The financial accounting framework can be used very effectively as the basis of a financial model of the business, and is thus at the heart of most systems of corporate planning or corporate strategy development. An understanding of the interrelationship of the main financial statements is necessary if full benefit is to be obtained from such a system. When coupled with the use of a computerized spreadsheet or other modelling package, the advantages of this approach become even more apparent, because of the facility to use techniques such as sensitivity analysis and scenario analysis.

Exercises

1 The balance sheet of Corplans Plc as at 31 December 2000 is as follows:

	Cost £	Depreciation £	Net £
Fixed assets			
Land and buildings			540,000
Plant and machinery	500,000	100,000	400,000
Vehicles	100,000	40,000	60,000
			1,000,000
Current assets			
Stock		100,000	
Debtors		150,000	
Cash		105,000	
		355,000	
Creditors: amounts falling due within 1 year			
Trade creditors		(120,000)	
Net current assets			235,000
Total assets less current liabilities			1,235,000
Creditors: amounts falling due after more than 1 year			
Loan capital: 10% debentures			200,000
			1,035,000

Capital and reserves

Ordinary share capital	800,000
Revenue reserves	235,000
	1,035,000

The directors are now considering their plans for the next financial year, and have asked you to assist in converting their ideas and assumptions into a financial forecast. In discussions with them you ascertain the following:

(i) During 2000, sales totalled £1,200,000 (200,000 units at £6 each), variable costs per unit were £3.50, and total fixed costs (including depreciation and interest) were £350,000. Depreciation was on the basis of 20% per annum on cost for both plant and machinery and vehicles. No depreciation was taken on land and buildings.

(ii) In 2001 the directors expect the volume of sales to increase by 20%. Selling price will probably need to fall to £5.70 per unit. Variable costs per unit are expected to increase by 5%, while fixed costs are expected to be subject to a 10% inflationary increase.

(iii) Working capital is expected to be maintained at similar levels to those existing at 31 December 2000, namely:
- stocks will be 1/7 of variable costs;
- debtors will be given $1\frac{1}{2}$ months' credit, on average;
- creditors will be 1/10 of sales.

Required

(a) Prepare a forecast profit and loss account for the year ending 31 December 2001.

(b) Prepare a forecast balance sheet as at 31 December 2001.

(c) Prepare a forecast cash flow statement for the year ending 31 December 2001.

2 The balance sheet of AFC Plans Plc as at 31 May 2000 is as follows:

	Cost £	Depreciation £	Net £
Fixed assets			
Land and buildings			1,000,000
Plant and machinery	800,000	400,000	400,000
Vehicles	200,000	60,000	140,000
			1,540,000
Current assets			
Stock		400,000	
Debtors		800,000	
Cash		400,000	
		1,600,000	

Creditors: amounts falling due within 1 year		
Trade creditors	(800,000)	
Net current assets		800,000
Total assets less current liabilities		2,340,000
Creditors: amounts falling due after more than 1 year		
Loan capital: 10% debentures		200,000
		2,140,000
Capital and reserves		
Ordinary share capital (£1 shares – fully paid)		1,000,000
Revenue reserves		1,140,000
		2,140,000

The directors are now considering their plans for the next financial year, and have asked you to assist in converting their ideas and assumptions into a financial forecast. In discussions with them you ascertain the following:

(a) The profit for the year ended 31 May 2000 was £800,000, made up as follows:

	£
Sales revenue (800,000 at £10)	8,000,000
Variable costs (800,000 at £7)	5,600,000
	2,400,000
Fixed costs (including depreciation and debenture interest)	1,600,000
Net profit (added to reserves)	800,000

(b) In the year to 31 May 2001 the directors expect sales to increase in volume by 15%. Selling price per unit is expected to remain the same. It is anticipated that additional advertising costing £150,000 will be needed to generate the volume increase identified above.

(c) The variable cost per unit of existing products is expected to rise by 5%, while the rate of change in fixed costs is expected to be 10%.

(d) The fixed costs shown in (a) above include depreciation of plant and machinery and vehicles. Depreciation is calculated at the rate of 20% on cost of all fixed assets (other than land and buildings) held at the year-end.

(e) Working capital levels at 31 May 2001 are expected to be:
- Stock   5% of sales
- Debtors   10% of sales
- Creditors   10% of sales

Required
(a) Prepare profit and loss, balance sheet and cash flow forecasts for the year ending 31 May 2001 to reflect the financial aspects of the plans.
(b) Discuss how the use of a spreadsheet could assist in this kind of exercise.
(c) Set up this exercise on a spreadsheet, with a facility to change a number of variables. What happens to the results if:
   (i) The advertising campaign results in an increase in sales volume of only 5%?
   (ii) Variable costs increase by 10% per annum (not 5%, as expected)?
   (iii) Both (i) and (ii) occur?
(d) Comment on the plans. Are they satisfactory? Would you change any aspects of the plans? Why/why not?

Note:

This question is fairly complicated, in terms of the number of variables which are subject to forecast. The question contains nothing, however, which should cause you any serious difficulties.

3 The balance sheet for Planning Ltd as at 31 May 2000, and the profit and loss account for the year ended 31 May 2000, are as shown below:

Balance sheet as at 31 May 2000

	Cost £	Depreciation £	Net £
Fixed assets			
Land and buildings	500,000	–	500,000
Plant and machinery	300,000	100,000	200,000
Vehicles	50,000	20,000	30,000
	850,000	120,000	730,000
Current assets			
Stock		50,000	
Debtors		40,000	
Cash		40,000	
		130,000	
Current liabilities			
Corporation tax (due 1/3/01)	28,000		
Creditors	35,000		
Ordinary dividends	25,000		

		(88,000)
		42,000
		772,000
Loans		200,000
		572,000

Capital and reserves		
Ordinary share capital		300,000
Reserves		272,000
		572,000

Profit and loss account for the year ending 31 May 2000

	£	£
Sales		500,000
Less expenses		
Cost of goods sold	250,000	
Wages	50,000	
Depreciation		
Plant and machinery	50,000	
Vehicles	10,000	
Loan interest	24,000	
Administration	20,000	
Marketing	16,000	
		420,000
Net profit		80,000
Appropriated as follows:		
Corporation tax	28,000	
Ordinary share dividend	25,000	
		53,000
Unappropriated profit added to reserves		27,000

Additional notes

1 Sales were made up of 50,000 units at £10 each.
2 Cost of goods sold, and wages, vary in direct proportion to the volume of output and sales (i.e. the cost of goods sold figure is made up of 50,000 units at £5 each, while the wages figure represents 50,000 units at £1 each).
3 Annual depreciation charges are based upon the following:

Land and buildings	– none;
Plant and machinery	– 1/6 of cost;
Vehicles	– 1/5 of cost.

4   The current loans carry interest at 10% per annum, and are repayable in equal instalments over the next five years.

The directors of the company are now considering their plans for the next few years, and have asked you to assist in converting their ideas into formalized financial plans. During discussions with them you ascertain the following facts:

1   A 10% increase in the sales volume of existing goods is expected for the next year. In passing, the directors indicate that the volume is expected to be stable for a further two years after this, with a decline being expected thereafter. A price rise of 5% is considered to be realistic for the next year.
2   The price indices for cost of goods sold and wages were 110 and 180 respectively, as at 30 November 19X5. The forecast indices for 30 November 19X6 are 120 and 190 respectively. It can be presumed that expenses for these two areas are incurred evenly throughout the year, so the use of averages is acceptable.
3   A new product is to be launched on 1 June 19X6. It is expected that 20,000 units of this product will be sold in its first year, at a price of £15 each. Cost of sales and wages are £3 per unit and £2 per unit respectively (i.e. both vary directly in proportion to output). The new product will require the purchase of new plant and machinery, expected to cost £150,000. Since it is expected to last six years, this new machinery will also be depreciated at 1/6 of cost each year. Old equipment which had originally cost £50,000, on which depreciation had been taken to date totalling £30,000, is to be sold for £25,000. (Assume that the purchase of the new asset, and the disposal of the old, will occur on 1 June 19X6.) The new product is likely to require additional marketing expenditure in the next year amounting to approximately £20,000, and will lead to increased administration expenses of £15,000. Existing administration and marketing expenses are expected to rise by 10% in the next year.
4   Dividends are expected to be at least maintained over the foreseeable future.
5   Corporation tax for the next accounting year can be assumed to be payable at the rate of 35% on profits for the year.
6   Working capital is expected to be maintained at the following levels:

- stock   10% of sales
- debtors   8% of sales
- creditors   7% of sales
- cash   4% of sales

Required
You are specifically asked to do the following:

(a) Prepare:
  (i) a forecast profit and loss account for the year ending 31 May 2001;
  (ii) a forecast balance sheet as at 31 May 2001;
  (iii) a forecast cash flow statement for the year ending 31 May 2001;
  so as to show the directors the results of their plans in financial terms.
(b) Make comments on the forecasts prepared; in particular, consider whether the decision to introduce the new product and to acquire new machinery is sensible. What advice would you give the directors in this area?
(c) Briefly indicate to the directors how the use of a computerized spreadsheet could assist in a planning exercise of this type.

Chapter 19

The analysis of financial statements: 1

19.1 **Introduction**	This chapter is concerned with the analysis of financial statements. It explains how financial ratios may be used to help assess the position and performance of a business.

19.2 **Objectives**	On completion of this chapter you should be able to: • identify the key areas in which financial ratios are employed; • calculate the major financial ratios; • discuss the significance of each ratio in assessing the financial position and performance of a business; • assess the strengths and weaknesses of ratios as tools of financial analysis.

19.3
Financial ratios

The purpose of calculating financial ratios is to help assess the position and performance of a business. An assessment of current or past position and performance is useful in determining whether or not the managers of the business have used the resources available in an efficient and effective manner. It can also help in formulating views about the future, which should be extremely valuable when making decisions. Ratios are an important and widely used tool of financial analysis. They are referred to frequently in newspapers, business journals and other literature. You should, therefore, be able to understand their uses and interpret their significance.

A ratio simply expresses the relationship of one figure with another figure and, provided the information is available, ratios can usually be calculated with little difficulty. In the case of financial ratios both figures used are often taken from the financial statements; however, a financial ratio can relate an item contained in the financial statements with some business resource (e.g. profit per employee, sales per square metre of floor space, etc.) or some output of the business (e.g. profit per passenger mile, etc.).

Ratios sketch out the financial profile of a business and are frequently employed by those who analyse accounting reports. While the *calculation* of financial ratios is a fairly straightforward process, the *interpretation* of ratios is often more complex. The analyst must exercise skill and judgement in deciding whether or not the changes in a financial ratio are significant and what the underlying cause of any change might be.

By calculating ratios which reflect key relationships (e.g. the relationship between profit and sales) it is possible to reduce the complexity of the profit and loss account and balance sheet to a small number of key indicators. These indicators provide the analyst with valuable clues concerning the financial health of the business. However, ratios alone do *not* provide a comprehensive analysis of financial condition. Rather, they provide a useful starting point for further analysis by highlighting areas which warrant investigation.

19.4 Standards of performance

A ratio by itself has no real significance. For example, if it was found that ordinary shareholders were receiving a 10% return on their investment in the business, it would not be possible (based on this information alone) to say whether such a return was good, bad or indifferent. It is only when this ratio is compared with some standard of performance that it can be properly evaluated.

There are three *standards of performance* by which ratios can be judged:

1 *Past periods.* This will indicate whether current ratios are better or worse than ratios of past periods. By employing past periods as a standard of performance it may be possible to detect trends which will be useful in predicting future performance. The major problem, however, is that economic conditions may differ significantly between periods and this will hinder a proper evaluation of current performance and position. There is also a potential problem that the results of past periods will reflect operating inefficiencies which have not been recognized.

2 *Planned performance.* This will indicate whether ratios for the current period meet with earlier, planned performance. The usefulness of this standard of comparison will, of course, depend on the validity of the assumptions employed in formulating earlier plans.

3 *Similar businesses within the same industry.* The advantage of this particular standard is that it offers an external basis for comparison. However, there may be problems in finding businesses providing similar services or products. No two businesses are identical. Furthermore, differences in accounting policies between businesses concerning stock valuation, depreciation, etc. may hinder comparisons. This problem, however, may be lessened where there is an interfirm comparison scheme operating for the industry. Such a scheme involves a central body adjusting the financial statements of each participating business to conform with particular income and asset measurement procedures. The central body will then calculate ratios based on the adjusted figures.

There is a counter-argument, however, for not standardizing accounting procedures between businesses in this way. This is that a business may have chosen particular policies which best reflect their economic characteristics and so standardization will hinder rather than help comparison.

It is clear from the above that there is no ideal standard of comparison. Nevertheless, some standard must be used and the skill and judgement of the analyst will be required to ensure that comparisons are properly interpreted.

19.5 Ratio classification

Ratios can be classified according to the particular aspect of a business's financial health it seeks to examine. There are four major classifications:

1 *Liquidity.* Liquidity ratios examine the ability of the business to meet its short-term commitments. It is vital that a business has the capacity to pay debts when they fall due. Even a profitable business may be forced to cease trading if it has insufficient liquid resources. Poor liquidity can lead to delays in paying debts which may, in turn, result in a loss of confidence among lenders and creditors.
2 *Gearing (leverage).* Gearing is important in the assessment of financial risk. Gearing ratios examine the financial structure and financial capacity of the business as well as the relative contributions of investors and lenders towards financing the business. In addition, they examine the capacity of the business to service and repay loans.
3 *Activity (efficiency).* Activity ratios measure the efficiency with which the business utilizes its assets. These ratios provide useful insights into management policy and operational efficiency.
4 *Profitability ratios.* Profitability ratios relate profit to other key figures in the financial statements. Profit represents the central measure of operating achievement and by relating this to other key figures a clearer view of performance can be gained.

The level of importance attached to each class of ratio will depend on the type of user and the purpose of the analysis. A trade creditor, for example, is likely to be interested in the short-term creditworthiness of the business and may concentrate attention on the liquidity ratios. An investor, on the other hand, is likely to be interested in the risks and returns associated with the business. Hence, the investor may have a particular interest in gearing and profitability ratios. It is therefore important to be clear when calculating ratios *for whom and for what purpose* the analysis is being undertaken.

Activity 1

Which classes of ratio are each of the following user groups most likely to be interested in and why?

User group	Class of ratio	Reason
Long-term lenders		
Government		
Employees		
Customers		
Management		

Your answer to this activity should be along the following lines:

User group	Class of ratio	Reason
Long-term lenders	Gearing profitability	Long-term lenders will be concerned with the extent to which they are financing the business and long-term viability
Government and Employees	Profitability	Government may use profit as a basis for taxation, grants and subsidies
	Profitability Liquidity Activity	Employees will be concerned with job security and wage bargaining
Customers	Liquidity	Customers will seek reassurance that the business can survive in the short term and continue to supply
Management	Profitability Liquidity Activity Gearing	Management is interested in all aspects of the financial health of the business

Details of the main ratios, under each of the above headings, are given in the sections which follow. In order to provide worked examples for each ratio, appropriate calculations are made, based on a set of accounts (for Abacus Ltd) as set out in Appendix 1 to this chapter. This appendix also provides details of the industry average for comparison purposes. Please refer to this appendix to make sure you are clear about the source of the figures used in each of the ratios.

19.6 Liquidity ratios

To assess the liquidity of a business two ratios are commonly used. These are current ratio and acid-test (quick) ratio.

Current ratio

This ratio is calculated as follows:

$$\text{Current ratio} = \frac{\text{Current assets}}{\text{Current liabilities (i.e. amounts due within 1 year)}}$$

Current assets include cash or assets intended to be converted into cash, such as stock and debtors. In dividing current assets by the current liabilities, an attempt is made to measure the amount of coverage available for short-term obligations.

The current ratio for Abacus is:

$$\frac{950}{450} = 2.11 (\text{sometimes expressed as } 2.11:1)$$

This means that Abacus Ltd has £2.11 worth of current assets for every £1 worth of current liabilities. This ratio compares with a ratio of 2.2 for the industry average. Thus, the current ratio of Abacus Ltd is near the average for the industry as a whole. In that sense, the ratio may be considered satisfactory.

Acid-test (quick) ratio

The current ratio discussed above has been criticized for not being a particularly stringent test of liquidity. This is because certain current assets such as stock and prepayments may not be easily converted into cash. Hence, it is argued that such assets should be excluded when assessing the ability of the business to meet its short-term obligations. The acid-test ratio is based on this line of reasoning and is calculated as follows:

$$\text{Acid-test ratio} = \frac{\text{Current assets} - \text{stock and prepayments}}{\text{Current liabilities}}$$

For Abacus Ltd the acid-test ratio is:

$$\frac{570}{450} = 1.27 (\text{sometimes expressed as } 1.27{:}1)$$

This means that Abacus Ltd has £1.27 worth of liquid current assets for every £1 worth of short-term obligations. The above ratio of 1.27 compares with an industry average of 0.90. Hence, Abacus Ltd has a satisfactory acid-test ratio which is higher than the industry average.

In evaluating these liquidity ratios it is worth noting that the relevant figures are taken from the balance sheet. This means the ratios only reflect the liquidity position at the point in time for which the balance sheet was prepared. A more detailed analysis of the business's liquidity position would involve monitoring cash flows over a period in time.

The lower the current and acid-test ratios, the lower the liquidity of the business. Clearly, liquidity ratios may be too low, thereby suggesting an inability to pay short-term obligations. However, it is also possible for liquidity ratios to be too high. A very high ratio may suggest that the business has excessive amounts tied up in current assets which could be used to more profitable ends. When examining liquidity ratios it is therefore useful to have in mind an acceptable range within which the ratios might occur.

Activity 2

From the information provided in Appendix 2 to this chapter, calculate the liquidity ratios of Vortex Ltd. What do you deduce from an analysis of these ratios over the three-year period?

Liquidity ratios	1998	1999	2000
Current ratio	24,000	27,000	31,000
	12,000	14,000	19,000
	2.0	1.93	1.63
Acid-test ratio	16,000	15,000	14,000
	12,000	14,000	19,000
	1.33	1.07	0.74

Both ratios reveal a declining trend in liquidity over the three-year period. The acid-test ratio has declined more sharply than the current ratio and this should be of particular concern. The acid-test ratio reveals that by 2000 there are insufficient liquid current assets to meet short-term obligations. The business should seek to reverse the declining trend in liquidity in order to maintain the confidence of creditors.

19.7 Gearing (leverage) ratios

The relationship between the amount of fixed-return capital (preference shares and loan stocks) and ordinary shares in the capital structure is usually referred to as capital gearing or leverage. The term gearing or leverage is used because employing fixed-return capital can have the effect of accentuating the returns to ordinary shareholders, as we shall see below.

Example

Power Plc, which always pays its entire net profit to its ordinary shareholders as a dividend, has the following long-term capital structure:

	£ m
5m ordinary shares of £1 each	£5
£5m loan stock (10%)	£5
	£10

Over 3 consecutive years, the net profits before loan stock interest were:

Year 1 £1.0m
Year 2 £2.0m
Year 3 £0.5m

The returns to the shareholders over the 3 years would be as follows:

Year	1	2	3
	£ m	£ m	£ m
Net profit (before interest)	1.0	2.0	0.5
Loan interest (£5m × 10%)	0.5	0.5	0.5
Net earnings	0.5	1.5	0.0
Earnings per share (EPS)	£0.10	£0.30	£0.00

(EPS = net earnings available to ordinary shareholders/number of ordinary shares.)

Note that the doubling of the profit from Year 1 to Year 2 has the effect of *trebling* the return to shareholders. Also, the halving of the profit from Year 1 to Year 3 has the effect of eliminating any return to shareholders.

Activity 3

Contrast the above returns with the position which would arise in each year if there were no fixed-return capital and all of the finance was provided by 10 million ordinary shares.

The position would be as follows for each year:

Year	1	2	3
	£ m	£ m	£ m
Net profit	1.0	2.0	0.5
Earnings per share	£0.10	£0.20	£0.05

Here the return to shareholders fluctuates exactly in line with profit fluctuations. We can see that the existence of a fixed-return element has the effect of accentuating fluctuations in the returns to ordinary shareholders. This is analogous to the effect of two meshing cog wheels of different sizes or of the movement of, and force exerted by, either end of a lever whose fulcrum is not at the centre of its length.

It is clear from the above example that a certain minimum profit before interest must be made before there is any return to the shareholders. This is because the use of debt carries with it an automatic and contractual expense (interest). In the above example, the profit before interest *must* be £0.5 million for the company to cover the interest payable, otherwise the shareholders will suffer a loss. Only if the profit before interest is in excess of this figure will the shareholders make a positive return. Clearly, while the use of gearing provides the opportunity for far greater returns to shareholders when profits are good, it also brings with it much lower returns to shareholders when profits are not so good. In sustained periods of recession, the use of debt is likely to lead to far greater pressures than the use of shareholder funds, since dividends can be stopped as conditions worsen, whereas interest payments cannot.

The introduction of gearing into a business should therefore be seen as introducing a further dimension to risk, as far as the shareholders are concerned. Any business is faced with risks inherent in the type of business in which it is engaged. Such risk is referred to as *business risk*, and will not change irrespective of how a business is financed. The introduction of gearing introduces an additional facet of risk for the shareholders, as has been illustrated above. This risk is referred to as *financial risk*. This means that the returns to equity for a business with financial gearing will fluctuate more

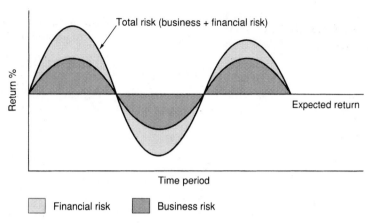

Figure 19.1

sharply than the fluctuating profits arising from business risk. This is depicted in Figure 19.1.

Shareholders must recognize there is a *risk–return trade-off* to be made. The higher the level of gearing, the higher the prospective returns to equity shareholders, but the higher the level of financial risk incurred (see Figure 19.1).

Activity 4

In the context of the above example, what relationship is there between the loan stock interest rate and the fact that, at some levels of profit, gearing is beneficial to other shareholders but at other levels it is not?

In the example given, the dividend per share is only the same in Year 1, when the net profit before interest is 10% of the net assets, which is the same as the interest payable on the loan. If the rate of return on assets exceeds the interest rate payable on the loan, the dividends per share will be higher, the higher the level of debt used. Year 2 provides an illustration of this. Where the rate of return on assets is less than the rate of interest on the loan, the opposite is true. In practice, taxation complicates this relationship, but the general principle remains valid.

High levels of gearing tend to be found where some of the following conditions exist:

- earnings are stable over time or show an increasing trend
- there is adequate security available for the debt
- there is a risk of a dilution of control with respect to existing shareholders if new ordinary shares are issued
- the market value of ordinary shares is low and would prove to be an unattractive investment

Debt-to-equity ratio

This ratio is concerned with the relative contribution of debt and equity (ordinary shareholders) in financing the business. It is calculated as follows:

$$\text{Debt-to-equity ratio} = \frac{\text{Total debt (i.e. long- and short-term liabilities)}}{\text{Total equity (ordinary share capital plus reserves)}}$$

For Abacus Ltd the debt-to-equity ratio is:

$$\frac{1{,}050}{1{,}800} = 0.58$$

This means that for every £1 contributed by equity shareholders to finance the business, lenders and creditors have contributed £0.58. The above ratio of 0.58 compares with a ratio of 0.85 for the industry average. Abacus Ltd is, therefore, well below the industry average.

Generally speaking, the higher the ratio (i.e. the higher the level of gearing), the less protection is being offered to lenders. However, this may not always be the case. Where lenders have been offered security for a loan by way of a charge on certain assets, they may feel well protected despite a high debt-to-equity ratio.

Debt-to-total assets ratio

This ratio measures the extent to which lenders and creditors are financing the assets of the business. It is calculated as follows:

$$\text{Debt-to-total assets} = \frac{\text{Total debt (i.e. long- and short-term liabilities)} \times 100}{\text{Total assets (i.e. fixed and current assets)}}$$

In the case of Abacus Ltd the ratio is

$$\frac{1{,}050 \times 100}{2{,}850} = 36.84\%$$

The ratio indicates that lenders and creditors are providing over 36% of the total funds required to finance the assets of the business. This compares with an industry average of 38%.

Where a company has lower gearing ratios than the industry average it may suggest there is unused debt capacity. This means the company may be able to borrow more, if it so wished, without incurring any adverse reaction from lenders and creditors. However, we have seen that other factors such as the availability of security for borrowings will also be important in determining debt capacity.

Interest coverage (times interest earned) ratio

This ratio examines the ability of the business to meet its regular financial commitments. It is calculated as follows:

$$\text{Interest coverage} = \frac{\text{Net profit before interest and taxation}}{\text{Interest charges}}$$

For Abacus Ltd the ratio is:

$$\frac{340}{60} = 5.67$$

This means that the business is generating £5.67 worth of profit to cover each £1 of interest charges. The above ratio of 5.67 compares with an industry average of 3.95. Thus, Abacus Ltd has a ratio well above the industry average.

This ratio is a *coverage* ratio similar to the liquidity ratios discussed earlier. It attempts to measure the amount of protection available to lenders. The higher the ratio, so it is argued, the greater the ability of the business to cover its interest payments. The lower the ratio, the greater the risk the business will default on its interest payments. This line of argument, however, is something of an oversimplification as the ability of a business to meet interest charges is related to cash flows rather than profit flows. A rough measure of cash flows for the year can be derived from the income statement by adding back to net profit items, such as depreciation, which do not involve any cash outlay. The cash flow coverage ratio is based on the above idea and is calculated as follows:

$$\text{Cash flow coverage ratio} = \frac{\text{Net profit before depreciation, interest and taxation}}{\text{Interest charges}}$$

For Abacus Ltd this ratio is:

$$\frac{400}{60} = 6.67$$

This compares with an industry average of 4.90. Thus, Abacus Ltd has a ratio well above the industry average and, in one sense, it is satisfactory. However, it also suggests the business may have the capacity to take on additional debt. Failure to do so may indicate the business is not availing itself of a relatively cheap form of finance.

Activity 6

From the information provided in Appendix 2 to this chapter, calculate three gearing ratios for Vortex Ltd. What do you deduce from an analysis of these ratios over a 3-year period?

Gearing ratios

Debt-to-equity ratio	$\frac{12,000}{22,000}$	$\frac{15,000}{22,100}$	$\frac{21,000}{22,150}$
	$= 0.55$	$= 0.68$	$= 0.95$
Interest coverage ratio	–	$\frac{2800}{100}$	$\frac{1700}{200}$
		$= 28$ *times*	$= 8.5$ *times*
Cash flow coverage ratio	–	$\frac{4000}{100}$	$\frac{3200}{200}$
		$= 40$ *times*	$= 16$ *times*

All three ratios reveal a trend towards higher levels of gearing. This is due partly to the issue of debentures in 1999 and 2000 and partly to a considerable increase in creditors in 2000. The coverage ratios (i.e. interest and cash flow coverage) have declined sharply between 1999 and 2000 because of the sharp fall in profits and the increase in interest charges which have occurred. This sharp decline will do little to inspire confidence among existing lenders. However, the coverage ratios have not yet declined to a point where lenders should be alarmed.

19.8 Activity (efficiency) ratios

Activity ratios are concerned with how efficiently the resources of the business are being managed. The most important activity ratios are as follows.

Ratios related to stock

The stock turnover ratio expresses the relationship between the average stock held and the cost of sales. The ratio is as follows:

$$\text{Stock turnover ratio} = \frac{\text{Cost of sales}}{\text{Average stock held}}$$

The average stock figure is usually calculated by taking the average of the opening and closing stock figures. However, where the business is seasonal in nature and closing stocks are not representative of average stock held, information concerning stockholdings throughout the year should be used (wherever possible) to calculate an average figure.

For Abacus Ltd the stock turnover ratio is:

$$\frac{2,500}{300} = 8.3$$

If required, the above ratio can be inverted to arrive at an average period of stockholding:

$$\text{Average period of stockholding} = \frac{\text{Average stock held} \times 12}{\text{Cost of sales}}$$

Multiplying by 12 will give the period in months for which the stock is held. If the period is to be expressed in days, the number will need to be 365.

For Abacus Ltd the period of stockholding is:

$$\frac{300}{2,500} \times 12 = 1.44 \text{ months}$$

This compares with 1.1 months for the industry average. Thus, Abacus Ltd has a ratio above the average, which may not be satisfactory. (Comparing the stock turnover rate of 8.3 with an industry figure of 10.9 should lead to an identical conclusion.)

Activity 7

What possible interpretations (positive or negative) may be placed on the following?

(a) a higher-than-average stockholding period
(b) a lower-than-average stockholding period

A high stockholding period may suggest the existence of slow-moving or obsolete stocks, or poor utilization of resources. However, other interpretations of this ratio may be possible. For example, management may acquire large amounts of stock, and thereby lengthen the stockholding period, if a shortage of supplies or a significant rise in the price of stocks is predicted. Management may also accumulate stocks in anticipation of higher sales in the following period as a result, for example, of a price-cutting campaign to be launched. Further investigation into stockholding policies and practice would, therefore, be required.

A low stockholding period may also suggest poor stock management. Where the level of stock is low in relation to sales this may indicate the company is understocked and this, in turn, can lead to lost sales and lost customer goodwill. On the other hand, it may indicate a very efficient management of stocks. If stock movements are carefully recorded and checked frequently and it is possible to obtain new stocks from suppliers quickly, it may be possible to reduce the amount of stocks held and, thereby, reduce the stockholding period.

Like the liquidity ratios discussed earlier, it is probably a good idea to establish an acceptable range within which this ratio might fluctuate.

Ratios related to debtors

Similar ratios can be calculated for debtors as for stock. In order to calculate debtors' turnover the following ratio is used:

$$\textbf{Debtors' turnover} = \frac{\textbf{Credit sales}}{\textbf{Trade debtors}}$$

For Abacus Ltd debtors' turnover would be:

$$\frac{3,200}{520} = 6.15$$

Inversion of the ratio will give a figure for the average credit period allowed. This ratio measures the average length of time it takes trade debtors to pay. It is calculated as follows:

$$\textbf{Average credit period allowed} = \frac{\textbf{Trade debtors}}{\textbf{Credit sales}} \times \textbf{12}$$

Once again, the ratio is multiplied by 12 to derive the average period in months. In calculating the ratio, the year-end trade debtors figure is usually employed as the appropriate figure. However, where demand is seasonal, or where there has been considerable sales growth during the year, some calculation of average debtors using monthly data is preferable.

For Abacus Ltd the average credit period allowed (based on year-end debtors) is:

$$\frac{520}{3,200} \times 12 = 1.95 \text{ months}$$

This compares with 1.90 months for the industry average. Hence, Abacus is very near the average for the industry and, in that sense, the ratio is satisfactory.

Activity 8

What possible interpretations (positive or negative) might be placed on:

(a) a higher-than-average credit period allowed?
(b) a lower-than-average credit period allowed?

If the debtors' turnover was much lower, or (using the inverse ratio) the period of credit much higher, than the industry average, this might suggest the business adopts a more liberal credit policy than its competitors, or that the business has weak credit control procedures. Conversely, a higher debtors' turnover period or lower credit period allowed may indicate tighter credit control standards and/or procedures. The decision concerning the appropriate credit control policy to adopt will involve weighing the expected benefits of a particular policy against expected costs. For example, a liberal credit policy may result in higher sales but may also result in higher credit administration costs and high levels of bad debts. A tight credit control, on the other hand, may reduce the level of bad debts but may also reduce the level of sales.

It is important to recognize that it is the average credit period allowed which is being calculated. This ratio may be influenced by a few large debtors who are slow to pay and, therefore, care must be taken in interpreting the results.

Ratios related to creditors

In addition to calculating ratios relating to debtors, it may also be useful to calculate ratios relating to creditors. The ratios calculated are similar to those calculated for debtors.

In order to calculate creditors' turnover the following ratio is used:

$$\textbf{Creditors' turnover} = \frac{\textbf{Credit purchases}}{\textbf{Trade creditors}}$$

For Abacus Ltd the creditors' turnover ratio is:

$$\frac{2,600}{380} = 6.84$$

In calculating this ratio, it is assumed that all purchases during the year have been made on credit.

Inversion of the ratio will give a figure for the average credit period taken. Thus:

$$\text{Average credit period allowed} = \frac{\text{Trade creditors}}{\text{Credit purchases}} \times 12$$

For Abacus Ltd the average credit period **taken** (in months) is:

$$\frac{380}{2,600} \times 12 = 1.75 \text{ months}$$

This compares with the industry average of 1.8 months and may therefore be regarded as satisfactory.

Activity 9

'A business should have a high average credit period for creditors as the amounts owed represent a free source of finance to the business.'

Do you agree with this statement?

It is often true that trade creditors provide a free source of finance for a business. However, there may be costs involved if a business takes an excessive time to pay. Such a policy may result in lost supplier goodwill which may, in turn, lead to withdrawal of credit, delays in processing orders, lower priority in the future and perhaps interest charged on overdue amounts. Where a supplier offers a cash discount for prompt payment, the benefits of delaying payment must be weighed against the discounts forgone.

A high average credit period taken may indicate the business has liquidity problems, i.e. creditors are not being paid because there is no cash available. It may therefore be a symptom of financial distress.

Fixed asset turnover ratio

This ratio measures how effectively the business is using its fixed assets to generate sales. The ratio is calculated as follows:

$$\text{Fixed asset turnover ratio} = \frac{\text{Sales}}{\text{Fixed assets}}$$

The year-end fixed asset figure is often taken as the appropriate one for this ratio. However, an average of the opening and closing fixed assets may also be used. This would be particularly relevant if the business were rapidly expanding.

For Abacus Ltd, the ratio (employing the year-end fixed asset figure) is

$$\frac{3,200}{1,900} = 1.68 \text{ times}$$

This means that for every £1 invested in fixed assets, the business is generating £1.68 in sales. The above ratio of 1.68 companies with an industry average of 1.60. Thus, Abacus Ltd is slightly above the industry average and, therefore, the ratio may be seen as satisfactory. It is important, however, to recognize that differences in the age and condition of fixed assets between businesses will complicate interpretation of this ratio. Given the same level of sales, a business with old, highly depreciated fixed assets will have a higher fixed asset turnover ratio than one with new, barely depreciated fixed assets.

Total asset turnover ratio

This ratio measures how effectively the business is using its assets to generate sales. It is calculated as follows:

$$\textbf{Total asset turnover ratio} = \frac{\textbf{Sales}}{\textbf{Total assets}}$$

For Abacus Ltd, the ratio (employing year-end asset figures, although an average figure can also be used) is:

$$\frac{3,200}{2,850} = 1.12 \text{ times}$$

This means that for every £1 invested in assets the business is generating £1.12 in sales each year. The above ratio of 1.12 compared with a ratio of 1.2 for the industry average. Abacus Ltd is, therefore, not performing as well as the industry average.

Too low a ratio may suggest the business is not using its assets productively. A very high turnover ratio, on the other hand, may suggest the business is overtrading on its assets, i.e. it has an inadequate amount of assets in relation to the sales generated. Overtrading will often arise when a new business attempts to expand too quickly. Sales may increase but the finance may not be available to invest in fixed assets and working capital. As a consequence, the business will suffer from liquidity problems and will be unable to supply customers as the funds will not be available to purchase the necessary stocks. These liquidity problems may ultimately force the business to cease trading if it is unable to meet its maturing debts.

Activity 10

From the information given in Appendix 2 to this chapter, calculate the activity ratios for Vortex Ltd. What do you deduce from an analysis of these ratios over the 3-year period?

Activity (efficiency) ratios

Stock turnover period	$\frac{7,500}{15,000} \times 12$	$\frac{10,000}{22,000} \times 12$	$\frac{14,500}{30,000} \times 12$
	6 months	*5.45 months*	*5.8 months*

Average credit period allowed	$\dfrac{6,000}{24,000} \times 12$	$\dfrac{9,000}{30,000} \times 12$	$\dfrac{14,000}{38,000} \times 12$
	3 months	3.6 months	4.42 months
Fixed asset turnover ratio	$\dfrac{24,000}{10,000}$	$\dfrac{30,000}{10,100}$	$\dfrac{38,000}{12,150}$
	2.4 times	2.97 times	3.13 times
Total asset turnover ratio	$\dfrac{24,000}{34,000}$	$\dfrac{30,000}{37,100}$	$\dfrac{38,000}{43,150}$
	0.71 times	0.81 times	0.88 times

The stock turnover period has remained fairly stable over the 3-year period. However, the ratio does seem very high and further investigation of stockholding policy is required. The average credit period allowed has sharply increased over the 3-year period. By 2000 trade debtors were taking, on average, almost 41/2 months to pay. This ratio again seems very high and further investigation of credit policy is required. Notice that over the 3-year period sales have increased by nearly 60%. This increase may have arisen, at least in part, as a result of a more liberal credit policy. Asset turnover ratios have increased over the period as a result of the increase in sales.

19.9 Profitability ratios

Profitability ratios help assess the operating performance of the business. The major profitability ratios are as follows.

Gross profit margin

This ratio expresses the gross profit as a percentage of sales. The ratio is, therefore:

$$\text{Gross profit margin} = \frac{\text{Gross profit}}{\text{Sales}} \times 100$$

The gross profit margin can be used to assess trading performance and pricing policy. For Abacus Ltd the gross profit margin is:

$$\frac{700}{3,200} \times 100 = 21.87\%$$

This means for every £1 of sales generated the business earns £0.22 (approx.) gross profit. The above ratio of 21.87% compares with an industry average of 21% and may, therefore, be regarded as satisfactory.

Net profit margin

This ratio expresses the net profit as a percentage of sales. It therefore measures the percentage return from sales after taking account of all expenses (including tax). The ratio is:

$$\text{Net profit margin} = \frac{\text{Net profit after tax}}{\text{Sales}} \times 100$$

For Abacus Ltd the ratio is:

$$\frac{210}{3,200} \times 100 = 6.56\%$$

This ratio is below the industry average of 8.2%. In view of the fact that the gross profit margin of Abacus Ltd is in line with the industry average, it would appear that the lower net profit margin can be attributed to higher than average overheads for the level of sales generated. It may be useful to express each overhead as a percentage of sales to see how much each absorbs of gross revenue. The percentages calculated can then be compared with those of similar businesses to assess relative efficiency.

Some businesses are prepared to work on very low profit margins in order to stimulate sales and thereby increase total profits. The early success of Tesco Plc, for example, was founded on the philosophy 'stack it high and sell it cheap'.

Return to equity

This ratio expresses the profit available to equity (ordinary) shareholders as a percentage of the equity shareholders stake in the business. The ratio is as follows:

$$\text{Return to equity} = \frac{\text{Net profit (after tax and preference dividends)}}{\text{Ordinary share capital plus reserves}} \times 100$$

This ratio measures the return the equity shareholders are receiving from their investment in the business. The ordinary share capital plus reserves figure used in the ratio is usually based on the year-end figures. However, an average of opening and closing balances can be used.

For Abacus Ltd, the return to equity (based on year-end figures) is:

$$\frac{210}{1,800} \times 100 = 11.67\%$$

This ratio is below the industry average of 13.11% and may be regarded as unsatisfactory.

Return on capital employed (ROCE)

This ratio expresses the profit available to suppliers of long-term capital as a percentage of the long-term capital employed. The profit available to long-term suppliers of capital is the net profit before interest (and taxation). It is an important and useful measure of performance as it measures *input* in the form of capital employed against *output* in the form of profit. The return to equity ratio discussed above is, of course, another example of an input/output ratio.

Return on capital employed is calculated as follows:

$$\text{ROCE} = \frac{\text{Net profit before interest and taxation}}{\text{Share capital + reserves + long-term loans}} \times 100$$

For Abacus Ltd, the ratio is:

$$\frac{340}{2,400} \times 100 = 14.17\%$$

This ratio is below the industry average of 16.59% and, therefore, may be regarded as unsatisfactory.

| Return on investment (ROI) | This ratio expresses the net profit (after tax) as a percentage of total assets. The ratio is therefore: |

$$ROI = \frac{\text{Net profit (after tax)}}{\text{Total assets}} \times 100$$

This ratio is also considered to be very important as it measures the profit available after all obligatory charges have been deducted in relation to the assets held by the business. The total assets figure used in the ratio is often the year-end figure but again, an average of opening and closing figures may be used.

For Abacus the ratio (based on year-end figures) is:

$$\frac{210}{2,850} \times 100 = 7.36\%$$

This compares with an industry average of 9.84%. Abacus Ltd's ratio is therefore below the industry average.

Differences between businesses in the age and condition of their fixed assets will complicate interpretation of this ratio. Given the same net profit after tax, a business with highly depreciated fixed assets will have a higher ROI than a business with newer, less depreciated, fixed assets.

Activity 11

From the information in Appendix 2 to this chapter, calculate the profitability ratios of Vortex Ltd. What do you deduce from an analysis of these ratios over the three-year period?

Profitability ratios

Gross profit margin	$\frac{9,000}{24,000} \times 100$	$\frac{8,000}{30,000} \times 100$	$\frac{8,000}{38,000} \times 100$
	37.5%	26.67%	21.05%
Net profit margin	$\frac{3,600}{24,000} \times 100$	$\frac{1,900}{30,000} \times 100$	$\frac{1,050}{38,000} \times 100$
	15%	6.33%	2.76%
Return to equity	$\frac{3,600}{22,000} \times 100$	$\frac{1,900}{22,100} \times 100$	$\frac{1,050}{22,150} \times 100$
	16.36%	8.6%	4.74%
ROCE	$\frac{5,200}{22,000} \times 100$	$\frac{2,800}{23,100} \times 100$	$\frac{1,700}{24,150} \times 100$
	23.64%	12.12%	7.04%

$$ROI \qquad \frac{3,600}{34,000} \times 100 \qquad \frac{1,900}{37,100} \times 100 \qquad \frac{1,050}{43,150} \times 100$$

$$10.59\% \qquad 5.12\% \qquad 2.43\%$$

There has been a sharp decline in all profitability ratios over the three-year period. The sharp decrease in the gross profit margin and the corresponding sharp increase in sales may suggest the business has lowered prices in order to stimulate sales. The fall in the net profit margin reflects, to a large extent, the fall in the gross profit margin. However, the net profit margin has not fallen by quite the amount of the gross profit margin as certain overhead expenses have not increased proportionately with sales. The fall in profit margins has not been adequately compensated for by increases in sales. Hence, the return to equity, ROCE and ROI ratios have declined. The sharp decline in these ratios is likely to cause concern among investors and lenders. Efforts to reverse the trends should therefore be made. The starting point may be to reconsider pricing policy over recent years.

19.10
Trend analysis

Ratios may be computed for a business over time and the results plotted on a graph. This can be useful when seeking to identify trends over time. An example of this form of trend analysis is shown in Figure 19.2.

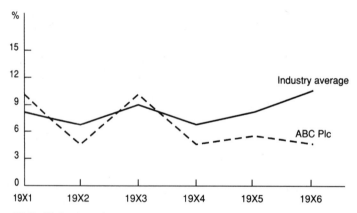

Figure 19.2. *Return on investment*

Self-assessment question 19.1

Bradbury Ltd is a family-owned clothes manufacturer based in the south-west of England. For a number of years the chairman and managing director of the company was David Bradbury. During his period of office the company's sales turnover had grown steadily at a rate of 2–3% each year. David Bradbury retired on 30 November 1999 and was succeeded by his son, Simon. Soon after taking office Simon decided to expand the business. Within weeks he had successfully negotiated a five-year contract with a large clothes retailer to make a range of sports and leisurewear items. The contract will result in an additional £2 million sales during each year of the contract. In order to fulfil the contract new equipment and premises were acquired by Bradbury Ltd.

Financial information concerning the company is given below:

Profit and loss account for the year ended 30 November

	1999	2000
	£000	£000
Turnover	9,482	11,365
Profit before interest and tax	914	1,042
Interest charges	22	81
Profit before tax	892	961
Taxation	358	385
Profit after tax	534	576
Dividends	120	120
Retained profit	414	456

Balance sheet as at 30 November

	1999		2000	
	£000	£000	£000	£000
Fixed assets				
Freehold premises at cost		5,240		7,360
Plant and equipment (net)		2,375		4,057
		7,615		11,417
Current assets				
Stock	2,386		3,420	
Trade debtors	2,540		4,280	
Cash	127		–	
	5,053		7,700	
Creditors: amounts falling due within 1 year				
Trade creditors	1,157		2,245	
Taxation	358		385	
Dividends payable	120		120	
Bank overdraft	–		2,424	
	1,635		5,174	
Net current assets		3,428		2,526
		11,033		13,943
Creditors: amounts falling due in more than 1 year				
Loans		1,220		3,674
Total net assets		9,813		10,269

Capital and reserves		
Share capital	2,000	2,000
Reserves	7,813	8,269
	9,813	10,269

Required
(a) Calculate for each year the following ratios:
    (i) Net profit margin.
    (ii) Return on capital employed.
    (iii) Current ratio.
    (iv) Debt ratio.
    (v) Days debtors (collection period).
    (vi) Net asset turnover.
(b) Using the above ratios, and any other ratios or information you consider relevant, comment on the results of the expansion programme.

19.11 The usefulness of financial ratios

The usefulness of ratio analysis will largely depend upon:

- the quality of the underlying financial statements, and
- the validity of the standards of comparison employed.

Where the underlying statements upon which the ratios are based are unreliable, the quality of the analysis will be undermined. Sometimes managers may wish to undermine the quality of financial statements prepared for users. For example, managers may seek to provide a healthier picture of the performance and position of the business than is really the case in order to be viewed in a favourable light, or they may seek ways of hiding contractual or financial obligations which are burdensome to the business in order to obscure the true level of financial risk taken by lenders and shareholders. It is therefore important for users not to rely exclusively on the annual financial statements in order to assess performance and position. Other sources of information available should be used to confirm the reliability of the financial statements and to provide a more detailed picture of the business.

Activity 12

What other sources of information might be used to confirm or supplement the information contained in the annual financial statements? (A similar question was posed in Chapter 1; however, at this stage in your studies you should be able to answer this question in more detail.)

The following sources of information may prove useful:

- *interim (i.e. half-yearly or quarterly) financial reports prepared by the company*
- *the financial statements of similar businesses in the same industry*

- *newspaper and journal articles relating to the business*
- *newspaper and journal articles relating to the industry and the economy as a whole*
- *industry reports*
- *announcements made by the directors of the company*
- *share price movements*
- *stockbrokers' reports*
- *rumours*
- *prospectuses/offers for sale*
- *discussions with directors/managers*

This is not an exhaustive list. You may have thought of others.

The standards used for comparison purposes must be valid for a proper interpretation of results. We saw earlier that there are three major standards which may be used, and considered some of their drawbacks. Information relating to similar businesses in the same industry provides an external source of data which many find useful. This information is becoming increasingly available through computerized databases produced by commercial companies and represents an easy and relatively cheap form of information. However, there may be problems with using such a database. Not all businesses may be included in it. For example, businesses considered to be less important to database customers such as small businesses or businesses whose shares are not traded on the Stock Exchange may be excluded. In addition, the classification methods used by the database may exclude or obscure valuable items of information relating to a company. There is also a risk that the database may not include up-to-date information or may contain recording errors. Users must be aware of these potential problems when employing this source of information.

Ratios have the advantage of controlling for differences in size. For example, two businesses may be quite different in size but can be compared in terms of profitability, liquidity, etc. by the use of ratios. Thus, Business A may have sales of £1m and a net profit of £100,000 and Business B may have sales of £10m and a net profit of £1m. The net profit margin ratio will reveal that the profitability of each business is identical. While this ability to control for size differences can be useful, it can also have its drawbacks. It may be, for example, that the size of a business is an important factor in identifying profitable businesses within a particular industry or in identifying businesses which are likely to fail. If we rely only on ratios, these kinds of relationships will not be picked up.

19.12 Summary

Financial ratios offer a useful means of highlighting the strengths and weaknesses of a business. As a result they provide useful signposts for further analysis. Although the calculation of financial ratios is fairly straightforward, skill and judgement are required in interpreting the results. A ratio has a numerator and denominator and changes in the ratio can occur from changes in either or both. It is therefore important to be clear why a ratio has changed.

It must be emphasized that ratios alone do not provide a sufficient basis for arriving at firm conclusions concerning the position and performance of a business. If an increase in stocks results in a higher stock turnover period we cannot say for sure that this reflects poor stock control. In certain circumstances an increase in stockholdings may be both desirable and deliberate, e.g. where future supplies will cost significantly more or are likely to be disrupted. Ratios provide a starting point for further investigation and conclusions based on ratios alone must be regarded as extremely tentative.

In this chapter only the more widely used ratios have been considered. Many more ratios may be computed to determine the financial health of a business. Some of these ratios relate figures on the financial statements to particular resources held by the business or particular outputs in order to measure efficiency. It has been mentioned above that measures of output such as sales and profit can be related to employee or floor space, passenger miles to devise ratios such as sales (profit) per employee, sales (profit) per square metre of floor space, profit per passenger mile, etc.

Exercises

1 White and Black are sole traders. Both are wholesalers dealing in a similar range of goods. Summaries of the profit calculations and balance sheets for the same year have been made available to you, as follows:

Profit and loss accounts for the year	White		Black	
	£000	£000	£000	£000
Sales		600		800
Cost of goods sold		450		624
		150		176
Administration expenses	64		63	
Selling and distribution expenses	28		40	
Depreciation – equipment and vehicles	10		20	
Depreciation – buildings	–	102	5	128
Net profit		48		48

Balance sheets as at end of the year	White		Black	
	£000	£000	£000	£000
Buildings		29		47
Equipment and vehicles		62		76
Stock		56		52
Debtors		75		67
Bank balance		8		–
		230		242

Creditors	38		78	
Bank balance	–	38	4	82
Capital		192		160

Required

Compare the performance and position of the two businesses on the basis of the above figures, supporting your comments where appropriate with ratios and noting what further information you would need before reaching firmer conclusions.

2 Joseph Brown Ltd is a medium-sized enginering company based in the north-east of England, an area of high unemployment. It has been owned by the Brown family for the last 120 years and has recently appointed James Barratt as its new managing director. Barratt, who previously worked very successfully as general manager of a similar company owned by a large group, has been hired to rationalize the company's activities. His first task is to tackle the company's high manning levels, and he has negotiated a redundancy deal with the unions which is expected to cost £400,000, payable over the next six months. This will, however, result in savings in labour costs of £300,000 per year.

Financial information relating to the company is as follows:

Profit and loss account – year ending 31 December

	1998	1999	2000
	£000	£000	£000
Turnover	12,430	10,874	11,450
Profit before interest and taxation	1,183	476	1,243
Term loan interest	(420)	(350)	(280)
Bank overdraft interest	(481)	(540)	(500)
Profit before taxation	282	(414)	463
Taxation	(132)	–	(15)
Profit after taxation	150	(414)	448
Dividend payable	(100)	–	–
Retained	50	(414)	448

Balance sheet at 31 December

	1998	1999	2000
	£000	£000	£000
Fixed assets			
Freehold premises	4,025	4,025	4,025
Plant and equipment	3,047	3,167	3,750
	7,072	7,192	7,775

Less depreciation	3,045	3,825	4,680
	4,027	3,367	3,095
Current assets			
Stock	2,590	3,625	2,863
Debtors	3,065	3,277	2,980
Cash	75	–	–
	5,730	6,902	5,843
Creditors: amounts falling due in under 1 year			
Trade creditors	(1,295)	(2,175)	(1,432)
Bank overdraft	(3,700)	(4,246)	(3,710)
	(4,995)	(6,421)	(5,142)
Total assets less current liabilities	4,762	3,848	3,796
Less creditors: amounts falling due			
in more than 1 year – loans	3,000	2,500	2,000
	1,762	1,348	1,796
Capital and reserves			
Share capital	1,000	1,000	1,000
Reserves	762	348	796
	1,762	1,348	1,796

To meet the costs of the redundancy scheme, and to allow for reasonable fluctuations in working capital requirements, the company has decided to approach its clearing bankers with a request to extend its overdraft limit from £4 million to £4.5 million.

Notes

1 The term loan is repayable to Venture Capital Ltd in instalments of £500,000 per year. It is secured on factory premises, which have a market value of £6,000,000.
2 The overdraft, which has been obtained from the Barland National Bank, is secured by a floating charge on the company's assets.
3 The net book value of plant and equipment is £1,875,000.

Required
(a) Calculate the following ratios from the accounts, using 19X6 figures:
    (i) Times interest earned.
   (ii) Debt/equity ratio.
  (iii) Acid-test ratio.
  (iv) Return on investment.

(v) Return on equity.

(vi) Days' debtors.

(b) Discuss the request for the extension to the overdraft from a banker's viewpoint. If the banker granted the request, what terms and conditions do you think he might impose?

3 Business A and Business B are both engaged in retailing, but seem to take a different approach to this trade according to the information available. This information consists of a table of ratios, shown below:

Ratio	Business A	Business B
Current ratio	2:1	1.5:1
Quick assets (acid-test) ratio	1.7:1	0.7:1
Return on capital employed	20%	17%
Return on owner's equity	30%	18%
Debtors' turnover	63 days	21 days
Creditors' turnover	50 days	45 days
Gross profit percentage	40%	15%
Net profit percentage	10%	10%
Stock turnover	52 days	25 days

Required

(a) Explain briefly how each ratio is calculated.

(b) Describe what this information indicates about the differences in approach between the two businesses. If one of them prides itself on personal service and one of them on competitive prices, which do you think is which and why?

4 You are given summarized results of an electrical engineering business, as follows. All figures are in £000.

Profit and loss account for the year ended 31 December

	1999	2000
Turnover	60,000	50,000
Cost of sales	42,000	34,000
Gross profit	18,000	16,000
Operating expenses	15,500	13,000
	2,500	3,000
Interest payable	2,200	1,300
Profit before taxation	300	1,700
Taxation	350	600
(Loss) profit after taxation	(50)	1,100
Dividends	600	600
Transfer (from) to reserves	(650)	500

Balance sheet for the year ended 31 December

	1999	2000
Fixed assets		
Intangible	500	–
Tangible	12,000	11,000
	12,500	11,000
Current assets		
Stocks	14,000	13,000
Debtors	16,000	15,000
Bank and cash	500	500
	30,500	28,500
Creditors due within 1 year	(24,000)	(20,000)
Net current assets	6,500	8,500
Total assets less current liabilities	19,000	19,500
Creditors due after 1 year	6,000	5,500
	13,000	14,000
Capital and reserves		
Share capital	1,300	1,300
Share premium	3,300	3,300
Revaluation reserve	2,000	2,000
Profit and loss	6,400	7,400
	13,000	14,000

Required
(a) Prepare a table of the following ratios, calculated for both years, clearly showing the figures used in the calculations.
 (i) Current ratio
 (ii) Quick assets ratio
 (iii) Stock turnover in days
 (iv) Debtors' turnover in days
 (v) Creditors' turnover in days
 (vi) Gross profit (%)
 (vii) Net profit (%; before taxation)
 (viii) Interest cover
 (ix) Return on owner's equity
 (x) Return on capital employed
 (xi) Gearing
(b) Making full use of the information given in the question, of your table of ratios, and your common sense, comment on the apparent position of the business and on the actions of the management.
5 Extracts from the accounts for the year ended 30 June 1999 of two companies appear below:

	Dover Printers Ltd	Folkestone Engineers Ltd
	£000	£000
Fixed assets	468	330
Current assets	580	870
	1,048	1,200
Less: Amounts due in under 1 year		
Creditors	(230)	(150)
Overdraft	(160)	(50)
Total assets less current liabilities	658	1,000
Less: Amounts due in over 1 year		
Loans	460	200
	198	800
Share capital and reserves		
Ordinary share capital	80	300
Reserves (note 1)	118	500
	198	800
Profit before interest and taxation	95	165
Interest (note 2)	62	45
Profit before taxation	33	120
Taxation	12	42
Profit after taxation	21	78
Less: Ordinary dividends	10	10
Retained	11	68
Note 1: Includes revaluation reserve –	300	
Note 2: Includes overdraft interest	16	15

Required

(a) For each company, calculate the two ratios listed below. You should describe the purpose of each ratio and state to whom they are of most interest. You should include brief notes explaining your calculations.

 (i) Return on capital employed.

 (ii) Return on equity.

(b) Explain the difficulties that may be encountered when attempting to compare the performance of each company on the basis of the ratios above.

(c) Explain the term gearing and demonstrate its impact on profitability using some illustrative numbers.

6 Threads Ltd is a company which manufactures nuts and bolts which are sold to industrial users. The abbreviated accounts for 2000 and 1999 are given below.

Threads Ltd
Profit and loss account for the year ended 30 June

	2000		1999	
	£000	£000	£000	£000
Sales		1,200		1,180
Cost of sales		(750)		(680)
Gross profit		450		500
Operating expenses	(208)		(200)	
Depreciation	(75)		(66)	
Interest	(8)		(–)	
		(291)		(266)
Profit before tax		159		234
Tax		(48)		(80)
Profit after tax		111		154
Dividend – proposed		(72)		(70)
Retained profit for year		39		84

Balance sheet as at 30 June

	2000		1999	
Fixed assets (note 1)		687		702
Current assets				
Stocks	236		148	
Debtors	156		102	
Cash	4		32	
	396		282	
Creditors (amounts due within 1 year)				
Trade creditors	(76)		(60)	
Other creditors and accruals	(16)		(18)	
Dividend	(72)		(70)	
Tax	(48)		(80)	
Bank overdraft	(26)		(–)	
	(238)		(228)	
Net current assets		158		54
Creditors (amounts due after more than 1 year)				

Bank loan (note 2)	(50)	–
	795	756

Ordinary share capital of		
£1 (fully paid)	500	500
Retained profits	295	256
	795	756

Note 1: Fixed assets

	Buildings £000	Fixtures and fittings £000	Vehicles £000	Total £000
Cost 1.7.1999	900	100	80	1,080
Purchases	–	40	20	60
Cost 30.6.2000	900	140	100	1,140
Depreciation 1.7.1999	288	50	40	378
Charge for year	36	14	25	75
Depreciation 30.6.2000	324	64	65	453
Net book value 30.6.2000	576	76	35	687

Note 2
The bank loan was taken up on 1 July 1999 and is repayable on 1 January 2005. It carries a fixed rate of interest of 12% per annum and is secured by a fixed and floating charge on the assets of the company.

Required
(a) Calculate the following financial statistics for *both* 1999 and 2000, using end-of-year figures where appropriate:
    (i) Return on capital employed
    (ii) Net profit margin
    (iii) Gross profit margin
    (iv) Current ratio
    (v) Liquid ratio
    (vi) Days' debtors
    (vii) Days' creditors
    (viii) Stock turnover ratio
(b) Comment on the performance of Threads Ltd from the viewpoint of a company considering supplying a substantial amount of goods to Threads Ltd on usual credit terms.
(c) What action could a supplier take to lessen the risk of not being paid should Threads Ltd be in financial difficulty?

Case study: Housewarm Central Heating Supplies Plc

Housewarm Central Heating Supplies Plc (HCHS) is a business which specializes in manufacturing and marketing oil-fired domestic central heating systems. All the company's sales are made to housebuilders and plumbers. The company was established on 1 August 1997 when three managers of United Industrial Trust Plc (UIT) negotiated a management buyout of Petersen Ltd, one of its subsidiaries. Most of the £2.5 million finance needed to fund the buyout had come from the Enterprise Finance Fund (EFF), though the managers themselves had raised between them about £500,000, mainly by second-mortgaging their homes. EFF is a consortium of City institutions which had been formed at the instigation of the government to provide finance for smaller businesses, particularly management buyouts.

Petersen Ltd had been long-established family-run heating engineers. When the last of the Petersen family died in 1973, UIT had bought the company but had not really taken very much interest in it subsequently. Throughout the period of UIT's ownership Petersen had lacked focus in its production and marketing, being a general provider of commissioned heating systems, both industrial and domestic. Petersen's high-quality workmanship had enabled the company to produce enough profit to satisfy UIT and to prevent interference from the parent company in its affairs.

The three managers involved with the buyout were James Atkinson, the production manager, Mike Wimborne, the sales manager, and Terry Pike, the chief accountant. Following the buyout, they had become the production, marketing and finance directors, respectively, with Wimborne also acting as chief executive and chairman. The membership of the board of directors was completed by the inclusion of a nominee of EFF, Arthur Peters, as a non-executive director. Peters had made it plain from the outset that neither he nor EFF was keen to interfere, provided that he was confident that EFF's investment was prospering. Generally the strategic decisions had been easy to take, since there had been little disagreement between the three executive directors as to the direction which the company should take, partly because Wimborne's strong personality and leadership qualities had influenced his more passive colleagues. Peters had been true to his word and had not sought to influence them.

Almost the first decision taken after the buyout was to focus more clearly on the company's target market. In the future the company was to produce a limited range of domestic central-heating systems to be sold only to the trade, i.e. to builders and plumbers. It was also decided to have a change of company name which would reflect more the nature of the work they were to undertake.

The board recognized that competition in the supply of central heating systems had grown in recent years and were anxious to ensure that the company established a competitive edge in terms of both price and quality.

During the three years since the management buyout the company had succeeded in increasing its market share each year. This had been achieved through a combination of aggressive marketing and the development of a very competitive range of products. The quality of workmanship and adherence to delivery dates had created goodwill among customers and the order book for the forthcoming year suggested that sales turnover would reach new peaks. Although this news was pleasing, the board also recognized that the company was experiencing a number of difficulties.

The financial position and performance for each of the first three years following the management buyout were as follows:

Abridged accounts for the three years ending 31 July 2000
Trading and profit and loss account

	1998	1999	2000
	£000	£000	£000
Sales	4,940.5	6,175.2	7,412.3
Less cost of sales	3,458.0	4,693.7	6,298.5
Gross profit	1,482.5	1,481.5	1,113.8
Less overheads	1,037.4	1,160.9	1,171.2
	445.1	320.6	(57.4)
Add income from investments	49.4	49.4	–
Net profit (loss)	494.5	370.0	(57.4)

Profit and loss appropriation account

Net profit (loss) for the year	(494.5)	(370.0)	(57.4)
Less: Dividend	(250.0)	(150.0)	–
Corporation tax	(167.5)	(136.1)	–
Retained profit (loss)	(77.0)	(83.9)	(57.4)
Add retained profit brought forward	–	77.0	160.9
Retained profit carried forward	77.0	160.9	103.5

	1998		1999		2000	
Balance sheet	£000	£000	£000	£000	£000	£000
Fixed assets						
Freehold land and buildings		494.5		494.5		494.5
Machinery and plant, net of depreciation		617.5		543.4		774.3
		1,112.0		1,037.9		1,268.8
Trade investments		294.0		294.0		–
		1,406.0		1,331.9		1,268.8
Current assets						
Stock-in-trade	637.3		938.6		1,468.6	
Sundry debtors	823.3		1,235.1		1,675.5	
Cash	451.4		336.2		–	
	1,912.0		2,509.9		3,144.1	

Less: *current liabilities*					
Sundry creditors	(741.0)		(1,180.9)		(1,729.1)
Bank overdraft	–		–		80.3
	(741.0)		(1,180.9)		(1,809.4)
		1,171.0		1,329.0		1,334.7
Net assets		2,577.0		2,660.9		2,603.5
Capital and reserves					
Ordinary £1 shares		2,500.0		2,500.0		2,500.0
Retained profit		77.0		160.9		103.5
		2,577.0		2,660.9		2,603.5

The non-executive director, Arthur Peters, was becoming increasingly concerned about the dividend policy of the board. He recognized that, while EFF saw the company as a long-term investment, the failure to pay any dividend for the year ended 31 July 2000 would cause EFF to take a closer interest in the company's affairs. Soon after publication of the accounts for the year ended 31 July 2000, representatives of EFF sought a meeting with the board. The board was concerned that EFF might begin to influence strategic decisions unless confidence in the company and its future direction could be restored.

In addition, the company recently had a loan application turned down. The board had hoped to borrow £1.0 million over a 15-year period in order to finance an expansion to its existing production facilities. The company was currently utilizing its production facilities almost to the full and the board was aware that this situation could constrain future growth. The prospective lender, however, felt that the programme was too ambitious and rejected the loan application. The board was now considering whether or not to approach another lender with its expansion plans.

During the past year the company had been relying on a bank overdraft to finance its working capital requirements. The overdraft limit had been raised on three separate occasions to accommodate the company's financing needs. However, the bank was becoming increasingly uneasy about the current level of the overdraft (now standing at £92,700) and the company had been asked to reduce the overdraft over the next six months to a maximum of £40,000.

A meeting of the board was scheduled in order to review the current strategy of the company and to deal with what appeared to be a crisis of confidence amongst investors and lenders.

Required
(a) Analyse the performance of Housewarm Central Heating Supplies Plc over the three years ended 31 July 2000.
(b) How might the board deal with the crisis of confidence among investors and lenders?

Appendix 1: Abacus Ltd	

Profit and loss account for the year ended 31 October 2000

	£000	£000
Sales		3,200
Less cost of sales		
Opening stock	250	
Purchases	2,600	
	2,850	
Closing stock	350	
		2,500
Gross profit		700
Less operating expenses		
Selling expenses	210	
Administrative expenses	90	
Interest payable	60	
Depreciation	60	
		420
Net profit before taxation		280
Less corporation tax		70
Net profit after taxation		210

Balance sheet as at 31 October 2000

	£000	£000	£000
Fixed assets			
Freehold land at cost			1,000
Plant and machinery at cost		1,500	
Less accumulated depreciation		600	
			900
			1,900
Current assets			
Stock		350	
Trade debtors		520	
Prepayments		30	
Cash at bank		50	
		950	
Creditors: amounts falling due within one year			
Trade creditors		380	
Corporation tax		70	
		450	
			500

Total assets less current liabilities		2,400
Creditors: amounts falling due		
after more than one year		
10% Debentures		600
		1,800
Capital and reserves		
£1 ordinary shares		600
Share premium account	200	
General reserve	680	
Profit and loss account	320	
		1,200
		1,800

Comparative ratios based on the industry average

	Abacus Ltd	Industry average
Liquidity		
Current ratio	2.11	2.2
Acid-test ratio	1.27	0.9
Gearing		
Debt/equity ratio	0.58	0.85
Debt/total assets	36.84%	38.00%
Interest coverage ratio	5.67	3.95
Cash flow coverage ratio	6.67	4.90
Activity		
Stock turnover	8.3	10.9
Period of stockholding	1.44m	1.1m
Debtors' turnover	6.15	6.3
Period of credit to debtors	1.95m	1.9m
Period of credit from suppliers	1.75m	1.8m
Fixed asset turnover ratio	1.68	1.6
Total asset turnover ratio	1.12	1.2
Profitability		
Gross profit margin	21.87%	21.0%
Net profit margin	6.56%	8.2%
Return to equity	11.67%	13.11%
Return on capital employed	14.17%	16.59%
Return on investment	7.36%	9.84%

Appendix 2: Vortex Ltd

The abridged accounts for Vortex Ltd for the past three years are as follows:

Profit and loss account

	1998		1999		2000	
	£000	£000	£000	£000	£000	£000
Sales		24,000		30,000		38,000
Less: Cost of sales		15,000		22,000		30,000
Gross profit		9,000		8,000		8,000
Less: Selling expenses	2,000		2,500		3,000	
Admin. expenses	1,000		1,500		1,800	
Interest payable	–		100		200	
Depreciation	800		1,200		1,500	
		3,800		5,300		6,500
Net profit before tax		5,200		2,700		1,500
Less: corporation tax		1,600		800		450
Net profit after tax		3,600		1,900		1,050
Less: Dividends		1,800		1,800		1,000
Retained profit for year		1,800		100		50

Balance sheet

	1998		1999		2000	
	£000	£000	£000	£000	£000	£000
Fixed assets						
Freehold land		2,000		2,000		2,000
Plant and machinery	12,000		13,300		16,850	
Less: Depreciation	4,000		5,200		6,700	
		8,000		8,100		10,150
		10,000		10,100		12,150
Current assets						
Stock	8,000		12,000		17,000	
Debtors	6,000		9,000		14,000	
Cash at bank	10,000		6,000		–	
	24,000		27,000		31,000	
Creditors: due within one year						
Sundry creditors	12,000		14,000		19,000	
		12,000		13,000		12,000
		22,000		23,100		24,150
Creditors: due after one year						
10% Debentures		–		1,000		2,000
		22,000		22,100		22,150
Capital						
Ordinary £1 shares		10,000		10,000		10,000
Reserves						
Profit and loss account		12,000		12,100		12,150
		22,000		22,100		22,150

Stock at beginning of 1998 – £7,000

Chapter 20

The analysis of financial statements: 2

20.1
Introduction

This chapter is concerned with further aspects of financial analysis. It examines ratios which are of particular value to investors and explains how techniques such as common-size financial statements can be used in the evaluation of performance.

20.2
Objectives

On completion of this chapter you should be able to:

- analyse the return on investment ratio into its component ratios and explain the significance of this form of analysis;
- prepare common-size financial statements and explain their usefulness;
- measure the variability of earnings;
- calculate the major investment ratios and explain their significance.

20.3
Return on investment

In the previous chapter the return on investment (ROI) ratio was examined. This is a primary ratio which measures the ability of the business to use its assets in a profitable way. It will be recalled that the ratio is calculated as follows:

$$\text{ROI} = \frac{\text{Net profit after tax}}{\text{Total assets}} \times 100$$

This ratio can be separated into two component ratios, the net profit margin and sales to total assets. Hence:

$$\frac{\text{Net profit after tax}}{\text{Total assets}} = \frac{\text{Net profit after tax}}{\text{Sales}} \times \frac{\text{Sales}}{\text{Total assets}}$$

The breakdown of ROI in this way reveals that the profitable employment of assets will be determined by both the net profit margin and the efficient use of assets. This may be useful in understanding trends in ROI. To illustrate this point, consider the financial data of Alpha Plc set out below:

	1998	1999	2000
Sales	£10 m	£20 m	£30 m
Net profit after tax	£2 m	£3 m	£4 m
Total assets	£16 m	£18 m	£20 m
ROI	12.5%	16.6%	20%
Net profit margin	20%	15%	13.3%
Sales/total assets	0.625	1.11	1.5

Table 20.1   Factors influencing return on investment

These data reveal that, over the three-year period, the net profit margin has declined. However, over the same period sales have increased at a faster rate than the increase in assets and, therefore, the sales/total assets ratio has increased. Because the increase in the sales/total assets ratio has been greater than the decrease in the net profit margin, the net effect has been that ROI over the period has increased. Thus, a decrease in net profit margins has been more than offset by more efficient use of assets.

The two component ratios can also be broken down to reveal, in detail, the factors influencing ROI. Table 20.1 shows that ROI can be influenced by changes in sales, expenses and assets.

Activity 1

Beta Plc and Gamma Plc are similar enterprises operating in the same industry. Extracts from their most recent accounts are set out below:

	Beta Plc	Gamma Plc
Sales turnover	£42 m	£74 m
Net profit after tax	£4 m	£6 m
Total assets	£28 m	£30 m

Do the following

(a) Calculate Return on Investment (ROI) for each enterprise.
(b) Analyse the ROI of each ratio into its component ratios.
(c) Discuss whether you feel ROI is sufficient for an equity shareholder to assess the profitability of the enterprise.

Your answer to this activity should be as follows:

	Beta Plc	**Gamma Plc**
(a) ROI $= \dfrac{\text{net profit after tax} \times 100}{\text{total assets}}$	14.29%	20.0%
(b) (i) Net profit/sales	9.52%	8.11%
(ii) Sales/total assets	1.5	2.47

(c) *Equity shareholders will be interested in the rate of return on equity as well as return on total assets. Maximizing return on assets is not necessarily the same as maximizing returns to equity shareholders. The latter will be affected by the level of gearing the business adopts.*

Activity 2

Indicate whether you would expect the component ratios of ROI to be high or low for each of the following enterprises:

	Net profit margins (High/Low)	**Sales/total assets** (High/Low)
(a) A supermarket chain		
(b) A motor manufacturer		
(c) A petrol station		
(d) A heavy engineering business		
(e) A professional firm of accountants		

Your answer should be as follows:

	Net profit margins	*Sales/total assets*
(a) A supermarket chain	Low	High
(b) A car manufacturer	High	Low
(c) A petrol station	Low	High
(d) A heavy engineering business	High	Low
(e) A professional firm of accountants	High	High

A professional firm of accountants is likely to be different from the other types of business mentioned. The professional rules for accountants demand that they must practise as either a sole proprietor business or a partnership. In both cases, any amounts payable to the owners (who usually work in the business) will not be shown as wages in the profit and loss account but as withdrawals of capital. This, in turn, means that a higher net profit margin will be shown than if the firm operated as a limited company and the owners were drawing salaries as directors of the company. A firm of accountants is likely to have few fixed assets and no stock-in-trade. So the return on investment may well be high, particularly given that the net profit margin is likely to be high.

Activity 3
How would each of the following affect ROI?

(a) An increase in administration expenses
(b) An increase in sales
(c) A decrease in stock levels
(d) An upward revaluation of land and buildings

Your answer should be as follows:

	Effect on ROI	
	Increase	*Decrease*
(a) An increase in administration expenses		Yes
(b) An increase in sales	Yes	
(c) A decrease in stock levels	Yes	
(d) An upward revaluation of land and buildings		Yes

**20.4
Common-size
financial
statements**

Common-size financial statements relate individual figures appearing on the conventional statements to some base figure. By relating all figures to a common base it may be possible to detect trends occurring within a business over time or to make useful comparisons between similar enterprises in the same industry for a particular period of time.

One form of common-size statement compares figures appearing on a conventional financial statement with a base figure taken from the same statement. This is referred to as *vertical analysis*. To illustrate this form of analysis, consider the financial data relating to Delta Plc set out below. The conventional and common-size profit and loss accounts for a four-year period are displayed. To prepare the common-size profit and loss accounts the sales figure for each year has been set at 100 and all other figures are expressed as a percentage of the sales for the relevant year.

Delta Plc
Conventional profit and loss account for the year ending 30 June

	1996		1997		1998		1999	
	£m	£m	£m	£m	£m	£m	£m	£m
Sales		130.0		150.0		170.0		200.0
Less cost of sales		78.0		93.0		108.0		130.0
Gross profit		52.0		57.0		62.0		70.0
Wages and salaries	13.0		18.0		22.5		28.0	
Rent and rates	6.5		7.5		8.5		8.0	
Heat and light	5.2		4.5		6.8		10.0	
Depreciation	2.6		3.0		3.4		4.0	
		27.3		33.0		41.2		50.0

Net profit before tax	24.7	24.0	20.8	20.0
Taxation	13.2	6.0	6.8	8.0
Net profit after tax	11.5	18.0	14.0	12.0
Dividends	9.0	3.0	12.0	6.0
Retained profit	2.5	15.0	2.0	6.0

Common-size profit and loss account for the year ending 30 June

	1996	1997	1998	1999
	%	%	%	%
Sales	100.0	100.0	100.0	100.0
Less cost of sales	60.0	62.0	63.5	65.0
Gross profit	40.0	38.0	36.5	35.0
Wages and salaries	10.0	12.0	13.2	14.0
Rent and rates	5.0	5.0	5.0	4.0
Heat and light	4.0	3.0	4.0	5.0
Depreciation	2.0	2.0	2.0	2.0
Net profit before tax	19.0	16.0	12.3	10.0
Taxation	10.2	4.0	4.0	4.0
Net profit after tax	8.8	12.0	8.3	6.0
Dividends	6.9	2.0	7.1	3.0
Retained profit	1.9	10.0	1.2	3.0

The common-size profit and loss accounts reveal that cost of sales, as a percentage of sales turnover, has risen steadily over the four-year period. This has resulted in a decline in both the gross profit margins and the net profit margin. Wages as a percentage of sales turnover have also increased steadily over the four-year period and this has contributed further to the decline in net profit margins. As can be seen, this form of analysis highlights why changes in profit margins have occurred and provides a starting point for further investigation.

Common-size balance sheets provide another useful form of analysis. By preparing such statements it is possible to see more clearly the distribution of assets held and the ways in which the enterprise is funded. The conventional and common-size balance sheets for Delta Plc for a four-year period are set out below. To prepare the common-size balance sheets the total assets and total liabilities figures are set at 100 and individual assets and liabilities are then expressed as a percentage of the base figure.

Delta Plc
Conventional balance sheet as at 30 June

	1996		1997		1998		1999	
	£m	£m	£m	£m	£m	£m	£m	£m
Fixed assets								
Freehold land and property		25.0		25.0		25.0		25.0

Plant and equipment	40.0	44.0	48.0	60.0
Motor vehicles	20.0	21.0	22.0	22.0
	85.0	90.0	95.0	107.0
Current assets				
Stock	52.2	59.0	64.8	51.0
Debtors	20.0	27.0	23.0	25.0
Cash	15.0	10.0	10.0	8.0
	87.2	96.0	97.8	84.0
	172.2	186.0	192.8	191.0
Financed by				
Share capital	70.0	70.0	70.0	70.0
Retained profit	5.0	20.0	22.0	28.0
	75.0	90.0	92.0	98.0
Creditors: due beyond 1 year				
Debentures	60.0	60.0	60.0	60.0
Creditors: due within 1 year				
Trade creditors	15.0	27.0	20.0	19.0
Tax and dividends	22.2	9.0	20.8	14.0
	37.2	36.0	40.8	33.0
	172.2	186.0	192.8	191.0

Common-size balance sheets as at 30 June

	1996 %	1997 %	1998 %	1999 %
Fixed assets				
Freehold land	14.5	13.4	13.0	13.1
Plant and equipment	23.2	23.7	24.9	31.4
Motor vehicles	11.6	11.3	11.4	11.5
Current assets				
Stock	30.3	31.7	33.6	26.7
Debtors	11.6	14.5	11.9	13.1
Cash	8.8	5.4	5.2	4.2
	100.0	100.0	100.0	100.0
Financed by:				
Share capital	40.7	37.6	36.3	36.6
Retained profit	2.9	10.8	11.4	14.7
Creditors: due beyond 1 year				
Debentures	34.8	32.3	31.1	31.4
Creditors: due within 1 year				
Trade creditors	8.7	14.5	10.4	10.0
Tax and dividends	12.9	4.8	10.8	7.3
	100.0	100.0	100.0	100.0

The common-size balance sheets above highlight the increasing investment in plant and equipment and the steady decline in cash over the four-year period. These statements also reveal the growing importance of retained profit in financing the business.

It is important to recognize that a change in the percentage figure for a particular item may be due to a change in either the absolute size of the figure or the size of the group of which it forms part. It is therefore important when examining common-size statements to examine also the conventional statements in order to ensure percentage changes are properly interpreted.

In the above examples, common-size statements were prepared for a single business over a four-year period. However, common-size statements can also be prepared using data from similar businesses within the same industry. Such statements may prove useful for comparing cost structures, profit margins, sources of finance and the distribution of assets between enterprises.

The common-size statements illustrated above were based on *a vertical analysis* of the conventional financial statements, i.e. figures appearing on a particular statement were compared to a base figure taken from the same statement. However, it is also possible to prepare common-size statements based on a *horizontal analysis* of the conventional statements. This involves selecting a base year and setting all the figures appearing within the financial statements for that year at 100. Figures appearing in the financial statements of subsequent periods are then compared to the relevant figures relating to the base year. Horizontal analysis can help reveal how a business has arrived at its current position.

To illustrate this form of analysis, the conventional profit and loss accounts of Delta Plc set out above have been used as a basis to perform horizontal analysis. The appropriate common-size statements are shown below. These statements reveal that the increase in sales for the period has been less than the increase in the cost of sales and therefore gross profit has not risen in line with sales. The statement also reveals the particularly high increase in wages over the four-year period. Common-size balance sheets may also be prepared using horizontal analysis. These statements will help highlight the relative changes in assets and sources of finance over time.

Delta Plc
Common-size profit and loss accounts for the year ending 30 June

	1996 %	1997 %	1998 %	1999 %
Sales	100	115.4	130.8	153.8
Less cost of sales	100	119.2	138.5	116.7
Gross profit	100	109.6	119.2	134.6
Wages and salaries	100	138.5	173.1	215.4
Rent and rates	100	115.4	127.8	123.1
Heat and light	100	86.5	130.8	192.3
Depreciation	100	115.4	130.8	153.8

Net profit before tax	100	97.2	84.2	81.0
Taxation	100	45.5	51.5	60.6
Net profit after tax	100	156.5	121.7	104.3
Dividends	100	33.3	133.3	66.7
Retained profit	100	600.0	80.0	240.0

Activity 4

Below are the conventional profit and loss accounts of Omega Plc for a four-year period:

Profit and loss account for the year ended 30 September

	1996		1997		1998		1999	
	£m	£m	£m	£m	£m	£m	£m	£m
Sales		140		160		190		240
Less cost of sales		90		96		105		122
Gross profit		50		64		85		118
Administration expenses	20		28		34		43	
Selling and distribution	22		31		46		68	
Finance charges	3		3		3		3	
		45		62		83		114
Net profit		5		2		2		4

Do the following

(a) Produce common-size profit and loss accounts for each year based on a vertical analysis of the above statements.

(b) Discuss the main points arising from an examination of these statements.

Your answer should be as follows:

(a) *Common-size profit and loss accounts – vertical analysis*

	1996	1997	1998	1999
	%	%	%	%
Sales	100.0	100.0	100.0	100.0
Cost of sales	(64.3)	(60.0)	(55.3)	(50.8)
Gross profit	(35.7)	(40.0)	(44.7)	(49.2)
Admin. expenses	(14.3)	(17.5)	(17.9)	(17.9)
Selling expenses	(15.7)	(19.4)	(24.2)	(28.3)
Finance charges	(2.1)	(1.9)	(1.6)	(1.3)
Net profit	3.6	1.2	1.0	1.7

(b) *Although the enterprise has managed to increase the gross margin substantially over the period, the benefits have not filtered through to the net profit margin. This is largely due to the fact that selling expenses as a percentage of sales have almost doubled over the four-year period. There has also been some increase in administration expenses as a percentage of sales. Although finance charges as a percentage of sales have decreased over the period, this has not been sufficient to prevent a fall in net profit margins.*

Activity 5

Refer to the conventional profit and loss accounts set out in Activity 4 above.
   Using this information:

(a) Produce common-size profit and loss accounts for each year based on an horizontal analysis of the conventional statements
(b) Explain what additional insights these statements provide to those mentioned in Activity 4(b)

Your answer should be as follows:

(a) Common-size profit and loss accounts – horizontal analysis

	1996	1997	1998	1999
	%	%	%	%
Sales	100.0	114.3	135.7	171.4
Cost of sales	100.0	106.7	116.7	135.6
Gross profit	100.0	128.0	170.0	236.0
Admin. expenses	100.0	140.0	170.0	215.0
Selling expenses	100.0	140.9	209.1	309.1
Finance expenses	100.0	100.0	100.0	100.0
Net profit	100.0	40.0	40.0	80.0

(b) Common-size statements, based on horizontal analysis, provide information concerning changes in items over time. For Omega Plc, these statements reveal that sales have increased by more than 70% over the four-year period whereas cost of sales have only increased by half this amount. Although finance charges have remained constant over the period, administration expenses have more than doubled and selling expenses have more than trebled.

20.5 Variability of earnings

In order to obtain some sort of 'feel' for the quality of earnings generated by a business it is useful to measure variability of earnings over time. A simple measure of earnings variability is as follows:

$$\text{Earnings variability} = \frac{\text{Range of earnings ratio over recent years (i.e. highest-lowest earnings ratio)}}{\text{Average (mean) earnings ratio}}$$

The higher the measure of variability obtained, the greater the level of risk and, therefore, the lower the quality of earnings.

In order to illustrate the application of this measure let us look at an example. Consider the net profit to sales ratios (expressed below as decimals rather than percentages as the variability ratio is not usually expressed in percentage form) of three companies over a five-year period:

Year	Red Ltd	Amber Ltd	Green Ltd
19X2	0.03	0.08	0.04
19X3	0.10	0.11	0.12
19X4	0.09	0.09	0.14
19X5	0.07	0.14	0.16
19X6	0.11	0.13	0.04

The earnings variability of Red Ltd can be calculated as follows:

$$\text{Earnings variability} = \frac{0.11 - 0.03}{0.08} = 1.0$$

This measure must be compared with the results of other companies in order to derive relative variability.

The net profit-to-sales ratio is used for illustration purposes; however, other earnings ratios could also be used.

Activity 6

Calculate the earnings variability of Amber Ltd and Green Ltd. Which of the three companies has the highest variability and which has the lowest variability of earnings? Can you think of any weaknesses of this measure?

The earnings variability of the other two companies is as follows:

	Amber Ltd	Green Ltd
Earnings variability =	$\dfrac{0.14 - 0.08}{0.11}$	$\dfrac{0.16 - 0.04}{1.0}$
=	0.55	1.2

From the measures derived, it can be seen that Green Ltd has the highest level of variability and Amber Ltd has the lowest variability of earnings.

Whilst this measure may be useful, it suffers from the major weakness that an extreme figure for just one period may seriously affect the measure of earnings variability even though earnings may vary little in other periods. Thus, the measure may not provide a truly representative picture.

20.6 Investment ratios

In addition to the ratios discussed in the preceding chapter, there are certain ratios designed specifically for the investor. These provide measures of return and coverage which may help in deciding whether to buy, hold or sell shares in a particular business. To show how these ratios are calculated, the financial data of Phi Plc, set out below, will be used. It will be seen that some of the ratios discussed employ the market value of equity shares in their calculation. This means that the application of these ratios is normally confined to businesses whose shares are traded on a stock market.

Phi Plc
Abridged profit and loss account for the year ended 31 October 1999

	£m
Sales	200
Net profit before taxation	100
Less corporation tax	35
Net profit after taxation	65
Dividends paid	30
Retained profit for the year	35

Abridged balance sheet as at 31 October 1999

	£m
Net assets	122
Financed by:	
Share capital and reserves	
200 million ordinary shares of 25p	50
Retained profit	57
	107
Creditors due beyond 1 year	
10% Debentures	15
	122

At 31 October 1999 the ordinary shares of Phi Plc were quoted at £2.50 each on the Stock Exchange.

Dividends per share	This ratio relates the dividends announced each year to the number of shares issued, to obtain a figure of the dividends which relate to each share. The ratio is calculated as follows:

$$\text{Dividends per share} = \frac{\textbf{Ordinary share dividends}}{\textbf{Number of ordinary shares issued}}$$

For Phi Plc the dividends per share are calculated as follows:

$$\frac{£30 \text{ m}}{200 \text{ m}} = 15 \text{ p per share}$$

Dividend yield	This ratio relates the dividends announced during the year to the market value of the shares. In effect, the ratio measures the cash return the investor will receive on his/her investment. The ratio is calculated as follows:

$$\text{Dividend yield} = \frac{\textbf{Dividends per share}}{\textbf{Market price per share}} \times 100$$

As was shown above, the dividends per share for Phi Plc are 15p. The dividend yield is therefore:

$$\frac{15\,p}{£2.50} \times 100 = 6\%$$

This yield can be compared with the yields obtained from alternative investment opportunities.

It is important to bear in mind that the total returns from an investment in shares is made up of two elements: the cash dividend and the increase (decrease) in share price. A company may have a low dividend yield because it ploughs back profit to strengthen its financial position further. However, this, in turn, should result in high future share price growth.

Dividends from UK businesses are distributed net of taxation. However, returns from other forms of investment are often shown on a pre-tax basis. To compare the returns from dividends with other forms of investment it is therefore useful to calculate the gross value of the dividend. Assuming a standard rate of taxation of 25%, the net dividend will represent 75% (i.e. 100% − 25%) of the gross dividend.

To 'gross up' the net dividend of Phi Plc the following calculation is required.

$$6\% \times \frac{100}{75} = 8\%$$

Dividend cover

This ratio relates the dividends announced during the year to the profit available for dividend in that year. The ratio may be useful in assessing the ability of the business to maintain its existing level of dividends. The dividend cover ratio is calculated as follows:

$$\text{Dividend cover} = \frac{\textbf{Profits for year available for dividends}}{\textbf{Dividends announced for the year}}$$

For Phi Plc the profit available for dividend to ordinary shareholders is the net profit after taxation. (If Phi had issued preference shares, the preference share dividend would also have to be deduced in arriving at the profit available for dividend to ordinary shareholders.) The ratio is therefore:

$$\frac{£65\,m}{£30\,m} = £2.17$$

This means that for every £1 of dividend, Phi has generated £2.17 in profits to cover it. Thus, profits would have to fall substantially before the current level of dividend would not be covered.

Earnings per share

The earnings per share (EPS) ratio is a widely used measure of performance. This ratio relates the profits available for dividend to ordinary shareholders to the number of ordinary shares issued. It is calculated as follows:

$$EPS = \frac{\text{Profits for year available for dividend to ordinary shareholders}}{\text{Number of ordinary shares issued}}$$

EPS represents the profits attributable to each share. In some cases, a business may report an increase in profits as a result of an injection of fresh capital in the form of ordinary shares. If, however, the growth in profits is less than the growth in ordinary shares the effect will be to decrease EPS. Hence, equity shareholders are unlikely to be pleased, even though profits have risen. For Phi Plc the EPS ratio is:

$$\frac{£65 \text{ m}}{200 \text{ m}} = 32.5 \text{ p}$$

Earnings yield ratio

This ratio relates the earnings per share to the market price per share. It is calculated as follows:

$$\text{Earnings yield} = \frac{\text{EPS}}{\text{Market price per share}} \times 100$$

For Phi Plc the earnings yield is:

$$\frac{32.5 \text{ p}}{£2.50} \times 100 = 13\%$$

The earnings yield represents an alternative measure of return to the dividend yield discussed earlier. The dividend yield focuses on the cash return to investors and will be influenced by the dividend policies of the particular business. The earnings yield, on the other hand, compares the total profits attributable to each share to the market price per share and is unaffected by the dividend policies of the particular business.

Price/earnings ratio

The price/earnings (P/E) ratio also relates the earnings per share to the market price per share. The ratio is calculated as follows:

$$\text{P/E ratio} = \frac{\text{Market price of ordinary shares}}{\text{EPS}}$$

For Phi Plc the P/E ratio is:

$$\frac{£2.50}{32.5 \text{ p}} = 7.69$$

The significance of this ratio lies in the fact that share prices normally reflect investors' expectations concerning future earnings. Thus, by comparing share price (which reflects expected future earnings) to current earnings a measure of future growth prospects is obtained. The higher the P/E ratio, the greater will be investors' expectations concerning future growth (other things being equal). Thus, differences in P/E ratios between businesses will reflect differences in investor perceptions concerning the growth prospects of each enterprise.

Activity 7

Below are extracts from the *Financial Times* share information service.

Financial Times – Tuesday, 17 March 1999

1998/9 HOTELS AND CATERERS

High	Low	Stock	Price	+ or −	Div. Net	C'vr	Y'ld Gr's	P/E
229	81	Friendly Hotels 10p	224	−2	0.7	3.1	0.4	10.2
608	332	Grand Metrop. 50p	485	−4	10.25	2.7	3.0	14.4
810	440	Lon. Park Hotels	809	+10	10.0	2.8	1.7	24.6
$79\frac{1}{4}$	48	Queens Moat 5p	79	−	1.33	2.3	2.4	20.8
405	348	Savoy 'A' 10p	400	+1	3.5	6.9	1.2	15.7
88	57	Stakes 10p	84	+4	1.4	3.0	2.3	18.5
$226\frac{1}{2}$	140	Trusthouse Forte	217	−2	6.0	1.8	3.9	17.5

Answer each of the following:

(a) Explain what you think each column represents.
(b) Identify which company has:
   (i) the highest cover for its dividends
   (ii) the best cash return on investment
   (iii) the best growth prospects

Your answer to this activity should be as follows:

(a) High   *The highest share price achieved during the year (in pence – unless otherwise indicated)*

Low   *The lowest share price achieved during the year (in pence – unless otherwise indicated)*

Stock   *The name of the listed company and the par value of the share.*

Price   *The price at which shares are currently being traded at the close of business.*

+/−   *The change in share price from the previous price at which shares were traded at the previous day's close of business.*

Div. net   *The net dividend per share (in pence – unless otherwise indicated).*

Cover   *The dividend cover.*

Y'ld Gr's   *The gross dividend yield.*

P/E   *The price/earnings ratio*

(b) (i)   Savoy A

(ii)   Trusthouse Forte

(iii)   Lon. Park Hotels

Self-assessment question 20.1

Conday and Co. Ltd have been in operation for three years and produce antique reproduction furniture for the export market. The most recent set of accounts is set out below:

Balance sheet as at 30 November

	£000	£000	£000
Fixed assets			
Freehold land and buildings at cost			228
Plant and machinery at cost		942	
Less: Accumulated depreciation		180	
			762
Current assets			
Stocks		600	
Trade debtors		820	
		1,420	
Less: *Creditors: amounts falling due within 1 year*			
Trade creditors	665		
Taxation	95		
Bank overdraft	385		
		1,145	
			275
			1,265
Less: *Creditors; amounts falling due more than 1 year*			
12% Debentures			200
			1,065
Capital and reserves			
Ordinary shares of £1 each			700
Retained profits			365
			1,065

Profit and loss account for the year ended 30 November

	£000	£000
Sales		2,600
Less: Cost of sales		1,620
Gross profit		980
Less: Selling and distribution expenses		
(see Note 2)	408	
Administration expenses	174	
Finance expenses	78	

	660
Net profit before taxation	320
Corporation tax	95
Net profit after taxation	225
Proposed dividend	160
Retained profit for the year	65

Notes

1 The debentures are secured on the freehold land and buildings.
2 Selling and distribution expenses include £170,000 in respect of bad debts.

An investor has been approached by the company to invest £200,000 by purchasing ordinary shares in the company at £6.40 each. The company wishes to use the funds to finance a programme of further expansion.

Required
(a) Analyse the financial position and performance of the company and comment on any features you consider to be significant.
(b) State, with reasons, whether or not the investor should invest in the company on the terms outlined.

**20.7
Summary**

This chapter has dealt with various aspects of financial analysis. It began by analysing the ROI ratio in rather more detail, and identifying the factors which can influence ROI. We have seen how profitability and productivity ratios interact to produce a measure of ROI for a business. We have examined common-size financial statements, using both vertical and horizontal methods, and seen how they can assist in analysing and interpreting results.

In order to try to assess the quality of earnings generated, a measure of earnings variability can be calculated. We have examined one such measure and the weakness of this measure has been discussed. Ratios have been discussed which relate specifically to the investor and which are widely quoted in financial journals and newspapers. Most of these ratios have particular relevance to those companies whose shares are traded on a Stock Exchange. All the techniques examined in this chapter should provide further insights into the performance of a business, and can be used in conjunction with the ratios discussed in Chapter 19.

Exercises

1 Rose Ltd operates a small chain of retail shops which sell high-quality teas and coffees. Approximately half of the sales are on credit. Abbreviated and unaudited accounts are given below.

Rose Ltd
Profit and loss accounts for the years ended 31 March

	2000 £000	2000 £000	1999 £000	1999 £000
Sales		12,080		7,800
Cost of sales		6,282		4,370
Gross profit		5,798		3,430
Labour costs	2,658		2,106	
Depreciation	625		450	
Other operating costs (note 1)	1,003		92	
		4,286		2,648
Net profit before interest		1,512		782
Interest payable		66		–
Net profit before tax		1,446		782
Tax payable		259		158
Net profit after tax		1,187		624
Dividend payable		300		250
Retained profit for year		887		374
Retained profit brought forward		872		498
Retained profit carried forward		1,759		872

Balance sheets as at 31 March

	2000 £000	2000 £000	1999 £000	1999 £000
Fixed assets (note 2)		2,728		1,536
Current assets				
Stocks	1,583		925	
Debtors	996		488	
Cash	26		312	
	2,605		1,725	
Creditors: amounts due within 1 year				
Trade creditors	(1,118)		(660)	
Other creditors	(417)		(321)	
Tax	(259)		(158)	
Dividends	(300)		(250)	
Overdraft	(180)		–	
Net current assets		331		336
Creditors: amounts due after more than 1 year				
Secured loan		(300)		–
		2,759		1,872

Capital and reserves

Share capital (50p shares, fully paid)	750	750
Share premium	250	250
Retained profit	1,759	872
	2,759	1,872

Note 1

The other operating costs include profit on sale of fixed assets of £20,000.

Note 2: Schedule of fixed assets

	Short leasehold	Fixtures and fittings	Motor vehicles	Total
	£000	£000	£000	£000
Cost				
At 1.4.1999	1,198	1,155	560	2,913
Disposals	–	–	(210)	(210)
Additions	947	780	120	1,847
	2,145	1,935	470	4,550
Depreciation				
At 1.4.1999	547	558	272	1,377
Disposals	–	–	(180)	(180)
Charge for year	329	178	118	625
At 31.3.2000	876	736	210	1,822
Net book value at 31.3.2000	1, 269	1, 199	260	2, 728

Required

(a) Calculate the following financial statistics for Rose Ltd for both 1999 and 2000, using end-of-year figures where possible.

    (i) Return on capital employed.

    (ii) Return on shareholders' funds.

    (iii) Dividend per share.

    (iv) Earnings per share.

    (v) Net profit margin.

    (vi) Gross profit margin.

    (vii) Current ratio.

    (viii) Liquid ratio.

    (ix) Days' debtors.

    (x) Days' creditors.

    (xi) Stock turnover.

(b) Comment on the performance of Rose Ltd from the viewpoint of:

    (i) a shareholder with a 5% holding who believes that Rose Ltd will announce a rights issue in the near future.

    (ii) the bank which has given Rose Ltd its current overdraft facility.

2 The following financial statements for Blackstone Plc are a slightly simplified set of published accounts. Blackstone Plc is an engineering firm, which developed a new range of products in 1998; these now account for 60% of turnover.

Blackstone Plc
Profit and loss account for the year ended 31 March 2000

	Notes	2000 £000	1999 £000
Turnover		11,205	7,003
Cost of sales		(5,809)	(3,748)
Gross profit		5,396	3,255
Operating expenses	1	(3,087)	(2,205)
Operating profit		2,309	1,050
Interest payable		(456)	2(216)
Profit before taxation		1,853	834
Taxation		(390)	(210)
Profit after taxation		1,463	624
Dividends		(400)	(300)
Retained profit for the year		1,063	324
Retained profit brought forward		685	361
Retained profit carried forward		1,748	685

Balance sheet as at 31 March 2000

	Notes	2000 £000	2000 £000	1999 £000	1999 £000
Fixed assets					
Intangible assets	2	700		–	
Tangible assets	3	7,535		4,300	
			8,235		4,300
Current assets					
Stocks		2,410		1,209	
Trade debtors		1,372		807	
Other debtors		201		134	
Cash		4		28	
		3,987		2,178	
Creditors: Amounts falling due within 1 year					
Trade creditors		1,306		607	
Other creditors		201		124	
Taxation		390		210	
Dividends		400		300	
Overdraft		1,625		–	
		(3,922)		(1,241)	

Net current assets	65	937
Creditors: Amounts falling due		
after more than 1 year		
Bank loan (repayable 2004)	(3,800)	(1,800)
	4,500	3,437

Capital and reserves			
Share capital	4	1,800	1,800
Share premium		600	600
Capital reserve		352	352
Retained profits		1,748	685
		4,500	3,437

Notes to the accounts

1 Operating costs include the following items:

	£000
Exceptional items	503
Depreciation	1,251
Administrative expenses	527
Marketing expenses	785

2 Intangible assets represents the amounts paid for the goodwill of another engineering business acquired during the year.

3 The movements in tangible fixed assets during the year are set out below.

	Land and buildings £000	Plant and machinery £000	Fixtures and fittings £000	Total £000
Cost				
At 1 April 19X0	4,500	3,850	2,120	10,470
Additions	–	2,970	1,608	4,578
Disposals	–	(365)	(216)	(581)
At 31 March 19X1	4,500	6,455	3,512	14,467
Depreciation				
At 1 April 19X0	1,275	3,080	1,815	6,170
Charge for year	225	745	281	1,251
Disposals	–	(305)	(184)	(489)
At 31 March 19X1	1,500	3,520	1,912	6,932
Net book value at 31 March 19X1	3,000	2,935	1,600	7,535

Proceeds from the sale of fixed assets in the year ended 31 March 2000 amounted to £54,000.

4 Share capital comprises 3,600,000 fully paid ordinary shares of 50p each.

Required

(a) Calculate the following financial statistics for Blackstone Plc, using year-end figures where possible, for both 1999 and 2000.

(a) Return on capital employed;
(b) Return on shareholders' funds;
(c) Gross profit margin;
(d) Net profit margin;
(e) Gearing ratio (total debt/total equity);
(f) Current ratio;
(g) Liquid ratio (acid-test ratio);
(h) Days' debtors;
(i) Days' creditors;
(j) Stock turnover.

(b) Comment on the performance of Blackstone Plc, using the published financial statements and the information prepared in 1 above, from the viewpoint of:
(a) an individual who owns 10% of the issued share capital;
(b) the bank which has granted Blackstone Plc its overdraft facility.

3. The financial statements for Harridges Ltd are given below for the two years ended 30 June 1999 and 2000. Harridges Ltd operates a department store in the centre of a small town.

Profit and loss account for the year ending 30 June

	2000		1999	
	£000	£000	£000	£000
Sales		3,500		2,600
Cost of sales		2,350		1,560
Gross profit		1,150		1,040
Expenses: Wages and salaries	350		320	
Overheads	200		260	
Depreciation	250		150	
		800		730
Operating profit		350		310
Interest payable		50		50
Profit before taxation		300		260
Taxation		125		105
Profit after taxation		175		155
Dividend proposed		75		65
Profit retained for the year		100		90

Balance sheet as at 30 June

Fixed assets (note 1)		1,525		1,265
Current assets				
Stock	400		250	
Debtors	145		105	
Bank	115		380	
	660		735	
Creditors: amounts falling due within 1 year				
Trade creditors	(300)		(235)	
Dividend	(75)		(65)	
Other	(110)		(100)	
	(485)		(400)	
Net current assets		175		335
Total assets less current liabilities		1,700		1,600
Creditors: amounts falling due after more than 1 year				
10% loan stock (19X8)		(500)		(500)
		1,200		1,100
Capital and reserves				
Share capital: £1 shares fully paid		490		490
Share premium		260		260
Profit and loss account		450		350
		1,200		1,100

Note 1: Fixed assets schedule

	Freehold property* £000	Fixtures and fittings £000	Motor vehicles £000	Total £000
Cost or valuation				
At 1.7.1999	905	620	80	1,605
Additions	–	480	30	510
Disposals	–	–	(20)	(20)
At 30.6.2000	905	1,100	90	2,095
Depreciation				
At 1.7.1999	–	300	40	340
Disposals	–	–	(20)	(20)
Charge for year	–	220	30	250
At 30.6.200	–	520	50	570
Net book value	905	580	40	1,525

*The freehold property is the department store operated by Harridges Ltd which was valued at £905,000 in June 1995. The directors consider the property to be worth at least this amount at June 2000.

Required

(a) Choose and calculate eight ratios which would be helpful in assessing the performance of Harridges Ltd. Use end-year values and calculate for 1999 and 2000.

(b) Using the ratios calculated in (a) above and any others you consider helpful, comment on the performance of Harridges Ltd from the viewpoint of a prospective purchaser of a majority of the shares of Harridges.

4. The following financial statements for Xenith Plc are based upon the financial statements of a UK company in the form in which they were published. The main activity of Xenith Plc is home retailing whereby customers can order, from a series of catalogues, goods which are delivered to their homes. Customers usually pay for the goods over a period of three or six months.

Xenith Plc
Group profit and loss account for the year ended 31 March 2000

Note		2000	1999
		£000	£000
	Turnover	140,166	126,568
	Cost of sales	68,277	62,965
	Gross profit	71,889	63,603
	Distribution costs	(14,320)	(12,239)
	Sales and administration expenses	(38,109)	(33,897)
	Operating profit	19,460	17,467
	Interest payable	(5,651)	(5,250)
	Income from listed investments	205	301
	Profit on ordinary activities before taxation	14,014	12,518
1	Taxation on ordinary activities	(4,414)	(4,184)
	Profit on ordinary activities after taxation	9,600	8,334
	Extraordinary items	–	70
	Profit for the year	9,600	8,264
	Dividends	(3,572)	(3,261)
	Retained profit	6,028	5,003

Group balance sheet at 31 March 2000

Note		2000	1999
		£000	£000
	Fixed assets		
2	Tangible assets	25,314	10,591
	Investments	1,797	1,907
		27,111	12,498

Current assets		
Stocks	23,948	20,249
Trade debtors	63,078	54,632
3 Other debtors	5,697	4,559
Cash at bank and in hand	2,445	472
	95,168	79,912
4 *Creditors: amounts falling due within 1 year*	33,219	30,517
Net current assets	61,949	49,395
Total assets less current liabilities	89,060	61,893
5 *Creditors: amounts falling due after more than 1 year*	48,028	35,065
6 Provisions for liabilities and charges	894	–
	40,138	26,828
Capital and reserves		
Called-up share capital (10p shares)	6,446	6,021
Share premium account	7,881	867
7 Revaluation reserve	3,168	3,278
8 Other reserves	1,884	1,931
Profit and loss account	20,759	14,731
	40,138	26,828

Notes to the accounts

1 The amount of tax actually paid in the year ended 31 March 2000 was £4,031.
2 Schedule of tangible fixed assets

	Freehold property	Long leasehold property	Equipment and motor vehicles	Total
	£000	£000	£000	£000
At cost or valuation				
At 1.4.1999	6,337	143	7,846	14,326
Additions	3,619	48	13,710	17,377
Disposals	–	–	(2,167)	(2,167)
At 31.3.2000	9,956	191	19,389	29,536
Accumulated depreciation				
At 1.4.1999	98	27	3,610	3,735
Charge for the year	32	5	890	927

Disposals	–	–	(440)	(440)
At 31.3.2000	130	32	4,060	4,222
Net book value				
at 31.3.2000	9,826	159	15,329	25,314

During the year ended 31 March 2000 the proceeds from fixed assets disposals amounted to £1,957,000.

3 Other debtors at 31 March 1999 included an amount for recoverable advance corporation tax of £263,000. During the year ended 31 March 2000 this amount has been written off against the deferred taxation provision.

4 Creditors falling due within 1 year include:

	2000	1999
	£000	£000
Bank loans and overdrafts	1,732	3,872
Trade creditors	17,072	13,836
Current taxation	3,474	4,248
Other creditors	8,362	6,348
Proposed dividend	2,579	2,213
	33,219	30,517

5 Creditors falling due after more than one year comprise bank loans which are repayable between two and five years.

6 Provisions for liabilities and charges comprise the provision for deferred taxation only.

7 Reserves

	Revaluation reserve	Other reserves
	£000	£000
Balance at 1.4.1999	3,278	1,931
Deficit on revaluation of listed investments	(110)	
Goodwill purchased and written off		(47)
Balance at 31.3.2000	3,168	1,884

8 Five-year review

	Turnover	Pre-tax profit	Earnings per share
	£m	£m	p
1996	73.4	9.2	11.5
1997	100.5	13.5	15.8
1998	107.7	6.1	7.1
1999	126.6	12.5	To be
2000	140.2	14.0	calculated

Required

1 Calculate the following financial statistics for Xenith Plc for both 2000 and 1999, using year-end figures where possible.
   (a) Return on capital employed
   (b) Earnings per share
   (c) Gross profit margin
   (d) Net profit margin
   (e) Gearing ratio
   (f) Current ratio
   (g) Liquid ratio
   (h) Days' debtors
   (i) Days' creditors
   (j) Stock turnover

2 Using the financial statements and the data that you have prepared in answer to question 1 above, comment on the performance of Xenith Plc from the viewpoint of:
   (a) a shareholder who owns 0.1% of the issued share capital (you should be aware that the board of directors of Xenith Plc have recently announced their intention of raising £16 million by a rights issue);
   (b) a bank which has made a substantial medium-term loan to Xenith Plc.

Chapter 21

The analysis of financial statements: 3

21.1 Introduction

This chapter is concerned with further aspects of financial analysis. The areas covered can be seen as non-traditional. In particular the chapter looks at DuPont analysis, the way in which ratios may be used to predict financial distress and vulnerability to takeover, and use of economic value added (EVA) and monetary value added (MVA).

21.2 Objectives

On completion of this chapter you should be able to:

- explain and utilize Du Pont analysis;
- explain how ratios and multivariate analysis may be used to predict financial distress;
- explain how ratios may be used to predict vulnerability to takeover;
- describe MVA and EVA;
- assess the usefulness of the techniques discussed in this chapter;
- identify the limitations of ratio analysis.

21.3 Du Pont system/decomposition analysis

In Chapter 20 return on investment was analysed in some detail, with Table 20.1 setting out the factors which influence return on investment. ROI was seen as being dependent on net profit margin and asset turnover. Net profit margin is influenced by both costs and revenues, and use of comparative common size profit and loss statements should provide useful information to assist businesses in the desire to improve overall return. Asset turnover is influenced by both sales and the amount of assets (of various types) in use by the business. Comparisons should focus on areas of difference and the potential for improvement.

The analysis developed within the Du Pont corporation takes this approach a little further. The analysis effectively adopts the following approach:

- the starting point is return on equity (ROE) – a profitability ratio
- ROE can be expanded as shown below:

$$\text{ROE} = \frac{\text{Net Income} \times 100}{\text{Ord. Shareholders' equity}} \times \frac{\text{Sales}}{\text{Sales}} \times \frac{\text{Total assets}}{\text{Total assets}}$$

$$= \frac{\text{NI} \times 100}{\text{Sales}} \times \frac{\text{Sales}}{\text{TA}} \times \frac{\text{Total assets}}{\text{OS equity}}$$

The first two of these are the same as we have used earlier, namely net profit margin and asset turnover. The third is new. It provides a measure of gearing and is known as the equity multiplier.

- Hence return on equity can be seen to be dependent on three factors, summarized in the following equation:

$$\text{ROE} = \text{NP margin} \times \text{asset utility} \times \text{equity multiplier}$$

Alternatively this can be viewed as:

$$\text{ROE} = \text{ROA} \times \text{equity multiplier}$$

Businesses which use high levels of debt will have a high equity multiplier. The greater the debt, the lower the equity used to fund total assets. If a firm funds 50% of its total assets from debt and 50% from equity it will have an equity multiplier of 2, whereas if it funds only 25% of its assets from debt the equity multiplier will be $100/75 = 1.33$.

The Du Pont system builds on this, linking and expanding these ratios. This would seem to provide a useful approach – improvements in one or all of the above sub-ratios will improve ROE. Stages of such an analysis might include:

- The net profit margin can be broken down to calculate every type of expense as a percentage of sales – NP margin can be improved by increasing revenues or reducing expenses.
- Improvements in asset utility will improve ROE, but which assets? It would seem sensible to break total asset turnover into current asset turnover and non-current asset turnover, each of which can be further broken down to identify the effectiveness of management of, say, inventory, debtors or cash.
- The equity multiplier section can link together the debt management ratios.
- The liquidity ratios then need to be calculated.
- Finally the market value ratios can be calculated.

The term decomposition analysis is also used to describe this kind of approach, since ROE is broken down into a full range of detailed factors all of which impact on the overall return figure.

Care needs to be taken using the Du Pont system. One possible implication of the model is that increased use of debt will lead to increased returns on equity. While this may be so, it also may *not* occur. It needs to be recognized that while net profit margin and asset turnover ratios (suitably sub-divided) may be relatively independent of each other, the same is not necessarily true of the equity multiplier. Increases in debt might well reduce the net profit margin with the overall result that ROE declines with an increase in debt (and therefore the equity multiplier).

21.4 Financial distress prediction

Increasing attention has been paid in recent years to testing the usefulness of financial ratios for decision making. As decision making involves predicting the future, it can be argued that the usefulness of ratios rests on their predictive ability. One area in which the usefulness of ratios has been tested is in predicting financial distress. This is an extremely important area to all those connected with the business. When a business is in financial difficulties investors, lenders, employees, suppliers and customers may all suffer loss.

In order to see whether financial ratios could help predict financial distress, Beaver (1966) matched 79 US businesses which failed during the period 1954-64 with similar businesses in the same industry which did not fail during that period. For each business he calculated thirty separate ratios for each of the five years prior to failure and then computed the means (averages) of each ratio for the failed group of businesses and the non-failed group. He found that there was a substantial difference, generally, in the behaviour of the mean ratios of each group. He summarized his findings thus:

> The ratio distributions of non-failed firms are quite stable throughout the five years before failure. The ratio distributions of the failed firms exhibit a marked deterioration as failure approaches. The result is a widening gap between the failed and non-failed firms. The gap produces persistent differences in the mean ratios of failed and non-failed firms, and the difference increases as failure approaches (p. 101).

Beaver recognized that differences in the mean ratios may be caused by a few extreme observations within either of the groups. He, therefore, ranked each ratio according to size to see whether it could successfully discriminate between failed and non-failed businesses. (When ranking liquidity ratios, for example, it may be expected that failed businesses would be ranked lower than non-failed businesses.) Beaver found that some ratios predicted failure better than others. A ratio of cash flow to total debt appeared to discriminate extremely successfully between failed and non-failed enterprises throughout the five years prior to failure, whereas liquidity ratios (somewhat surprisingly) did not perform well. In the first year prior to bankruptcy there was a 13% misclassification rate which increased significantly as the time horizon lengthened.

One problem with the approach adopted by Beaver is that it examines each ratio individually (a univariate approach). Thus, one ratio might predict failure whereas another might not. In order to avoid possible conflicts of this nature attempts have been made to combine ratios in such a way that a single index or score is produced which will point to either failure or non-failure. However, in the absence of any theory of financial distress it is difficult to determine which ratios should be combined or how they might be combined. 'Multivariate' analysis can combine ratios in such a way that a single score can be produced which can point to failure or non-failure. The inevitable question that emerges is 'what ratios should be combined?' With no real theory to help, researchers initially had to use trial and error. Discriminant analysis has been used to identify the most critical relationships. Essentially discriminant analysis focuses on those issues which provide the boundary of the two categories, in this case failed and non-failed firms.

Arguably the best known of the bankruptcy prediction studies is that by Altman (1968). This study produced a z-score, which is the value associated with the following discriminant analysis equation:

$$z = 1.2\frac{(\text{Working capital})}{(\text{Total assets})} + 1.4\frac{(\text{Retained earnings})}{(\text{Total assets})}$$

$$+ 3.3 \frac{\text{(EBIT)}}{\text{(Total assets)}} \quad + 0.6 \frac{\text{(Market value of equity)}}{\text{(book value of debt)}}$$

$$+ 1.0 \frac{\text{(Sales)}}{\text{(Total assets)}}$$

A z-score of less than 2.675 signals bankruptcy.

Analysis of misclassifications resulted in three zones being identified:

- z-score >2.99 clearly non-bankrupt
- z-score <1.81 bankrupt
- z-score in between a grey area.

Altman *et al.* (1977) developed a more refined model but the parameters of the 'zeta' model remain private, for commercial reasons. Apparently zeta is far more effective in predicting bankruptcy early. Interestingly it is worth noting that zeta used adjusted rather than reported accounting data, with two important adjustments being:

- off-balance-sheet debt – all non-cancellable operating and capital leases are added to firm assets and liabilities
- intangible assets – capitalized items such as R&D, interest, goodwill etc. are expensed.

In the UK Taffler (1983) has shown how a z-score model may be used to predict financial distress. (The work of Taffler was based on the earlier work of Altman in the USA.) The z-score of a business is derived by calculating four key ratios, attaching weights to each ratio, and then adding together the weighted ratios. If the z-score is greater than 0 this means the enterprise is solvent and will not fail in the forthcoming year. If, on the other hand, the z-score is less than 0 the business is considered 'at risk' which, according to Taffler, means a more than 50/50 chance of failure at some future time.

Taffler states that separate z-score models are required for quoted manufacturing, quoted distribution and privately owned companies because of their differing financial structures. The z-score model for quoted manufacturing businesses, which is broadly similar to the other models, is as follows:

$$z = C_0 + C_1 \frac{\text{PBT}}{\text{CL}} + C_2 \frac{\text{CA}}{\text{TL}} + C_3 \frac{\text{CL}}{\text{TA}} + C_4 \text{NCI}$$

where:

$$z = \text{the } z \text{ score}$$
$$C_0 = \text{a constant}$$
$$C_1 - C_4 = \text{the ratio weights}$$
$$\text{PBT} = \text{profit before tax}$$
$$\text{CL} = \text{current liabilities}$$
$$\text{TL} = \text{total liabilities}$$
$$\text{TA} = \text{total assets}$$

$$\text{NCI} = \text{no-credit interval, i.e. } \frac{\text{liquid current assets}}{\text{daily operating expenses}}$$

The no-credit internal ratio reveals how long, in days, the enterprise can finance its operations in the event of a complete cessation of revenues. It is, therefore, a liquidity ratio for extreme circumstances.

Although a negative z-score indicates a business is at risk, it does not necessarily mean the business will fail. According to Taffler, failure will depend on how bad the z-score is, how many years the z-score has persisted, and the trend in the z-score. Taffler claims the z-score model works extremely well and provides z-score information to clients on a commercial basis. The ratio weights for the model are not made publicly available by Taffler and must usually be purchased in order to make the model operational.

Activity 1

How might each of the following groups use the z-score of a particular business?

(a) Shareholders
(b) Trade creditors
(c) Management
(d) Customers
(e) Auditors of the business

Shareholders *may use z-scores to provide an early-warning signal of failure. (If shares are traded on the stock market, however, it is likely that share prices will reflect any financial difficulties a business is experiencing.) The z-scores will be useful in assessing the degree of risk attached to the investment.*

Trade creditors *will be interested in using z-scores to assess the creditworthiness of a business. It may be useful in establishing the degree of risk associated with the credit allowed and in establishing the terms and conditions of trade credit.*

Management *have a general interest in the position and performance of the business relative to similar enterprises in the same industry. A poor z-score may prompt management into taking corrective action. This may involve restricting the business or seeking a suitable business with which to merge.*

Customers *may be interested in the continuity of future supplies. A poor z-score may prompt customers to seek alternative sources of supplies. Where the customer is another business, it may be prepared to offer financial help or to take over the supplier business, particularly if it is the sole supplier of important items.*

Auditors *must satisfy themselves that the accounts of the enterprise show a true and fair view. Usually accounts are prepared on the basis that the business is a going concern. If, however, the z-scores suggest the impending failure of the business, the auditors may feel the accounts should not be prepared according to the going concern convention. As a result assets may be valued at realizable values rather than acquisition values (less any amounts written off).*

Activity 2

Should z-scores be publicly available? What are the advantages and disadvantages of publishing z-scores for enterprises with negative z-scores?

z-scores are based on ratios which, in turn, are based on publicly available accounting information. Hence, it is difficult to argue that z-scores should not be published. It has been shown above that various groups may find z-scores useful for decision-making purposes. However, there is a danger that poor z-scores will become a self-fulfilling prophecy, i.e. because z-scores are poor, lines of credit and investment will be withdrawn from the business which will result in its financial collapse.

More recently Taffler has released a new model, and a number of other models have been developed and are used commercially. Clearly these models are used and are seen as adding value. The evidence is that these approaches can identify companies with some characteristics similar to those displayed by companies that have failed in the past, and can provide a framework in which failures can be studied. Expert systems have been developed. The biggest danger is that of self-fulfilment.

No one particular model has proved to be so robust as to be generally accepted and used.

The models developed using discriminant analysis do however, have a number of *weaknesses*:

- they use traditional accounting so absorb its weaknesses;
- there is usually some delay in reporting, so timeliness is a problem;
- the fuzziness of definitions of success;
- the use of a past time frame in an ever-changing world – none of the formulae include any reference to external conditions;
- proponents suggest that these measures can be used as objectives – note that you can't measure anything without interfering with it.

As against this:

- it can be argued that the success reaffirms the usefulness of conventional accounting;
- further improvements could be obtained by considering the score relative to the market, providing more grades rather than simply fail–non-fail, tailoring the formulae to specific industries or markets.

21.5 Financial ratios and vulnerability to takeover

Another area in which financial ratios have been widely used has been in explaining or predicting vulnerability to takeover by a predator company. One such study has been carried out in the UK by Barnes (1990). This study matched 92 companies taken over during the period 1986–7 with companies in the same industry and of similar size which were not taken over. Barnes found that, using the following five ratios, it was possible to obtain a 68.48% level of accuracy in classifying companies between takeover target and non-takeover target companies:

- Return on equity
- Gross profit margin before tax
- Net profit margin after tax
- Current ratio
- Acid-test ratio

As you can see, the study suggests profitability and liquidity ratios provide the key to explaining vulnerability to takeover.

Activity 3

Why do you think each of the five ratios identified above may be useful in identifying a takeover target?

In answering this activity you may have thought of the following:

- ***Return on equity.*** *A poor return on equity may attract the interest of another company because the managers of the predator company may feel the target company is not fully exploiting profitable opportunities and that they could do a better job. A high return, on the other hand, would make a company a more difficult target as shareholders of that company may not feel a predator company could match or improve profitability.*
- ***Gross profit margin before tax.*** *Profit may indicate an ability to generate cash and to meet maturing obligations as they arise. Thus, a relatively low margin may be a sign of financial weakness whereas a high margin may suggest a strong independent company which can survive as a separate entity. However, this need not always be the case. Some companies may deliberately adopt a lower profit margin in order to increase sales demand.*
- ***Net profit margin after tax.*** *As we saw earlier, a company with high profitability will mean it is more difficult for a predator company to convince shareholders of the target company that a takeover is in their interests. Moreover, if profits after tax are high, the company will also have profits available to distribution. A predator company may find it difficult to match a high dividend policy adopted by the target company. However, there is a counter-argument which states that high profit margins can actually attract predators, thereby making the company more vulnerable to takeover. Thus, the reliability of this measure in predicting takeovers may be affected by these conflicting forces.*
- ***Current ratio.*** *The liquidity of a business, as mentioned earlier, provides a measure of ability to meet short-term obligations. A company with liquidity problems may require outside funding and thereby be more vulnerable to takeover. The current ratio, however, may not be a very reliable measure of liquidity as stocks are regarded as liquid assets, which is not always the case. A high level*

of stocks may simply indicate a high number of slow-moving and obsolete items being held.

- **Acid-test ratio.** *This is a more stringent test of liquidity as stocks are excluded from the calculation. However, there can be problems in interpreting this ratio in so far that a high debtors figure (resulting in a high acid-test ratio) may indicate poor credit control and a low creditors figure (also resulting in a high acid-test ratio) may indicate that suppliers are unwilling to provide credit on normal industry terms.*

In the USA, Wansley, Roenfelt and Cooley (1983) developed a multivariate model to explain and predict vulnerability to takeover. The sample was based on 44 companies that were taken over during the period 1975–6 and a further 44 companies randomly selected from the population of companies which had the same year-end dates as the companies acquired. The variables used in the model were:

- P/E ratio
- Market value of equity to total assets
- Compound growth in net sales
- Long-term debt to total assets
- Natural log of net sales (in millions)

Using these variables it was possible to obtain a 75% level of accuracy overall in classifying companies between takeover and non-takeover targets. It is interesting to note that the size of the companies was seen as an important variable in this particular study.

Perhaps the most interesting part of the study was the second stage, which used the multivariate model developed to predict from a sample of 754 companies which were most likely to be taken over. Although, during the time period under review (1977–8), none of those identified by the models as having a high likelihood of being taken over were actually taken over, the researchers found that it was possible to make higher than normal returns by investing in those companies which were identified as acquisition targets.

21.6 MVA and EVA

MVA and EVA were developed by Joel Stern and Bennett Stewart, co-founders of the consulting firm Stern Stewart & Company. EVA is very similar in concept to 'residual income', an earlier accounting concept.

It is generally held that the primary goal of most businesses is to maximize shareholders' wealth. Shareholder wealth is maximized by maximizing the difference between the market value of equity and the amount contributed by shareholders over the years – including retentions. This difference is known as *market value added* (MVA). Hence:

(MVA) = Market value of the equity − equity capital supplied

where equity capital supplied is the capital plus reserves. MVA measures the effects of managerial actions since the inception of a company.

Economic value added (EVA) focuses on managerial effectiveness in a given year. It recognizes that there is an opportunity cost for the capital used. When interpreting a set of accounts it is important that we look at the profit figure and ask: 'Is this profit enough?' Opportunity cost of capital includes obvious things such as the interest costs associated with use of debt capital, and dividends associated with preference shares. Clearly the opportunity costs don't stop there. An ordinary shareholder who invests in a company forgoes the opportunity to invest elsewhere. In an efficient market such as is provided by the Stock Exchange the opportunity cost is provided by the earnings lost through not investing elsewhere. Given the efficiency of the market it should be relatively easy to work out what kind of returns are being earned in the market for companies carrying certain degrees of risk. A business of a particular type, bearing risk of a particular category, would be expected to yield a return of a certain level. The higher the risk, the higher the likely return and vice versa. The required return represents the typical sort of return that similar businesses would earn in the market, and as such represents an opportunity cost for the investor. Unless the business is making enough to cover all the constituent costs of capital, including the opportunity cost of equity capital, it is not performing adequately. In other words, it is not adding any economic value.

In fact at any one time a comparison of earnings with price enables us to calculate an earnings yield which effectively measures the return earned in the market for a particular company, with a particular risk profile, at a particular time. Different assumptions about growth may impact on these return figures, with higher growth rates giving higher returns. As circumstances change, and risk patterns vary, the required rate of return will vary. However, some fairly good estimates can be made of the opportunity cost of capital. (A detailed coverage of share valuation methods is beyond the scope of this book, and some simplifying assumptions follow, but what follows aims to provide you with an understanding of some general principles.)

The basic formula for EVA is:

EVA = operating profit after taxes − cost of all capital

= (sales revenues − operating costs − taxes)

− (total capital supplied multiplied by the cost of capital)

EVA is an estimate of a business's true profit for the year, and it differs substantially from accounting profit. It represents the residual income after *all* opportunity costs of capital are covered. A positive EVA indicates that the business is creating value, whereas a negative EVA indicates that the firm is destroying value. EVA is the residual income remaining after deducting the cost of all the capital that has been used in generating profit. Thus it can be said that EVA depends on both operating efficiency and efficient balance sheet management.

Example

The following information is available for a business:

	1999	2000
Profit figures		
Net operating profit before interest and taxes		
	2,488,000	3,248,000
Less interest (8% × 600,000)	48,000	48,000
	2,440,000	3,200,000
Tax	610,000	800,000
Net profit after tax	1,830,000	2,400,000
Preference dividend	30,000	30,000
Ordinary share earnings	1,800,000	2,370,000
Net operating profit after taxes	1,878,000	2,448,000
Tax rate	25%	25%
Balance sheet/market value figures		
Share price (ordinary shares)	10	12
Number of ordinary shares (£1 shares)	1 million	1 million
Reserves	5 million	6 million
Share price (10% preference shares)	1.25	1.25
Number of preference shares (£1 shares)	300,000	300,000
Debt (8%) Book value	600,000	600,000
Debt (8%) Market value	800,000	800,000
The *calculation of* MVA is as follows:		
Market value of the ordinary equity is		
Number of shares × share price	10,000,000	12,000,000
Book value	6,000,000	7,000,000
Market value added	4,000,000	5,000,000

Note that this is a lifetime figure, giving the total market value added over the life of the business. The MVA during 2000 is £1 million.

Before calculating EVA it is necessary to digress slightly to estimate the cost of the various sources, namely debt, preference share capital and ordinary share capital. The cost to the business is effectively the same as the return earned by the investor, subject to any taxation differences. So if we can calculate the return earned by the investor we should be able to derive the cost to the business.

1 *Cost of debt.* The return earned by debenture holders is the interest divided by the market value of debt which equals:

$$48,000/800,000 = 6\%$$

You should note that while the interest rate is formally 8% on book debt of £600,000, the market is prepared to pay more (£800,000) and thus the market rate of return of a security of this type is currently only 6%. The cost to the company is therefore 6% on a before-tax basis. As interest is a tax deductible expense the after tax cost is $6\%\ (1 - 0.25) = 4.5\%$.

2 The return earned on the market value for preference shares is:

$$30,000/(300,000 \times 1.25) = 30,000/375,000 = 8\%$$

i.e. the preference dividends/market value of preference shares.

Hence the cost of preference capital is 8% as dividends are not tax deductible.

3 For 1999 the earnings yield is $£1,800,000/£10,000,000 = 18\%$ i.e. the return relative to the market value of equity.

If this return is sustainable indefinitely in the future it would be reasonable to interpret this as saying that an investment in a company of this risk category will earn 18% in the market. 18% represents an appropriate opportunity cost of equity capital. Of course there may be an expectation of growth, with the consequent return being higher.

4 The weighted average cost of capital can be derived as follows:

Type of funds	Market value	Weight	Cost
Ordinary share capital	10,000,000	89.5%	18%
Preference share capital	375,000	3.4%	8%
Debt	800,000	7.1%	4.5%
	11,175,000	100%	

So the weighted average cost of funds is:

$$(89.5 \times 18\%) + (3.4\% \times 8\%) + (7.1\% \times 4.5\%) = (16.1 + 0.27 + 0.32) = 16.7\%$$

This gives a reasonable approximation of the current cost of funds. To the extent that conditions do not dramatically change (especially regarding the risk associated with the business) it will also provide an indication of likely future costs.

Economic value will be added when business yield returns greater than this. So for 2000 the company will earn a net operating profit after taxes of £2,448,000. The initial invested capital is £11,175,000. This needs to earn 16.7% so the business needs to earn $11,175,000 \times 16.7\% = £1,866,225$.

As the company earned £2,448,000 the EVA is £581,775.

An alternative calculation is:

Profit after taxes	2,448,000	
less interest	36,000	covers interest component after tax
	2,412,000	
less preference dividend	30,000	covers required return
	2,382,000	
less ordinary capital	1,800,000	i.e.10m @ 18%
	582,000	

Positive EVA effectively builds up the price, as investors will bid up the share price. The bigger the EVA, the higher the market value of the business and the share price. Stock price effectively reflects future EVA expectations.

A number of advantages are claimed, including the following:

- It provides a means of differentiating between performance of divisions or sections which carry different risks and therefore have different costs of capital
- It has a behavioural dimension in which managers can be encouraged to act in a way which is virtually guaranteed to be in the best interest of shareholders
- Simplicity

Activity 4

1 How would sales managers react if they were held accountable for working capital required to support a new product line?
2 How would managers of divisions react if the opportunity cost of capital were different across divisions?
3 How might the treatment of research and development expenditure be influenced by EVA?

---

1 They are much more likely to consider the implications of these requirements in making a recommendation.

2 They would become much more conscious of the specific costs associated with their division and adjust their thinking accordingly.

3 Research and development expenditure is often seen as discretionary, and is often reduced when adverse conditions occur. This can be done in the short-term, but is potentially disastrous in the medium and long term. An EVA orientation should encourage a long-term approach to problems of this type.

Many successful firms now use compensation schemes based on EVA. This is because it is seen as providing an incentive to take actions that contribute strongly to shareholder wealth. EVA is also increasingly used in capital budgeting, target setting and planning. Targets can now be set by reference to expectations embedded in the share price.

In many ways EVA is more than just another appraisal system. It needs to be put at the heart of the financial management system, and become more than just a performance measure. It needs to drive business in a significant way.

An alternative view is that EVA is simply a repackaged and well-marketed application of a standard investment technique known as net present value. There are certainly dangers in its use, not least of which is where current earnings are achieved at the cost of future earnings.

21.7 Limitations and problems with the use of ratios

While ratios are potentially extremely useful, their limitations must be recognized. Potential limitations include the following.

1 Ratios are based on financial accounts, so they contain almost all the deficiencies of these accounts.
2 Some ratios are open to manipulation and need to be interpreted with care, e.g. stock levels may be kept artificially low at the year-end thus creating

an impression of high efficiency in this area. Window dressing must be recognized.

3 Inter-firm comparisons are faced with the problem that different businesses might use different accounting policies.

4 A financial analysis is particularly concerned with estimating the likely future cash flows of a business. Traditional financial statements are not presented in the most appropriate form for projection purposes, and some regrouping by type of flows is frequently required, e.g. expenses may need to be split into those which are variable, semi-variable or fixed.

5 Detailed knowledge of a business's markets is seldom obtainable from the published accounts, yet such knowledge is important for assessing future profitability.

6 Recognition of any cycles which relate to particular industries is important in forecasting. Short-term cyclical movements may well over-ride long-term trends and must be built into forecasts.

7 Ratios are useful when comparing similar businesses operating under similar conditions. Comparisons with different types of organizations can be misleading.

8 There is a real danger that ratio analysis can lead to conclusions which are oversimplified, e.g. a high current ratio is seen as good, while high credit periods allowed to debtors are seen as bad. Very little attention is paid to determining optimal values for ratios, yet in practice some kind of balancing between various ratios must be done.

In analysing a set of financial statements you must recognize that good analysis requires a lot more than simply calculating and interpreting numbers. There are a range of factors that might be considered including the following:

- the extent to which success is tied to one major product
- the extent to which success is tied to one major customer (or a small number of customers)
- the extent to which success is tied to one supplier
- the proportions of the market which is domestically based
- the proportions of the market which is offshore
- stability (both economic and political) of the markets
- the nature of the industry, i.e. competitive, oligopolistic, monopolistic
- future prospects in various markets
- future prospects with regard to product development
- research and development activity and its consequences
- the legal and regulatory environment
- openness of the offshore markets
- degree of market penetration through strategic alliances with partners (often offshore)

The list could go on. Suffice it to say that an effective analysis requires a detailed understanding of the business and its environment.

21.8 Summary

This chapter builds on the approach to ratios which was introduced in the previous two chapters. All the ideas in this chapter provide interesting insights into performance appraisal.

The chapter provided an overview of the Du Pont method of analysis. This method provides a systematic and detailed way of analysing return on shareholders' equity. The chapter also provided an examination of the use of ratios in predicting financial distress and company takeovers. The concepts of economic value added and market value added were then examined and assessed. Finally the limitations of ratios were discussed.

Exercises

1. Explain how the Du Pont system can be used to analyse return to equity, and discuss how it can be used to obtain improved performance.
2. What is the equity multiplier?
3. Choose a company you know fairly well. List some qualitative factors that should be considered when evaluating performance.

References

Altman E.I. Financial ratios, discriminant analysis and the prediction of corporate bankruptcy. *Journal of Finance*, September 1968, pp 589–609.

Barnes P. The prediction of takeover targets in the UK by means of multiple discriminant analysis. *Journal of Business Finance and Accounting*, Spring 1990.

Beaver W.H. Financial ratios as predictors of failure. *Empirical Research in Accounting: Selected Studies*, 1966, pp 71–111.

Taffler R.J. The z-score approach to measuring company solvency. *The Accountants Magazine*, March 1983, pp 91–96.

Wansley J., Roenfelt R. and Cooley P. Abnormal returns from merger profiles. *Journal of Financial and Quantitative Analysis*, June 1983, pp 149–162.

Additional reading

G. Bennett Stewart III (1994). EVA: Fact and Fantasy. *Journal of Applied Corporate Finance*, Summer, pp 71–84

Also

www.evanomics.com

Chapter 22

The conventions and the conceptual framework

22.1 Introduction

The accounting conventions suffer from a number of weaknesses which undermine their usefulness. This has led to attempts to develop a conceptual framework in order to place accounting on a sounder footing. The nature of a conceptual framework is examined in this chapter and its potential usefulness assessed. This chapter aims to review the framework on which accounting statements are built and to identify both the strengths and weaknesses of accounting information. This should make you more able to interpret accounting information and to search out additional information where appropriate.

22.2 Objectives

At the end of this chapter you should be able to:

- explain the problems associated with the major conventions of accounting;
- explain the purpose of a conceptual framework;
- discuss the problems in deriving a workable conceptual framework for accounting;
- outline the major features of FRS 3, *Reporting Financial Performance*.

22.3 Derivation of the traditional framework

The conventions of accounting which provide the framework in which accounting is practised, virtually throughout the world, have evolved as they have in order to satisfy a need. An analogy is language. Living languages have developed, new words have been introduced and redundant words fallen into disuse as the need has arisen or receded. For example, the word 'television' has been introduced to meet a need to refer to a phenomenon which came into existence only relatively recently. Language provides a good analogy for accounting since accounting can itself be seen as a kind of language. This is because it is a means of collecting, storing, analysing and communicating information, albeit information of a particular type.

Accounting, as it is currently practised, is undoubtedly found to be useful by most users. However, the fact that it has emerged from practice, rather than being the result of a thoroughgoing assessment of what framework would be most useful, may have led to the fact that in some aspects it is less useful than it might otherwise be.

22.4 A review of the conventions of accounting

The principal conventions which provide the framework on which modern accounting in the UK is based will now be reviewed. Although you will have encountered these conventions in earlier chapters, the problems associated with these conventions have not yet been discussed in detail.

Money measurement

Items in accounting statements are described in terms of money. Items or factors which are incapable of being described in this way, perhaps because they are qualitative, rather than quantitative, must therefore be excluded from accounting statements. Thus the money measurement convention can lead to somewhat limited information. It is like a primitive language which has not developed a word for certain phenomena. In such a language reference to those phenomena would be impossible, or at least, difficult.

It is perhaps easy to overstate the deficiency of adherence to the money measurement convention. Accounting seeks to deal with information of an economic nature. Most information of this type can be expressed in monetary terms. Money is also a useful common denominator of much economic activity. Describing and assessing economic activities and phenomena in a quantitative manner does, it has been argued, give accounting a rigour of analysis which it might otherwise lack. In any case, there are other means of communicating information besides the use of accounting statements. Such means, which include narrative statements, are available to those who need to communicate information which cannot be communicated through accounting statements.

Self-assessment question 22.1

A narrative statement to supplement the accounts produced may be extremely valuable to users. It could help in analysing the performance and position of a business and assessing its future prospects. Some large companies now produce a mainly narrative statement (known as an operating and financial review) as a supplement to the accounts.

What kind of information do you think such a statement might usefully include?

Business entity

This convention simply says that, from an accounting point of view, the business is to be treated as a self-contained entity, separate from all who are connected with it. The most striking effect of this is that the owner(s) of the business and the business itself are viewed as being separate for accounting purposes. One way in which this separateness manifests itself is that in the balance sheet of the business, the capital of the owner(s) is dealt with essentially in the same way as the claim of all other claimants.

Note that the business entity convention says nothing about the legal relationship between the business and its owner(s). In unincorporated business forms (e.g. sole proprietorships and partnerships) there is no legal distinction between the business and its owner(s). With companies there is a legal distinction between the company and its shareholders. Both unincorporated businesses and companies follow the business entity convention.

The business entity convention is seen by most people as necessary and useful. Without this convention it would be difficult, if not impossible, to look at the position and performance *of the business* without including personal matters relating to the owner(s), or other business activities engaged in by the owner. These are irrelevant to assessing position and performance *of the business*. The convention sets boundaries to what is being accounted for.

Activity 1

During a period of trading the owner of a small business did the following:

(a) Paid for her private house to be decorated using a cheque drawn on the business bank account;
(b) Bought a photocopying machine for the business using her personal bank account cheque to pay for it.

How would each of these transactions be dealt with in the accounts of the business?
    What effect does the business entity convention have on the treatment of these transactions?

Your answer should be as follows:

(a) *The business cash would be reduced and this would be treated as drawings of the owner and so deducted from capital.*
(b) *This would be treated as an injection of capital into the business. Capital would be increased and the acquisition of the photocopier would be shown as an asset.*

In effect, the business entity convention causes the capital to reflect, in each of these transactions, the fact that private assets of the owner had been affected by a transaction which also affected the business.

Duality

This convention requires that each transaction concerning the business has two effects on the accounts (double entry). It rather emphasizes the self-contained nature of the business, from an accounting point of view. Without the convention of duality, the business entity convention could not really function (and vice versa). This is because the full effect on the business of each transaction would not be recorded.

The duality convention is linked to the existence of the balance sheet equation:

$$\text{Assets} = \text{capital plus liabilities}$$

Historic cost

This convention holds that assets should normally be shown in accounts at their outlay cost to the business. This approach has the advantage that what a business actually paid out to acquire the asset is typically a matter of demonstrable fact. Any other value placed on the asset is likely to involve some expression of opinion. Defenders of the historic cost approach to accounting argue that this approach is very suitable as a basis of managers reporting to owners on their stewardship of the owners' assets. The traditional balance sheet, in essence, shows from where the business obtained its resources (the claims portion of the balance sheet) and how those resources have been deployed (the assets). Using historic cost to describe the assets, it is argued, is entirely logical since that value represents the amount of resources which were actually deployed. This is much the same as the way in which an individual might explain how a sum of money was spent. Reporting in this way leads to a much greater level of objectivity since the managers' opinions are reduced to a minimum. Any other approach than one based on historic cost inevitably increases the level of subjectivity involved.

Though the use of the historic cost convention may lead to objectivity, it is questionable if it always promotes the provision of useful, relevant information, as can be seen from the following examples.

Example

Jenkins Garage occupies a fairly large site in the centre of an attractive market town. The business was acquired by George Jenkins in 1971 when he bought an existing garage business. The garage sells petrol, undertakes repairs and buys and sells second-hand cars. The premises appear in the accounts of the business at what George paid for them – £30,000.

Following the advice of a friend, George recently applied to his local council for outline planning permission to demolish the garage buildings and erect a block of luxury flats. The application was successful and as soon as it became public knowledge George was approached by Property Developments Plc who offered him £250,000 for the site as it stands. George has decided not to sell the site but to continue to operate the business for a few more years while he considers his future.

Clearly, to continue to show the premises in the accounts at £30,000 is potentially misleading. The original cost may have been £30,000 but that figure has become useless and irrelevant. For example, if George wishes to assess his return on capital employed, to base the capital employed on the £30,000 would be thoroughly misleading.

Activity 2

Precision Engineering Plc has just paid £2 million to buy, and have installed, a highly specialized piece of equipment. The equipment is expected to help generate buoyant profits for the business for a number of

years. The equipment is very highly specialized to the company's work. It would also be very expensive to move the equipment to other premises. Consequently, the equipment has virtually no realizable value.
At what value should the equipment be shown in the accounts?

It would obviously be misleading to show the asset at its realizable value. To Precision Engineering Plc the equipment is very valuable. It would probably be more appropriate to show it at historic cost, less an allowance for depreciation. It could be argued that better still would be to show the equipment at its value to the company, which could easily be above cost.

Example

Telesales retails television sets and other electrical equipment. It has just sold a popular model of television set for £300. This had cost £210 from the manufacturer a month earlier. The manufacturer has announced a price increase on the model. All future purchases of the model by Telesales will cost £250 each.

The traditional (historic cost) approach to profit (income) measurement would calculate the gross profit on the television sold at £90 (i.e. £300 − 210). This could be misleading because at the time of making the sale the effective cost of the television was £250, implying a gross profit of £50. The reason why the £250 cost is more appropriate is that leading directly from the sale of this set will be the need to replace it (it is a popular model). Thus the effective cost of making the sale is £250. Had the set not been sold, the need to replace it would not have arisen.

To view this from a slightly different angle, ask yourself what Telesales would feel itself deprived of if the particular television was stolen just before it was due to be delivered to the customer. The answer is £250, since this is what it will cost to replace the set and make the sale.

These three examples serve to show that the historical cost convention is not always effective in providing the most useful information. In none of the three examples does historic cost provide a particularly meaningful result. In none of these cases would historic cost be the most useful basis to help a user to make a rational decision.

Activity 3
Can you think of any advantages in applying the historic cost convention when preparing accounts?

The advantage that this convention has is that it leads to the use of figures which are, generally speaking, objective (capable of independent verification). Use of the convention can lead to readers having confidence that the figures have not been manipulated to give one impression rather than another. For this reason it is often

> *seen as relevant to the stewardship function in accounting. The use of any other basis than historical cost does raise questions about the choice of the alternative. There is no consensus concerning a method of valuation which should replace historic cost.*

In spite of these advantages, the problems raised above have led the accounting profession to look at alternative measurement bases much more seriously. The period of rapid inflation in the UK that occurred in the 1970s and 1980s resulted in many businesses revaluing their land and buildings. Such increases in value were not recorded in the profit and loss account, but were reflected in an increase in equity through an increase in a capital reserve (which was generally not distributable as a dividend). Only when the asset was sold was the profit on sale recognized and included in the profit and loss account. Also during the 1970s and 1980s a series of debates occurred within the accounting profession (and beyond) regarding measurement of profit and maintenance of capital. The essence of this debate is summarized in the next chapter. A major thrust of this debate was centred around the appropriateness of historic cost as a measurement base, with alternative valuation bases being proposed. Current value was often the favoured alternative. Current value could take several forms, namely the replacement cost of the asset, the current cost of an asset which can perform at the same level as the existing asset, resale value, or the present value of future cash flows. Clearly the first two could be substantially different if technology is changing rapidly. Resale value would differ depending whether it was the price associated with an orderly liquidation or a 'fire sale'. Present value of future cash flows might be appropriate in a small number of cases, but is generally highly subjective.

In spite of these problems the importance of alternatives to historic cost is being increasingly recognized. By way of illustration, in a recently published Draft Statement of Accounting Principles for Financial Reporting (Accounting Standards Board) two measurement bases are included for assets and liabilities; historical cost or current value. The statement points out that:

> most assets and liabilities arise from arm's length transactions. In such circum-stances and regardless of the measurement basis used, the carrying amount assigned on initial recognition will be the transaction cost.

In other words historic cost and current cost will initially be the same. They will usually only diverge later down the track. At this later stage it is necessary to decide which basis to use. The statement recognizes that a mixed measurement system may result, with some balance sheet categories using historical cost and other using current value. It goes on to say:

> that the measurement basis used for a category of assets or liabilities will be determined by reference to factors such as the objective of financial statements, the nature of assets or liabilities concerned and the particular circumstances involved.

Re-measurement may be necessary. For example, if historical cost is used it will be necessary to ensure that the lower of cost or market value is applied.

Clearly historic cost still remains as the most likely measurement base for most assets, but alternatives are now an accepted part of the accounting process, as long as these alternatives can be justified.

Stable monetary unit

Closely related to the historic cost convention is the assumption that the measurement unit in accounting, the unit of currency, retains a stable value relative to other assets over time. However, in recent times this has not usually been the case.

Example

Apex Property Company owns two identical buildings on the same site in central London. The first was bought ten years ago for £1 million; the second was bought last year for £3 million. They are each let as office space for the current commercial rent of £0.5 million, with the tenant responsible for all costs in both cases.

The stable monetary unit convention holds that it is assumed that the value of each pound sterling was the same when each of the buildings was bought. This would lead to the balance sheet of the business including an amount of £4 million for the sum of the two buildings. In fact, it is known that the value of the pound sterling has fallen in every year since the Second World War, not necessarily relative to other currencies but relative to the amount of goods and services which each pound will buy. In recent years, particularly during the 1970s and 1980s, the effect of inflation has been very dramatic. Obviously, the aggregation of assets expressed in pounds of different purchasing power leads to meaningless figures appearing in the accounts.

Following the stable monetary unit convention can lead to more than merely the presentation of anomalous figures; it can give misleading figures. If a user of the accounts wanted to assess the relative effectiveness of the two investments above the conclusion might be reached that the first building yields a return of 50% p.a. (i.e. £0.5m/1.0 × 100%), whereas the second one only generates a return of 16.7% p.a. (i.e. £0.5m/3 × 100%). Since the value of money, the yardstick of measurement, has altered, these return figures are each misleading and they are not comparable. It is illogical to seek to relate the rent from either building (an amount measured in pounds of one value), with the cost of the buildings (amounts measured in pounds of another value). Even worse, perhaps, is to try to compare the two rates of return.

In the next chapter we shall consider some suggestions which have been made to try to overcome the misleading effects of both the historic cost and stable monetary unit conventions.

Going concern convention	This convention holds that, unless there is reason to take a different view, the business should be treated as if it will continue for the foreseeable future. The relevance of the convention tends to be in the area of asset valuation for inclusion in the balance sheet. Broadly, where an asset is expected to be realized (turned into cash) in the near future it should be valued at its net realizable value, or at cost if relevant and if cost gives a lower figure. So, for example, stock in trade is typically valued at the lower of cost and net realizable value. Similarly, trade debtors are usually valued at net realizable value (i.e. the amount of the unpaid debts less any debts written off as uncollectable, also less a provision for doubtful debts). By contrast, fixed assets are typically valued at cost, less an allowance for depreciation. It is often the case that no real attempt is made to value fixed assets on a current market value basis except just before their planned disposal date. The reason for this is the fact that fixed assets, by definition, are not bought with the *intention* of disposing of them. If the going concern status of the business is in question, the possibility arises that fixed assets may need to be sold to meet creditors' claims. At that point any excess of book value over current market value will have to be treated as an expense so as to reduce the fixed asset value to its net realizable value.

In effect, the going concern convention supports the use of historic cost as the valuation base for fixed assets. It is argued that, since realizable value is only important when the asset is to be realized in the relatively near future, the assumption that the business will continue beyond that time horizon means that the fixed assets can be reasonably valued on the basis of historic cost rather than realizable values.

Activity 4
Is this last argument concerning support for the historic cost convention valid? Can you think of a counter-argument?

It can be argued that a business will adapt to a changing environment by selling assets in the normal course of business and buying new ones. So, even if the business is expected to continue operations for the foreseeable future, information concerning the current realizable values of assets held may still be useful. Some argue that the realizable value of assets held can provide users with an indication of the financial adaptability of a business which can be extremely useful.

Realization	The convention of realization maintains that revenues should be recognized when they are actually realized. This tends to be interpreted as:

- when the amount of the revenue is capable of objective measurement;
- when the work necessary to earn the revenue is substantially completed;
- the receipt of cash (or other asset) in consideration is fairly certain.

Thus revenues tend to be recognized when the goods or services pass to, and are accepted by, the customer. However, there are certain industries where a different point in the production/selling cycle is taken.

Activity 5
Can you think of a type of business where revenue could be recognized:

• when the goods are produced?
• after goods have been passed to the customer but before payment is made?
• After payment is made?

• **When the goods are produced.** A gold-mining business may recognize the revenue as soon as they have extracted the metal from the earth. This is presumably because at that point the sale is virtually certain and there is a known current market price. There may also be no selling and marketing costs to be incurred. Civil engineering businesses tend to recognize part of the revenue from protracted contracts as the contract progresses rather than at the end.
• **After the goods have been passed to the customer.** A business which operates on a mail-order basis such as a book or record club, a language-tuition centre, etc. may offer customers a certain period (e.g. seven days) of free trial before they have to make an irrevocable commitment to buy. If the goods are returned within the stated period no payment is required. Recognition of revenue may then take place at the end of the trial period.
• **After payment is made.** Some businesses which operate on a mail-order basis, such as those identified above, may ask for payment before the goods are despatched. However, return of the goods within a specified period will require repayment of monies received. Once again, revenue will be recognized after the trial period.

While the realization convention is generally seen as being sensible and prudent, there are circumstances in which it can give misleading results. These circumstances arise because the convention prevents the reporting of changes in wealth which are not verified by a market transaction.

Example

A building firm recently bought a small plot on which it erected two identical houses. Though the property market was very buoyant, the firm was short of cash and had to sell one of the houses immediately for £100,000. The firm decided that it would retain the second house because it was felt that property prices were likely to increase. The total cost of both houses, including the cost of the land, was £120,000. Following the realization convention, as it would typically be applied, the profit on the sold house (£100,000 − £60,000 = £40,000) would be recognized, but the other house would be shown as an asset at its cost (£60,000). If these two houses represented the only work undertaken by the firm in a particular accounting period, the gross profit would be £40,000. This is despite a buoyant market in which the second house could be sold easily.

This example not only illustrates the point that the realization convention can have a misleading effect. It also shows that the realization convention is closely related to the historic cost convention, since the fact that no profit is typically recognized until the goods pass to the customer means that assets tend to be shown at historic cost rather than at historic cost, plus expected profit.

Matching

This convention holds that expenses should be matched to the revenues which they helped to generate such that the revenue and its associated expenses are set against one another in deducing the income of a business for a particular accounting period. Clearly this is a logical approach to take. Without the matching convention there would be no rule which, for example, advocated that in deducing the income for a period the cost of the stock sold must be deducted from the sales revenue to which it gave rise. With direct expenses (i.e. expenses linked directly to sales) like cost of sales, matching is a fairly easy process. The problems with the matching convention start to show when expenses such as depreciation must be matched. In most cases, the depreciation of a fixed asset does not relate directly to a particular revenue or set of revenues. This means that the accountant is forced to use some fairly arbitrary basis of matching. Several bases of deducing the depreciation expense for particular accounting periods are found in practice. All of them rely very substantially on judgements of expected useful life of the asset and potential residual value as well as the choice of the actual method used.

In practice, the allocation of expenses to accounting periods is a major problem of accounting.

Activity 6

What is the effect of the matching convention on the portrayal of fixed assets on the balance sheet? Does this undermine the usefulness of the balance sheet?

Some argue that the matching convention can undermine the usefulness of the balance sheet as a statement of financial position. This is because the effect of the matching convention is to show the fixed assets at their unexpired cost (i.e. cost less accumulated depreciation). In other words, the balance sheet portrays to users what is left of the fixed assets after matching (i.e. the depreciation of these assets in past periods) has occurred, which may not be particularly useful for decision-making purposes. The amounts remaining which are shown on the balance sheet will be matched against revenues generated in future periods.

In the draft Statement of Principles for Financial Reporting (referred to earlier) it is envisaged that matching will continue to play an important role in the revenue-recognition process. However, the statement argues that assets should only be carried forward if there are economic benefits still to be derived from them.

Accruals

This convention maintains that profit (or loss) for a period is the difference between revenues earned and expenses incurred during the period, *not* the difference between cash receipts and payments for the period. It really adds support to the matching convention by stating that expenses should be matched to revenues within a time period on the basis of the wealth consumed in generating revenues, not on the basis of cash (if any) relating to an expense paid during the period.

Prudence

This convention maintains that preparers of accounting statements should take a pessimistic rather than an optimistic view of future events to the extent that it is necessary to view future events in the preparation of those statements. Put another way, losses should be anticipated and included, but profits should not be taken into account until they are realized. Prudence is arguably the most important valuation principle in accounting. Where there is a conflict between prudence and another valuation convention (such as historic cost or realization) it is the former which will usually prevail. However, the role of prudence in financial reporting has been questioned increasingly over the years. This convention was considered important in financial reporting in the past when the emphasis was on the protection of lenders and creditors. However, in more recent times the emphasis in financial reporting has shifted towards providing information for investors.

Activity 7
What is the problem with adopting this convention? Could this convention work to the disadvantage of an investor?

The problem with the convention is that it encourages the production of accounting statements which show a systematic bias towards understatement of profit (or overstatement of loss) and understatement of asset values. Moreover, it is not always clear how much bias has been applied in measuring profit or loss. This understatement of profit and asset values may work to the advantage of an investor purchasing shares (who may pay less than if more realistic figures were used in the accounts) and to the disadvantage of investors who are selling shares in the company (as they may sell the shares too cheaply).

There may be some logic for this approach, in that it may be beneficial to exercise caution in business life. It is probably better, however, to produce unbiased information and let the decision maker exercise caution to the extent required in making any decisions based on the information. It has been argued that, if the future events which bear on accounting statements are uncertain, it might be more appropriate to give users statements based on a range of possible outcomes and let the users make their own judgements.

Consistency

Where a particular transaction or event could legitimately be treated in more than one way, the convention of consistency says that the same treatment should be applied from one accounting period to the next. Comparison of that which is shown by accounting statements will be easier where the same accounting policies are consistently applied over time.

Depreciation provides an example of following the convention. When a business acquires a depreciating fixed asset it should, in order to follow the convention, use the same method (e.g. straight-line or reducing-balance) as is applied to other *similar* assets owned by that business. The method should then be applied throughout the life of the asset. This is not to say that it is never acceptable to alter an accounting policy, such as the depreciation method. If, in the light of other conventions, there seems good reason for a change, then a change should be made and the new policy regarded as standard for the foreseeable future. It should be noted that the convention does not seek to establish comparability between the accounting reports of different businesses, though many would argue that such comparability is very useful.

The consistency convention probably leads to the provision of more useful information, but it can encourage adherence to accounting policies which may be difficult to support on grounds other than consistency.

Materiality

Where strictly following a particular convention involves only immaterial amounts, then the convention concerned need not be followed. A problem lies in assessing what is meant by 'immaterial'. This would normally be interpreted as an amount so trivial as not to be capable of having an effect on the judgements of a reader of the accounts.

An area where the materiality convention is often involved is in the strict interpretation of the matching convention.

Example

A business bought a box of paperclips costing £1 during a particular financial year. At the end of the year most of the paperclips had been used. Strictly following the matching convention requires that the remaining paperclips should be counted and valued to deduce the part of the £1 cost which is an expense for the year and the part which should be treated as an asset. Clearly, to follow the matching convention will involve use of staff time in counting paperclips and other similarly insignificant items. The effect that strictly following the matching convention would have on the usefulness of the accounts is almost certainly zero. Thus ignoring the matching convention and treating the cost of the paperclips as an expense of the year in which they were bought seems much more practical.

Activity 8

To what extent is the convention of materiality related to the idea of relevance which we considered in Chapter 2?

It can be argued that the convention of materiality is closely related to the idea of relevance. You may recall that relevance is concerned with providing information which has the ability to influence the decisions of users. The convention of materiality is concerned with what should be disclosed for decision-making purposes. It also involves deciding between what is likely to have an influence on decisions and what is not. Too much information may be as difficult for users to deal with as too little information. There is often a danger that important items in the financial statements may be submerged by less important items. By applying the convention of materiality, less important items may be aggregated in order to allow the key items to be highlighted and to make the financial statements more relevant for decision-making purposes.

Objectivity

This convention maintains that accounting statements should be based on unbiased, verifiable facts, rather than on matters of judgement.

Adherence to this convention has obvious appeal. Surely we should all regard the provision of unbiased verifiable facts as preferable to expressions of opinion? However, the preparation of accounting statements does inevitably rely to some extent – sometimes to a great extent – on opinions. For example, it is necessary to take account of depreciation of fixed assets to achieve some sensible assessment of the trading success or efficiency of a business. Calculation of the depreciation expense for an accounting period in respect of a particular fixed asset relies on four factors:

1. The cost of the asset
2. The economic life of the asset
3. The residual value of the asset at the end of that economic life
4. The method (e.g. straight-line, reducing-balance, etc.) of allocating the cost less the residual value over the economic life of the asset.

At the time that it is necessary to deduce the depreciation expense for the period, only the cost of the asset is typically a verifiable fact. The other three factors are matters of judgement.

The discussion of the deficiencies of both the historic cost and stable monetary unit conventions, earlier in this chapter, includes examples of circumstances where, using verifiable facts, the historic cost of an asset could seriously mislead a user of an accounting statement. Substitution of a figure based on judgement and opinion, e.g. current market value, could make the statement much more useful. Clearly, there can be a conflict between verifiability and objectivity, on the one hand, and usefulness, on the other.

Activity 9
Can you think of three accounting conventions which emphasize the use of subjective rather than objective facts in preparing financial reports?

Three particular conventions which seem to promote subjectivity are matching, prudence and materiality. All of these require making judgements rather than reliance on unbiased, verifiable facts. This emphasis on subjective judgement provides an example of conflict between conventions.

22.5 Towards a conceptual framework

The conventions of accounting discussed above were developed over many years by accountants in order to deal with the practical problems which are encountered in the preparation of financial reports. Until relatively recently, these conventions have provided the only agreed framework available to deal with accounting issues and problems. The conventions offer the accountant some practical guidance concerning *what to record* and *how to record* financial transactions. The conventions are rather broad in nature and do not provide detailed guidelines. Moreover, they do, at times, conflict with each other. However, the fact that they represent a distillation of practical experience in preparing financial reports is viewed by some as a major strength.

There has been an increasing recognition, however, of the limitations of conventions in providing an adequate foundation for the development of accounting. Although it is true that the conventions offer guidance concerning what and how to record, they do not provide guidance concerning why we should record transactions in certain ways or, indeed, why we should record at all. What is required, it is argued, is a clear rationale for accounting, i.e. we need to have a framework which clearly defines the purpose of accounting and the nature and content of financial reports. Such a framework would address fundamental questions such as:

- What are the objectives of accounting?
- For whom are accounting reports prepared?
- What kind of accounting reports are required?
- What should these accounting reports contain?

By answering such questions it is believed that a more logical and systematic approach to the development of accounting practice can be achieved.

In recent years there have been attempts to develop a framework for accounting which deals with the fundamental questions identified above. Perhaps the most notable attempt has been by the Financial Accounting Standards Board (FASB) in the USA. Work on this project began in the early 1970s. The impetus for the FASB effort can be traced to the dissatisfaction of the business community with the quality of accounting reports produced. This dissatisfaction was due to a number of reasons which included:

- the fact that more than one method of accounting could be applied to the same basic data, with each method producing quite different results;
- that less conservative accounting methods were being used in preparing financial reports compared with earlier periods;
- that too much emphasis was being placed on the form of financial statements rather than the underlying economic substance.

As a result of this dissatisfaction, the FASB felt that it was necessary to identify more clearly the aims of accounting in order to provide a basis for developing more consistent accounting policies. The FASB hopes that its efforts will help restore the credibility of accounting in the eyes of users of accounting information and will help ensure that standard-setting in the USA remains free of government intervention.

The FASB has attempted to develop what it has referred to as 'a conceptual framework'. This has been defined as

> a constitution, a coherent system of interrelated objectives and fundamentals that can lead to consistent standards and that prescribes the nature, function, and limits of financial accounting and financial statements (FASB, 1977).

The conceptual framework developed consists of a number of elements which are as follows:

- *Objectives of financial reporting.* This element identifies for whom and for what purpose financial reports are prepared. It also sets out in broad terms what financial statements should contain in order to be of value to users. This provides the logical starting point for a fundamental examination of the nature and content of financial reports.
- *Qualitative characteristics of financial information.* This element establishes criteria by which financial policies and reports can be judged and sets out such qualities as relevance, reliability, comparability, etc. The development of such criteria helps to distinguish between 'good' and 'bad' accounting.
- *Elements of financial statements.* This examines the nature of capital, assets and liabilities and the nature of revenue and expenses. These items form the basic building blocks of financial statements.
- *Recognition criteria.* This examines the process by which an item should be incorporated into the financial statements as an asset, liability, revenue, expense, etc.
- *Measurement.* This element examines the methods of measuring assets and liabilities such as historic cost, constant purchasing power, current cost, net realizable value, etc.
- *Form and content of financial statements and reports.* This element considers the form and content of the statements and reports that should be published and whether it is necessary for all organizations, irrespective of size, to publish the same information.

- *Income reporting.* This examines the nature of 'comprehensive income' and identifies its components (revenue, expense, gains and losses). This element also examines which capital maintenance concept should be adopted, i.e. whether financial or physical capital should be maintained.
- *Funds flow and liquidity.* This element examines how information concerning liquidity should be presented to users.

Activity 10

Explain how a conceptual framework may be of value to:

- a standard-setting body such as the Accounting Standards Board (ASB)
- the auditors of a company
- preparers of financial statements
- users of financial statements

In answering this activity you may have thought of the following:

- **Standard-setting body.** *A body, such as the ASB, should find a conceptual framework useful in developing a more consistent approach to the development of accounting standards as it will provide a clearer basis for deciding between alternative accounting methods. It should also help in reviewing existing standards.*
- **The auditors of a company** *should find a conceptual framework useful in forming an opinion as to whether financial statements conform with accounting standards. The underlying principles should also provide a guide to the application of particular standards.*
- **Preparers of financial statements** *should find it useful in deciding how to apply financial standards. A conceptual framework, which sets out broad principles, may also be helpful in dealing with issues not falling within the scope of particular standards.*
- **Users of financial statements** *should find a conceptual framework useful in interpreting financial reports which are prepared in accordance with accounting standards. The adherence to underlying principles should help eliminate or reduce any uncertainty concerning the treatment of particular items appearing in the accounts.*

The FASB is not alone in attempting to develop a conceptual framework for accounting. There have also been attempts by accounting bodies in other countries such as those in Canada and Australia. In addition, the International Accounting Standards Committee (IASC) has also produced a conceptual framework. The development of this framework follows a similar pattern to that of the FASB framework above.

In the UK, the ASB produced in 1991 a statement on the principles that underpin accounting and the preparation of financial reports for external users. This statement recognized, and drew heavily on, the work produced by the other accounting bodies referred to above. In developing a statement of principles, the ASB identified the following areas as being relevant:

- the objectives of financial statements
- the attributes or qualities of financial statements that enable them to fulfil their purpose
- the elements that make up financial statements
- when items are to be recognized in financial statements
- how resources and performance are to be measured
- how items can best be presented in the financial statements
- the principles underlying the consolidation of groups of companies.

The first stage of the work of the ASB was to set out their views on the first two of the areas mentioned, i.e. the objectives of financial statements and the qualitative characteristics of financial statements. The objective of financial reports according to the ASB was:

> to provide information about the financial position, performance and adaptability of an enterprise that is useful to a wide range of users in making economic decisions.

In addition, the financial statements should also show:

> the results of the stewardship of management, that is, the accountability of management for the resources entrusted to it.

These objectives did not provoke a great deal of debate. They were broad in nature, they emphasize the user-orientation of accounting which has gained increasing acceptance over the years and are similar to objectives proposed by various leading bodies in the past. However, they were criticized for making a distinction between economic decisions and the stewardship function. A wider view of stewardship, based on whether management was acting in the best interests of the owners, would mean that the distinction between economic decision-making and stewardship was really an artificial one.

The ASB statement identified relevance and reliability as the two key qualities of financial statements. The main qualities of financial statements were considered in Chapter 2 and so will not be discussed here. However, a diagram produced by the ASB showing the factors which influence relevance and reliability is shown (as Figure 22.1). The figure also identifies secondary characteristics of accounting which, if lacking, would limit the usefulness of the information.

In 1995 the ASB produced a further exposure draft – *Statement of Principles for Financial Reporting*. The main objective identified was revised to take into account earlier criticisms, and became:

> The objective of financial statements is to provide information about the financial position, performance, and financial adaptability of an enterprise that

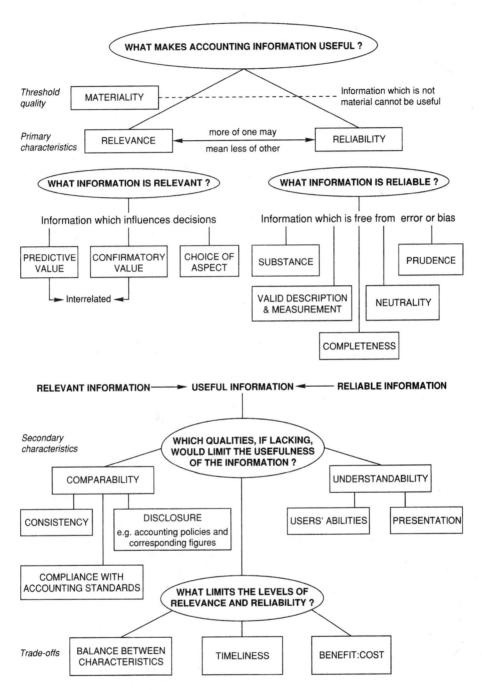

Figure 22.1. *The qualitative characteristics of accounting information*

is useful to a wide range of users for assessing the stewardship of management and for making economic decisions.

The primary qualitative characteristics relating to content were reaffirmed as relevance and reliability. The primary qualitative characteristics relating to presentation were identified as comparability and understandability. Reliability was seen as subsuming faithful representation, substance, neutrality, prudence and completeness, all of which were covered in Chapter 2.

In 1999 the ASB produced a revised exposure draft, together with an introductory booklet *Some questions answered*. Changes were fairly subtle and in the nature of a fine-tuning exercise. For example:

> The objective of financial statements is to provide information about the reporting entity's financial performance and financial position that is useful to a wide range of users for assessing the stewardship of management and for making economic decisions.

The user groups targeted by the statement mirror very closely those identified in Chapter 1. The qualitative characteristics are largely a mirror of those discussed in Chapter 2. The issue of measurement bases has already been discussed earlier in this chapter under historic cost, when the mixed measurement system was discussed. Exactly where the statement goes from here is less clear. It may be that the development of a conceptual framework has gone as far as it can, for reasons discussed below. The problem of measurement remains, and that is the topic of the final chapter.

22.6 Problems in developing a conceptual framework

While many may agree that, in principle, the development of an agreed conceptual framework would be extremely valuable, they remain sceptical that such a framework can actually be developed. Others believe that, in order to secure widespread agreement, a conceptual framework would have to be couched in such broad terms that it would prove meaningless as a guide to action. Certainly a number of difficulties are encountered when seeking a framework which would command broad support. For example, in recent years there has been a number of studies which have attempted to define the objectives of financial reports and/or to identify the users of these reports and their information needs. These studies have, at times, reached similar conclusions but at other times have displayed marked differences in the conclusions reached.

There are also problems of resolving conflicts involving the exercise of judgement. The preparation of financial statements will always involve a need to exercise judgement due to such problems as the allocation of items over time and the existence of uncertainty concerning future outcomes which, nevertheless, have to be taken into account in the current period. As a result, disputes are likely to continue concerning the most appropriate way of dealing with these problems.

Activity 11
Can you think of four areas where judgement is required in the preparation of financial statements and which may have a significant effect on the calculation of profit and financial position?

Four areas which require the exercise of subjective judgement are as follows:

1 **Depreciation.** *The calculation of depreciation requires making estimates concerning the useful life of the asset, the residual value of the asset, and judgement is required as to the most appropriate depreciation method to employ.*
2 **Stocks.** *The calculation of stock requires that an appropriate stock flow assumption is made (i.e. FIFO, LIFO, etc.). It also requires that a judgement be made as to the net realizable value of stocks. If this is lower than cost then the net realizable value becomes the reported figure.*
3 **Goodwill.** *Goodwill paid for on the acquisition of a going concern should be written off. It can either be written off immediately or over a number of years. Judgement is required on the appropriate write-off policy.*
4 **Bad and doubtful debts.** *Judgement is required in determining the debts which are bad and which are doubtful.*

Some find it is difficult to believe that a conceptual framework, if adopted by the accounting profession, would eliminate fundamental debates concerning the nature and purpose of accounting. It has been suggested that, in one sense, a conceptual framework can be compared to the Bible. The Bible, as you probably know, sets out the basic tenets of Christian faith and provides guidelines on how Christians should live. However, the contents of the Bible are interpreted by different Christian sects in different ways and this can sometimes lead to quite profound differences in viewpoints.

This tendency for us to interpret the same things differently has been highlighted by Horngren (1981) who states:

> most of us have an incredible talent for processing new facts in such a way that our prior conclusions remain intact. Therefore, no matter what conceptual framework is developed, its success will be heavily affected by individual interpretations.

A conceptual framework, once developed, would have to adapt to economic, social and political changes. It cannot become a static framework with an indefinite life. However, the nature of possible changes to the framework and the pace of any change are likely to provoke further debate. What some may regard as progress, others are likely to regard as a backward step.

In view of the problems discussed, we should perhaps not expect too much from a conceptual framework, even though such a framework would be desirable. The major benefit so far derived from recent efforts in developing a conceptual framework is that it has helped to identify the important issues in accounting. It has stimulated an investigation into the purpose of accounting reports, the users of accounting information and their likely needs. Thus, it can be argued that we are now, at least, beginning to ask the right sort of questions. However, it seems unlikely that an agreed conceptual framework for accounting will emerge in the foreseeable future.

**22.7
Reporting
financial
performance**

In October 1992 the Accounting Standards Board published FRS 3, *Reporting Financial Performance*. At this stage of your studies you probably need to be aware of the main implications of this standard. It focuses on presentation of the profit and loss, and also introduces the notion of a statement of total recognized gains.

In presenting the profit and loss account a 'layered' format is to be used which highlights a number of important components of financial performance, including:

1 results of continuing operations;
2 results of discontinued operations;
3 profits or losses on the sale or termination of an operation, costs of a fundamental reorganization, and profits or losses on the sale of fixed assets;
4 extraordinary items, being unusual items outside normal activities.

In addition, where there is a material difference between the result disclosed in the profit and loss account and the result on an unmodified historical cost basis, a note of the historical cost profit or loss for the period should be presented. We saw earlier that the treatment of assets (in terms of the measurement base) is not consistent. This requirement goes some way to enabling comparability to be achieved for businesses which use different measurement bases in their published reports.

FRS 3 also required publication of a statement of total recognized gains and losses. The importance of this will become even clearer after completion of the next chapter, but a number of observations can be made now. If a business revalues an asset upwards, the amount of the revaluation will be credited to a capital reserve, known as a revaluation reserve. This will typically be seen as an unrealized gain for purposes of profit calculation. The inclusion of the revalued figure and its corresponding revaluation reserve effectively means that the gain is recognized, albeit not as a profit and loss item. The complete statement of total recognized gains and losses clearly identifies all of the gains or losses, whether these gains go through the profit and loss or not, and this is an important step forward. An example of such a statement is as follows:

Statement of total gains and losses

Profit for the year	x
Unrealized surplus on revaluation of properties	x
Unrealized loss on trade investments	(x)
Total recognized gains and losses relating to the year	x

22.8 Summary

In this chapter the major conventions of accounting have been examined. It has been seen that they suffer from a number of serious weaknesses which undermine their usefulness. They tend to be rather broad in nature and may conflict with one another. A number of problems and limitations were highlighted, the most noteworthy being the convention of historic cost. In fact, it was shown that current value is increasingly seen as an appropriate measurement base. This has a number of implications for profit measurement.

The development of a conceptual framework was then discussed, and the work done in the UK was outlined. Generally it can be seen that the approach taken in this book is consistent with the work to date. The problems of developing such a framework were then addressed, though no consensus appears to exist on the future of such a framework.

Finally FRS 3 was outlined, primarily as a natural development of the debates on measurement bases introduced in this chapter, and as a link with the final chapter of the book.

References

Financial Accounting Standards Board. *Objectives of Financial Reporting and Elements of Financial Statements of Business Enterprises.* FASB, 1977.

Accounting Standards Board. *Exposure Draft – Statement of Principles.* 1991.

Accounting Standards Board. *Exposure Draft – Statement of Principles for Financial Reporting.* 1995.

Accounting Standards Board. *Revised Exposure Draft – Statement of Principles for Financial Reporting.* 1999.

Horngren C.T. Uses and limitations of a conceptual framework. *Journal of Accountancy.* 1981. pp 86–95.

Chapter 23

Measurement of profit and capital maintenance

<table>
<tr><td>

**23.1
Introduction**

</td><td>

This chapter discusses the nature of profit, in particular the problems that arise in a period of rising prices. Various alternative approaches to profit measurement are explored, together with their underlying concept of capital maintenance. In the course of this exploration the chapter examines the two main proposals for dealing with the effect of changing prices in financial reports. The greater awareness of the measurement issues, and the differentiation between income and other gains, should enable the development of a better understanding of financial position and performance.

</td></tr>
<tr><td>

**23.2
Objectives**

</td><td>

At the end of this chapter you should be able to:

- define (profit) income;
- explain what is meant by capital maintenance;
- differentiate between financial and physical capital maintenance;
- prepare a simple set of accounts using CPP accounting;
- prepare a simple set of accounts using CCA;
- review the various proposals relating to accounting for changing prices made in the UK and summarize the current position;
- use the principles developed in this chapter to better analyse position and performance.

</td></tr>
<tr><td>

**23.3
Measurement of profit and the maintenance of capital**

</td><td>

It was shown in Chapter 22 that following the historic cost and stable monetary conventions can lead to the production of accounting reports which could seriously mislead a user. The misleading effects tend to be particularly concerned with questions of profit measurement (see, for example, the Telesales example which was considered in the context of the historic cost convention, in Chapter 22). There are also distortions in asset valuation and assessment of performance (see the Apex Property Company example which was discussed in Chapter 22 in the context of the stable monetary unit convention).

It was established in the early chapters of this book that revenues are trading events which increase capital and that expenses are trading events which reduce it. The net effect of revenues and expenses over a period is a profit or a loss and this has the effect of increasing capital or of decreasing it, respectively. This leads to an alternative version of the definition of profit. This version says that profit is the *net amount of assets which the owner(s) of the*

</td></tr>
</table>

business can withdraw (*as dividend, etc.*) *during the period and leave the business, or the owners, as well off at the end of the period as at the beginning.* This is an important version of the definition of profit in that it relates to the general desire of the owners of the business not to let the business, or their investment in it, decline in size as a result of capital withdrawals by the owners. This is effectively the traditional economics definition of income. You should note that the terms profit and loss account and income statement mean the same and can be interchanged.

When there is an environment of changing price levels, either general or specific to a particular asset, profit measurement becomes difficult. Inappropriate profit measurement could lead to owners taking out (as drawings or dividends) more than is sensible, with possible adverse effects on long-term survival. It is important to ensure that capital is worth as much at the end of the period as it was at the beginning. The problem is what we mean by capital, and what we mean by worth as much (in effect as well off). Are we talking about the capital of the owner, or the business? Are we talking about well-offness in terms of dollars? Are we talking about maintenance of purchasing power over goods and services generally, or over the particular goods and services that the business uses? In measuring profit we need to be very clear exactly which capital maintenance concept we are using.

Before exploring these alternative approaches in detail, it is important why changing prices create problems in profit measurement. The major problems that arise when prices change are given below:

- Capital gains will be overstated, because part of any gain will usually represent an inflation component – when an asset has been held for many years the effect of inflation is likely to be substantial, with much of the gain being attributable to inflation.
- Cost of sales are likely to be understated, because stock will be matched with revenues of a later period.
- Depreciation is likely to be understated.
- The effect of holding monetary assets and liabilities is considerable – such items do not need to be adjusted at the balance sheet date, as they are current at that time – however, holding of monetary assets in a time of inflation will lead to a loss of purchasing power while holding of monetary liabilities will give a gain in purchasing power.
- Historic cost figures soon become out of date, with the result that the balance sheet ceases to have any real meaning.
- Historic cost figures for different periods are not comparable.

The net effect of these is that profits will often be overstated in a time or rising prices, because input costs are matched with revenues of a later date. For real profit determination there must be a matching of revenues with the *current* costs of the assets used up to create those revenues.

Put another way, a system of profit calculation needs to be devised, such that users will know whether capital has been maintained or not. Profit measures the increase in capital accruing in a period. The price-level problem is concerned with the elimination of the 'price' effect from profit, and the calculation of the 'real' profit.

This brings us to the crux of the matter. It is clear that capital needs to be maintained, but are we looking at shareholders' equity, and concerning ourselves with maintenance of the shareholders purchasing power (the proprietory view)? Or are we concerned with maintaining the operating assets and the operating capacity of the firm (the entity view)? Either view is possible. Both have merits. The problems in the debate arise because of confusion and disagreement on these capital maintenance concepts.

Two major approaches have been proposed to try to deal with the problem of changing prices, though other methods have been put forward as well. Which of the two major methods is preferred is essentially concerned with whether it is the 'well-offness' or wealth of the owners which the definition of profit seeks to save from decline, or whether it is the ability of the business to continue at existing levels of activity which the definition of profit seeks to protect. This point and the two methods will now be explained. Before doing this it is worth noting that in some of the later proposals elements of each of the two main approaches are found.

23.4 Preserving owners' wealth – current (constant) purchasing power (CPP) accounting

If the wealth of the *owners* which is invested in the business is to be as much at the end of the accounting period as at the start, then the owners should be able to buy as much with their wealth at the end of the accounting period as they could at the beginning.

If all the prices of goods and services which the owners may wish to buy remain constant over the accounting period, then profit is fairly easy to measure.

Example

Jackie Jones runs a small business during her spare time, buying crockery and selling it at a local street market. She started it a year ago when she cashed in an insurance policy for £1,200 which she used to open a bank account for the business. Jackie had decided not to take any of her capital out of the business as drawings during the first year.

The balance sheet, which her accountant drew up as at the end of Jackie's first year of trading, included the following, under the heading of 'Capital':

Capital introduced	£1,200
Net profit for the year	3,574
Capital at the end of the year	£4,774

This implies that if Jackie were now to withdraw her £3,574 of profit, that part of her wealth remaining invested in the business (£1,200) would be equal to that which she started with. If general prices of goods and services had remained constant over the year, the £1,200 which she invested to start the business would have the same value to her as £1,200 at the end of the year.

Suppose, however, that during the year the price of goods and services within the economy had increased in price by a factor of 10% of the start-of-the-year prices. This would mean that to obtain the same amount of goods and services at the end of the year that £1,200 would have bought at the start would cost £1,200 plus 10%, i.e. £1,320. In this case, would it still be true to say that Jackie could take £3,574 out of the business and still be as well off in terms of her investment in the business as at the start of the year? Of course she would not be as well off in these circumstances. Given the definition of profit which is being adopted here, the profit is £3,454 [£3,574 − (£1,320 − £1,200)].

23.5 Preserving the ability of the business to trade at existing levels – current cost accounting (CCA)

The second approach defines profit as the amount which the owners of the business can withdraw and leave the *business* as well off, in terms of its ability to continue to trade, at the end of the period as it was at the beginning.

Example

Suppose that Jackie Jones (the street market crockery trader from the last example) needed her original capital of £1,200 because that was how much she felt it necessary to spend on crockery stocks each week. Out of her takings she would pay her rent to the local authority and the hire of the stall to the person from whom she rented it. Although the general level of consumer prices may have moved up by 10% over the year, suppose that the type of crockery in which Jackie trades has increased in price by 20% over that period.

In these circumstances, for the *business* to be as well off at the end of the year as it was at the start, in terms of its ability to continue to trade at the same level, at least £1,440 (£1,200 × 120/100) must be left after Jackie has withdrawn her profit. This means that according to the CCA version of the definition of profit, the profit is £3,334 (£3,574 − £240). Any more than this will not enable the business to trade at the original level, should all the profit be withdrawn.

You should note that CPP and CCA are based upon different definitions of profit. Both have advantages and disadvantages. However, it is important to recognize that one is not right and the other wrong. They both provide useful, but different, insights into profit measurement. Indeed, it is possible to obtain more information by using both methods, or at least certain aspects of them. For example, Jackie Jones' profit on a CPP basis was measured as £3,454, whereas on a CCA basis it was £3,334. This means that if Jackie wishes to continue in business at the same level of activity as at the start of the year, she can only withdraw £3,334. She must retain capital in the business of £1,440. However, this investment is £120 more than is needed to preserve her own personal purchasing power. This £120 therefore represents an increase in *her* purchasing power (as distinct from that of the business) which cannot be distributed without impairing the ability of *the business* to continue at the same level of activity.

Activity 1

You run a garage business. You start your year with 10,000 gallons of fuel which cost you £1.50 per gallon. Your capital is £17,000. Immediately following the start of the year the buying price of petrol increases to £2.00 per gallon as a result of which you increase the price to your customers. At the end of your first month of trading you refill the tanks with 10,000 gallons at £2.00 per gallon. Your profit and loss account for the first month of the year, on an historical cost basis is as follows:

		£
Sales	10,000 gallons @ £2.50	25,000
Cost of sales	10,000 gallons at £1.50	15,000
Gross profit		10,000
Overheads (including rent of premises and tank, paid at the start of the month)		2,000
Net profit		£8,000

(a) What would be the profit on a CCA basis?
(b) How much would you feel able to take out as drawings for the first month?
(c) By how much would you as the owner feel better off if the cost of goods and services which you regularly buy increased by 1% on the month?

(a) *On a* **CCA** *basis, the profit and loss account would be:*

		£
Sales	*10,000 gallons @ £2.50*	*25,000*
Cost of sales	*10,000 gallons @ £2.00*	*20,000*
Gross profit		*5,000*
Overheads		*2,000*
Net profit		*£3,000*

(b) *If you wish to continue to hold stocks at the level of the start of the month so that your ability to trade is not reduced, the maximum which can be withdrawn is the £3,000 CCA profit.*

(c) *Under* **CPP**, *assuming a rate of inflation of 1% over the month, the profit and loss account would be as follows:*

		£
Sales	10,000 gallons @ £2.50	25,000
Cost of sales	10,000 gallons @ £1.50 × 101/100	15,150
Gross profit		9,850
Overheads	(£2,000 × 101/100)	2,020
Net profit		£7,830

The £170 difference between the historical cost and the CPP profit arises because it will cost £17,170 (£17,000 × 101/100) to buy goods and services at the end of the month which would have cost £17,000 at the start. Thus to preserve the purchasing power of your capital, the maximum withdrawal is £7,830.

Before moving on to a more detailed example, it is important to note that the increases in expenses and assets that were recorded above in deriving CPP or CCA profit must have a balancing second entry. In the case of part (a) of Activity 1 the increase in the stock and purchases, which led to the increase in the cost of sales of £500, would be balanced by an increase (a credit) in a current cost reserve (i.e. an increase in equity).

This means that if we were to prepare a statement of total gains and losses we would get:

	HCA	CCA	CPP
Net profit	8,000	3,000	7,830
Current cost reserve		5,000	
CPP capital adjustment			170
	8,000	8,000	8,000

The total gain is the same. The crux of the question is how much of this is distributable as a dividend while keeping capital intact.

- If you are happy to simply maintain the dollar amount of capital £8,000 can be distributed.
- If you wish to maintain the real purchasing power (over goods and services generally) of the capital then £7,830 can be distributed.
- If you wish to maintain real purchasing power, in terms of the goods and services that are essential to the business – physical operating capacity), you can only distribute £3,000.

Of course, the current cost reserve can be seen as a holding gain. This gain is likely to be realized by the owner(s) of the business if and when the business is sold. Also, it should be noted that the CPP and CCA approaches could be combined as follows:

Net profit on a CCA basis		3,000
Current cost reserve split		
– general inflation adjustment	170	
– real gain	4,830	
		5,000
Total gain		8,000

In effect, part of the specific increase in current price of £5,000 is attributable to general inflation. The rest, while not distributable by the business without serious harm to the business, nevertheless represent a real profit to the owner.

Activity 2

A business starts with £50,000 capital.

Consider the situation that the company purchases 10,000 units of a good at a cost of £5 each. It sells them at a price of £10, by which time the cost has increased to £7. The general rate of inflation is 20%.

What possible income figures could be given?

Which one of these do you think is most useful?

Would it make any difference if:

- the business was a trading company which purchased goods on an opportunistic basis, with no continuing lines of business;
- the business was trading in the goods for the indefinite future.

Is there any role for adjustments for general inflation?

Historic cost profit = sales less historic cost of sales = £100,000 − £50,000 = £50,000

Current cost profit = sales less current cost of sales = £100,000 − £70,000 = £30,000. This amount could be distributed while leaving enough to replace the inventory at current cost.

In order to calculate the CPP profit we would have to know when the goods were sold and the general price index movements over the year (or at least those at the start and end of the year and at the time of sale).

Current cost is arguably the most useful in that it identifies the profit from operations. A holding gain of $20,000 would also be recognized but capitalized (i.e. transferred to current cost reserve). The historic cost profit includes both together which makes comparability difficult.

If the business was an opportunistic trading company as described the difference between holding and operating gains is irrelevant, as the idea of physical operating capability has no real meaning.

If the business is a continuing business trading in the same goods current cost profit is useful as a measure of distributable profit.

If general inflation is 20% the capital of the owners needs to be 20% higher than it was at the start of the year, if the owners' command of general goods and services is to be maintained. This means that capital would need to be $10,000 higher.

This means that the $50,000 profit on an historic cost basis could usefully be split as :

- *$10,000 general index adjustment*
- *$10,000 as a further specific price adjustment needed to ensure that operating capital could be maintained*
- *$30,000 current operating profit – distributable while preserving operating capital.*

Only the last two should be seen as 'real' profit to the shareholders in terms of general purchasing power.

Only the last one would be seen as 'real' profit to the business in terms of specific purchasing power.

23.6 CPP – a more detailed consideration

A closer look will now be taken at CPP accounting. When this approach is used in the preparation of final accounts, all the figures in the accounts are usually expressed in pounds of purchasing power as at the balance sheet date (end of the profit and loss account period). This operation, which can be a little laborious (but is not typically too difficult), is effected through the use of a general price index. This is simply a statistical device which relates the cost (in pounds) of a set of goods and services at various points in time. The one whose use is usually advocated in the context of CPP is the retail price index (RPI) which is compiled and published by the UK government and updated monthly.

Under CPP each expense and revenue is revised from the original historical cost figures. The revision is based on the price index used. In practice, it is not usually considered necessary to identify each sale on an individual basis. Usually, the view is taken that to adjust the sales figure as if all the sales took place at the mid-point in the financial year is acceptable, provided that the sales were spread fairly evenly over the year. Where this is not the case or the sales are in large discrete units, as they might be, say, for a small housebuilder, each revenue should be dealt with on an individual basis.

The balance sheet figures are also revised so that they are all expressed in terms of pounds at the year-end value. This includes the fixed assets, so that the depreciation charge for the year, in the profit and loss account, will be calculated with reference to the revised figures. Some of the items in the historical cost account balance sheet will not need adjustment since they are already expressed in terms of pounds of year-end value. These are those assets and claims whose amount is fixed in money terms. These include all forms of debtor and creditor, both long- and short-term, and cash itself. Such items are usually referred to as *monetary items*.

There is one more adjustment necessary, to reflect the fact that a business with assets whose value is fixed in money terms loses during a period of inflation, while one with such liabilities gains. This is because a debtor of £100 (or £100 in cash) held for a period is worth less in terms of purchasing power at the end of the period than it was at the beginning. Similarly, a liability loses value in terms of purchasing power, which is to the benefit of the business, since it will have to give up less in real terms to settle the obligation, if inflation has been present during the period that the liability was outstanding. Thus the profit will be reduced where the business has an excess of monetary assets over monetary liabilities and the profit will be increased where the opposite is the case.

It should be emphasized that the final profit and loss account and balance sheet prepared under CPP simply take the original, historic cost versions of these statements and translates them into pounds of balance sheet date value. In principle, this is much the same as would be necessary to convert final accounts prepared in one currency, say French francs, into another, say pounds sterling.

Activity 3

Honest John deals in a fairly small way in second-hand cars. John started the year with no cars in stock and during the year the following transactions took place:

	RPI at date of transaction	Bought	Sold
1 January	317	Ford (£800)	–
1 February	321	Rover (£3,000)	–
1 April	325	Jaguar (£2,500)	Rover(£3,300)
			Ford (£1,000)
1 May	327	Renault (£1,500)	–
1 June	331	Nissan (£2,000)	–
1 August	340	BMW (£5,000)	Nissan (£2,100)
1 September	344	Citroen (£2,000)	Renault (£1,400)
1 October	347	Fiat (£900)	Jaguar (£2,000)
			BMW (£5,200)
1 December	353	Skoda (£1,000)	Fiat (£1,100)
			Citroen (£2,400)
31 December	357	–	–

You are required in respect of the year to 31 December:

(a) to deduce the total CPP sales figure
(b) to deduce the total CPP cost of sales figure
(c) to deduce the CPP closing stock figure

Your answer should be as follows:

CPP cost of sales		**CPP sales**	
	£		£
£800 × 357/317	901	£4,300 × 357/325	4,723
£3,000 × 357/321	3,336	£2,100 × 357/340	2,205
£2,500 × 357/325	2,746	£1,400 × 357/344	1,453
£1,500 × 357/327	1,638	£7,200 × 357/347	7,407
£2,000 × 357/331	2,157	£3,500 × 357/353	3,540
£5,000 × 357/340	5,250		
£2,000 × 357/344	2,076		
£900 × 357/347	926		
	£19,030		£19,328

Closing stock
£1,000 × 357/353   £1,011

A more detailed example

The following are the balance sheets for the beginning of the year and end of the year, together with a profit and loss account (income statement) for the year, for a company. All figures are in £000.

Balance sheet	Start	End
Stock	800	800
Monetary assets	3,000	6,000
Non-current assets		
Cost	15,000	15,000
Depreciation provision	(1,500)	(3,000)
	17,300	18,800
Current monetary liabilities	1,800	800
Debentures	2,000	2,000
Capital and reserves	13,500	16,000
	17,300	18,800

Profit and loss account/income statement for the year

Sales		15,000
Opening stock	800	
Purchases	9,600	
	10,400	
less closing stock	800	
Cost of sales		9,600
Gross profit		5,400
Depreciation	1,500	

Other expenses	1,400	
		2,900
Net profit		2,500

Notes

1 The company was formed and the fixed assets purchased, at a time when the general price index was 75.
2 At the start of the year the index was 100.
   At the end of the year the index was 112.
   The general index had moved up 12% over the year, 1% a month.
3 Sales and purchases were made evenly over the year, as are other expenses, other than rent of £200, which was paid on the first day of the year. For ease of calculation you may assume that the opening and closing stocks were bought at the end of the respective years, when the price index was 100 and 112.
4 Depreciation is 10% straight line.

The first stage would be to revise the opening balance sheet as follows:

Balance sheet	Revised	Adjustment
Stock	800	
Monetary assets	3,000	
Non-current assets		
Cost	20,000	15,000 × 100/75
Depreciation provision	(2,000)	1,500 × 100/75
	21,800	
Current monetary liabilities	1,800	
Debentures	2,000	
Capital and reserves	18,000	13,500 × 100/75
	21,800	

The monetary items clearly cannot be changed. The real cost of the assets needs to be adjusted to reflect the inflation adjustment. The increase in the capital and reserves reflects an inflation adjustment which exactly reflects the adjustments made elsewhere, i.e. the £5,000 increase in the assets less the £500 increase in depreciation provision.

The profit and loss account (income statement) would be revised as follows:

Profit and loss account for the year			Adjustment
Sales		15,849	15,000 × 112/106
Opening stock	896		800 × 112/100
Purchases	10,143		9,600 × 112/106
	11,039		
Less closing stock	800		

Cost of sales		10,239
Gross profit		5,610
Depreciation	2,240	
Rent	224	$200 \times 112/100$
Other expenses	1,268	$1200 \times 112/106$
Loss on monetary items	118	see workings below
		3,850
Net profit		1,760

Notes

1 The sales which occurred evenly over the year (i.e. on average mid-way through the year when the index was 106) are adjusted by 112/106. Strictly we should split the sales by month (or other shorter period) and adjust them appropriately – i.e. the first month's sales would be adjusted by 112/101 with the last one being 112/112. The above approximation is acceptable when sales are spread evenly.

2 The opening stock is adjusted by 112/100 reflecting the fact that this stock was purchased when the index was 100. Purchases are adjusted in the same way as sales, an approximation which is acceptable as long as purchases are made evenly over the year. Closing stock is effectively adjusted by 112/112 as it was assumed to have been purchased when the index was 112.

3 Rent is adjusted by 112/100 as it was paid when the index was 100. Other expenses are adjusted by 112/106.

4 The *loss on monetary items* can be calculated in a number of different ways. It must be recognized that holding monetary assets in a time of inflation will result in a loss of purchasing power, and holding monetary liabilities will result in a gain. For example, the holding of debentures – a liability fixed in money terms – of £2,000, at a time when the index has gone from 100 to 112, means that in order to maintain the purchasing power constant the debenture would need to be restated to £2000 × 112/100 = £2,240. This restatement will not occur, as the debenture is fixed in money terms, which means that the company has made a gain of £240 in terms of end-of-year purchasing power. The debenture holder has made a loss of the same amount.

The *calculations of the loss on monetary items* are now given.

Method 1

The net monetary assets were £3,000 at the start of the year, less an immediate payment of rent – so £2,800. This was increased on average mid-year to £6000, an increase of £3,200.

The monetary liabilities were $3,800 at the start of the year and decreased to £2,800 mid-way through. This information can be set out as follows:

	Assets	Liabilities	Net
Held throughout the year	2,800	2,800	–
Held for first six months		1,000	(1,000)
Increase held for last six months	3,200		3,200

There will be a gain on the net liabilities held for the first six months, amounting to $1,000 \times 6/100 = £60$, but this is expressed in mid-year purchasing power so needs to be adjusted by $112/106 = £63$.

There will be a loss on the monetary assets held over the last six months of $3,200 \times 112/106 - 3200 = £181$

Overall loss on monetary items is therefore $£181 - £63 = £118$

Method 2

Tabulate as follows:

	Assets	Liabilities	Net
Held for first six months	2,800	3,800	(1,000)
Held for last six months	6,000	2,800	3,200

The calculations are similar to the above to give a loss of £118.

Method 3

All transactions which involve monetary items are adjusted to reflect the amounts they would need to have been to have maintained purchasing power. The resulting figure is then compared with the actual year-end figure and the difference represents a gain or loss.

Monetary assets/(liabilities) at the beginning (net)	$800 \times 112/100 =$	(896)
less payment of rent	$200 \times 112/100 =$	(224)
		(1120)
Plus sales (increases in cash or debtors)	$15,000 \times 112/106 =$	15,849
less other outflows		
Purchases	$9,600 \times 112/106 =$	(10,143)
Expenses	$1,200 \times 112/106 =$	(1,268)
Gives updated balance		3,318
Actual net monetary assets		3,200
Loss in purchasing power		118

The year-end balance sheet can be adjusted as follows:

Balance sheet	Revised	Adjustment
Stock	800	
Monetary assets	6,000	
Non-current assets		
Cost	22,400	$20,000 \times 112/100$
Depreciation provision	(4,480)	$2,000 \times 112/100$
		plus 2,240 depn for year
	24,720	

Current monetary liabilities	800	
Debentures	2,000	
Capital and reserves	21,920	see below
	24,720	

The *reserves* need to be broken down as follows:

Opening balance	20,160	$18,000 \times 112/1000$
Plus net (real) profit	1,760	
	21,920	

For those of you who like to track things through into ledger accounts the following revaluation account (or capital maintenance account) could be useful.

Revaluation/capital maintenance account

Depreciation provision	240	Fixed assets	2,400
Sales	849	Opening stock	96
		Purchases	543
		Rent	24
		Other expenses	68
Capital or balance c/d	2,160	Loss on monetary items	118
	3,249		3,249

Note that the balance reflects exactly the amount of adjustment needed to the opening capital and reserves to preserve purchasing power.

Advantages and disadvantages of CPP

The advocates of using the CPP approach argue that:

- It is relatively objective. It is based on historic costs which are adjusted by using a statistical index derived outside the business.
- Using a general index to make the adjustments makes those adjustments standard across businesses.
- It emphasizes the cost and benefits of holding monetary items during inflationary periods.
- It attempts to deal with the distortions caused by general inflation.
- As it is based on historic accounts, it is more evolutionary than other methods proposed.

Its detractors point out that:

- It is of dubious value for managerial decision-making purposes since decisions are likely to involve replacement of the *specific* assets of the business, rather than with goods and services generally.

- Using a general price index to make adjustments is considered irrelevant since this is likely to reflect price changes in a way which is quite different from those experienced by various users of the accounts.
- It is regarded by many as conceptually difficult to understand and to interpret the results from CPP.
- As the CPP accounts represent an adjustment to the historic cost accounts, they can only be regarded as supplementary statements. They cannot replace the historic cost accounts.
- The assets are shown in the CPP balance sheet at their adjusted historic cost. However, this is not the same (or as useful) as the current value of the assets.

23.7 CCA – a more detailed consideration

In practice, not all businesses are as simple as that of Jackie Jones, which was used earlier to illustrate the principles of CCA. They are much more likely to have fixed assets and other current assets, as well as stock. When the CCA approach is used to prepare the final accounts the general principle is that the expenses which are charged against the revenues, in the profit and loss account, should represent the current cost of the assets used to achieve those revenues. With stock sold this amounts to identifying, strictly in respect of each sale, the current cost of the stock sold. With most other expenses it is simply the actual amount spent on them. Depreciation is typically based on the current cost of the asset to the business at the mid-point in the year, this being regarded as a reasonable approximation. Current cost is typically (though not always) the amount that it would cost the business to replace the asset *at the time of its sale or use*.

The balance sheet shows the assets at their value to the business at balance sheet date. Value to the business has been defined as the lower of the replacement cost of the asset and its recoverable amount. The recoverable amount is the higher of the net realizable value and its value in use (present value). The value to the business of assets would typically (though not necessarily, given changes in technology) be their replacement cost since, if the business were deprived in some way of any of its assets, it would typically replace them.

In the basic CCA accounts, gains and losses on monetary asets and liabilities are ignored.

There is no attempt made with CCA to reflect year-end values in the profit and loss account. Revenues are left unadjusted and the expenses reflect the cost of replacing the asset consumed *at the date of the expense*, hence the tendency is towards the profit and loss account to reflect the average revenues and expenses for the year.

We will illustrate the broad principles of CCA by use of an example. This is basically the same as was used to illustrate CPP, but with specific figures used instead of a general index.

Example

The following are the balance sheets for the beginning of the year and end of the year, together with an income statement for the year, for a company. All figures are in £000.

Balance sheet	Start	End
Stock	800	800
Monetary assets	3,000	6,000
Non-current assets		
Cost	15,000	15,000
Depreciation provision	(1,500)	(3,000)
	17,300	18,800
Current monetary liabilities	1,800	800
Debentures	2,000	2,000
Capital and reserves	13,500	16,000
	17,300	18,800

Profit and loss (income statement for the year)

Sales		15,000
Opening stock	800	
Purchases	9,600	
	10,400	
less closing stock	800	
Cost of sales		9,600
Gross profit		5,400
Depreciation	1,500	
Other expenses	1,400	
		2,900
Net profit		2,500

Notes

1 Replacement cost of the fixed assets was £20,000 at the beginning of the current year.

2 At the start of the year all indexes were 100.
   The following specific indexes are available at the year end:

fixed assets	115
stock	118
rent	110

3 The general price index of 112 is seen as providing a fair guide to movements in general expenses. All these price movements have occurred evenly through the year.

4 Sales and purchases were made evenly over the year, as are other expenses, other than rent of £200, which was paid on the first day of the year. For ease of calculation you may assume that the opening and

closing stocks were bought at the end of the respective years, when the price index was 100 and 112. Depreciation is 10% straight-line.

The first stage would be to revise the opening balance sheet as follows:

Balance Sheet	Revised	Adjustment
Stock	800	
Monetary assets	3,000	
Non-current assets		
Cost	20,000	current cost
Depreciation provision	(2,000)	10% of current cost
	21,800	
Current monetary liabilities	1,800	
Debentures	2,000	
Capital	13,500	
Current cost reserve	4,500	see below
	21,800	

The monetary items clearly cannot be changed. The assets needs to be adjusted to reflect the current cost. The current cost reserve reflects the £5,000 increase in the assets less the £500 increase in depreciation provision.

The income statement would be revised as follows:

Profit and loss account/Income statement for the year			Adjustment
Sales		15,000	
Opening stock	872		800 × 109/100
Purchases	9,600		
	10,472		
less closing stock	739		800 × 109/118
Cost of sales		9,733	
Gross profit		5,267	
Depreciation	2,150		
Rent	210		200 × 105/100
Other expenses	1,200		
		3,560	
Net profit		1,707	

Notes

1 Under CCA revenues are not adjusted, but expenses are matched against them to arrive at the cost which is current at the time of sale. Since sales are deemed to have occurred evenly over the year (i.e. on average mid-year) as are purchases, only the opening and closing stocks need to be adjusted to put them in at average of the year current cost.

2 Rent is adjusted by 105/100 as it was paid when the index was 100 while the average of the year index was 105. Other expenses are assumed to have occurred evenly and are current at the time of sale.

3 Depreciation is based on the appropriate percentage (in this case 10%) of the average of the year current cost of the fixed asset. The current cost at the start of the year is £20,000 and at the year end is £20,000 × 115/100 = £23,000. The average of the year current cost is £21,500, giving a depreciation figure of £2,150.

In fact a more usual way of presenting this statement is as follows:

CCA *Profit and loss account*

Historic cost profit		2,500
Current cost adjustments		
Stock/cost of sales	133	
Depreciation	650	
Rent	10	
		793
CCA profit		1,707

This form of presentation clearly reconciles the historic cost profit with the current cost profit.

The year-end balance sheet can be adjusted as follows:

Balance sheet	Revised	Adjustment
Stock	800	
Monetary assets	6,000	
Non-current assets		
Cost	23,000	20,000 × 115/100
Depreciation provision	(4,600)	see below
	25,200	
Current monetary liabilities	800	
Debentures	2,000	
Capital	13,500	
Current cost reserve	7,193	see below
Profit & loss	1,707	from the P & L
	25,200	

The current cost reserve account would appear as follows

Previous year

Depreciation provision	500	Non-current asset	5,000
Balance c/d	4,500		
	5,000		5,000

Current year

		Balance b/d	4,500
Depreciation provision (1)	300	Non-current asset (1)	3,000
Depreciation provision (2)	150	Opening stock (3)	72
		Closing stock (3)	61
Balance c/d	7,193	Rent	10
	7,643		7,643
		Balance b/d	7,193

Notes

1 The net revaluation is effectively of an asset which has already been depreciated by 10% – an asset which was shown in the opening balance sheet at a current cost of £20,000 – £2,000 depreciation provision = £18,000. This adjusted by 15% gives a net £2,700 holding gain, which is £3,000 – £300.
2 This figure, known as backlog depreciation, is necessary in order to ensure that the figures in the end-of-year balance sheet are adjusted to the full year's charge – remember that the profit and loss account only included depreciation on average of the year current cost.
3 These figures simply reflect the opening and closing stock adjustments. These will be clarified in a later example.

The illustration given above is effectively a pure 'replacement cost' system. It can be argued that in a system of CCA the costs of maintaining the specific purchasing power of monetary items need to be incorporated. For example the Australian standard on CCA, which is clearly based on a concept of operating capability maintenance, recommends inclusion of an adjustment for monetary items. Under this standard gains or losses on holding monetary items should be calculated as follows:

(a) for trade debtors and creditors, by reference to appropriate measures (e.g. indexes) of changes in the current costs of relevant goods and services that are principally responsible for the balance of trade debtors and creditors during the period;
(b) for loan capital, by reference to movements in a general price index;
(c) for other monetary assets and monetary liabilities, by reference to appropriate measures of changes in the current cost of relevant goods and services during the period. Where this is not practicable, a general price index may be used.

Activity 4

1 How do you think that the current cost of an asset subject to technological change would be addressed?
2 Is ensuring that the general purchasing power of monetary items is maintained not mixing two different capital maintenance concepts – especially loan capital?

1 *The term current cost is potentially ambiguous – does it mean the price at which an identical asset can be purchased or the price at which equivalent service potential can be purchased?*
   Generally it is the second of these views which has the highest support.
2 *This is an interesting point. Most CCA advocates do not see it as a mixing of concepts. Certainly it is easy to adjust net monetary working capital by an appropriate index and argue that it is an operating capital maintenance adjustment. To argue the same for loan capital is more difficult. It is theoretically justifiable if a target capital structure exists and is maintained and this is far from clearly justifiable.*

A further argument that has been used in the past is that the adjustments to historic cost profit do not necessarily need to be retained to preserve operating capability. If a business typically funds, say 50%, of its net assets by debt, it does not have to retain the full adjustment. For example, using the above figure £793 of the profit of £2,500 typically needs to be retained in order to preserve operating capability. If 50% of assets are funded by debt, it can be argued that only half of the £793 needs to be retained, since the other half will be funded by debt. This adjustment, if used, is referred to as a gearing adjustment.

Advantages and disadvantages of CCA

Those who favour CCA point out that:

- Since it relates to specific costs as they affect the business concerned, it is more relevant and helpful as an aid to management decision making.
- It gives a more valid measure of how much capital can be withdrawn so that the business is as well off at the end of the period as it was at the beginning. Thus, it helps to ensure the productive capacity of the business is maintained.
- The balance sheet gives a realistic measure of the assets employed in the business on which to assess returns.

The critics of CCA argue that:

- The profit measure does not necessarily reflect the efficiency of management.
- Gains and losses on monetary items are ignored and so some useful information is omitted.
- Determining value to the business (typically replacement cost) can be difficult and inevitably strays into areas of subjectivity.
- CCA does not really deal with the distortions caused by general inflation.

23.8 Accounting for changing price levels in the UK

The history of the last twenty years of the UK accounting profession is littered with unsuccessful attempts to establish a means of accounting for inflation, which could command sufficient general support for it to be regarded as the standard approach.

The Sandilands Committee in the UK (1975) made the following points:

1 It is essential that accounts should allow for changes in costs and prices.
2 Existing conventions do not do so adequately, and tend to present the affairs of companies in a misleading way.
3 The most fruitful line of development in inflation accounting is a system based on the principles of value accounting, which shows the specific effect of inflation on individual companies.

Sandilands regarded measurement of assets for most purposes in terms of their 'value to the business'. Operating profit was to be derived by charging against revenues the 'value to the business' of assets consumed in generating these amounts. It is interesting to note that Sandilands clearly thought that including adjustments for depreciation and cost of sales was sufficient.

While the Sandilands Report was accepted in principle, implementation took a bit longer. The 'Morpeth' Committee was charged with implementation and produced Exposure Draft 18 – *Current Cost Accounting*. The Sandilands Committee proposals had been criticized for (among other things) not dealing with accounting for inflation, and ignoring gains/losses on monetary items. Morpeth attempted to deal with most of the problems and criticisms. The Exposure Draft ran to 93 pages and the guidance manual to 273 pages. A summary of the ED18 proposals is given below. It can be argued that this particular proposal is the most thorough proposal that has ever been devised (at least of those that are feasible). The main points were:

- Fixed assets were to be shown in the balance sheet at their *value to the business* and not at their depreciated original cost; stocks were to be shown at their value to the business and not at the lower of original cost and net realizable value.
- Depreciation for the year was to be calculated on the value to the business of the fixed assets – on average of the year figures.
- Cost of sales was to be calculated on the basis of value to the business of the inventory at the date of consumption and not purchase.
- Effects of the loss or gain from holding monetary assets or owing liabilities was to be shown in a '*statement of the gain or loss in the value of the shareholders' net equity interest after allowing for the change in the value of money*'.
- The distinction between real and apparent growth insofar as the equity interest is concerned was also made clear in this statement.
- Directors were to appropriate to a *revaluation reserve* amounts required to maintain the scale of the business – main components to be:
  - increased replacement cost of fixed assets and inventories
  - increased requirements for monetary working capital
  - depreciation unprovided in the past on fixed assets because prices have risen since the depreciation was provided.

- The distinction between '*operating*' and '*holding*' gains/losses were recognized, and operating profit was defined as 'revenue less current expenses, including in those expenses the value to the business of the physical assets consumed during the year, but before interest, tax or extraordinary items'.
- The *profit and loss account* suggested would have shown:
  - operating profit or loss for the year
  - interest payable less receivable
  - current cost profit before tax (CCP)
  - tax
  - CCP before extraordinary items
  - extraordinary items for the year
  - CP for the year.
- Holding gains were to go to revaluation surpluses (net of minority interests) and subsequently to the appropriation account.
- The *appropriation account* brought together 'the current cost profit for the year; the net surplus arising from the revaluation of assets; the amount which the directors... decided to appropriate to revaluation reserve; the dividends paid for the year; and the net balance transferred to or from general reserve', i.e.

CCP for the year		*x*
net surplus for year on revaluation of assets	*x*	
less appropriated to revaluation reserve	*x*	*x*
available for distribution and general reserve		*x*
dividends		*x*
Added to/subtracted from general reserve		*x*

- Additionally, the accounts were to include a statement, by way of a note, 'setting out prominently the *gain or loss for the period of account in the shareholders' net equity interest after allowance has been made for the change in the value of money during the period*'. This took the following form:

Net equity interest at the beginning of the year	*x*
New equity capital introduced in the course of the year	*x*
	x
Amount required to compensate for the change in the value of money during the year	*x*
	x
Net equity interest at the end of the year before dividends on equity capital	*x*
Gain/loss for the year after allowing for the change in the value of money	*x*
Dividends on equity capital for the year	*x*
Gain/loss for the year after allowing for the change in the value of money and dividends	*x*

- In addition an analysis of the *gain or loss on holding monetary assets and liabilities* was to be provided, showing separately the figures for long-term liabilities, overdrafts and non-equity share capital.

This proposal was comprehensive and complicated, but had the effect of putting people off. Criticisms seemed to be concentrated on the appropriation account, which had not been seriously considered by Sandilands. Sandilands had implied that revaluation reserves would be capitalized, but Morpeth did not necessarily see it that way. This, coupled with the supplementary statements (gain/loss on monetary items – changes in net equity), caused serious misgivings. Some critics claimed that CCA accounts would not be auditable. Others felt that too much discretion was left with directors, with consequent scope for manipulation. Other concerns raised were the cost of implementation and the confusion between CCA and CPP.

Strength of feeling against Morpeth was such that in 1977 members of the ICAEW passed a resolution at a special meeting 'that members of the ICAEW do not wish any system of current cost accounting to be made compulsory'.

Activity 5

It may be that in attempting to deal with the debate in a comprehensive manner that Morpeth was ahead of his time. Many of the issues raised and dealt with recurred later. In order to put this proposal in perspective consider the following questions.

1 Do you think that CCA and CPP approaches are irreconcilable?
2 Can one be used to the exclusion of the other? If this occurs are there useful insights which will be missed?
3 Do the supplementary statements add value?
4 Do you consider that revaluation reserves should automatically be capitalized, or does the Morpeth proposal recognize reality?

1 While it may be difficult (though not impossible) to devise an accounting system which encapsulates both CPP and CCA, Morpeth showed that both systems provide useful but different insights. Both are necessary if we are to maximize the information. More strictly, CPP as a system is less useful, but the kind of overarching approach used by Morpeth enables potentially useful information to be conveyed.
2 They can be mutually exclusive – but need not be. One on its own will miss some insights.
3 They do, in that they focus on management of monetary items and on 'real' profits from a shareholder perspective.
4 Morpeth recognizes reality – when conditions change why should cost increases necessarily be capitalized?

The demise of ED18 created an embarrassing vacuum which was filled by a set of interim guidelines (the Hyde Guidelines, 1977) which could be relatively easily agreed. Basically a supplementary statement was required showing the financial results as amended by the following adjustments:

1   depreciation – the difference between depreciation based on current cost and historic cost;
2   cost of sales – the difference between current cost at the time of sale and historic cost;
3   a gearing adjustment.

The first two were non-controversial. With regard to the gearing adjustment the following comments were made.

> It is recognized that there are differing views on the question of how monetary items should be dealt with in inflation adjusted statements and that such differences are unlikely to be resolved quickly or without experiment. Nevertheless, it is considered that it would not be acceptable for the statement recommended to be limited to adjustments for depreciation and cost of sales. Such limitation would result in an incomplete and potentially misleading figure being given to shareholders and other users of accounts. Accordingly, the description of the gearing adjustment given below. . . are intended as an interim guide as to how this adjustment might be approached.
> There are two different situations to be met, each of which calls for a different treatment:
>
> (a)   if the total liabilities of the business, including for this purpose preference share capital, exceed its total monetary assets, so that part of its operating capability is effectively financed by the net monetary liabilities, an adjustment should be made to reflect the extent to which the depreciation and cost of sales adjustments do not need to be provided in full from the current revenues of the business in showing the profit attributable to the shareholders.
> (b)   if the total monetary assets of the business exceeds its total liabilities, an adjustment should be made to reflect the increase in net monetary assets needed to maintain its scale of operation.
> The adjustment suggested for (a) was:

$$\frac{\text{Net balance of monetary liabilities}}{\text{Net balance plus equity share capital plus reserves}} \times \begin{array}{c}\text{Sum of the cost of the}\\\text{sales and depreciation}\\\text{adjustments}\end{array}$$

> For (b) an appropriate index should be applied to net monetary assets

In spite of some misgivings about the gearing adjustment, there was a sense of relief that something simple had been proposed.

What was interesting about the ED18 and Hyde discussions was the blurring of some of the capital maintenance concepts. While it is conceptually quite easy to include maintenance of net working capital as one of those areas that need to be maintained in deriving operating profit, the debates concerning gains/losses on monetary items have their genesis in CPP accounting. The gearing adjustment attempts to deal with the issue – recognized squarely by Morpeth – that not all revaluation surpluses need to be capitalized and retained. All these issues clearly impacted on discussions going on around the world, e.g. on the Australian recommendations.

Eventually, after much more debate, SSAP 16 was issued by the UK Accounting Standards Committee in 1980. The proposals, in common with the Hyde guidelines, proposed that a separate statement be given showing the current cost adjustments made to historic cost profit in respect of depreciation, cost of sales and gearing. However, SSAP 16 went further by introducing, separate from the gearing adjustment, an adjustment, the monetary working capital adjustment (MWCA), which in effect extends the cost of sales adjustment to the other working capital items. The MWCA was not an adjustment for general inflation but for the effect of specific price changes. The gearing adjustment was concerned with the determination of CCP attributable to shareholders. The net operating assets shown in the balance sheet will usually have been partly financed by borrowings. Where such borrowings are fixed in monetary terms, any liability to repay is not effected by changes in the price of assets which they have partly financed. This provides a benefit to shareholders during a period of increasing prices which is not brought into CCOP.

This benefit was recognized by a gearing adjustment. This reduced the total of the adjustments for depreciation, cost of sales and monetary working capital, in the proportion which net operating assets financed by borrowing bear to total net operating assets.

This adjustment was a long way from being an adjustment for the effect of inflation on long-term monetary liabilities. In fact the explanation (echoed above) is not very compelling and suggests some confusion of capital maintenance concepts. It might be better to simply explain the gearing adjustment as the proportion of current cost increases that do not need to be transferred to a capital reserve, because the increases would be financed from borrowings. By implication some optimal capital structure will be targeted. In fact stability of gearing ratios is a dubious assumption which weakens the argument.

SSAP16 did not deal with the maintenance of financial capital in general purchasing power terms. It was recognized that some users may be interested in a statement of the change in the shareholders' net equity interest after allowing for the change in the general purchasing power of money, and a supplementary statement was permitted.

In 1985 the mandatory status of SSAP 16 was withdrawn.

Over the years CPP, CCA and hybrid versions of the two have been proposed by standard setters but none of these has gained general acceptance. This is seen by many as particularly unfortunate since the last twenty years have also seen rates of price inflation in the UK which are historically unprece-dented. The objections to proposals can probably be classified broadly as:

- genuine objections to a particular proposal on the grounds that it was not appropriate to user needs;
- a belief that the benefits of producing adjusted accounts, in terms of making the information more useful as a basis for decision making, do not justify the cost of producing the adjusted accounts;
- reluctance from some commercial and industrial directors to publish final accounts adjusted for inflation since almost inevitably such adjustments have the effect of showing lower profit numbers.

Whether a generally agreed approach to accounting for changing price levels will ever emerge is doubtful and this is probably unfortunate. Despite this many progressive companies publish inflation-adjusted accounts of one sort or another, or use such accounts for internal management purposes.

It is important to recognize the implications of the two major approaches, and the associated problems of historic cost accounting. Shareholders should certainly be aware of the impact of general inflation on their investments, and associated returns. Specific changes in costs and revenues associated with a particular business may also provide investors with both opportunities and threats. Managers must consider the implications of current cost accounting as regards the amount of profit which is distributable, without reducing the ability of a business to continue, in the same line of business, without further recourse to new funds. The two alternative systems provide useful but different viewpoints of profit.

Self-assessment question 23.1

In this chapter we have dealt with two important issues: the development of a conceptual framework and accounting during a period of changing prices. We have seen that both of these issues provoke considerable controversy and many believe that progress in each area is only likely to be made if broad agreement can be reached on how we should proceed. This raises an issue about how accounting *should* develop in the future.

On the one hand, it can be argued that accounting is a *political process* where the interests of different groups (users, preparers, government etc.) have to be reconciled in order to make progress. On the other hand, it can be argued that the role of accounting is to report objective reality. Thus we should consider what is *technically correct* and not be concerned with the views of the particular interest groups.

Which of these two views (if either) do you support and why? Are these two views irreconcilable?

23.9 Summary

The chapter showed that profit (income) can be defined in more ways than one, with potentially considerable differences in the profit calculations resulting. Two main schools of thought were examined regarding the appropriate way of accounting for changing price levels. It was shown that each approach has something useful to add. Both need to be considered in some way if we are to obtain a good understanding of financial performance and position. The stance of the UK accounting profession on accounting for price-level changes is discussed.

References

The Sandilands Report – *Report of the Inflation Accounting Committee.* London: HMSO 1975.

The Morpeth Report – Inflation Accounting Steering Group. *Guidance Manual on Current Cost Accounting including the Exposure Draft.* London: Tolley 1976.

The Hyde proposals – Accounting Standards Steering Committee. *Inflation Accounting – Interim Recommendations.* 1977.

Accounting Standards Steering Committee. *Statement of Standard Accounting Practice 16 – Current Cost Accounting.* 1980.

Exercises

1 Three men, H, M, and A, each invests £10,000 in securities (shares) on 1 January. Their transactions, and those for the rest of the year, are as follows:

H	1 January	Buys equity shares costing £10,000
	30 June	Receives £1,100 in dividends, which is reinvested in further shares
M	1 January	Buys government loan stock for £10,000
	30 June	Receives £1,100 interest, which he puts on current account in his bank
A	1 January	Borrows £7,500 at 10%
		Buys equity shares costing £10,000 (i.e. puts in £2,500 of his own funds)
	30 June	Receives £1,100 in dividends, which is reinvested in more equities
	31 December	Pays (from his overdraft) £750 interest

The retail price index stood at 100 on 1 January, 110 on 30 June, and 121 on 31 December. Assume that equity prices keep pace with inflation, as measured by this index.

Required

Compare the three ventures by setting out profit and loss accounts and balance sheets for each, based on:

(i) historic cost accounting conventions;
(ii) CPP accounting conventions (in pounds stabilized at 31 December).

Ignore accrued revenue.

2 A company has the following purchases and sales in a period:

1 January	Purchases 150 units at £10 each
31 January	Sells 50 units at £12 each
1 February	Receives notification of an increase in the purchase price of goods to £11 per unit, to take effect immediately
28 February	Sells 50 units at £13 each
1 March	Purchases 100 units at £11 each
31 March	Sells 50 units at £14 each
1 April	Buys 100 units at a new price of £12 per unit
30 April	Sells 50 units at £15 each

Prepare a profit and loss account using:

(i) conventional accounts, assuming that stock is sold in the order in which it was bought;
(ii) costs current at the time of sale.

3 Modernity Ltd issues its shares, buys its fixed assets and commences business on 1 January 2000. Its accounts for 2000, prepared on an historic cost basis, are as follows:

Profit and Loss for the year

Sales		100,000
less cost of sales, interest etc.	65,000	
Depreciation	20,000	
		85,000
Net profit		15,000

Balance sheet as	*1 Jan.*	*31 Dec.*
Non-current assets – cost	80,000	80,000
– Depreciation provision	(–)	(20,000)
Cash	20,000	55,000
	100,000	115,000
Share capital	50,000	50,000
Reserves	–	15,000
Debentures (10%)	50,000	50,000
	100,000	115,000

The retail price index for the year is as follows:

1 January	100
30 June	110
31 December	121

Trading transactions can be assumed to take place on average on 30 June.

Required
1 Prepare a profit and loss account for the year and a balance at the year-end on a current purchasing power basis.
2 Discuss the meaning and usefulness of the revised accounts.

4 The following are the balance sheets for Modems Ltd for the beginning of the year and end of the year, together with an income statement for the year. All figures are in £000.

Balance sheet	Start	End
Non-current assets		
Cost	20,000	20,000
Depreciation provision	(2,000)	(4,000)
Stock	1,000	1,200
Monetary Assets	3000	9700
	22,000	26,900
Capital	10,000	10,000
Reserves	5,000	10,700
Debentures	4,000	4,000
Current monetary liabilities	3,000	2,200
	22,000	26,900

Profit and loss account/income statement for the year

Sales		25,000
Opening stock	1,000	
Purchases	14,600	
	15,600	
less closing stock	1,200	
Cost of sales		14,400
Gross profit		10,600
Depreciation	2,000	
Other expenses	2,900	
	4,900	
Net profit		5,700

Notes

1 Replacement cost of the fixed assets was £24,000 at the beginning of the current year
2 At the start of the year all indexes were 100.
3 The following specific indexes are available at the year-end:

fixed assets	115
stock	118

4 The general price index of 112 is seen as providing a fair guide to movements in general expenses. All these price movements have occurred evenly through the year.

5 Sales and purchases were made evenly over the year, as are other expenses. For ease of calculation you may assume that the opening and closing stocks were bought at the end of the respective years, when the stock price index was 100 and 118.

6 Depreciation is 10% straight-line.

Required
Prepare current cost accounts.

Answers to self-assessment questions

Chapter 2

Self-assessment question 2.1

Profit and loss account (income statement) for Day 1

	£	£
Sales of ice cream		120
Purchase of ice cream	100	
Less: closing stock of ice cream	20	
Cost of ice cream sold		80
Net profit (increase in wealth)		40

Cash flow statement for Day 1

	£
Receipts from sales	120
Less: payment for stock	100
Net increase in cash	20
Opening balance	100
Closing balance	120

Balance sheet (position statement) as at end of Day 1

	£
Stock of unsold ice cream	20
Cash (closing balance on Day 1)	120
	140

Therefore:

Russell's business wealth is	140

Profit and loss account (income statement) for Day 2

	£	£
Sales of ice cream		165
Opening stock of ice cream	20	
Purchase of ice cream	100	
	120	
Less: closing stock of ice cream	10	
Cost of ice cream sold		110
Net profit (increase in wealth)		55

Cash flow statement for Day 2

	£
Receipts from sales	165
Less: payment for stock	100
Net increase in cash	65
Opening balance	120
Closing balance	185

Balance sheet (position statement) as at end of Day 2

	£
Stock of unsold ice cream	10
Cash (closing balance on Day 2)	185
	195

Therefore:

Russell's business wealth is	195

Profit and loss account (income statement) for Day 3

	£	£
Sales of ice cream		60
Opening stock of ice cream	10	
Purchase of ice cream	100	
	110	
Less: closing stock of ice cream	70	
Cost of ice cream sold		40
Net profit (increase in wealth)		20

Cash flow statement for Day 3

	£
Receipts from sales	60
Less: payment for stock	100
Net decrease in cash	(40)
Opening balance	185
Closing balance	145

Balance sheet (position statement) as at end of Day 3

	£
Stock of unsold ice cream	70
Cash (closing balance on Day 3)	145
	215

Therefore:

Russell's business wealth is	215

Profit and loss account (income statement) for Day 4

	£	£
Sales of ice cream		56
Opening stock of ice cream	70	
Purchase of ice cream	–	
	70	
Less: closing stock of ice cream	–	
Cost of ice cream sold		70
Net loss (decrease in wealth)		14

Cash flow statement for Day 4

	£
Receipts from sales	56
Less: payment for stock	–
Net increase in cash	56
Opening balance	145
Closing balance	201

Balance sheet (position statement) as at end of Day 4

	£
Stock of unsold ice cream	–
Cash (closing balance on Day 4)	201
	201

Therefore:

Russell's business wealth is	201

We can see that, for the first three days, Russell managed to make a profit on each day of his venture and his business wealth rose steadily. However, on the fourth day he made a loss and there was also a corresponding decrease in his business wealth. Overall his wealth increased from £100 at the beginning of the venture to £201 after four days and so he may feel satisfied with the venture.

Chapter 3

Self-assessment question 3.1

	Assets	Claims
(a)	+ vehicle	
	– cash	
(b)	– cash	– creditor
(c)	+ equipment	+ creditor
(d)	+ cash	
	– debtor	
(e)	+ cash	+ loan
(f)	+ stock	
	– cash	
(g)	+ stock	+ creditors
(h)	– cash	– capital (drawings)

Self-assessment question 3.2

		Assets	Claims
(a)	Office equipment	*	
(b)	Fixtures and fittings	*	
(c)	Creditors		*
(d)	Debtors	*	
(e)	Loan from E. Mac		*
(f)	Outstanding bill for fuel		*
(g)	Bank balance	depends on whether cash in hand or overdrawn. If it is cash in hand it is an asset. If it is an overdraft it is a liability.	

Self-assessment question 3.3

(a) Reference to conventions of business entity and duality.

(b)
Capital	£10,000
Capital	£18,000
Liabilities	£15,000
Liabilities	£8,000
Assets	£20,000
Assets	£35,000

(c) The answer depends on whether the car is for his personal use (in which case it will not appear in the business balance sheet), or for business use (in which case it will appear in the business balance sheet).

(d) Refer to convention of business entity.

Self-assessment question 3.4

(a), (d), (f) and (h).
(b), (c) and (g) are fixed assets.
(e) is an intangible asset.

Self-assessment question 3.5

Balance sheet as at 31 December 1999

Fixed assets	£	£		£
Premises		20,000	Capital	25,000
Equipment		8,000	+ Retained profits	9,250
		28,000		34,250
Current assets			Long-term loan	12,000
Stock	10,000			
Debtors	15,000		Current liabilities	
Bank	3,000		Creditors	10,000
Cash	250			
		28,250		
		56,250		56,250

Since Assets = capital + liabilities
Capital = assets − liabilities
Therefore Capital = 56,250 − 22,000 = 34,250
Since £25,000 was put into the business originally, a further £9,250 profit must have been retained in the business since that time.

Chapter 4

Self-assessment question 4.1

James & Co
Balance sheet as at 30 November 1999

	+ £	− £	Net £		+ £	− £	Net £
Fixed assets				*Capital*			
Premises	35,000		35,000	Opening balance	35,000		35,000
Fixtures	5,000		5,000	Net profit	600		600
							35,600
Vehicles	3,600	3,600j	5,000	less drawings		100m	600
	5,000k		45,000			500m	
							35,000
Current assets							
Stock	7,000	6,500g	3,450				
	3,200e	100m					
		150n		Loans	15,000	2,000b	15,500
					2,500k		
Debtors	5,000	3,000a	6,000				
	4,000d			*Current liabilities*			
				Creditors	10,600	5,600f	8,200
Cash	5,000	2,000b	4,250		3,200e		
	3,000a	5,600f					
	7,000c	1,200h					
	3,000j	1,800i					
	100n	2,500k					
		250l					
		500m					
			58,700				58,700

Profit and Loss account for November 1999

Expenses	+ £	− £	Net £	Revenues	+ £	− £	Net £
Cost of sales	6,500g		6,650	Sales	7,000c		11,100
	150n				4,000d		
					100n		
Wages	1,200h		1,200				
Other expenses	1,800i		1800				
Loss on vehicle	600j		600				
Interest	250l		250				
			10,500				
Net profit			600				
			11,100				11,100

<table>
<tr><td>Self-assessment
question 4.2</td><td>

(a) Revenue – sales – £1,500
     Current assets – debtors £1,500
(b) Revenue – rent receivable £6,000
     Current assets – debtors (rent receivable) – £1,000
(c) Revenue – rent receivable – £6,000
     Current liabilities – deferred revenue (rent) – £1,500

</td></tr>
</table>

<table>
<tr><td>Self-assessment
question 4.3</td><td>

(a) Expense – £350
     Asset – stationery under the heading current assets £150
(b) Expense – £550
     Current liabilities – accrued expenses (accruals) £100
     (This relates to the period November/December 1999)
     Note that although a bill has been received which relates to January, as well as November and December, an accrual is only set up for that part which relates to the period of account
(c) Expense – £100
     Current liabilities – accrued expenses £100

</td></tr>
</table>

<table>
<tr><td>Self-assessment
question 4.4</td><td>

Revenues/expenses for the year ending 31 December 1999

Expenses

Rent	£2,000	*Note:* The first payment clears last year's accrual
Electricity	£460	i.e. £50 relating to January 1999 +£120 + £70 + £120 + an estimate of £100 for November/December 1999

</td></tr>
</table>

Rates   £875   i.e. £200 prepaid in 1998 + £450
                               +£225 relating to the period October to
                                  December 1999

Revenues

Interest   £800   i.e. £200 deferred revenue in 1998 + £400
                               +£200 owing at year-end to cover
                               October–December 1999

Balance sheet extracts as at 31 December 1999

Current assets		*Current liabilities*	
Prepayments – rent	£500	Accrued electricity	£100
(covering the quarter ending 31 March 2000))			
Prepayments – rates	£225		
(covering the quarter ending 31 March 2000)			
Debtors – interest receivable	£200		
(covering the quarter ending 31 December 1999)			

Chapter 5

Self-assessment question 5.1

Trading and profit and loss account for the year ended 31 December

	£	£	*Workings*
Sales		59,700	
Less cost of sales		27,500	
Gross profit		32,200	
Less *other expenses*			
Wages	7,700		8,000 – 300
Rates	1,500		2,000 – 500
Carriage	300		
Rent	3,200		3,000 + 200
Stationery	100		250 – 150
General expenses	2,750		2,500 + 250
Fuel and electricity	1,150		1,000 + 150
Motor expenses	1,150		1,250 – 100
Depreciation – equipment	800		
Depreciation – vehicles	1,000		
Interest	1,000		
		20,650	
Net profit		11,550	

Balance sheet as at 31 December

Fixed assets		
Premises	25,000	
Equipment	5,200	6,000 – 800
Vehicles	2,500	3,500 – 1,000
	32,700	

Current assets			
Stock		4,000	3,000 + 30,000
			−27,500 − 1,500
Debtors		5,200	4,500 + 59,700
			−59,000
Prepayments		250	100 + 150 Stat.
Cash		9,700	2,000 − 300
		19,150	−3,000 − 8,000
			−5,000 − 2,000
			−250 − 2,500
			+59,000−
			−28,000 − 1,000
			−1,250
Less liabilities due within 1 year			
Creditors	4,000		2,000 + 30,000
			−28,000
Accruals	1,400		150 + 250
		5,400	+1,000
			loan interest
Net current assets		13,750	
		46,450	
Less liabilities due more than 1 year from now			
Loans		10,000	
Net assets		36,450	
Financed by:			
Capital − opening balance		31,400	
Net profit		11,550	
		42,950	
Less drawings		6,500	
		36,450	

Chapter 6	Cost £20,000, disposal value £4,000. Total to be depreciated £16,000. Using straight-line depreciation, a full year's depreciation would be £3,200.
Self-assessment question 6.1	(a) *1997 entries* Since the lorry was acquired on 1 July, depreciation will be on a pro-rata basis, i.e. £1600.

- Include depreciation expense in profit and loss account, £1,600.
- Increase depreciation provision by £1,600.

The *balance sheet* would show:

Vehicles (cost)	£20,000
Depreciation provision	£1,600
	£18,400

1998 entries
- include depreciation expenses in profit and loss account, £3,200
- increase depreciation provision by £3,200

The *balance sheet* would show:

Vehicles (cost)	£20,000
Depreciation provision	£4,800
	£15,200

(b) *1999 entries*
- increase cash by £11,000
- reduce asset (vehicles) by £20,000
- reduce depreciation provision (vehicles) by £4,800
- increase expense (loss on disposal) by £4,200

(c) There is an almost infinite number of methods that could be used. Either the reducing-balance or the sum-of-the-digits methods might be more appropriate in the case of an asset like a lorry. This is because such an asset is likely to require increasing amounts of maintenance and repairs as it becomes older. Use of one of these two methods would tend to lead to a more equal total lorry expense to be matched against revenues, each year. Assuming that the lorry is helping to generate equal amounts of revenues each year, this would probably lead to a fairer matching of expenses to revenues.

Chapter 7

Self-assessment question 7.1

(a) See text
(b) **FIFO method**

Trading and profit and loss account

	1997 £	1998 £	1999 £
Sales	16,000	25,000	36,000
Cost of sales	10,000	14,000	21,000
Gross profit	6,000	11,000	15,000
Overheads	4,000	5,000	6,000
Net profit	2,000	6,000	9,000

Stock account	1997			1998			1999		
	Qty	Price	£	Qty	Price	£	Qty	Price	£
Opening balance		–		100 @ £50		= 5000	150 @ £60		= 9000
Purchases	300 @ £50		= 1500	300 @ £60		= 1800	250 @ £80		= 20000
Issues (cost of sales)	200 @ £50		= 10000	100 @ £50		= 5000	150 @ £60		= 9000
				150 @ £60		= 9000	150 @ £80		= 12000
Closing stock	100 @ £50		= 5000	150 @ £60		= 9000	100 @ £80		= 8000

LIFO method

Trading and profit and loss account

	1997 £	1998 £	1999 £
Sales	16,000	25,000	36,000
Cost of sales	10,000	15,000	23,000
Gross profit	6,000	10,000	13,000
Overheads	4,000	5,000	6,000
Net profit	2,000	5,000	7,000

Stock account	1997			1998			1999		
	Qty	Price	£	Qty	Price	£	Qty	Price	£
Opening balance		–		100 @ £50		= 5000	100 @ £50		= 5000
							50 @ £60		= 3000
Purchases	300 @ £50		= 15,000	300 @ £60		= 18,000	250 @ £80		= 20,000
Issues (cost of sales)	200 @ £50		= 10,000	250 @ £60		= 15,000	250 @ £80		= 20,000
							50 @ £60		= 3000
Closing stock	100 @ £50		= 5000	100 @ £50		= 5000	100 @ £50		= 5000
				50 @ £60		= 3000			

AVCO method

Trading and profit and loss account

	1997 £	1998 £	1999 £
Sales	16,000	25,000	36,000
Cost of sales	10,000	14,375	21,468
Gross profit	6,000	10,675	14,532
Overheads	4,000	5,000	6,000
Net profit	2,000	5,675	8,532

Stock account	1997			1998			1999		
	Qty	Price	£	Qty	Price	£	Qty	Price	£
Opening balance	–			100 @ £50		= 5000	150 @ £57.5		= 8625
Purchases	300 @ £50		= 15,000	300 @ £60		= 18,000	250 @ £80		= 20,000
Therefore AVCO	15000/300		= 50	23000/400		= 57.5	28625/400		= 71.56
Issues (cost of sales)	200 @ £50		= 10,000	250357.5		= 14,375	300 @ 71.56		= 21,468
Closing stock	100 @ £50		= 5000	150 @ 57.5		= 8625	100 @ 71.56		= 7156

Chapter 8

Self-assessment question 8.1

2001

First, we need to write off the bad debts, with the following entries:

- increase an expense – bad debts   £300
- decrease the debtors   £300

Then deal with the doubtful debts. The amount of provision required is £1,455 (i.e. £300 + (£23,400 − 300) × 5%). The entries are:

- increase an expense – creation of doubtful debts provision (£1,455)
- increase doubtful debts provision (£1,455)

The expense 'creation of doubtful debts provision' will be included in the profit and loss account. In the balance sheet debtors will appear as follows:

	£
Debtors	23,400
Less doubtful debts provision	1,455
	21,945

The net amount of £21,945 represents the expected future benefit associated with debtors, taking a prudent view.

It may be that you linked this question with Activity 2, and presumed that a bad debts provision was brought forward from the previous year, amounting to £1,070. If you made this assumption, any remaining balance on the bad debts provision will need to be eliminated by transferring it to the profit and loss account.

2002

When the sales were made the entries are:

- increase the revenues (sales) by £147,800*
- increase debtors by £147,800

When the cash was received the entries are:

- increase cash by £143,700*
- decrease debtors by £143,700

When the 2001 debts go bad the entries are:

- decrease debtors by £910*
- decrease the provision for doubtful debts by £910

When the 2002 debts go bad the entries are:

- increase the expense (bad debts written off) by £890
- decrease debtors by £890* (i.e. £1,800 − £910)

(*These will not all occur at one point, e.g. the sales total will be made up of lots of individual sales which will be recorded as they happen.)
At the end of the year the remaining provision against the 2001 doubtful debts will no longer be required. The entries are:

- reduce doubtful debt provision by £545 (i.e. £1, 455 − £910)
- increase revenues (doubtful debt provision no longer required) by £545.

Lastly, create a provision for doubtful debts as at 31 December 2002. The balance of debtors at 31 December 2002 is:

Debtors at 1 January 2002	£23,400
add: Sales for the year	147,800
	171,200
less: Cash received during the year	143,700
	27,500
less: Bad debts written off	1,800
Debtors at 31 December 2002	£25,700

The entries are:

- increase an expense (creation of doubtful debts provision) £1,285 (i.e. £25,700 × 5%)
- increase doubtful debts provision by £1,285.

In the balance sheet debtors will appear as follows:

	£
Debtors	25,700
Less doubtful debts provision	1,285
	24,415

If you use *the short-cut method*, and assume that this question is a continuation of Activity 2, the entries will be as follows:

2001
The bad debts will be dealt with as follows:

- increase an expense – bad debts   £300
- decrease the debtors   £300

Then deal with the doubtful debts. The amount of provision required is £1,455 (i.e. £300 + (£23,400 − £300) × 5%). However, a provision of £1,070 already exists, so the entries become:

- increase an expense – increase in doubtful debts provision (£1,455 − £1,070 = £285).
- increase doubtful debts provision (£285)

2002
The bad debts will be dealt with as follows:

- increase an expense – bad debts   £1,800
- decrease the debtors   £1,800

Then deal with the doubtful debts. The amount of provision required is £1,285 (i.e. £25,700 × 5%). However, a provision of £1,455 already exists, so the entries become:

- decrease doubtful debts provision (£170)
- increase a revenue – decrease in doubtful debts provision (£1,455 − £1,285 = £170).

The net effect on profit and loss account and balance sheet should be the same.

Chapter 9

Self-assessment question 9.1

Stage 1 – open accounts, enter opening balances and record summary transactions for month. Balance off accounts where necessary.

Premises

		£			£
October 31	Balance b/d	35,000			

Fixtures

		£			£
October 31	Balance b/d	5,000			

Vehicles

		£			£
October 31	Balance b/d	3,600		Disposal	3,600
	Cash	2,500	November 30	Balance c/d	5,000
	Loan	2,500			
		8,600			8,600
November 30	Balance b/d	5,000			

Stock

		£			£
October 31	Balance b/d	7,000		Cost of sales	6,500
	Creditors	3,200		Drawings	100
				Cost of sales	150
			November 30	Balance c/d	3,450
		10,200			10,200
November 30	Balance b/d	3,450			

Debtors

		£			£
October 31	Balance b/d	5,000		Cash	3,000
	Sales	4,000	November 30	Balance c/d	6,000
		9,000			9,000
November 30	Balance b/d	6,000			

Cash

		£			£
October 31	Balance b/d	5,000		Loan	2,000
	Debtors	3,000		Creditors	5,600
	Sales	7,000		Wages	1,200
	Disposal	3,000		Other expenses	1,800
	Sales	100		Vehicle	2,500
				Interest	250
				Drawings	500
			November 30	Balance c/d	4,250
		18,100			18,100
November 30	Balance b/d	4,250			

Capital

		£			£
			October 31	Balance b/d	35,000

Loans

		£			£
	Cash	2,000	October 31	Balance b/d	15,000
November 30	Balance c/d	15,500		Vehicle	2,500
		17,500			17,500
			November 30	Balance b/d	15,500

Creditors

		£			£
November 30	Cash	5,600	October 31	Balance b/d	10,600
	Balance c/d	8,200		Stock	3,200
		13,800			13,800
			November 30	Balance b/d	8,200

Sales

		£			£
				Cash	7,000
				Debtors	4,000
				Cash	100
					11,100

Disposal

		£			£
	Vehicles	3,600		Cash	3,000
			November 30	Balance c/d	600
		3,600			3,600
November 30	Balance b/d	600			

Drawings

		£			£
	Cash	500			
	Stock	100			
		600			

Cost of sales

		£			£
	Stock	6,500			
	Stock	150			
		6,650			

Wages

		£			£
	Cash	1,200			

Other expenses

		£			£
	Cash	1,800			

Interest

	£		£
Cash	250		

Step 2 – Draw up a trial balance

Trial balance as at 30 November	Debit	Credit
Premises	35,000	
Fixtures	5,000	
Vehicles	5,000	
Stock	3,450	
Debtors	6,000	
Cash	4,250	
Capital		35,000
Drawings	600	
Loans		15,500
Creditors		8,200
Sales		11,100
Cost of sales	6,650	
Wages	1,200	
Other expenses	1,800	
Disposal	600	
Interest	250	
	69,800	69,800

Step 3 – Open trading and profit and loss accounts, close off the revenues and expenses to the appropriate account, transfer the net profit and drawings to capital.

Sales

		£			£
	Trading	11,100		Cash	7,000
				Debtors	4,000
				Cash	100
		11,100			11,100

Disposal

		£			£
	Vehicles	3,600		Cash	3,000
			November 30	Balance c/d	600
		3,600			3,600
November 30	Balance b/d	600	November 30	Profit and loss	600

Cost of sales

		£			£
	Stock	6,500	November 30	Trading	6,650
	Stock	150			
		6,650			6,650

Wages

		£			£
	Cash	1,200	November 30	Profit and loss	1,200

Other expenses

		£			£
	Cash	1,800	November 30	Profit and loss	1,800

Interest

		£			£
	Cash	250	November 30	Profit and loss	250

Trading

		£			£
November 30	Cost of sales	6,650	November 30	Sales	11,100
November 30	Gross profit	4,450			11,100
		11,100			11,100

Profit and loss

		£			£
November 30	Wages	1,200	November 30	Trading – GP b/d	4,450
	Other expenses	1,800			
	Loss on disposal	600			
	Interest	250			
	Net profit – to capital	600			4,450
		4,450			4,450

Drawings

		£			£
	Cash	500	November 30	Capital	600
	Stock	100			
		600			600

Capital

		£			£
November 30	Drawings	600	October 31	Balance b/d	35,000
November 30	Balance c/d	35,000	November 30	Profit and loss	600
		35,600			35,600
			November 30	Balance b/d	35,000

Step 4 – The balance sheet can then be prepared by listing the closing balances.

Balance sheet as at 30 November

Fixed assets			*Capital*		
Premises	35,000		Opening balance	35,000	
Fixtures	5,000		Net profit	600	
Vehicles	5,000			35,600	
Current assets			less drawings	600	
Stock	3,450			35,000	
Debtors	6,000		*Current liabilities*		
Cash	4,250		Creditors	8,200	
	58,700			58,700	

Chapter 10

Self-assessment question 10.1

Rent receivable

1997		£	1998		£
June 30	Balance b/d	375		Cash	1,875
1998					
June 30	Profit and loss	1,500			
		1,875			1,875
1999			1999	Cash	1,125
June 30	Profit and loss	1,500	June 30	Balance c/d	375
		1,500			1,500
June 30	Balance c/d	375	2000	Cash	2,250
2000					
June 30	Profit and loss	1,500			
	Balance c/d	375			
		2,250			2,250
			June 30	Balance b/d	375

Rent payable

1997		£	1998		£
June 30	Balance b/d	1,000	1998		
1998	Cash	4,000	June 30	Profit and loss	4,000
				Balance c/d	1,000
		5,000			5,000
June 30	Balance b/d	1,000	1999		
1999	Cash	3,000	June 30	Profit and loss	4,000
		4,000			4,000
2000	Cash	3,000	2000		
June 30	Balance c/d	1,000	June 30	Profit and loss	4,000
		4,000			4,000
			June 30	Balance b/d	1,000

Self-assessment question 10.2

LIFO

Stock

	Debit – goods received			Credit – goods issued			Balance		
Date	Quantity	Cost/unit	Total cost	Quantity	Cost/unit	Total cost	Quantity	Cost/unit	Total cost
	60	1	60				60	1	60
				40	1	40	20	1	20
	60	1.10	66				60	1.10	66
							20	1	20
				60	1.10	66			
				10	1	10	10	1	10

AVCO

Stock

	Debit – goods received			Credit – goods issued			Balance		
Date	Quantity	Cost/unit	Total cost	Quantity	Cost/unit	Total cost	Quantity	Cost/unit	Total cost
	60	1	60				60	1	60
				40	1	40	20	1	20
	60	1.10	66				20	1	20
							60	1.10	66
							80	1.075	86
				70	1.075	75.25	10	1.075	10.75

Self-assessment question 10.3

Stage 1 – Open accounts, enter opening balances and record summary transactions for month. Balance off accounts where necessary.

Buildings

		£			£
December 31	Balance b/d	8,000			

Equipment

		£			£
December 31	Balance b/d	5,000			

Vehicles

		£			£
December 31	Balance b/d	3,000			

Stock

		£			£
December 31	Balance b/d	5,000			

Debtors

		£			£
December 31	Balance b/d	3,000	1999	Cash	36,000
1999	Sales	40,000	December 31	Balance c/d	7,000
		43,000			43,000
December 31	Balance b/d	7,000			

Cash

		£			£
December 31	Balance b/d	4,500	1999	Creditors	35,000
1999	Sales	10,000		Wages	5,000
	Debtors	36,000		Other expenses	3,000
				Rent	1,500
				Rates	750
				Drawings	2,500
			December 31	Balance c/d	2,750
		50,500			50,500
December 31	Balance b/d	2,750			

Capital

		£			£
			December 31	Balance b/d	20,000

Loans

		£			£
			December 31	Balance b/d	5,000

Creditors

		£			£
1999	Cash	35,000	December 31	Balance b/d	3,500
December 31	Balance c/d	10,500	1999	Purchases	42,000
		45,500			45,500
			December 31	Balance b/d	10,500

Sales

		£			£
			1999	Cash	10,000
				Debtors	40,000
					50,000

Drawings

		£			£
	Cash	2,500			

Wages

		£			£
1999	Cash	5,000			

Other expenses

		£			£
1999	Cash	3,000			

Purchases

		£			£
	Creditors	42,000			

Rent

		£			£
1999	Cash	1,500			

Rates

		£			£
1999	Cash	750			

Step 2 – Draw up a trial balance

Trial balance as at 30 November	Debit	Credit
Buildings	8,000	
Equipment	5,000	
Vehicles	3,000	
Stock	5,000	
Debtors	7,000	
Cash	2,750	
Capital		20,000
Drawings	2,500	
Loans		5,000
Creditors		10,500
Sales		50,000
Purchases	42,000	
Wages	5,000	
Other expenses	3,000	
Rent	1,500	
Rates	750	
	85,500	85,500

Step 3 – Open trading and profit and loss accounts, close off the revenues and expenses to the appropriate account, after incorporating the year end adjustments, transfer the net profit and drawings to capital.

Sales

1999		£	1999		£
December 31	Trading	50,000		Cash	10,000
				Debtors	40,000
		50,000			50,000

Drawings

1999		£	1999		£
1999	Cash	2,500	December 31	Capital	2,500

Wages

1999		£	1999		£
1999	Cash	5,000	December 31	Profit and loss	5,000

Other expenses

1999		£	1999		£
1999	Cash	3,000	December 31	Profit and loss	3,000

Stock

1998		£	1999		£
December 31	Balance b/d	5,000	December 31	Trading	5,000
	Trading (closing)	20,000			

Purchases

		£	1999		£
1999	Creditors	42,000	December 31	Trading	42,000

Rent

1999		£	1999		£
1999	Cash	1,500	December 31	Profit and loss	1,200
		1,500	December 31	Balance c/d	300
		1,500			1,500
December 31	Balance b/d	300			

Rates

1999		£	1999		£
1999	Cash	750	December 31	Profit and loss	1,000
December 31	Balance c/d	250			
		1,000			1,000
			December 31	Balance b/d	250

Depreciation – equipment

1999		£	1999		£
December 31	Dep–prov. – equipment	1,000	December 31	Profit and loss	1,000

Depreciation provision – equipment

		£	1999		£
			December 31	Depreciation	1,000

Depreciation – vehicles

1999		£	1999		£
December 31	Dep–prov. – equipment	600	December 31	Profit and loss	600

Depreciation provision – vehicles

		£	1999		£
			December 31	Depreciation	600

Trading

1999		£	1999		£
December 31	Stock (opening)	5,000	December 31	Stock (closing)	20,000
	Purchases	42,000	December 31	Sales	50,000
	Gross profit c/d	23,000			
		70,000			70,000

Profit and loss

		£			£
November 30	Wages	5,000	November 30	Trading – GP b/d	23,000
	Other expenses	3,000			
	Rent	1,200			
	Rates	1,000			
	Depreciation – equipt	1,000			
	Depreciation – vehicles	600			
	Net profit – to capital	11,200			
		23,000			23,000

Capital

1999		£	1998		£
December 31	Drawings	2,500	December 31	Balance b/d	20,000
	Balance c/d	28,700	1999		
			December 31	Profit and loss	11,200
		31,200			31,200
			December 31	Balance b/d	28,700

The remaining accounts are unaltered.

Step 4 – The balance sheet can then be prepared by listing the closing balances. The trading and profit and loss account will be rewritten for ease of communication.

Balance sheet as at 31 December 1999

Fixed assets			*Capital*		
Buildings		8,000	Opening balance	20,000	
Equipment	5,000		Net profit	11,200	
Less depn prov.	1,000			31,200	
		4,000	less drawings	2,500	
				28,700	
Vehicles	3,000				
Less depn prov.	600				
		2,400	*Loans*	5,000	
		14,400			

Current assets		Current liabilities	
Stock	20,000	Creditors	10,500
Debtors	7,000	Accrued rates	250
Prepaid rent	300		
Cash	2,750		
	44,450		44,450

Chapter 11

Self-assessment question 11.1

The answer is given below:

(a) Paul – credit the total sales in the sales account. Matthew – debit each debtor account with the appropriate amount for each sales invoice.

(b) Sales would be overstated by £1,000 so credits would exceed debits by this amount.

(c) Eventually he will write (or originate) a letter to the customer asking for payment. This is likely to provoke a reaction from the customer which might well lead to investigation into James' behaviour.

(d) No. Because he could then pocket cash received and write off the customers account as bad, thus preventing (c) above.

(e) Liaise with James to commit a joint fraud.

(f) No. Because of the possibility in (e).

Chapter 12

Self-assessment question 12.1

(a) £2.

(b)

Assets	£	Claims	£
Net assets	450,000	Ordinary share capital	200,000
		Reserves	100,000
		Share premiums account	150,000
	450,000		450,000

(c) £2.25.

(d) Book value per share reflects the share of net assets, which are shown at cost less depreciation. As such it is not a particularly meaningful figure. Market price per share reflects expected earnings, perceived risk, financial strength, market value of assets, etc. Since it results from the interaction of supply and demand it may be considered an efficient current price.

Self-assessment question 12.2

Corfu Ltd

Assets	£	Claims	£
Net assets	950,000	Ordinary share capital (600,000 shares of £1 each fully paid)	600,000
		Share premium account	50,000
		Revaluation reserve	200,000
		Revenue reserves	100,000
	950,000		950,000

The bonus issue results in a decrease in reserves and an increase in share capital of £100,000. Since the share premium has limited uses, and cannot be distributed as a dividend, it is sensible to convert this account first.

The rights issue results in an increase of £100,000 in share capital (the bonus issue had increased share capital to £500,000), making it £600,000; cash increases by £150,000, while the share premium account needs to be increased by £50,000.

Chapter 13

Self-assessment question 13.1

RAC Ltd

Trading profit and loss and appropriation account for the year ended 31 December 2000

	£	£
Sales		530,000
Opening stock	30,000	
Purchases	300,000	
	330,000	
Less closing stock	35,000	
Cost of sales		295,000
Gross profit		235,000
Less *other expenses*		
Directors' remuneration	31,000	
Selling and distribution expenses	29,000	
Loan interest	4,000	
Administration	42,000	
Wages and salaries	50,000	
Bad debts	2,000	
Depreciation – equipment	5,000	
Depreciation – fittings	5,000	
		168,000
Net profit		67,000
Profit and loss balance brought forward		25,000
Total available for appropriation		92,000

Appropriated as follows:

General reserve	25,000	
Preference dividends	5,000	
Ordinary dividends	40,000	
		70,000
Unappropriated profit carried forward		22,000

Balance sheet as at 31 December 2000

	£	£	£
Fixed assets			
Premises			200,000
Equipment – cost		50,000	
– depreciation provision		25,000	
			25,000
Fittings – cost		50,000	
– depreciation provision		30,000	
			20,000
			245,000
Current assets			
Stock	35,000		
Prepayments	1,000		
Debtors	50,000		
Cash	100,000		
		186,000	
Less Creditors due within 1 year			
Creditors	30,000		
Accruals	4,000		
Proposed pref. dividends	5,000		
Proposed ord. dividend	40,000		
		79,000	
Net current assets			107,000
			352,000
Creditors due in more than 1 year			
Loans			40,000
Net assets			312,000
Financed by:			
Capital			
Ordinary share capital			200,000
Preference share capital			50,000
			250,000
Reserves			
General reserve		40,000	
Profit and loss account		22,000	
			62,000
			312,000

<table>
<tr><td>

Chapter 14

Self-assessment question 14.1

</td><td>

(a) Marina Plc

Profit and loss account for the year ended 31 December 2000

	£000	£000
Sales		5,000
Opening stock	250	
Purchases	3,000	
	3,250	
Less closing stock	300	
Cost of sales		2,950
Gross profit		2,050
Less expenses		
Wages and salaries		
– Production/warehousing	200	
– Administration	200	
– Selling and distribution	400	
Motor expenses		
– Administration	20	
– Distribution	80	
General distribution expenses	350	
General administration expenses	150	
Debenture interest	28	
Directors' remuneration	200	
Bad debts	120	
Depreciation		
– Plant and machinery	24	
– Motor vehicles	50	
		1,822
Net profit		228
Less corporation tax		58
		170
Plus profit and loss balance b/f		50
		220
Appropriated as follows:		
General reserve	20	
Preference share dividend	50	
Ordinary share dividend	60	
		130
Profit and loss balance c/f		90

</td></tr>
</table>

(b) **Profit and loss account for the year ended 31 December 2000**

	£000
Turnover	5,000)
Cost of sales*	(3,150)
Gross profit	1,850)
Distribution costs*	(894)
Administration costs*	(700)
Interest payable	(28)
Corporation tax	(58)
Profit for the year after tax	170)
Transfer to general reserve	(20)
Dividends	(110)
Added to reserves	40

Workings

Expense	Cost of sales £000	Distribution £000	Administration £000
Cost of sales	2,950		
Wages and salaries	200	400	200
Motor expenses	–	80	20
General expenses	–	350	150
Directors' remuneration	–	–	200
Bad debts	–	–	120
Depreciation			
– Plant and machinery	–	24	–
– Motor vehicles	–	40	10
Total	3, 150	894	700

Balance sheet as at 31 December 2000

Fixed assets	Note	£000	£000	£000
Land and buildings				1,800
Plant and machinery	1			66
Motor vehicles	2			100
				1,966
Current assets				
Stock			300	
Debtors			600	
			900	

Creditors: amounts falling due within 1 year

Loans		100	
Overdraft		13	
Trade creditors		200	
Taxation		58	
Dividends	3	85	
			456
Net current assets			444
Less: Creditors falling due			
after more than 1 year			
Debenture loans	4		400
			44
Net assets			2,010
Capital and reserves			
Ordinary share capital	5		1,000
Preference share capital	6		500
Share premium			200
General reserve	7		220
Profit and loss account			40
			1,960

Notes

1 The plant and machinery figure comprises:

Plant and machinery – cost	£120,000
Less depreciation provision	£54,000
	£66,000

2 The motor vehicles figure comprises:

Motor vehicles (at cost)	£200,000
Less depreciation provision	£100,000
	£100,000

3 The dividends relate to the final preference dividend of £25,000 and the ordinary dividend of £60,000.
4 Debenture loans carry a 7% interest rate.
  They are redeemable in 1995.
5 The ordinary share capital consists of 2 million shares of £0.50 each, fully paid.

6 The preference share capital consists of 500,000 £1 preference shares, fully paid, which carry a dividend entitlement of 10%. The shares are cumulative.

7 £20,000 has been transferred to the general reserve, increasing it to £220,000.

Chapter 15	
Self-assessment question 15.1	

Goodwill on consolidation

Paid	£29m
Got	£16m (£12m ordinary share capital + £4mreserves − 80% at time of acquisition)
Goodwill	£13m

Reserves

Matt	£10m
James	£4m (80% of post-acquisition reserves)
	£14m

Minority interests

Capital James	£15m
Reserves James	£10m
	£25m ×20% = £5m

Balance sheet as at 31 December 2000

	£000	£000
Fixed assets		24,800
Goodwill on consolidation		13,000
Current assets	2,300	
Current liabilities	1,100	
		1,200
		39,000
Ordinary share capital		20,000
Reserves		14,000
Minority interests		5,000
		39,000

Typically the goodwill will be written off against the reserves.

Chapter 16

Self-assessment question 16.1

Group profit and loss account for the year ended 31 December 2000

	£000	£000	
Turnover		9,000	(6,000 + 3,000)
Cost of sales		(4,000)	(3,000 + 1,000)
Gross profit		5,000	
Distribution	(1,400)		(1,000 + 400)
Administration	(1,200)		(800 + 400)
Investment income	600		(1,000 − 400)
		(2,000)	
Profit before tax		3,000	
Tax		(1,000)	(700 + 300)
After-tax profit		2,000	
Minority interests		(260)	[pref. divs 100 + 20% (900 − 100)]
Profit attributable to the group		1,740	
Profit and loss balance b/f		820	[500 + 80% (500 − 100)]
		2,560	
Transfer to general reserve	(560)		[400 + 80% (200)]
Preference dividends	(300)		
Ordinary dividends	(600)		
		(1,460)	
Profit and loss account balance c/f		1,100	

Chapter 17

Self-assessment question 17.1

Cash flow statement for the year ending 28 February 2001

	£	£
Net cash inflow from operating activities (note 1)		12,000
Returns on investment and servicing of finance		−
Taxation		−

Capital expenditure

Payments to acquire fixed assets – plant and equipment	(21,000)	
– motor vehicles	(3,000)	
Net cash inflow (outflow) from capital expenditure activities		(24,000)
Dividends paid		–
Financing		
Issue of debentures	10,000	
Net cash inflow (outflow) from financing		10,000
Increase (decrease) in cash and cash equivalents		(2,000)

Analysis of changes in cash and cash equivalents during the year

Cash at beginning of period	3,000
Net cash outflow during the year	(2,000)
Cash at end of period	1,000

Note

1 Net cash flow from operations

	£	£
Net profit before taxation		5,000
Add Depreciation for the year		15,000
		20,000
(Increase)/decrease in stock held	(3,000)	
(Increase)/decrease in debtors	(2,000)	
Increase/(decrease) in creditors	(3,000)	(8,000)
Net cash flow from operating activities		12,000

Self-assessment question 17.2	**Cash flow statement for the year ending 31 March 2001**		

		£	£
Net cash inflow from operating activities (note 1)			350,000
Returns on investment and servicing of finance			–
Taxation			
Corporation tax paid (note 3)			(120,000)
Capital expenditure activities (note 4)			
Payments to acquire fixed assets			
– plant and equipment		(180,000)	
– land		(80,000)	
Sale of plant		14,000	
Net cash outflow from capital expenditure activities			(246,000)
Dividends paid (note 2)			(70,000)
Net cash inflow (outflow) before financing			(86,000)

Financing
Issue of shares (note 5)   –
Net cash inflow (outflow) from financing   –

Increase (decrease) in cash and cash equivalents   (86,000)

Analysis of changes in cash and cash equivalents during the year
Cash at beginning of period   30,000
Net cash outflow during the year   (86,000)
Overdraft at end of period   (56,000)

Notes

	£	£
1 Net cash flow from operations		
Net profit before taxation		334,000
Add Depreciation for the year/loss on sale		132,000
		466,000
Increase in stock held	(142,000)	
Increase in debtors	(14,000)	
Increase in creditors	40,000	(116,000)
Net cash flow from operating activities		350,000

2 Dividends paid are assumed to be last year's proposed dividends and the current year's interim dividends.
3 Tax paid is assumed to be the amount owing at the beginning of the year, on the assumption of a 9-month lag between provision and payment.

4 **Plant and equipment**	Cost	Depreciation provision	Net
	£000	£000	£000
Opening balance	560	230	330
Less disposals	−80	−58	−22**
	480	172	308
Plus new acquisitions at cost	180*	–	$x = 180$
	660	172	$308 + x = 388$
Less depreciation for the year	–	124	−124
Closing balance	660	296	−364

*Missing figure.
**Plant with a book value of £22,000 is sold at a loss of £8,000. Sale proceeds must therefore be £14,000.

Freehold land	£
Cost at beginning of year	700,000
Cost at end of year	780,000
Acquisitions	80,000

5 Movements in share capital are all the result of the bonus issue. None are attributable to a cash offer.

Chapter 18

Self-assessment question 18.1

GO Ahead and Co. Ltd

Profit and loss account

	2000 £	2001 £	Notes
Sales	3,000,000	3,600,000	20% increase
Less variable costs	1,500,000	1,890,000	50% of sales
			+5% inflation
Contribution	1,500,000	1,710,000	
Less fixed costs (see below)	1,000,000	1,230,000	
Profit before tax	500,000	480,000	
Taxation	120,000	120,000	25% of profit
Profit after tax	380,000	360,000	
Dividends	100,000	120,000	12% of nominal capital
Added to reserves	280,000	240,000	

Workings

Fixed costs	£	
Current year's total	1,000,000	
Less depreciation	100,000	
Current year's cash costs	900,000	
Inflation adjustment	45,000	5%
	945,000	
Depreciation	135,000	10% of cost
Additional fixed costs in new year	150,000	
	1,230,000	

Forecast balance sheet as at 31 December

	2000 £	£	2001 £	£
Fixed assets				
Cost	1,000,000		1,350,000	
Depreciation provision	200,000		335,000	
		800,000		1,015,000
Current assets				
Stock	360,000		432,000	
Debtors	600,000		720,000	
Cash	150,000		63,000	
	1,110,000		1,215,000	

Creditors due within 1 year

Creditors	300,000		360,000	
Dividends proposed	100,000		120,000	
Corporation tax	120,000		120,000	
	520,000		600,000	
Net current assets		590,000		615,000
		1,390,000		1,630,000

Capital and reserves

Ordinary share capital		1,000,000		1,000,000
Reserves		390,000		630,000
		1,390,000		1,630,000

Workings

	%	2000	2001	Change
Current assets				
Stock	12	360,000	432,000	+72,000
Debtors	20	600,000	720,000	+120,000
Current liabilities				
Creditors	10	300,000	360,000	+60,000

Forecast cash flow statement for 2001

	£	£
Operating activities		
Net profit before tax	480,000	
Depreciation	135,000	
Increase in stock	(72,000)	
Increase in debtors	(120,000)	
Increase in creditors	60,000	
Net cash inflow from operating activities		483,000
Returns on investment and servicing of finance		–
Taxation		
UK corporation tax paid		(120,000)
Capital expenditure activities		
Purchase of fixed assets		(350,000)
Dividends		(100,000)
Net cash outflow before financing		(87,000)
Financing activities		–
Decrease in cash and cash equivalents		(87,000)

The plans are feasible, other than with regard to cash. The figures projected would lead to a decrease in cash of £82,000, as compared with the desired increase of £30,000. Some thought should be given to this problem, before the plans proceed. The profits, in spite of the expansion, are expected to fall, giving rise to some concern. Questions will need to be asked about this, although these results may well be much better than a 'do nothing new' policy.

	Chapter 19
	Self-assessment question 19.1

	1999	2000
Net profit margin	9.4%	8.5%
ROCE	8.3%	7.5%
Current ratio	3.1T	1.5T
Debt/total assets ratio	22.5%	46.3%
Days' debtors	98 days	138 days
Total asset turnover	0.75	0.59

Although the net profit has increased in absolute terms, there has been a decline in the net profit margin in 2000. This, in turn, has led to a decline in the ROCE ratio in 2000. The increase in sales for 2000 is probably due to the new contract. However, to support this increased level of activity, the company has increased its asset base by a more than proportionate amount. As a result, the sales to total assets ratio of the business has shown a significant decline. The increase in assets has been financed mainly by borrowing and the debt/total assets ratio has more than doubled over the period. However, this ratio may still be within acceptable limits.

The current ratio has shown a substantial decline in 2000 and this should be cause for concern. There has also been a corresponding fall in the acid-test ratio. This fall in liquidity has been accompanied by reliance on a large bank overdraft in order to finance the activities of the business. The continuing goodwill of the bank is now an important factor for the business to consider.

The increase in sales arising from the new contract has resulted in a large increase in the average days' debtors. The funding of this additional level of debtors is causing a strain on the company's liquidity and steps should be taken to reduce the days' debtors if possible. If this cannot be achieved for contractual or other reasons, the company must consider an injection of new long-term capital to ensure it can support the trading policies adopted.

	Chapter 20
	Self-assessment question 20.1

The following ratios may be calculated:

Profitability

Net profit margin	12.3%
Gross profit margin	37.7%
Return to equity	21.1%

Gearing

Debt to total assets	55.8%

Liquidity

Current ratio	1.2
Acid-test ratio	0.7

Efficiency

Stockholding period	135 days
Average credit period allowed	115 days

Investment ratios

Earnings per share	32.1p
Dividend cover	1.4T
Dividend yield	4.8%

The gross profit margin appears to be quite high and the return to equity seems to be reasonable. However, it is clear that a large amount of the gross profit is taken in overheads and this should cause some concern. The liquidity ratios reveal that the company liquidity is low and this, coupled with the fact that the bank overdraft seems very high, may be a problem for the company. The continuing support of the bank in the short term is of vital importance to the company. The efficiency ratios suggest room for improvement in the use of resources. The average credit period allowed seems high and this may be partly due to the fact that Conday and Co. Ltd operates an export business. However, when this ratio is viewed along with the high level of bad debts, it suggests weak credit control or excessive concern for making sales. The stock turnover ratio also seems rather high and a question must arise over the level of stock control operated by the company. The earnings per share seems reasonable but the dividend cover is rather low. The high level of dividend payout is puzzling given the liquidity problems of the company. The level of gearing is not high and so it may be possible to borrow more; however, it is not clear whether or not the company has sufficient security to do this.

While the company is profitable, it is difficult to recommend investment in the company on the terms mentioned. The company really needs to strengthen its financial base rather than expand at this point. Further expansion without improvements in liquidity and efficiency could prove fatal for the company. In addition, the dividend policy of the company should be reconsidered. If any money raised, however, was employed simply to reduce the bank overdraft there is unlikely to be a significant improvement in profits and so the returns to equity may actually reduce. A value per share of £6.40 suggests a P/E ratio for the company of nearly 20, which seems rather high. This suggests the company has overvalued the shares being offered.

Chapter 22

Self-assessment question 22.1

In answering this question you may have thought of the following matters which could be included in such a review:

- *Operating results*. This could include a discussion of the results of the business as a whole as well as individual segments. Any changes in the business or industry resulting from factors such as market conditions, new products, changes in exchange rates, changes in market share or profit margins would be useful.
- *Dynamics of the business*. Any factors which may affect future results such as scarcity of materials or skilled labour, new legislation, exchange rate fluctuations, dependence on major customers or suppliers, etc. could be discussed.
- *Investment in the future*. Steps taken to increase or maintain profits in the future such as capital investment expenditure, staff training

programmes, marketing campaigns, research and development, and refurbishment programmes could be identified.

- *Accounting policies.* Any areas where subjective judgement has been used and where this may have a significant effect on the measurement of performance and position could be mentioned.
- *Dividends.* Some discussion on the dividends announced in relation to profits may be useful.
- *Capital structure.* A discussion of the type of debt raised, interest rate structure and maturity dates of debt could be included.
- *Treasury policy.* A discussion of such matters may include foreign currency borrowings and the ways in which foreign currency risk is dealt with, the extent to which fixed interest borrowing is used and the currencies in which cash or near cash is held.
- *Cash flows.* Any special circumstances affecting cash flows from operations or other sources could be discussed.
- *Liquidity.* Any factors affecting the liquidity of the business and any future commitments which will reduce liquidity could be identified.
- *Unquantified resources.* Any resources not shown on the balance sheet but which are of value to the business such as brands or other intangible items could be identified.

Chapter 23

Self-assessment question 23.1

Three closely related arguments in favour of the political approach are:

- By introducing accounting policies and rules on how to do things, the rule-making bodies are placing restrictions on how individuals and businesses must behave. These restrictions should be introduced only after gaining the acceptance of those affected.
- In a democratic society, rule-making bodies such as the ASB should only gain their authority through general acceptance. Unless this is done, they really do not have the right to expect others to obey their rules.
- Rules will only work if they receive general acceptance by those affected. Hence, a process of negotiation and compromise should be undertaken in order to secure widespread acceptance.

The arguments for a technical approach (or against the political approach) are:

- The political approach is unlikely to produce the sort of radical shift in policies which may, at times, be required. The need for compromise suggests that any change in policy will be incremental.
- The rules developed using the political approach may have to be very broad in nature in order to secure agreement and this may result in a lack of rigour.
- Accounting should be neutral and should not bow to the requirements of particular interest groups. This would damage the confidence of users in the credibility of the information produced.

Some believe the two views can be reconciled. It can be argued that rule making is a two-stage process. First, a solution to an accounting problem which is technically correct must be found. Having done this it is then necessary to secure broad agreement among interested parties for the solution proposed. Hence, accounting rules should be regarded as being determined by both a technical and a political process rather than simply one or the other.

Index